Hana-Kimi

For You in Full Blossom

6

story and art by
HISAYA NAKAJO

HANA-KIMI
For You in Full Blossom
VOLUME 6
STORY & ART BY HISAYA NAKAJO

Translation/David Ury
English Adaptation/Gerard Jones
Touch-Up Art & Lettering/Gabe Crate
Design/Izumi Evers
Editor/Jason Thompson

Managing Editor/Megan Bates
Editorial Director/Elizabeth Kawasaki
Editor in Chief/Alvin Lu
Sr. Director of Acquisitions/Rika Inouye
Senior VP Marketing/Liza Coppola
Exec. VP of Sales & Marketing/John Easum
Publisher/Hyoe Narita

Hanazakari no Kimitachi he by Hisaya Nakajo © Hisaya Nakajo 1998
All rights reserved. First published in Japan in 1998 by HAKUSENSHA,
Inc., Tokyo. English language translation rights in America and Canada
arranged with HAKUSENSHA, Inc., Tokyo. New and adapted artwork
and text © 2005 VIZ Media, LLC. The HANA-KIMI logo is a trademark of
VIZ Media, LLC. All rights reserved. The stories, characters and incidents
mentioned in this publication are entirely fictional.

Published by VIZ Media, LLC, P.O. Box 77010, San Francisco, CA 94107

Shôjo Edition
10 9 8 7 6 5 4 3 2

First printing, May 2005
Second printing, March 2006

T 251165

www.viz.com
store.viz.com

CONTENTS

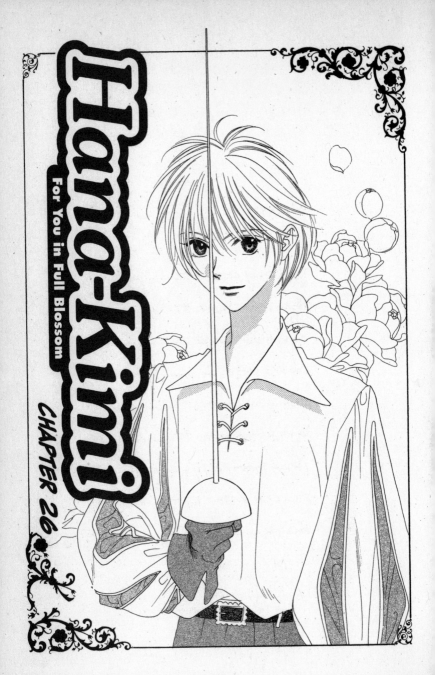

Hana-Kimi
For You in Full Blossom

CHAPTER 26

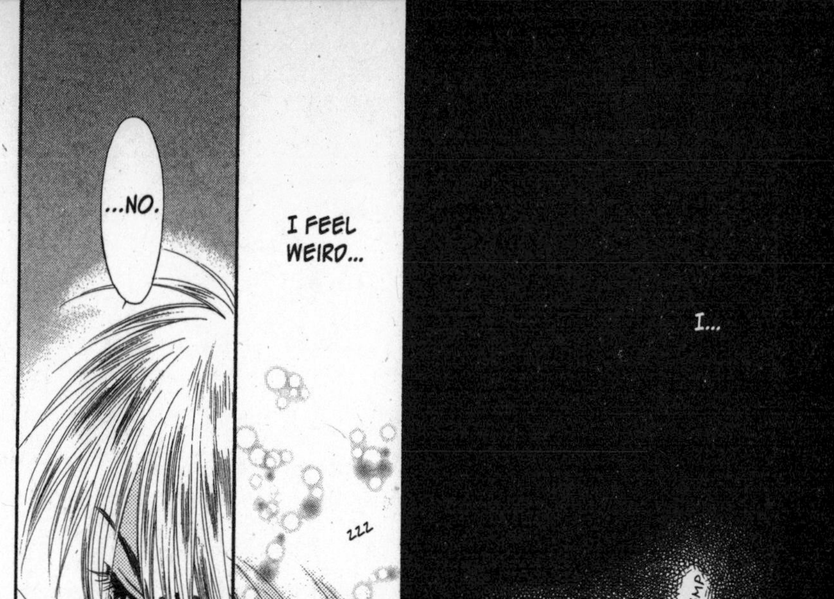
I...
B-BMP
B-BMP
B-BMP
I FEEL WEIRD...
zzz
...NO.

STUFF I LOVE

PART 1

「CAT GOODS」

RIGHT NOW WHAT I'M REALLY INTO ARE THESE CAT GOODS SHOWN ON THE RIGHT!! I ESPECIALLY LIKE THE ORIGINAL PIECES MADE BY NAOMI TOGAKI! ♡ I ALSO LOVE THE ALUMINUM TOILETRY AND TIN BOXES THAT ARE PAINTED WITH CATS, BEARS, AND RABBITS! ✿

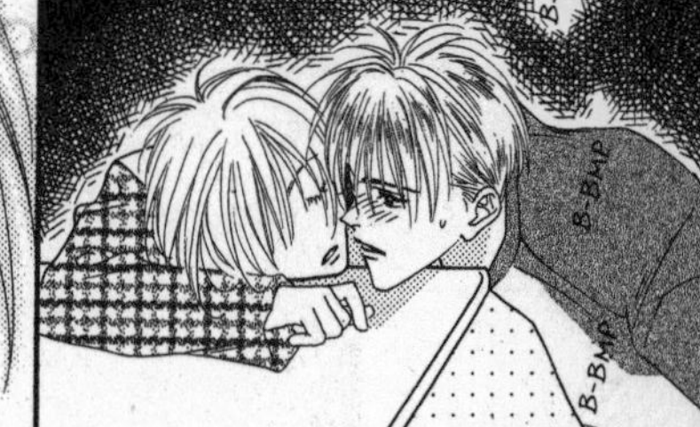
Bathroom sign
bath
je suis Sharon
je suis Sharon
Togaki's stuff has this mark on it.
On the bottom of the cups and stuff.

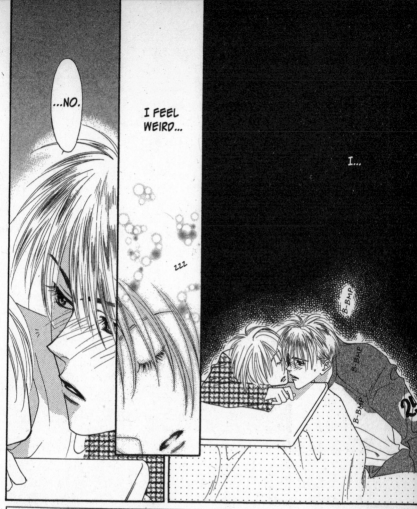

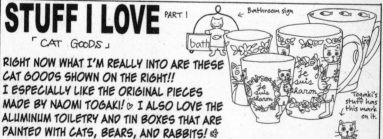

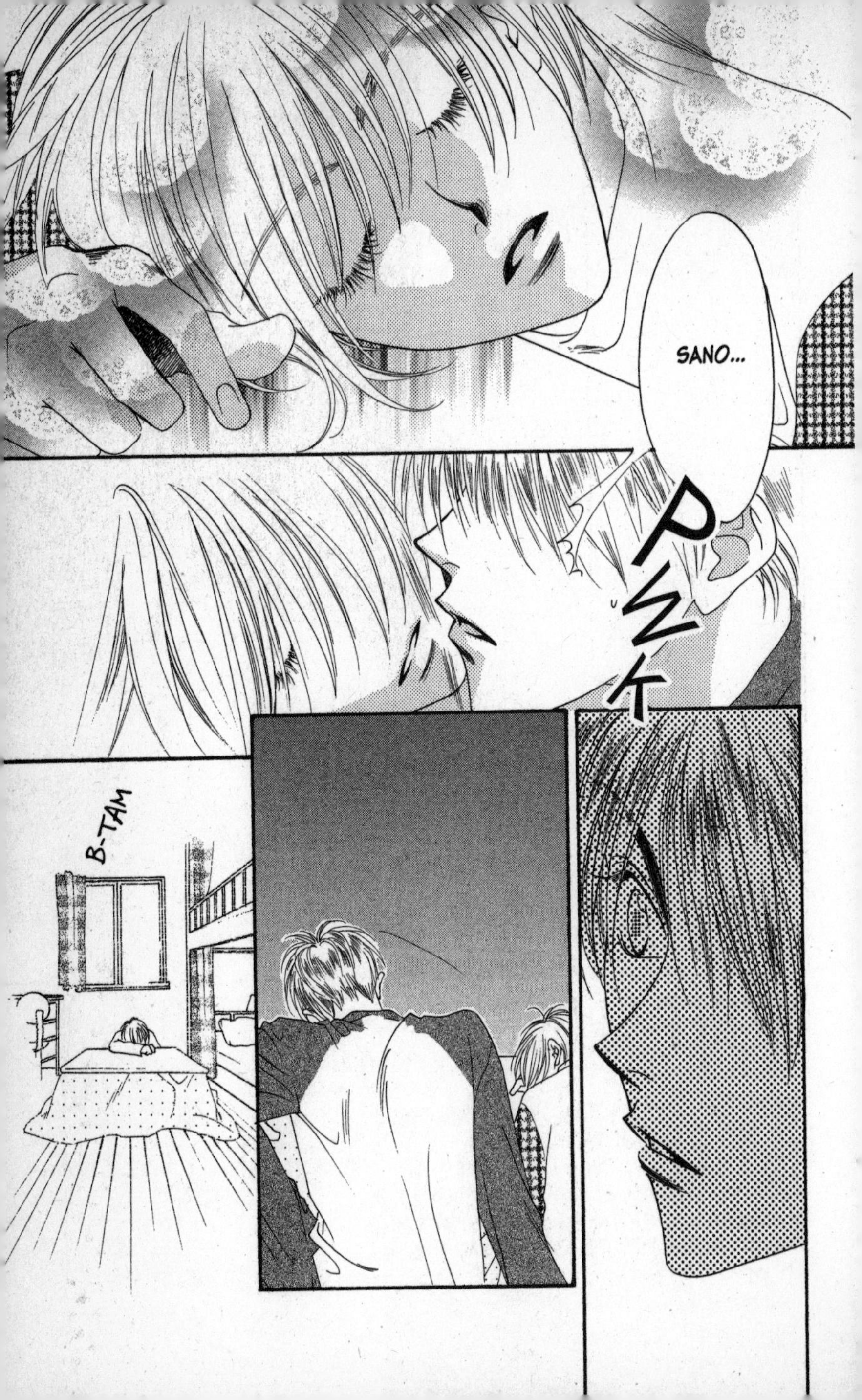
SANO...
PWK
B-TAM

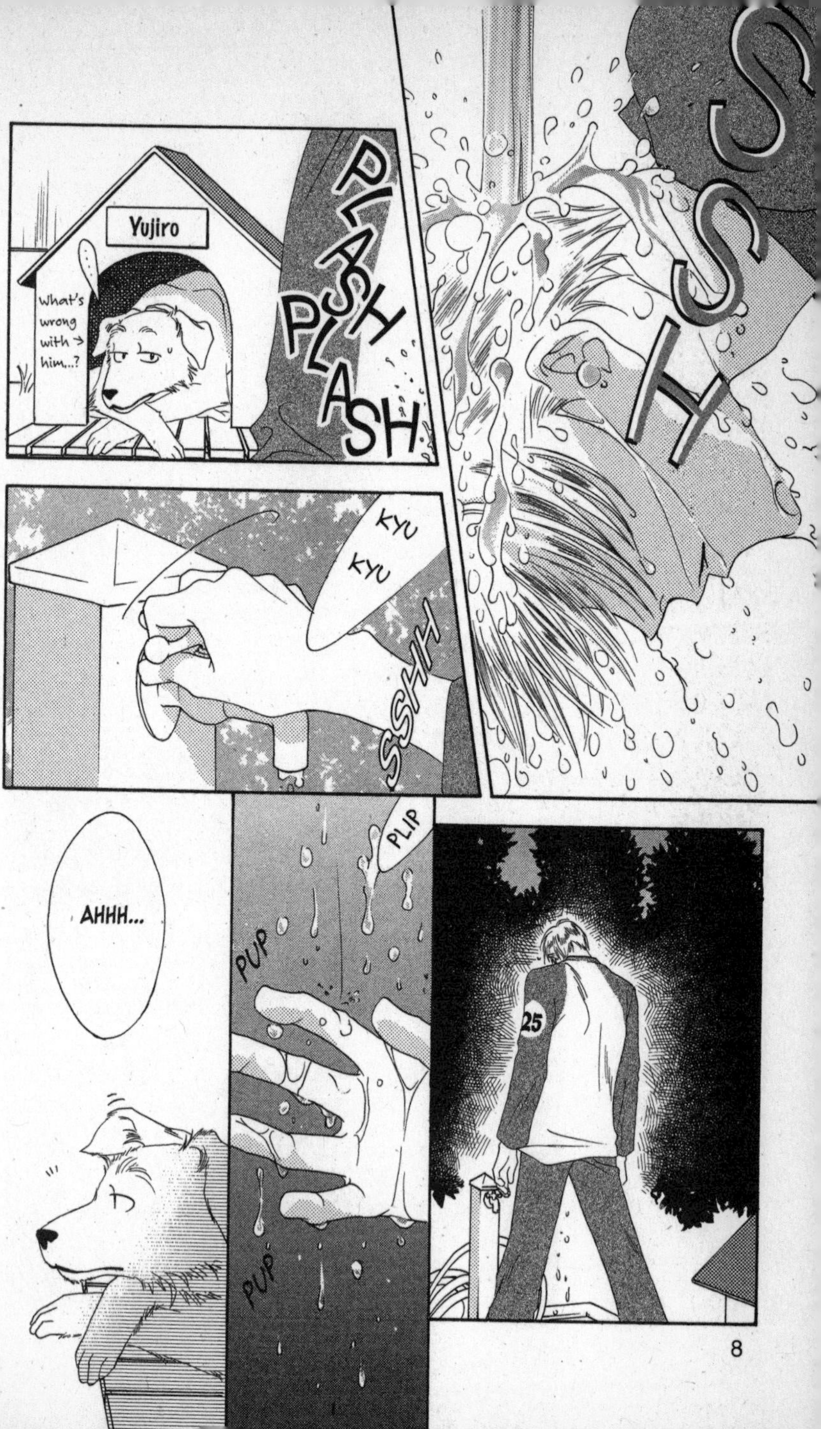
SSHH
SPLASH
SPLASH
Yujiro
...
What's wrong with → him...?
KYU
KYU
SSHH
PLIP
PUP
PUP
AHHH...

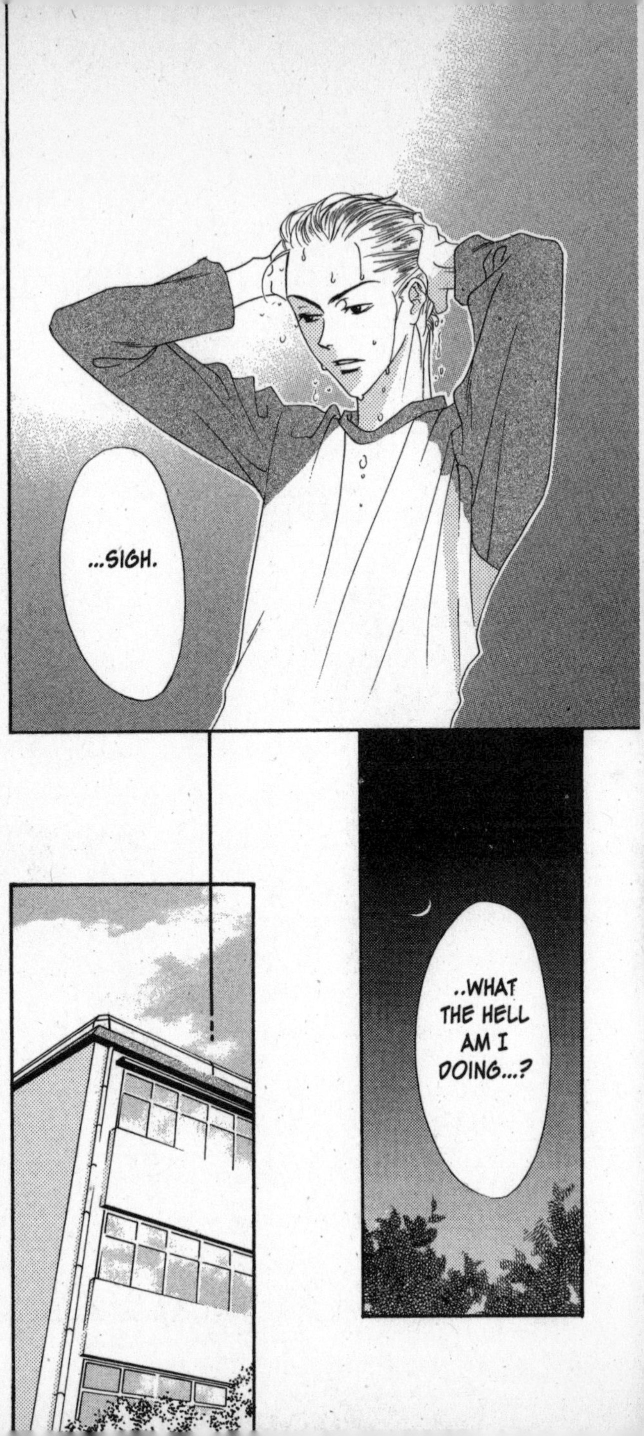
...SIGH.
..WHAT THE HELL AM I DOING...?

WHISPERED SECRETS

THAT'S RIGHT!

HELLO HELLO! IT'S HANA-KIMI VOL. 6! THIS VOLUME'S COVER FEATURES UMEDA, THE MOST REQUESTED CHARACTER. I DREW IT ESPECIALLY FOR THIS BOOK!! MY EDITOR TOLD ME THAT IT WAS SCARY. (WHY?) THIS IS UNRELATED, BUT SOMEBODY POINTED OUT THAT UMEDA'S FAMILY LOOKS A LOT LIKE THE FAMILY FROM SAZAE-SAN. AND I GUESS THEY'RE RIGHT! THIS MEANS UMEDA IS KATSUO, RIO IS WAKAME, AND NANBA IS TARA-CHAN! HA HA!

IN THIS BOOK, NOE AND SEKIME IMITATE THE (FEMALE) IDOL GROUP PAIRETSU (SEE PAGE 10). THEY WEREN'T THAT POPULAR WHEN I WROTE THIS, SO I WASN'T SURE IF ANYONE WOULD GET IT OR NOT.

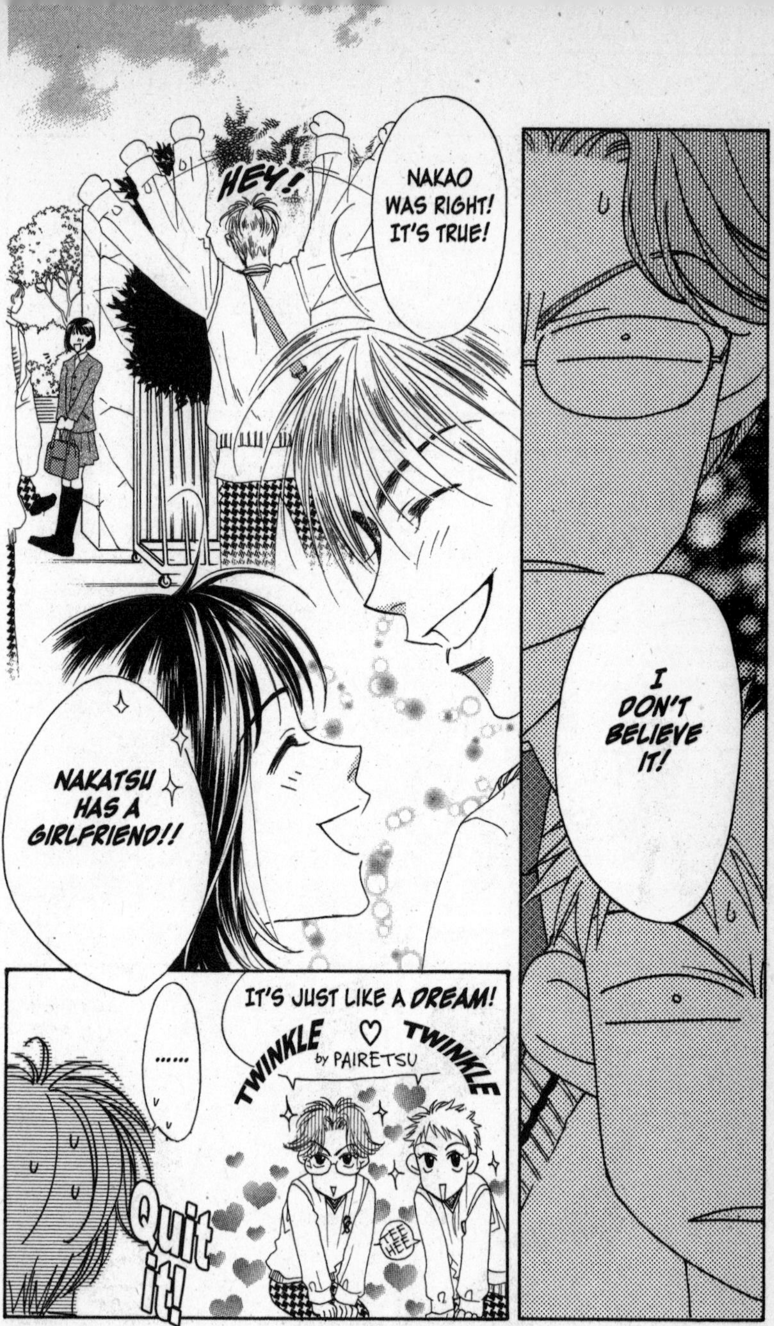
I DON'T BELIEVE IT!
HEY!
NAKAO WAS RIGHT! IT'S TRUE!
NAKATSU HAS A GIRLFRIEND!!
IT'S JUST LIKE A DREAM!
TWINKLE ♡ TWINKLE
by PAIRETSU
TEE HEE
......
Quit it!

...DID I MENTION I LIKE PAIRETSU?

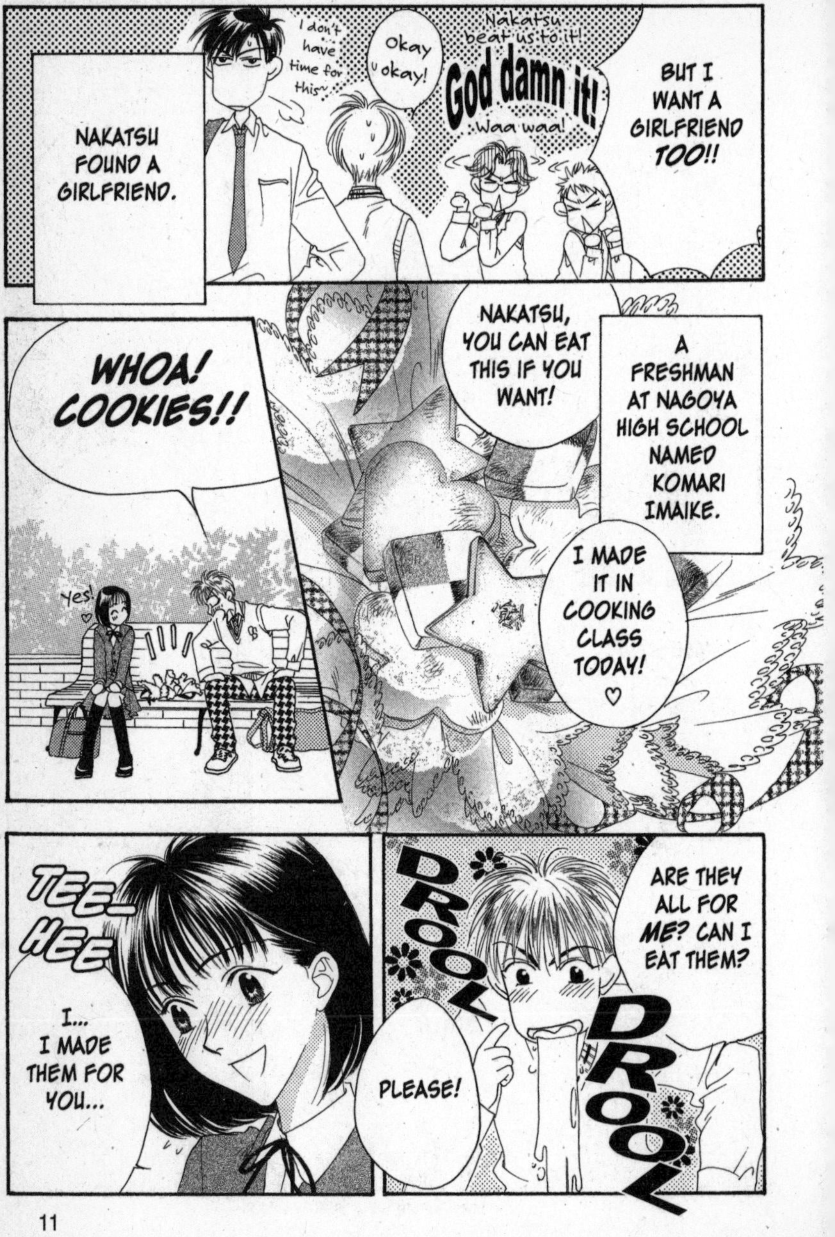
BUT I WANT A GIRLFRIEND TOO!!
Nakatsu beat us to it!
God damn it!
Waa waa!
Okay okay!
I don't have time for this~
NAKATSU FOUND A GIRLFRIEND.
A FRESHMAN AT NAGOYA HIGH SCHOOL NAMED KOMARI IMAIKE.
NAKATSU, YOU CAN EAT THIS IF YOU WANT!
I MADE IT IN COOKING CLASS TODAY! ♡
WHOA! COOKIES!!
Yes! ♡
ARE THEY ALL FOR ME? CAN I EAT THEM?
DROOL
DROOL
PLEASE!
TEE-HEE
I... I MADE THEM FOR YOU...

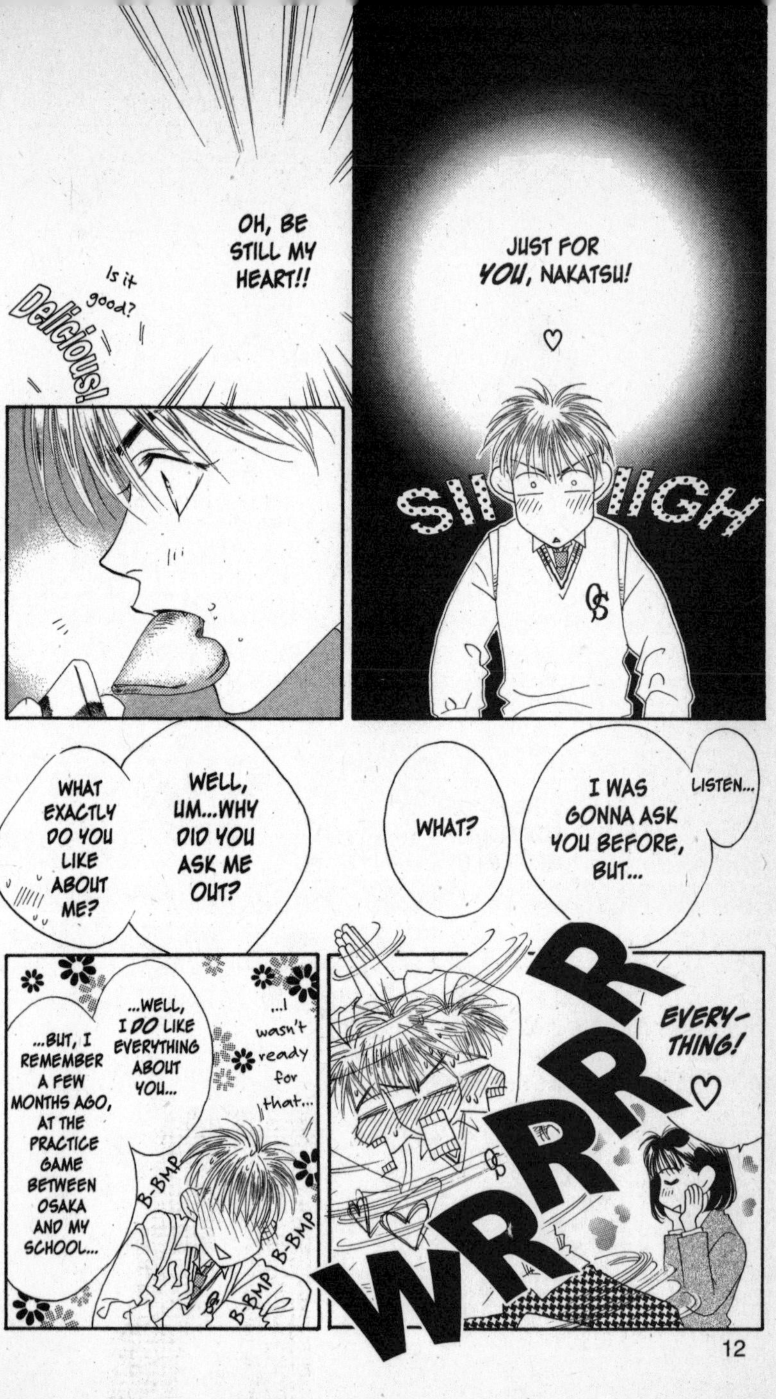

JUST FOR YOU, NAKATSU! ♡
SIIIIGH
OH, BE STILL MY HEART!!
Is it good?
Delicious!
LISTEN...
I WAS GONNA ASK YOU BEFORE, BUT...
WHAT?
WELL, UM...WHY DID YOU ASK ME OUT?
WHAT EXACTLY DO YOU LIKE ABOUT ME?
EVERY-THING! ♡
WRRRR
...I wasn't ready for that...
...WELL, I DO LIKE EVERYTHING ABOUT YOU...
...BUT, I REMEMBER A FEW MONTHS AGO, AT THE PRACTICE GAME BETWEEN OSAKA AND MY SCHOOL...
B-BMP B-BMP B-BMP B-BMP

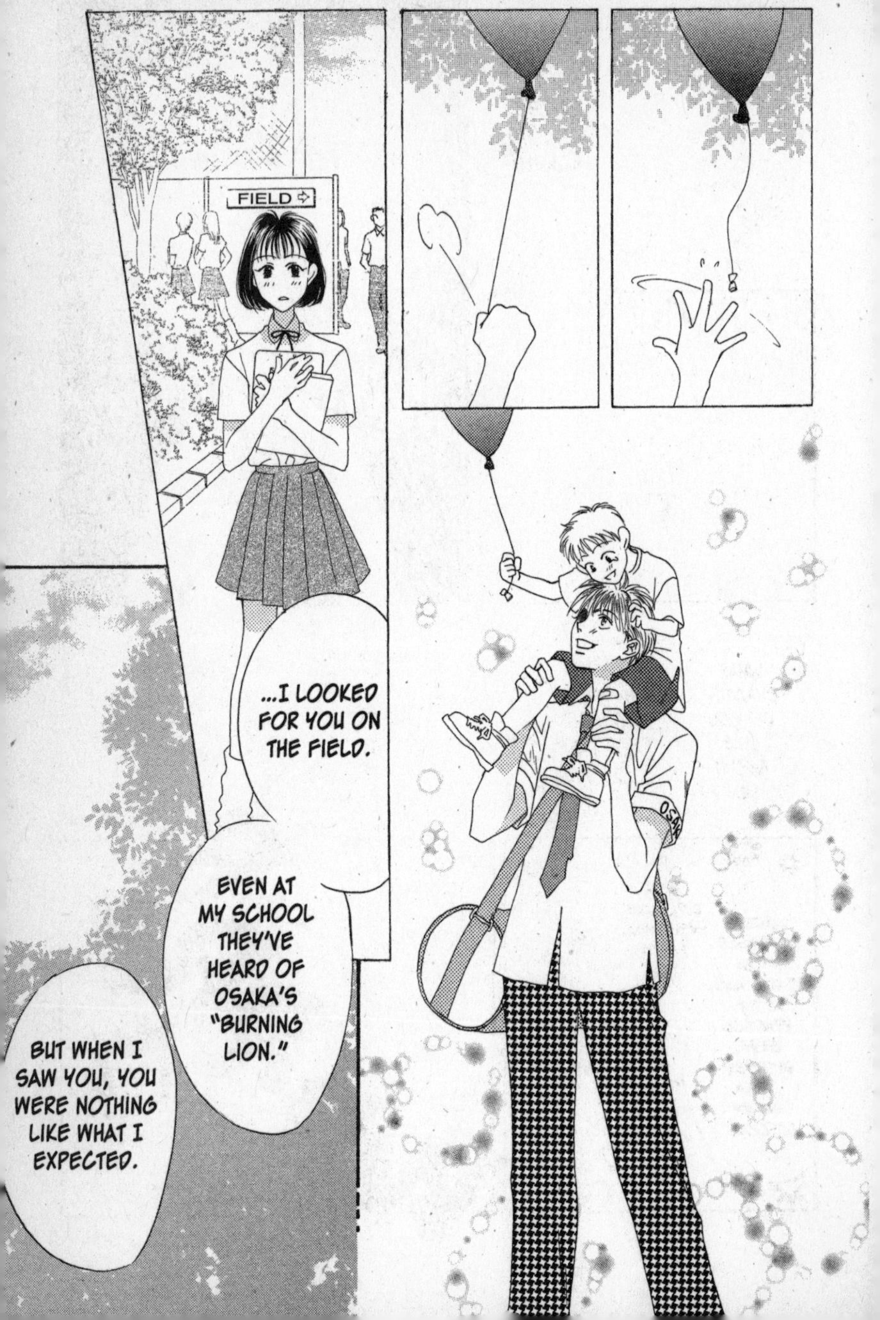
FIELD
...I LOOKED FOR YOU ON THE FIELD.
EVEN AT MY SCHOOL THEY'VE HEARD OF OSAKA'S "BURNING LION."
BUT WHEN I SAW YOU, YOU WERE NOTHING LIKE WHAT I EXPECTED.

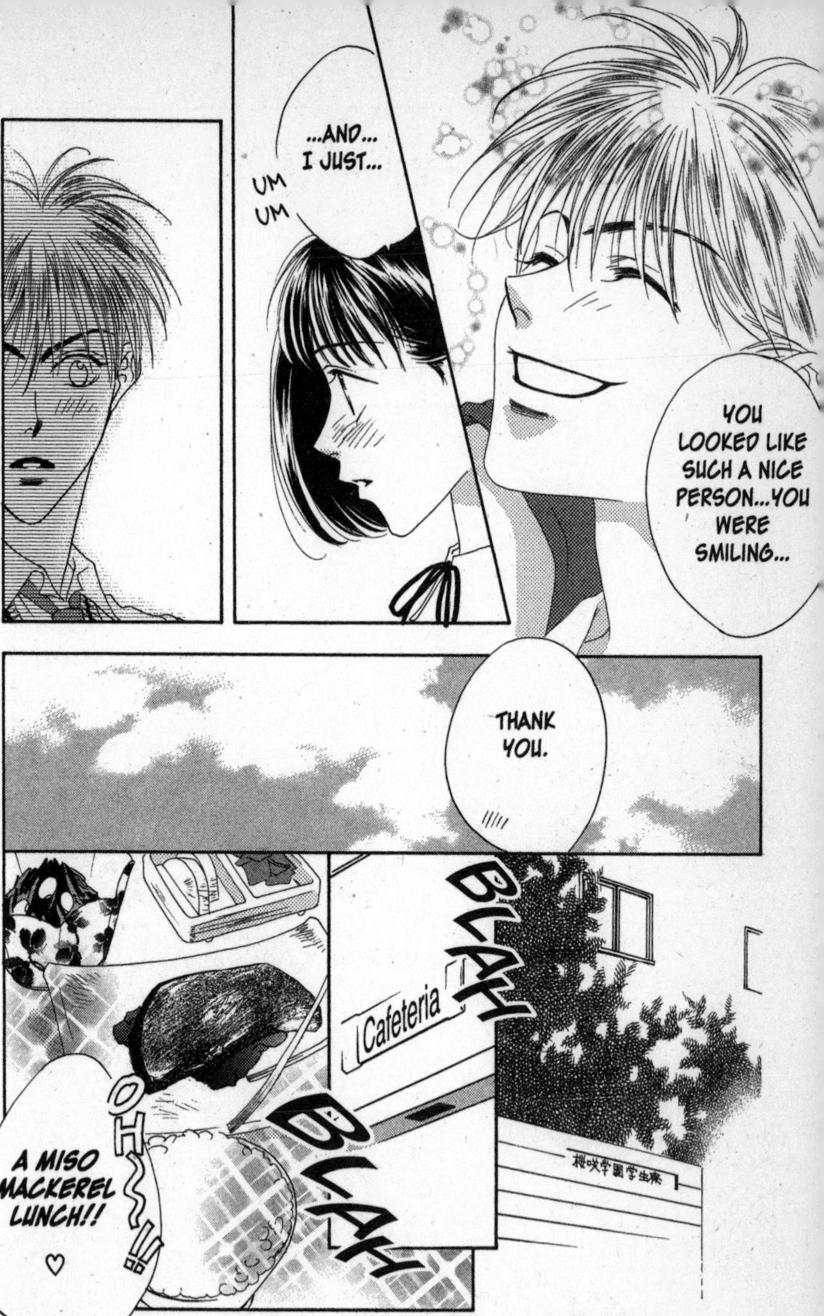
YOU LOOKED LIKE SUCH A NICE PERSON...YOU WERE SMILING...
...AND... I JUST...
UM UM
THANK YOU.
BLAH BLAH
Cafeteria
桜咲学園学生寮
OH~!!
A MISO MACKEREL LUNCH!! ♡

* Dormitory

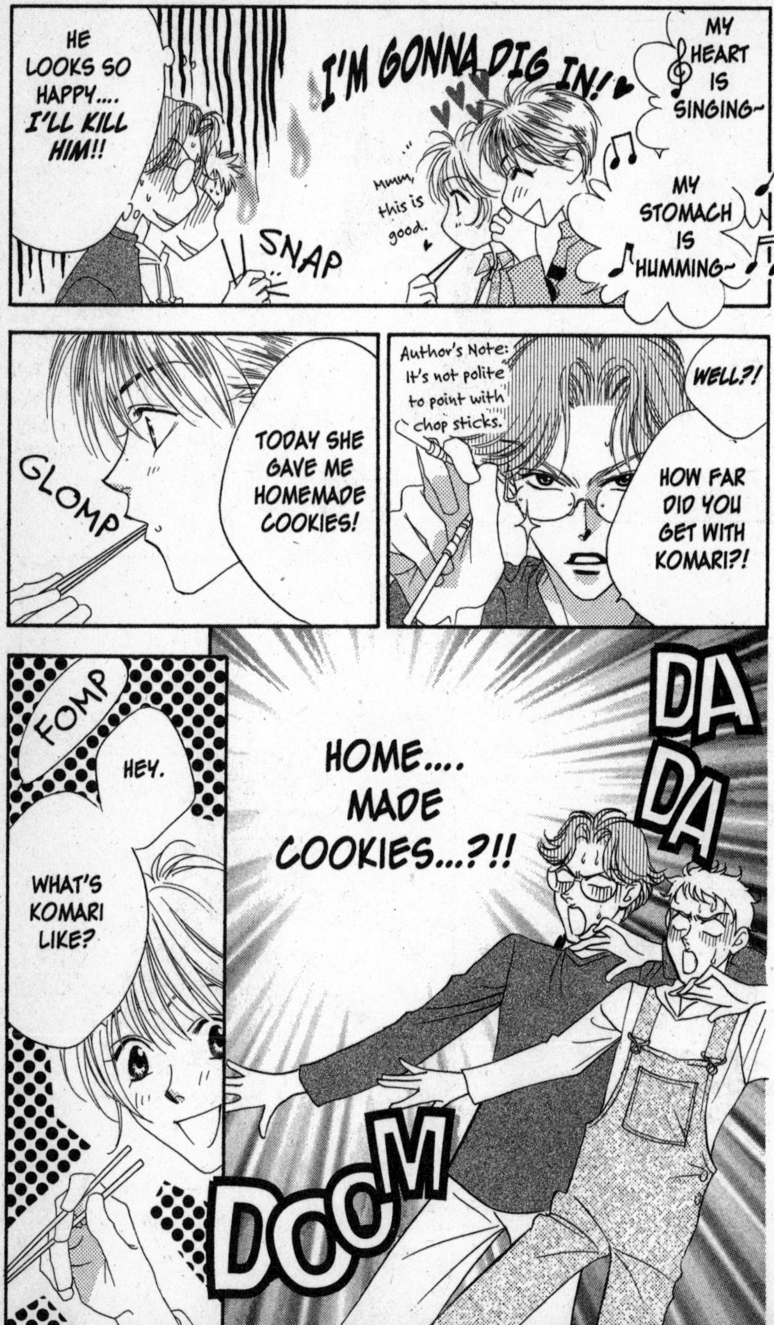
MY HEART IS SINGING~
MY STOMACH IS HUMMING~
I'M GONNA DIG IN!
Mmm, this is good.
SNAP
HE LOOKS SO HAPPY.... I'LL KILL HIM!!
WELL?!
HOW FAR DID YOU GET WITH KOMARI?!
Author's Note: It's not polite to point with chop sticks.
TODAY SHE GAVE ME HOMEMADE COOKIES!
GLOMP
DA
DA
HOME.... MADE COOKIES...?!!
DOOM
FOMP
HEY.
WHAT'S KOMARI LIKE?

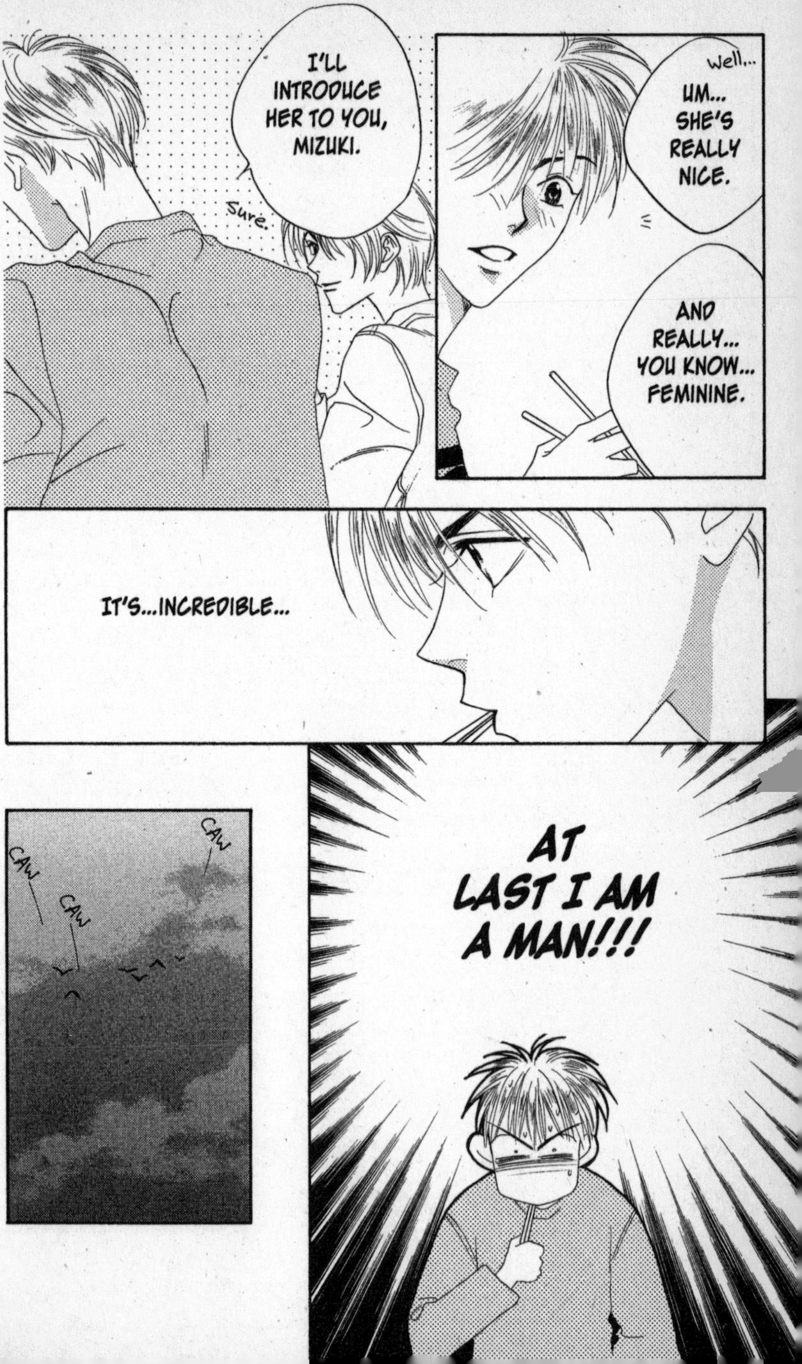
Well...
UM... SHE'S REALLY NICE.
AND REALLY... YOU KNOW... FEMININE.
I'LL INTRODUCE HER TO YOU, MIZUKI.
Sure.
IT'S...INCREDIBLE...
AT LAST I AM A MAN!!!
CAW
CAW
CAW

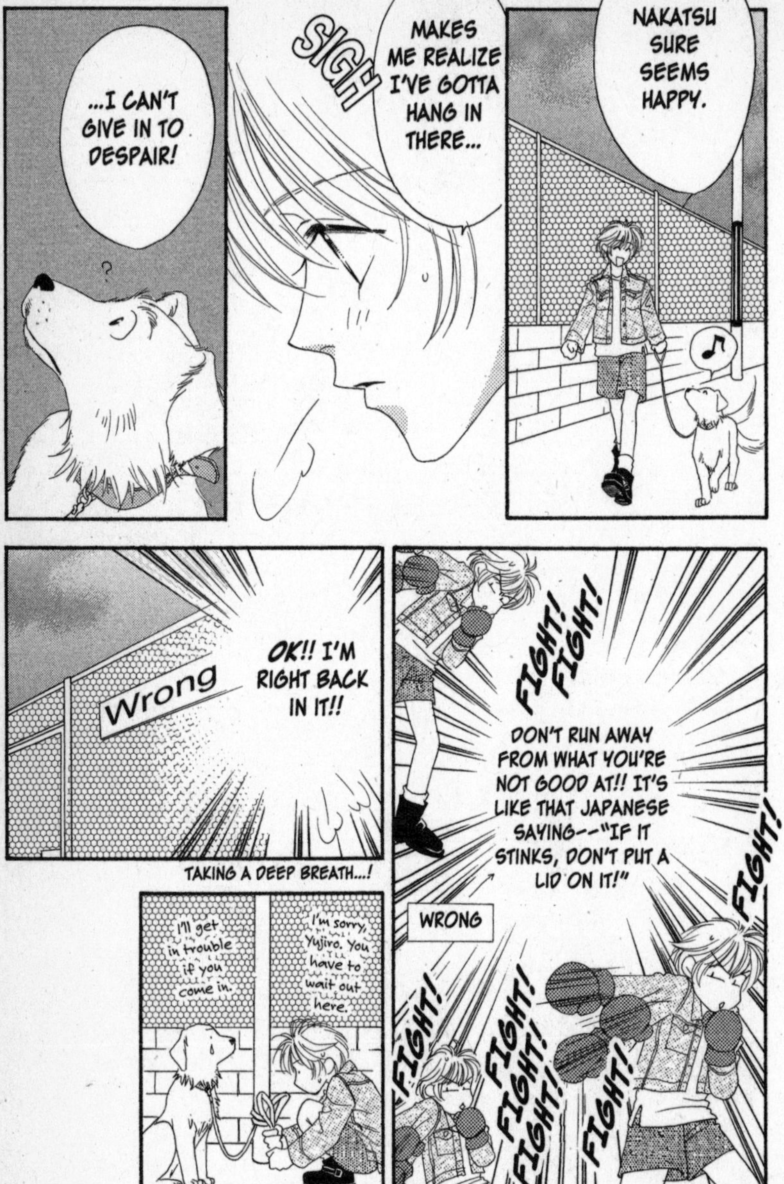
NAKATSU SURE SEEMS HAPPY.
SIGH
MAKES ME REALIZE I'VE GOTTA HANG IN THERE...
...I CAN'T GIVE IN TO DESPAIR!
FIGHT! FIGHT!
DON'T RUN AWAY FROM WHAT YOU'RE NOT GOOD AT!! IT'S LIKE THAT JAPANESE SAYING--"IF IT STINKS, DON'T PUT A LID ON IT!"
WRONG
FIGHT!
FIGHT!
FIGHT! FIGHT! FIGHT!
FIGHT!
OK!! I'M RIGHT BACK IN IT!!
Wrong
TAKING A DEEP BREATH...!
I'm sorry, Yujiro. You have to wait out here.
I'll get in trouble if you come in.

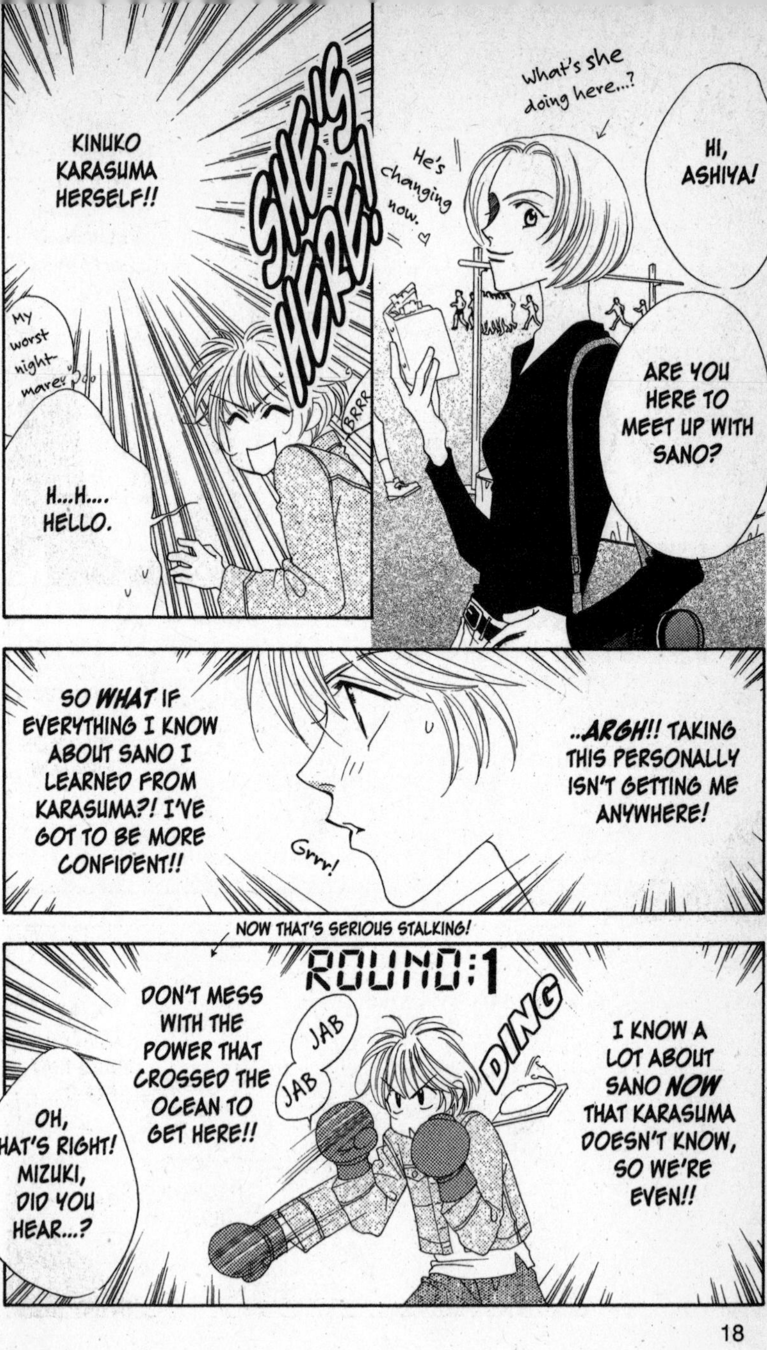
What's she doing here...?
HI, ASHIYA!
He's changing now. ♡
ARE YOU HERE TO MEET UP WITH SANO?
SHE'S HERE!!
KINUKO KARASUMA HERSELF!!
BRRR
My worst night-mare!
H...H.... HELLO.
...ARGH!! TAKING THIS PERSONALLY ISN'T GETTING ME ANYWHERE!
SO WHAT IF EVERYTHING I KNOW ABOUT SANO I LEARNED FROM KARASUMA?! I'VE GOT TO BE MORE CONFIDENT!!
Grrr!
NOW THAT'S SERIOUS STALKING!
ROUND:1
DING
I KNOW A LOT ABOUT SANO NOW THAT KARASUMA DOESN'T KNOW, SO WE'RE EVEN!!
JAB
JAB
DON'T MESS WITH THE POWER THAT CROSSED THE OCEAN TO GET HERE!!
OH, THAT'S RIGHT! MIZUKI, DID YOU HEAR...?

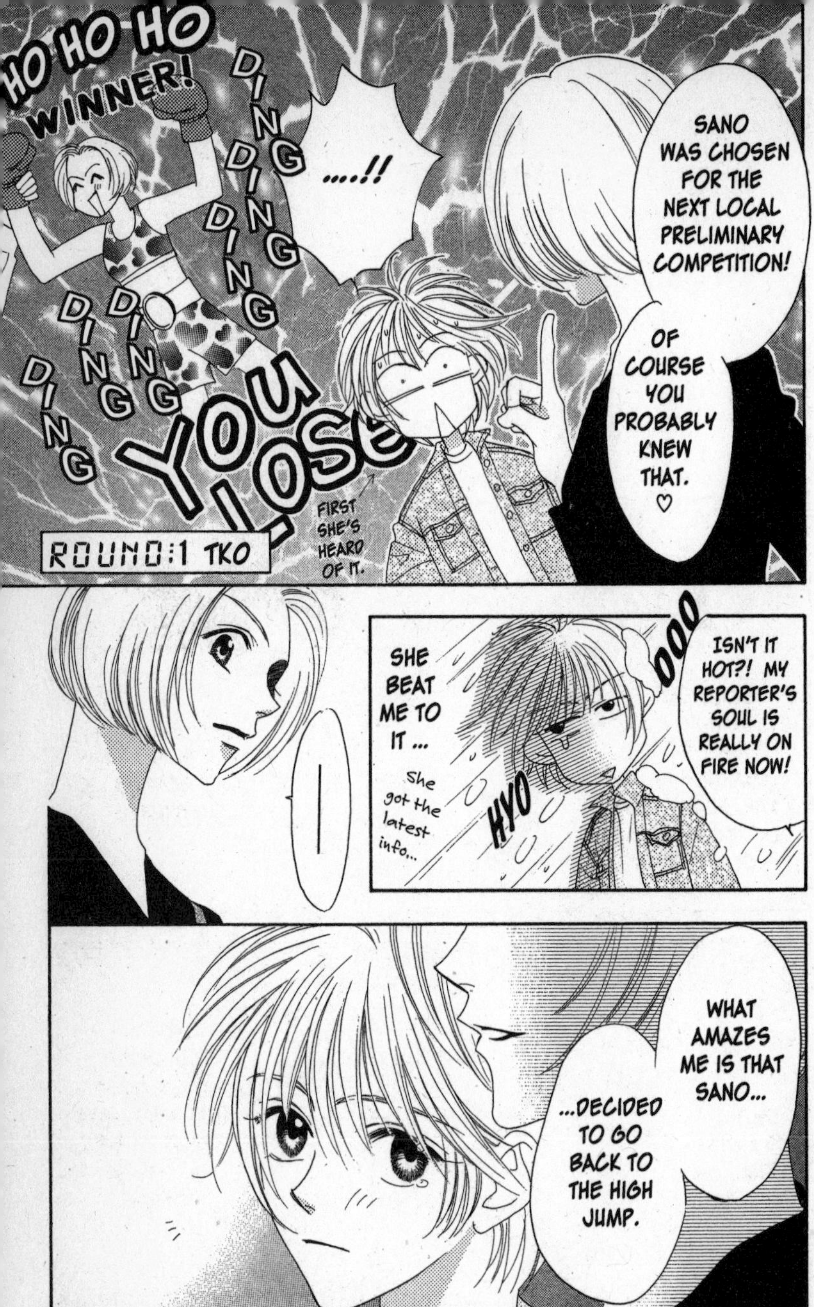
SANO WAS CHOSEN FOR THE NEXT LOCAL PRELIMINARY COMPETITION!
OF COURSE YOU PROBABLY KNEW THAT. ♡
....!!
HO HO HO
WINNER!
DING DING DING DING DING DING
YOU LOSE
FIRST SHE'S HEARD OF IT.
ROUND:1 TKO
ISN'T IT HOT?! MY REPORTER'S SOUL IS REALLY ON FIRE NOW!
OOO
HYO
SHE BEAT ME TO IT ...
She got the latest info...
—
WHAT AMAZES ME IS THAT SANO...
...DECIDED TO GO BACK TO THE HIGH JUMP.

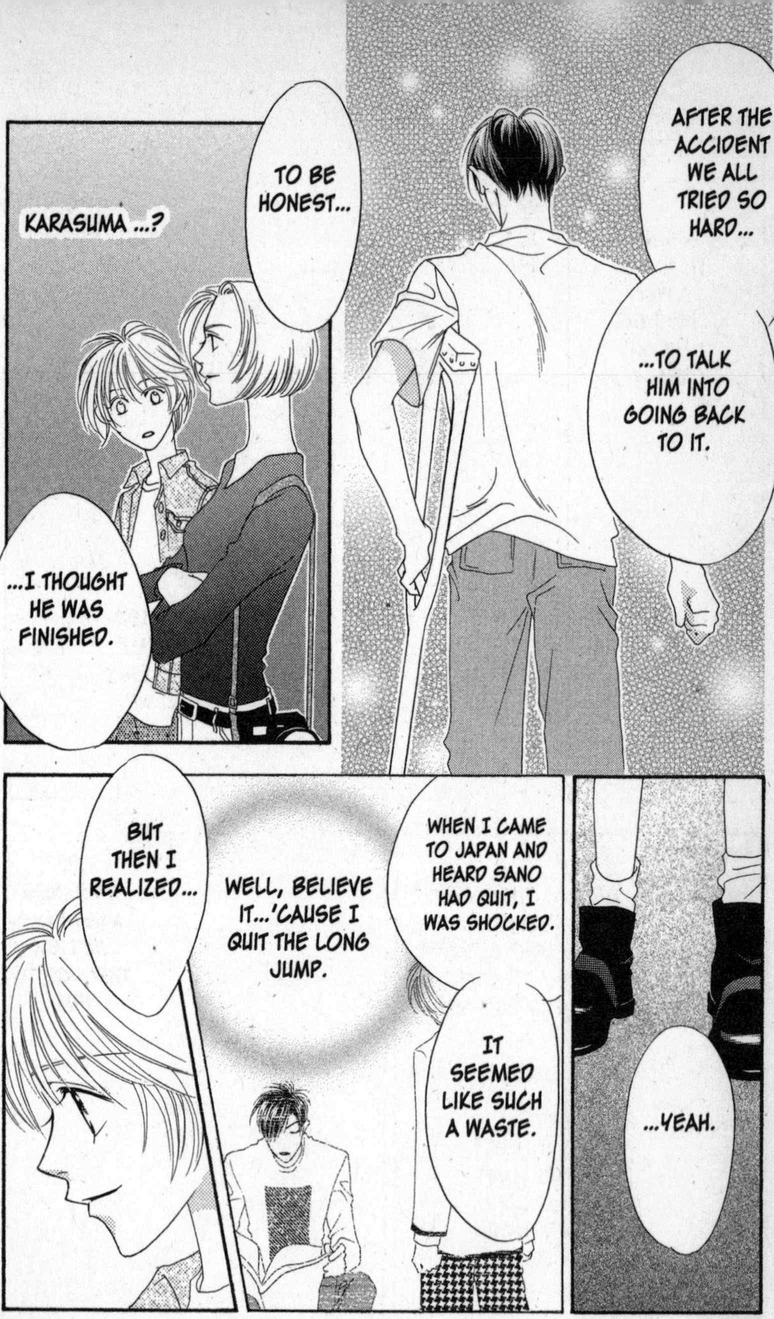
AFTER THE ACCIDENT WE ALL TRIED SO HARD...
...TO TALK HIM INTO GOING BACK TO IT.
TO BE HONEST...
KARASUMA ...?
...I THOUGHT HE WAS FINISHED.
...YEAH.
WHEN I CAME TO JAPAN AND HEARD SANO HAD QUIT, I WAS SHOCKED.
IT SEEMED LIKE SUCH A WASTE.
WELL, BELIEVE IT...'CAUSE I QUIT THE LONG JUMP.
BUT THEN I REALIZED...

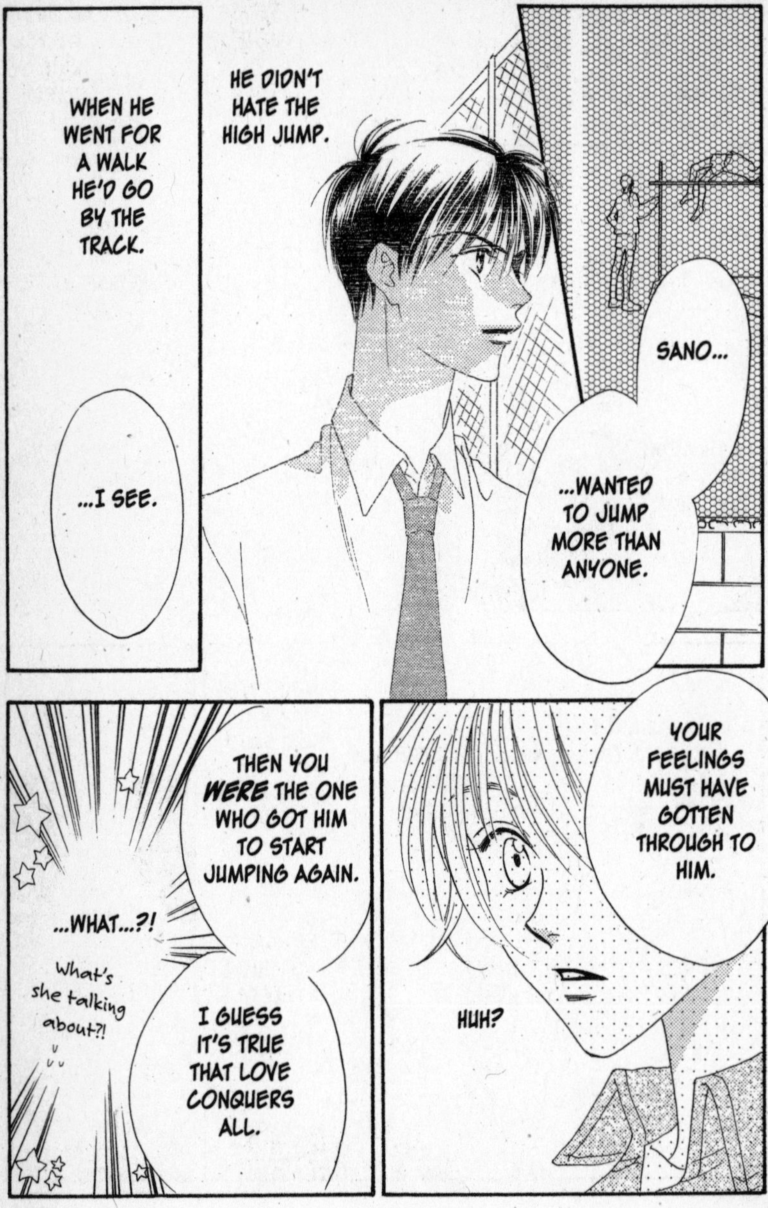
SANO...
...WANTED TO JUMP MORE THAN ANYONE.
HE DIDN'T HATE THE HIGH JUMP.
WHEN HE WENT FOR A WALK HE'D GO BY THE TRACK.
...I SEE.
YOUR FEELINGS MUST HAVE GOTTEN THROUGH TO HIM.
HUH?
THEN YOU *WERE* THE ONE WHO GOT HIM TO START JUMPING AGAIN.
...WHAT...?!
What's she talking about?!
I GUESS IT'S TRUE THAT LOVE CONQUERS ALL.

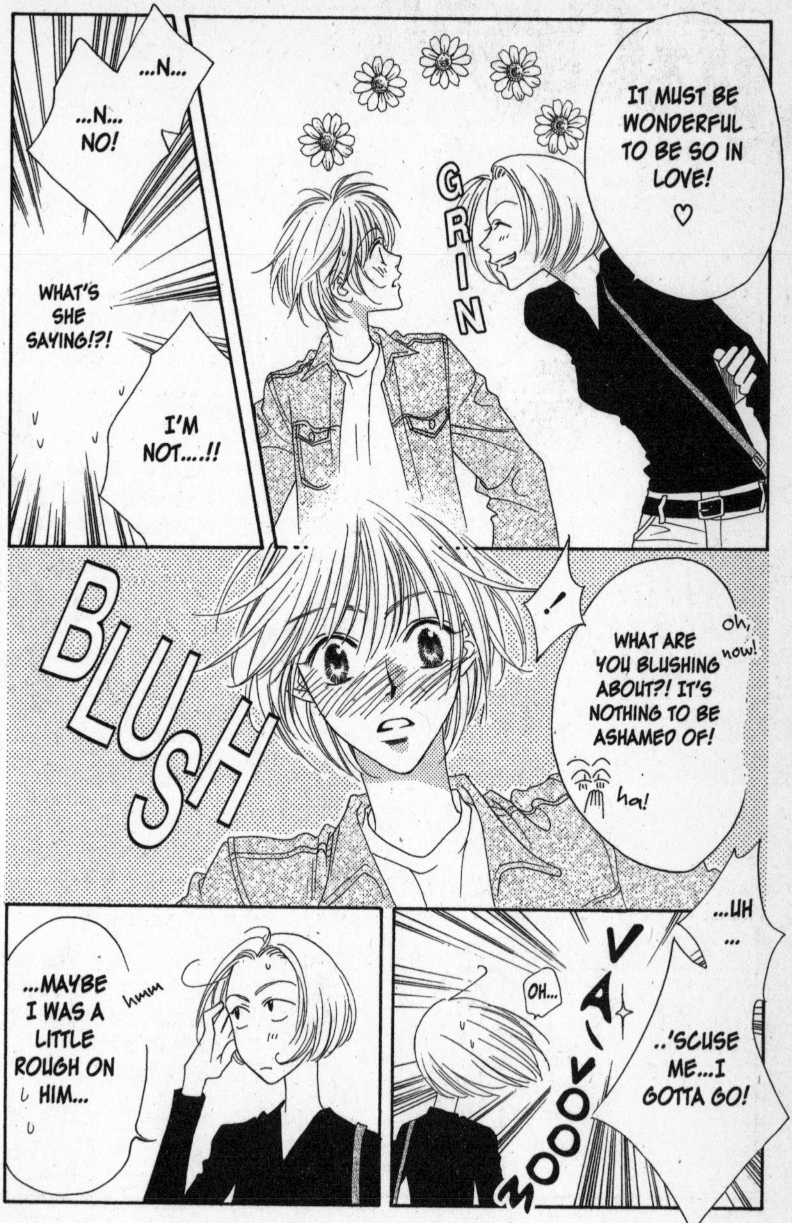
IT MUST BE WONDERFUL TO BE SO IN LOVE! ♡
GRIN
...N...
...N... NO!
WHAT'S SHE SAYING!?!
I'M NOT....!!
!
WHAT ARE YOU BLUSHING ABOUT?! IT'S NOTHING TO BE ASHAMED OF!
oh, now!
ha!
BLUSH
...UH ...
OH...
..'SCUSE ME...I GOTTA GO!
...MAYBE I WAS A LITTLE ROUGH ON HIM...
hmm

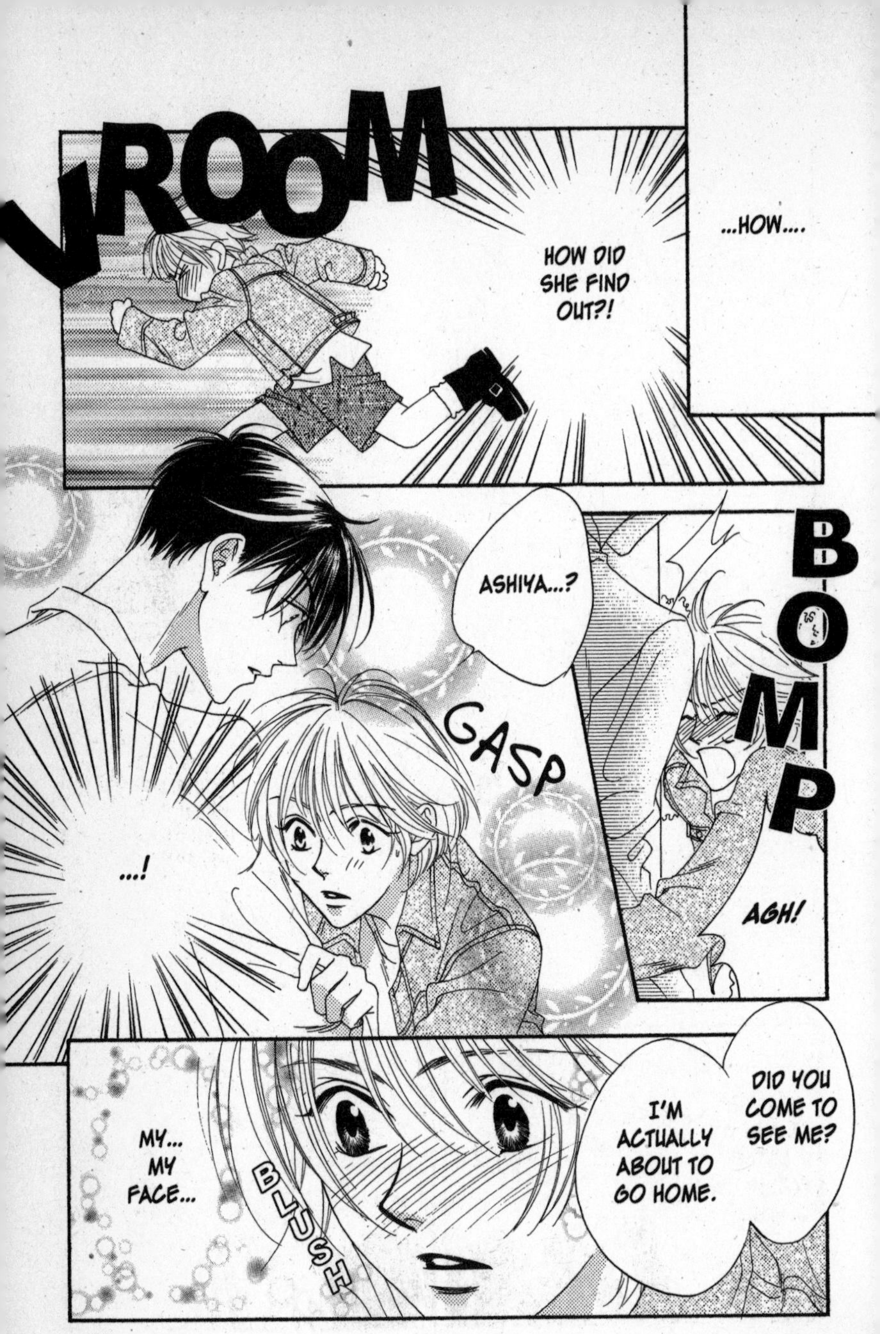
...HOW....
VROOM
HOW DID SHE FIND OUT?!
BOMP
AGH!
ASHIYA...?
GASP
...!
DID YOU COME TO SEE ME?
I'M ACTUALLY ABOUT TO GO HOME.
BLUSH
MY... MY FACE...

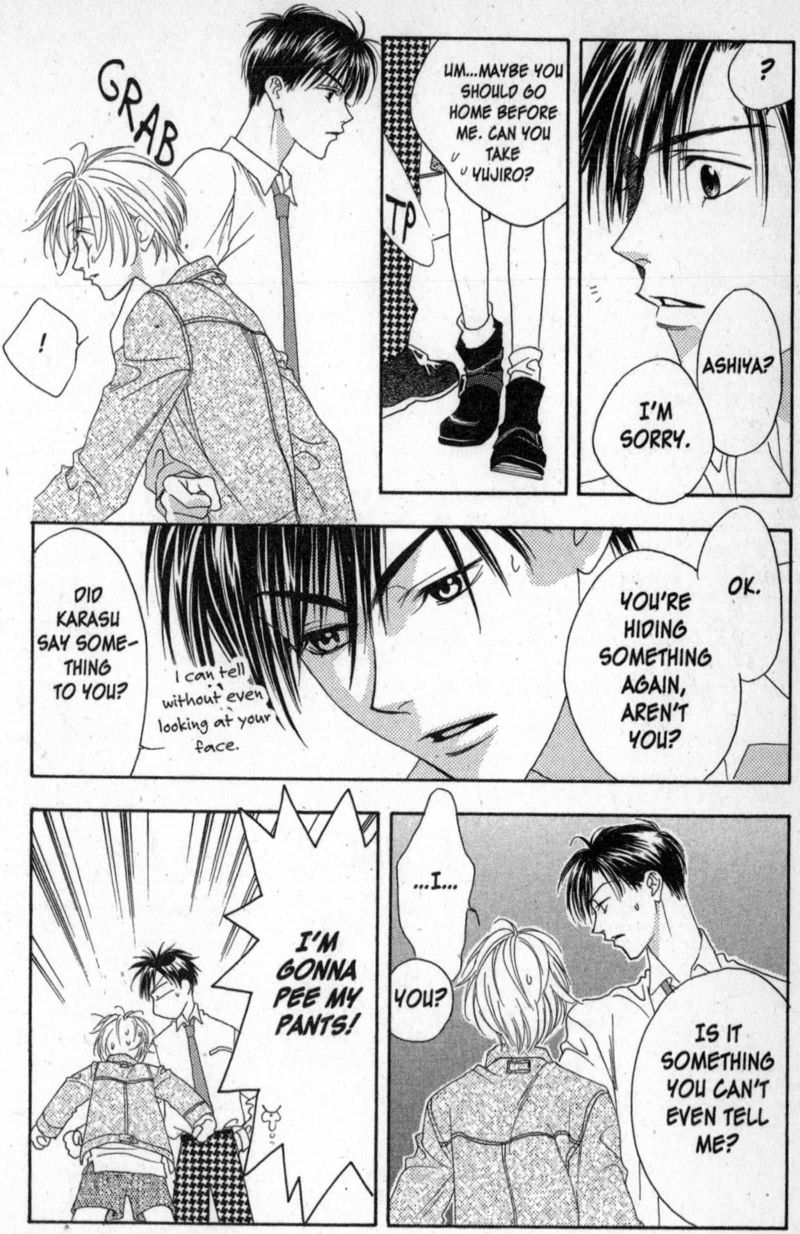
?
ASHIYA?
I'M SORRY.
UM...MAYBE YOU SHOULD GO HOME BEFORE ME. CAN YOU TAKE YUJIRO?
TP
GRAB
!
OK.
YOU'RE HIDING SOMETHING AGAIN, AREN'T YOU?
DID KARASU SAY SOME-THING TO YOU?
I can tell without even looking at your face.
...I...
YOU?
IS IT SOMETHING YOU CAN'T EVEN TELL ME?
I'M GONNA PEE MY PANTS!

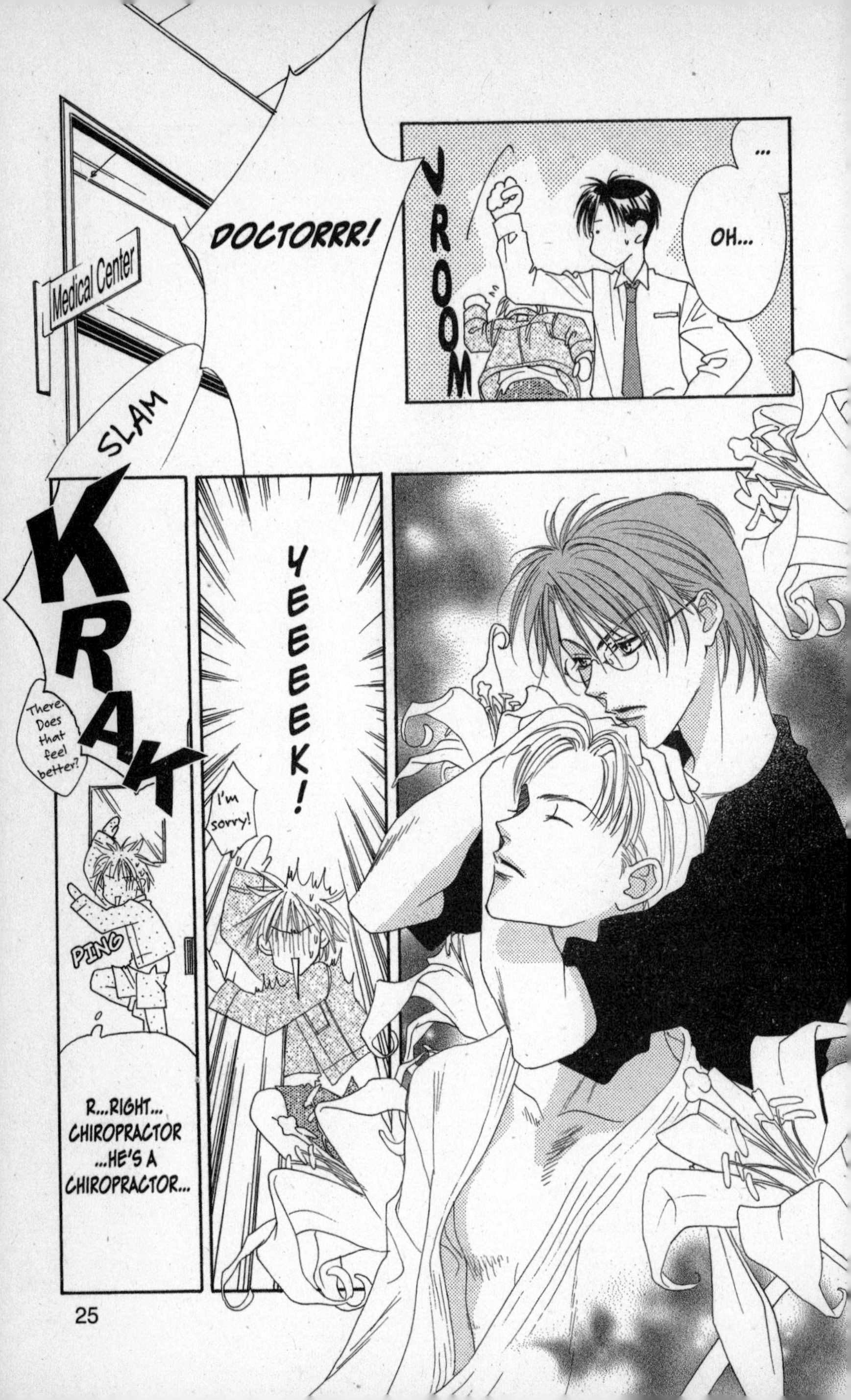

...
OH...
VROOM
DOCTORRR!
Medical Center
SLAM
YEEEEK!
I'm sorry!
KRAK
There. Does that feel better?
PING
R...RIGHT... CHIROPRACTOR ...HE'S A CHIROPRACTOR...

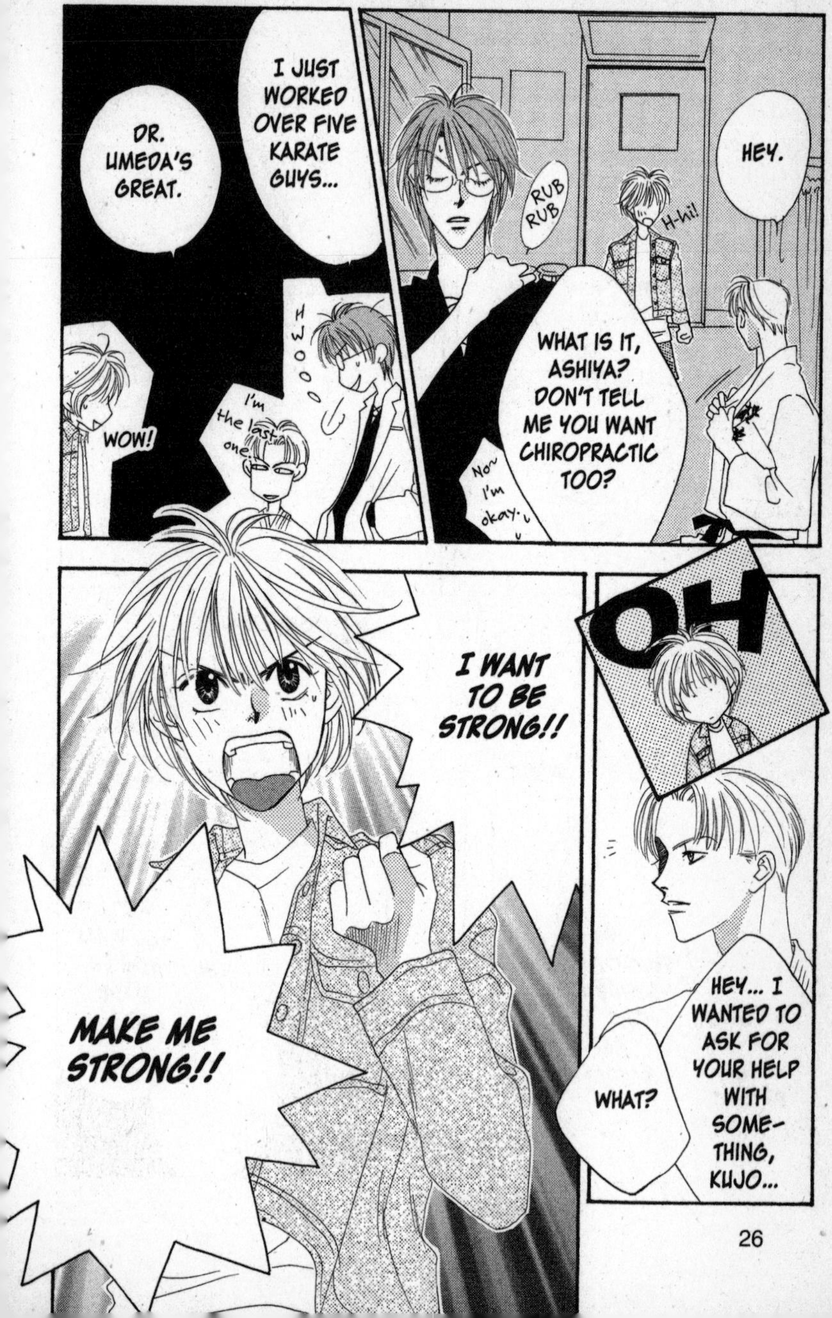
HEY.
H-hi!
RUB RUB
WHAT IS IT, ASHIYA? DON'T TELL ME YOU WANT CHIROPRACTIC TOO?
No~ I'm okay.
I JUST WORKED OVER FIVE KARATE GUYS...
DR. UMEDA'S GREAT.
HWOOO
I'm the last one.
WOW!
OH
HEY... I WANTED TO ASK FOR YOUR HELP WITH SOME-THING, KUJO...
WHAT?
I WANT TO BE STRONG!!
MAKE ME STRONG!!

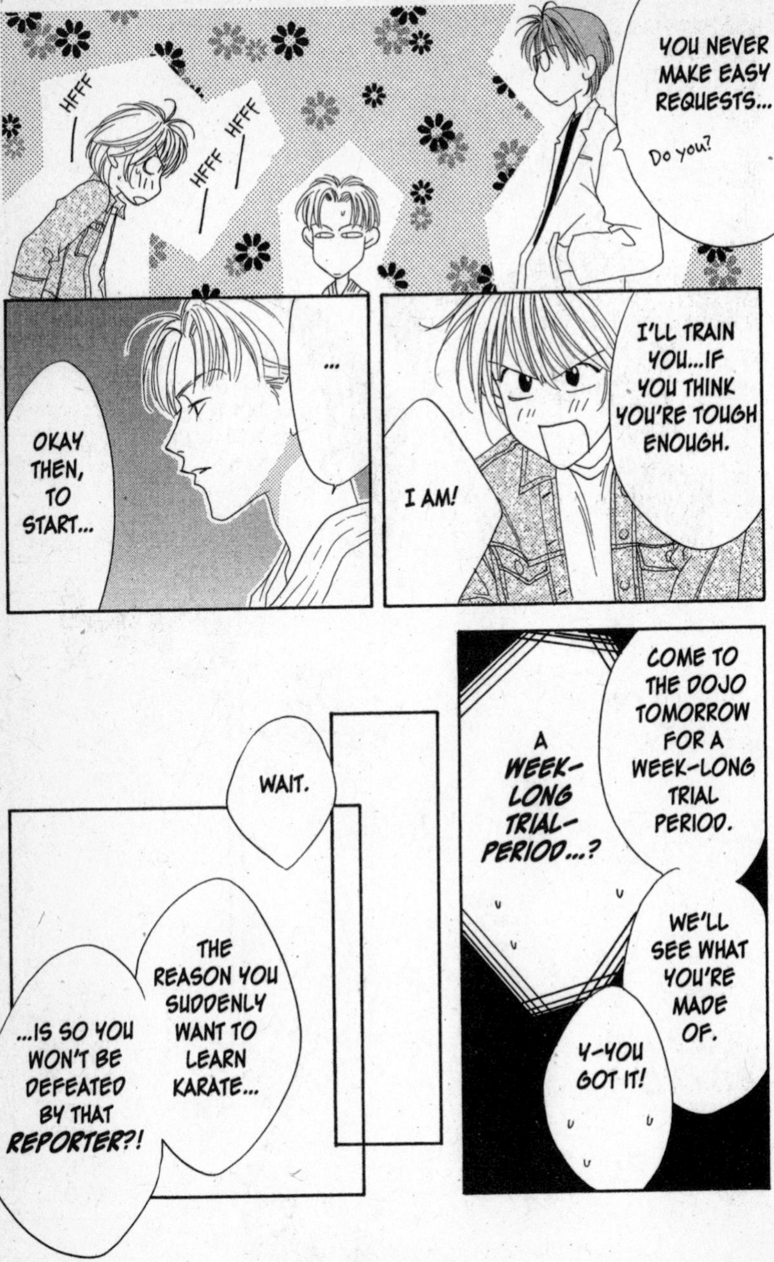
YOU NEVER MAKE EASY REQUESTS...
Do you?
HFFF
HFFF
HFFF
I'LL TRAIN YOU...IF YOU THINK YOU'RE TOUGH ENOUGH.
I AM!
...
OKAY THEN, TO START...
COME TO THE DOJO TOMORROW FOR A WEEK-LONG TRIAL PERIOD.
A *WEEK-LONG TRIAL-PERIOD*...?
WE'LL SEE WHAT YOU'RE MADE OF.
Y-YOU GOT IT!
WAIT.
THE REASON YOU SUDDENLY WANT TO LEARN KARATE...
...IS SO YOU WON'T BE DEFEATED BY THAT *REPORTER*?!

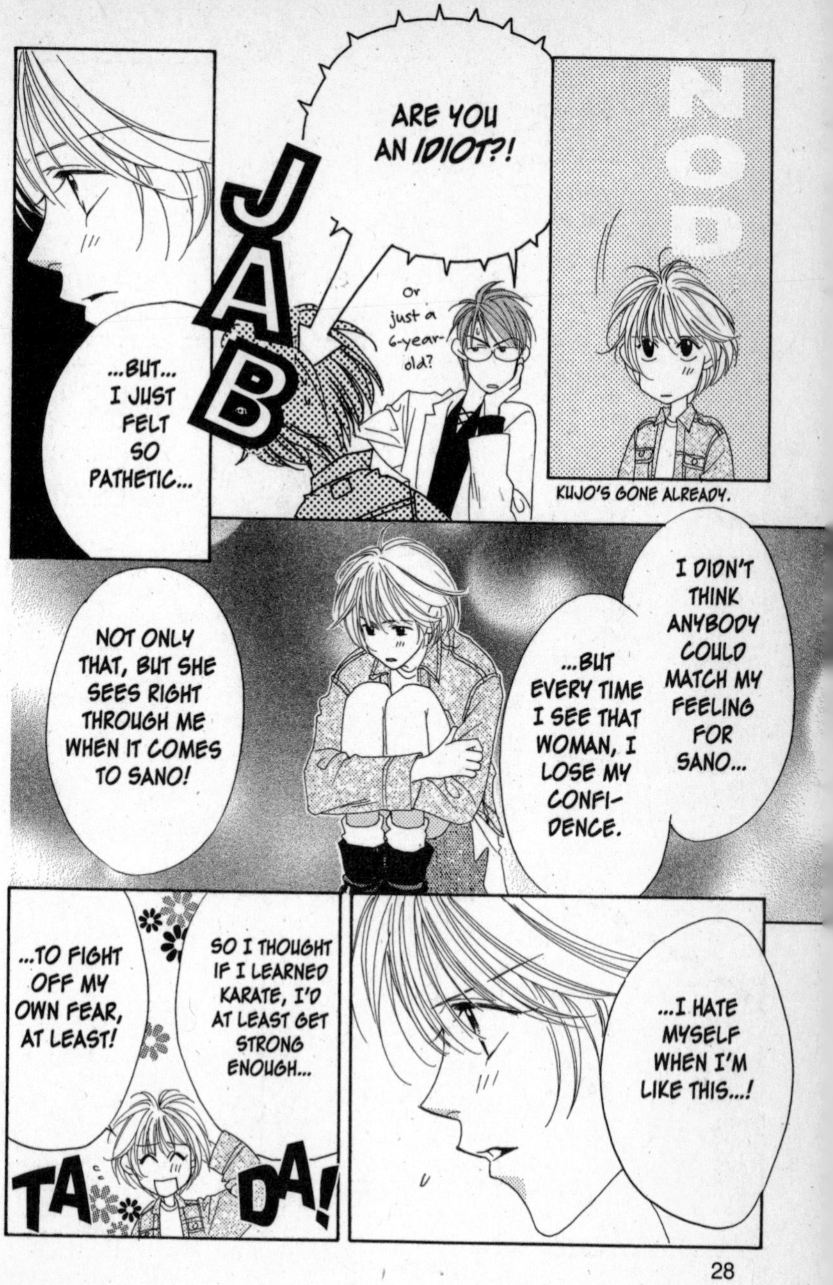
NOD
KUJO'S GONE ALREADY.
ARE YOU AN *IDIOT?!*
Or just a 6-year-old?
JAB
...BUT... I JUST FELT SO PATHETIC...
I DIDN'T THINK ANYBODY COULD MATCH MY FEELING FOR SANO...
...BUT EVERY TIME I SEE THAT WOMAN, I LOSE MY CONFIDENCE.
NOT ONLY THAT, BUT SHE SEES RIGHT THROUGH ME WHEN IT COMES TO SANO!
...I HATE MYSELF WHEN I'M LIKE THIS...!
SO I THOUGHT IF I LEARNED KARATE, I'D AT LEAST GET STRONG ENOUGH...
...TO FIGHT OFF MY OWN FEAR, AT LEAST!
TA DA!

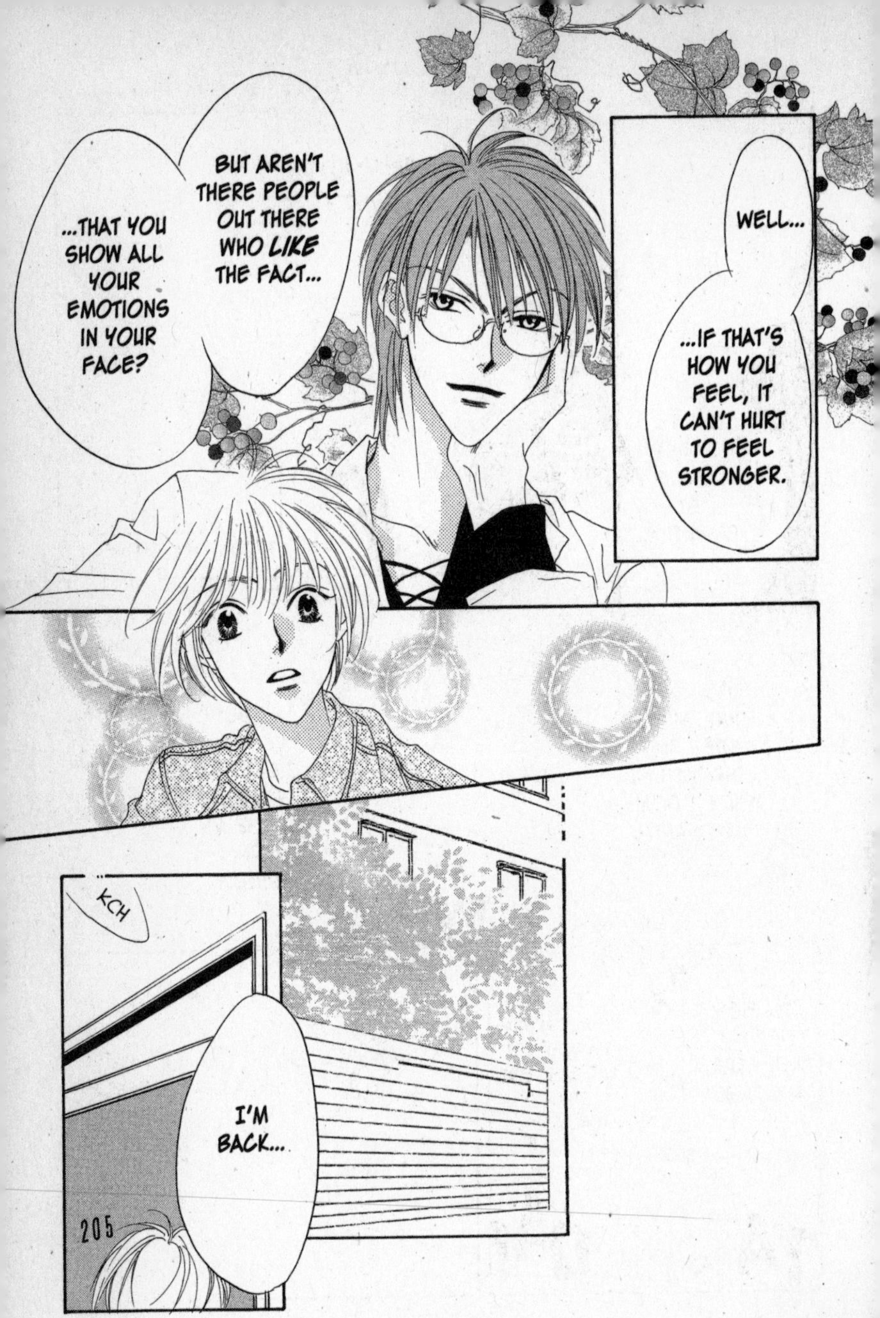
WELL...
...IF THAT'S HOW YOU FEEL, IT CAN'T HURT TO FEEL STRONGER.
BUT AREN'T THERE PEOPLE OUT THERE WHO *LIKE* THE FACT...
...THAT YOU SHOW ALL YOUR EMOTIONS IN YOUR FACE?
KCH
I'M BACK...
205

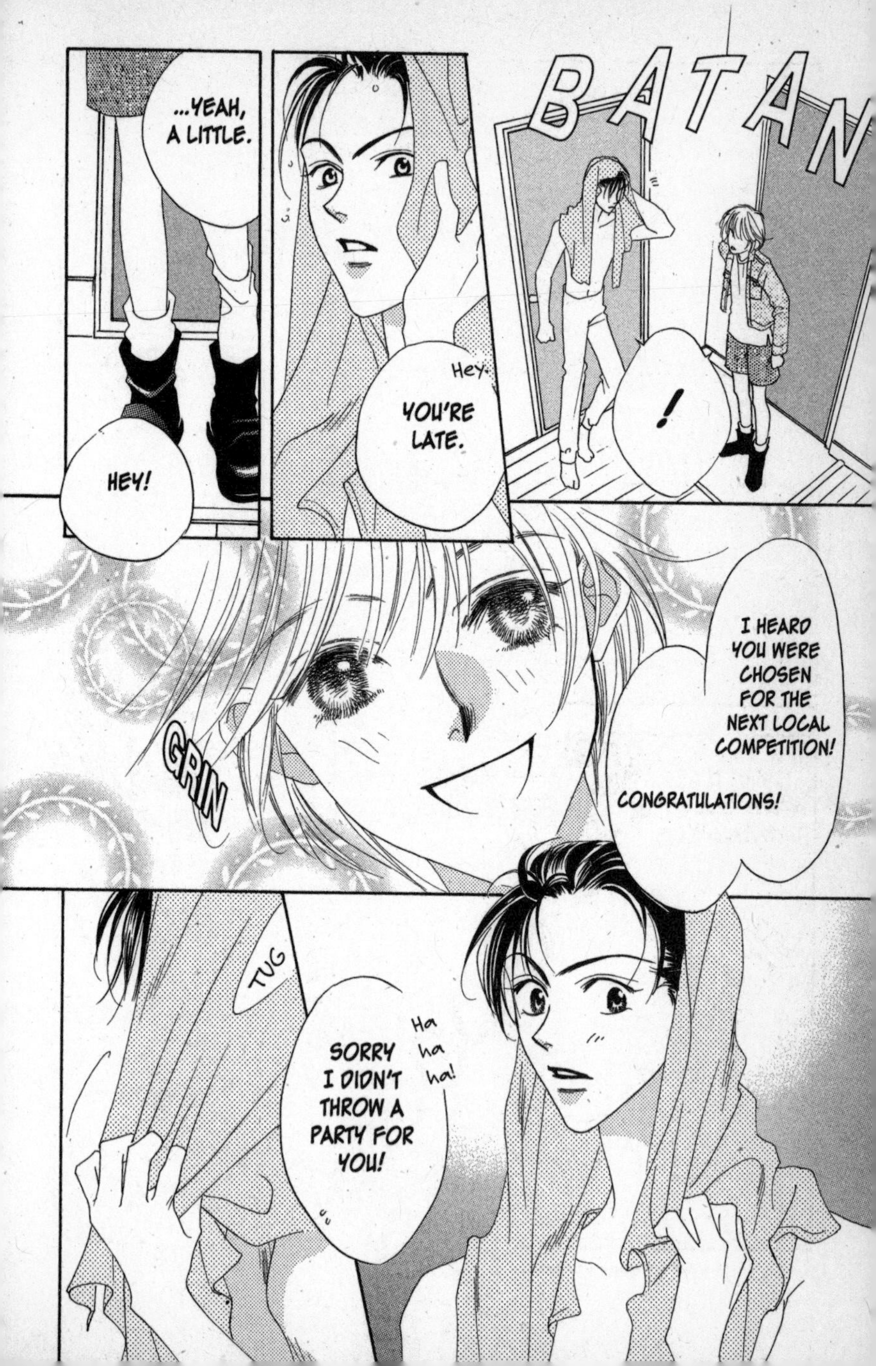
BATAN
!
Hey.
YOU'RE LATE.
...YEAH, A LITTLE.
HEY!
I HEARD YOU WERE CHOSEN FOR THE NEXT LOCAL COMPETITION!
CONGRATULATIONS!
GRIN
TUG
Ha ha ha!
SORRY I DIDN'T THROW A PARTY FOR YOU!

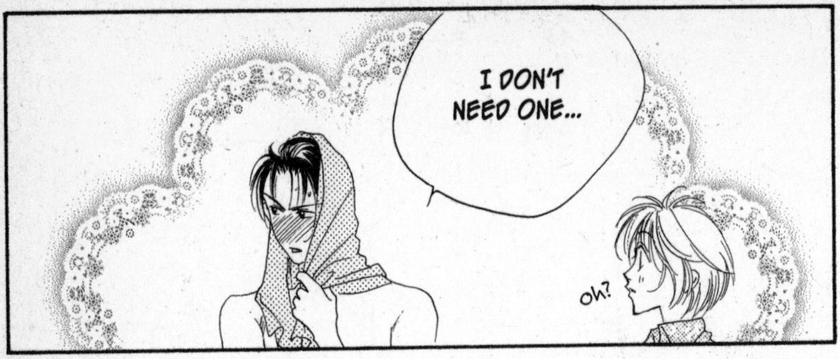
I DON'T NEED ONE...
Oh?

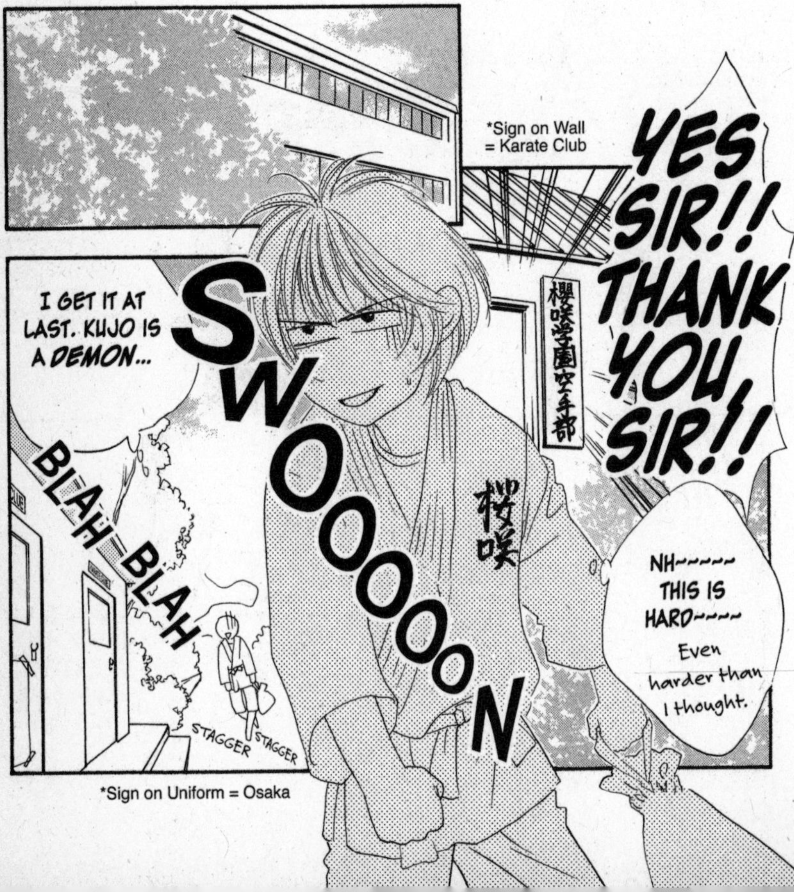
*Sign on Wall = Karate Club
YES SIR!! THANK YOU SIR!!
NH~~~~ THIS IS HARD~~~~
Even harder than I thought.
SWOOOOOON
I GET IT AT LAST. KUJO IS A DEMON...
BLAH BLAH
STAGGER STAGGER
*Sign on Uniform = Osaka

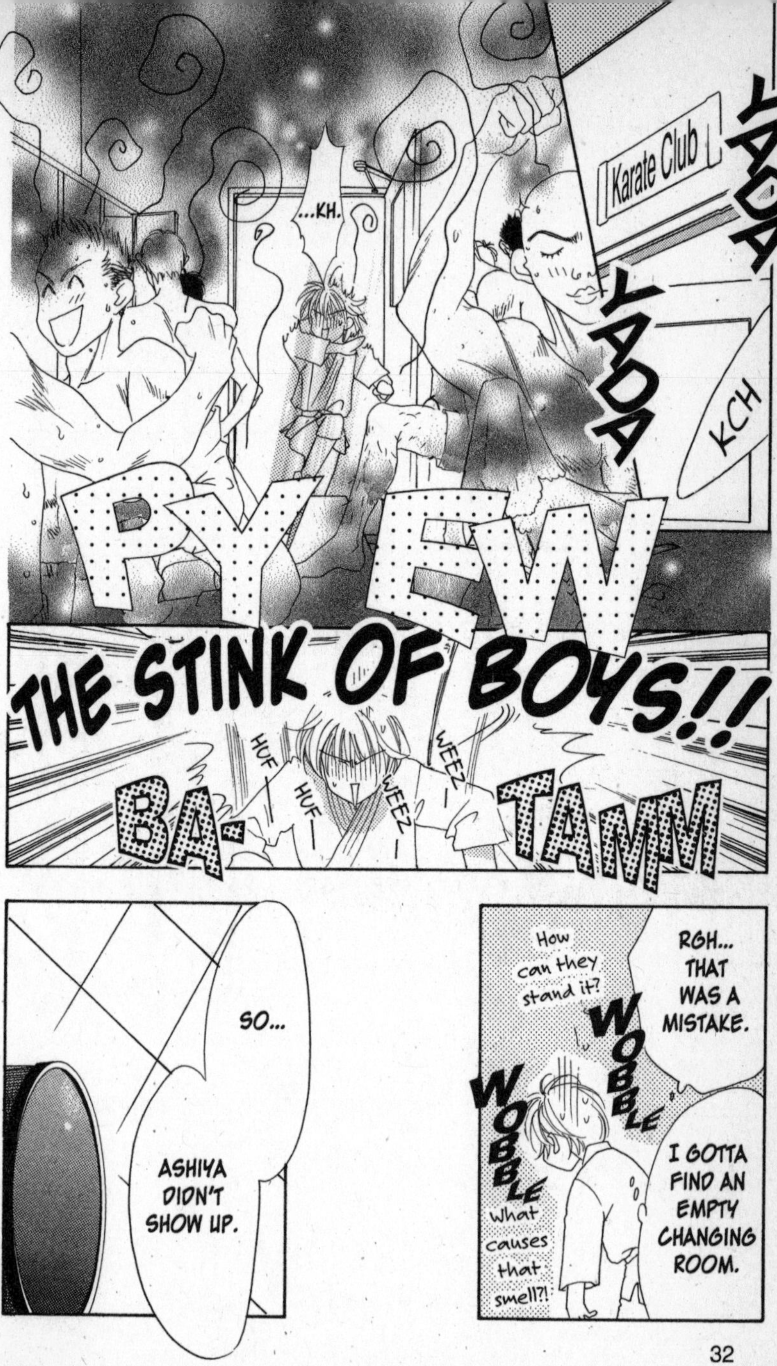

Karate Club
YADA
YADA
KCH
...KH.
PYEW
THE STINK OF BOYS!!
WEEZ WEEZ
HUF HUF
BA-TAMM
RGH... THAT WAS A MISTAKE.
How can they stand it?
WOBBLE
WOBBLE
I GOTTA FIND AN EMPTY CHANGING ROOM.
What causes that smell?!
SO...
ASHIYA DIDN'T SHOW UP.

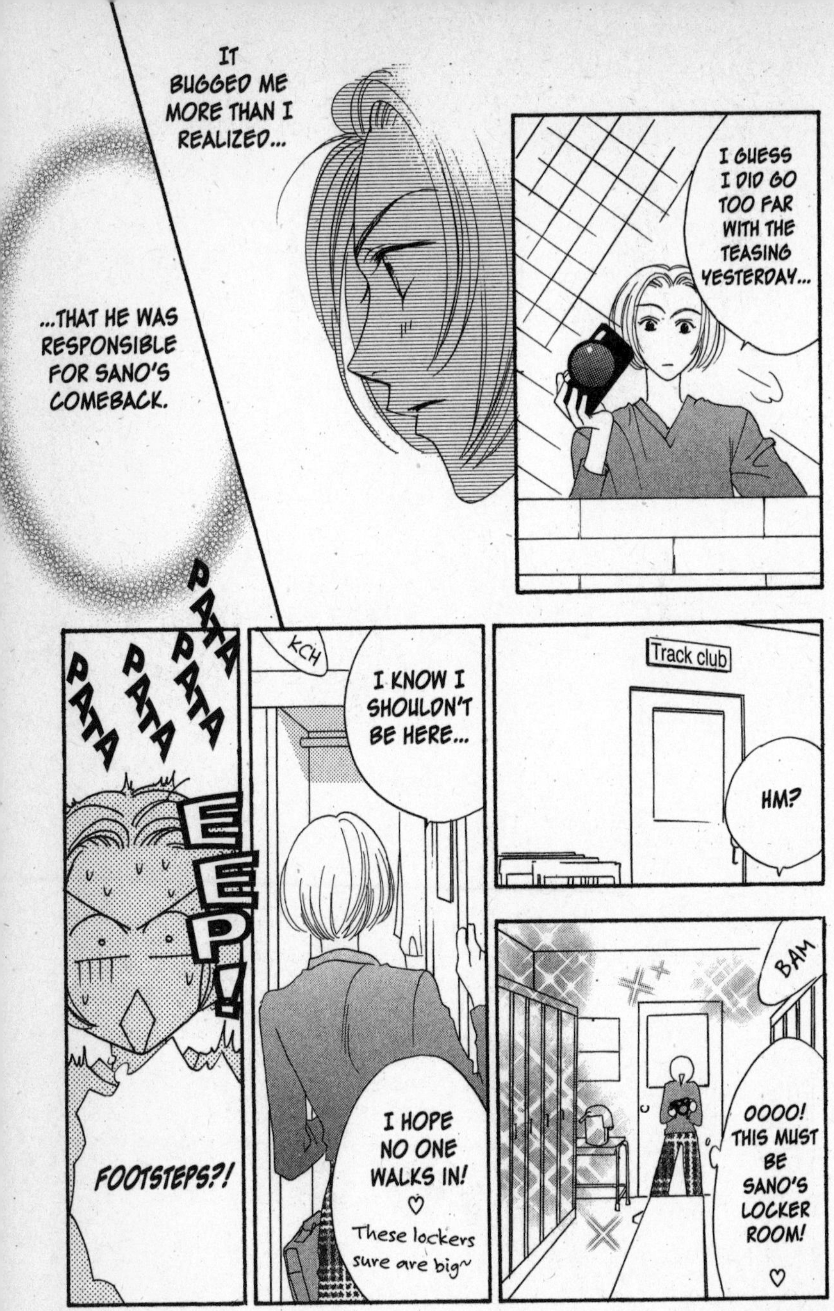
I GUESS I DID GO TOO FAR WITH THE TEASING YESTERDAY...
IT BUGGED ME MORE THAN I REALIZED...
...THAT HE WAS RESPONSIBLE FOR SANO'S COMEBACK.
Track club
HM?
BAM
OOOO! THIS MUST BE SANO'S LOCKER ROOM! ♡
KCH
I KNOW I SHOULDN'T BE HERE...
I HOPE NO ONE WALKS IN! ♡
These lockers sure are big~
PATA PATA PATA PATA
EEP!!
FOOTSTEPS?!

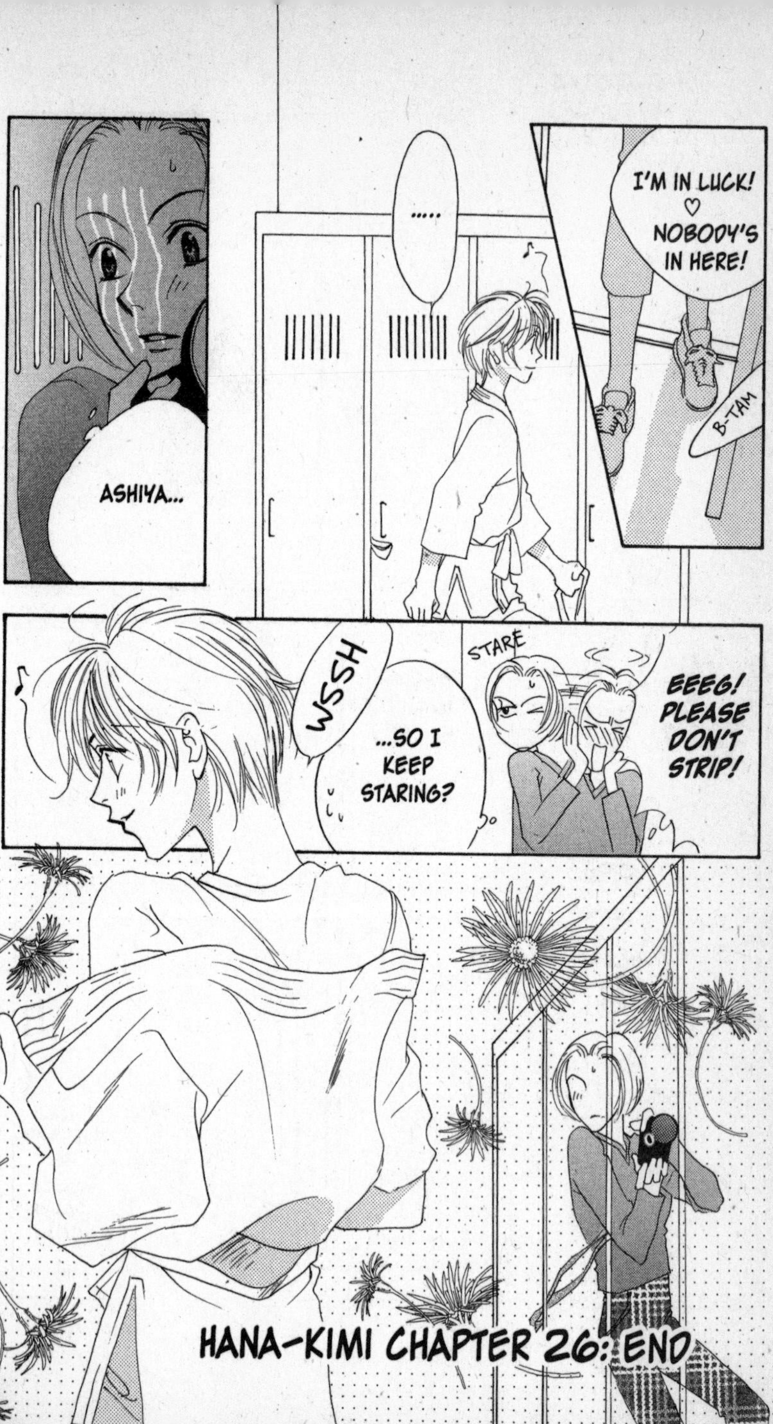
I'M IN LUCK! ♡ NOBODY'S IN HERE!
B-TAM
.....
ASHIYA...
STARE
EEEG! PLEASE DON'T STRIP!
WSSH
...SO I KEEP STARING?
HANA-KIMI CHAPTER 26: END

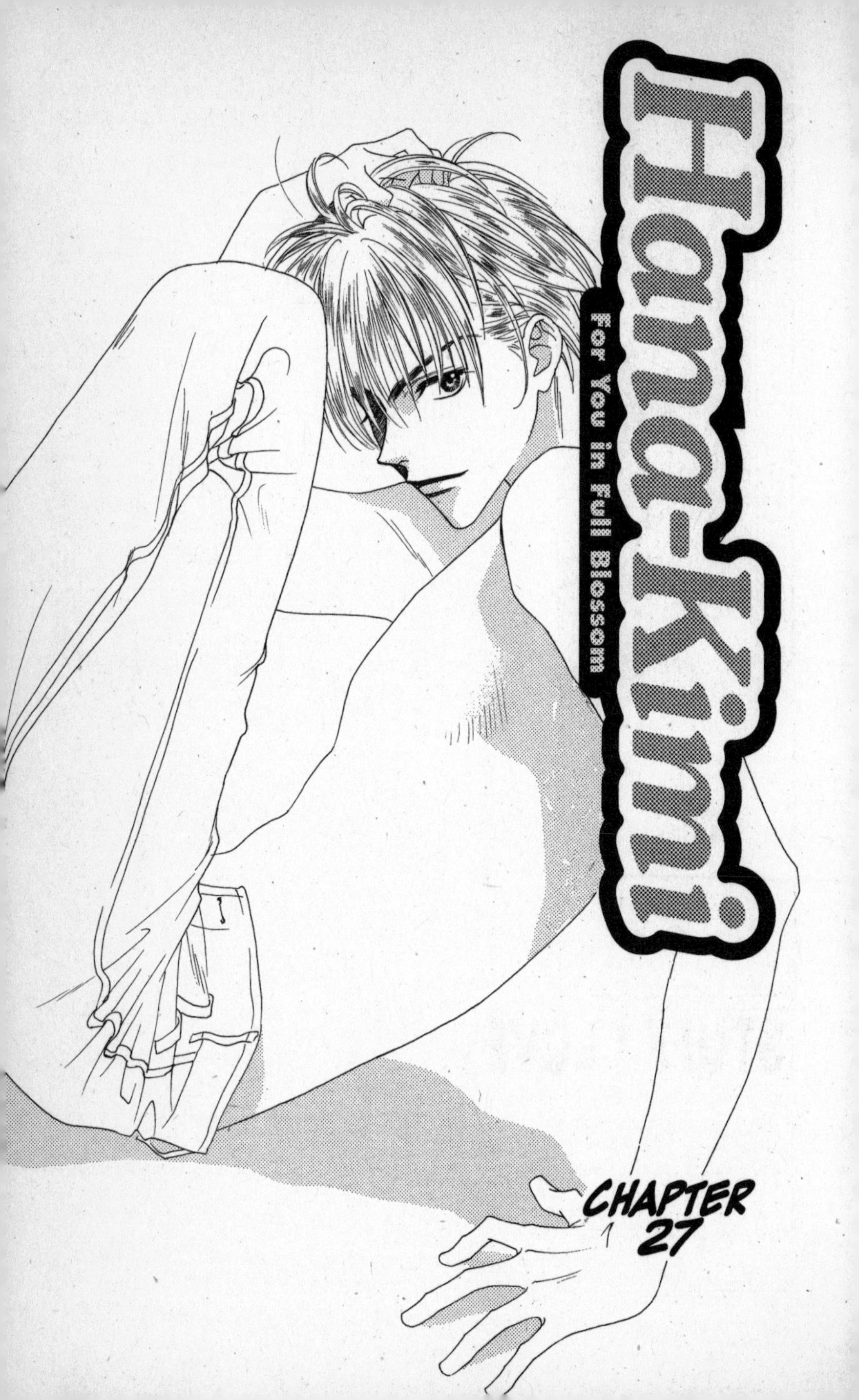
Hana-Kimi
For You in Full Blossom
CHAPTER 27

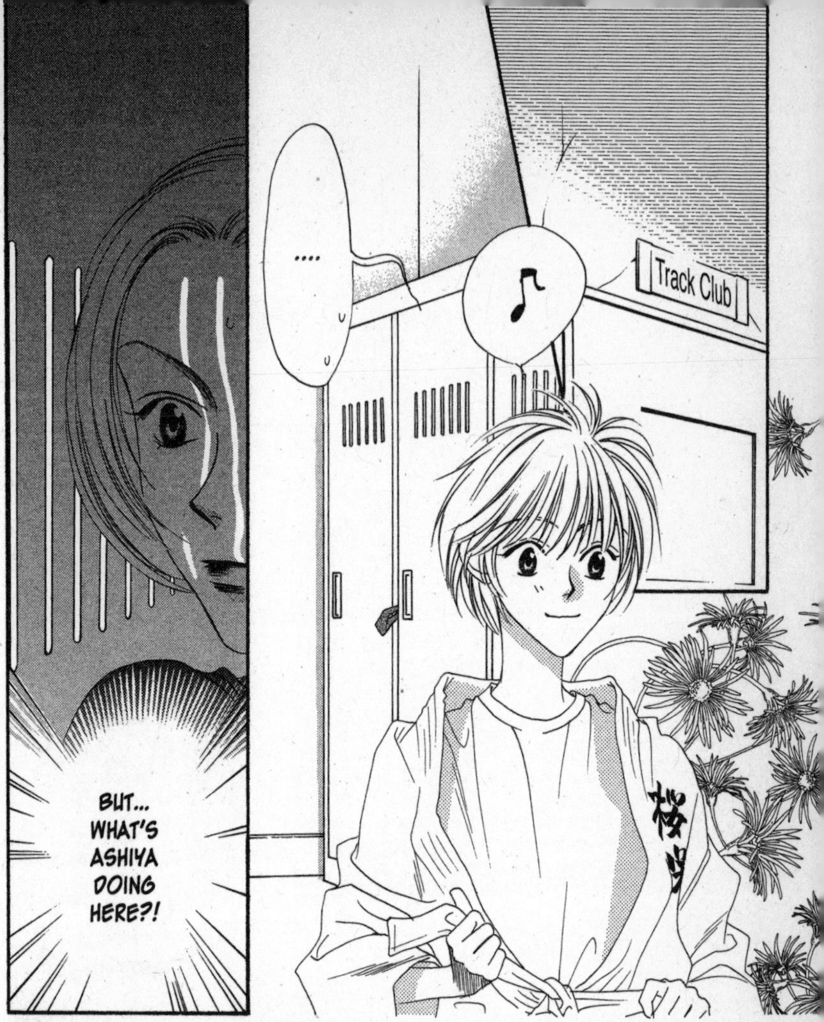

....
♪
Track Club
BUT... WHAT'S ASHIYA DOING HERE?!

STUFF I LOVE PART 2

「Bath GooDs」

When it comes to bath goods, I especially like stuff you pour in your bath. There's all kinds of fruit and flower bath soaps, but my favorite is sea salt! I recommend Sazabi or Mary Quant! For regular soap, I like what they have at the Body Shop and Buryjo.

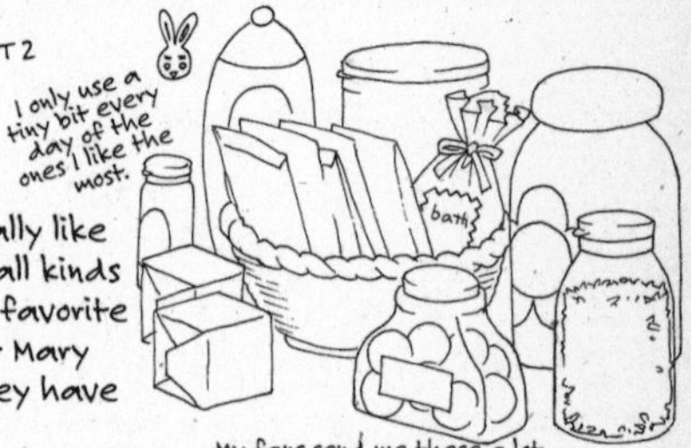

I only use a tiny bit every day of the ones I like the most.
bath
My fans send me these a lot, which makes me really happy!

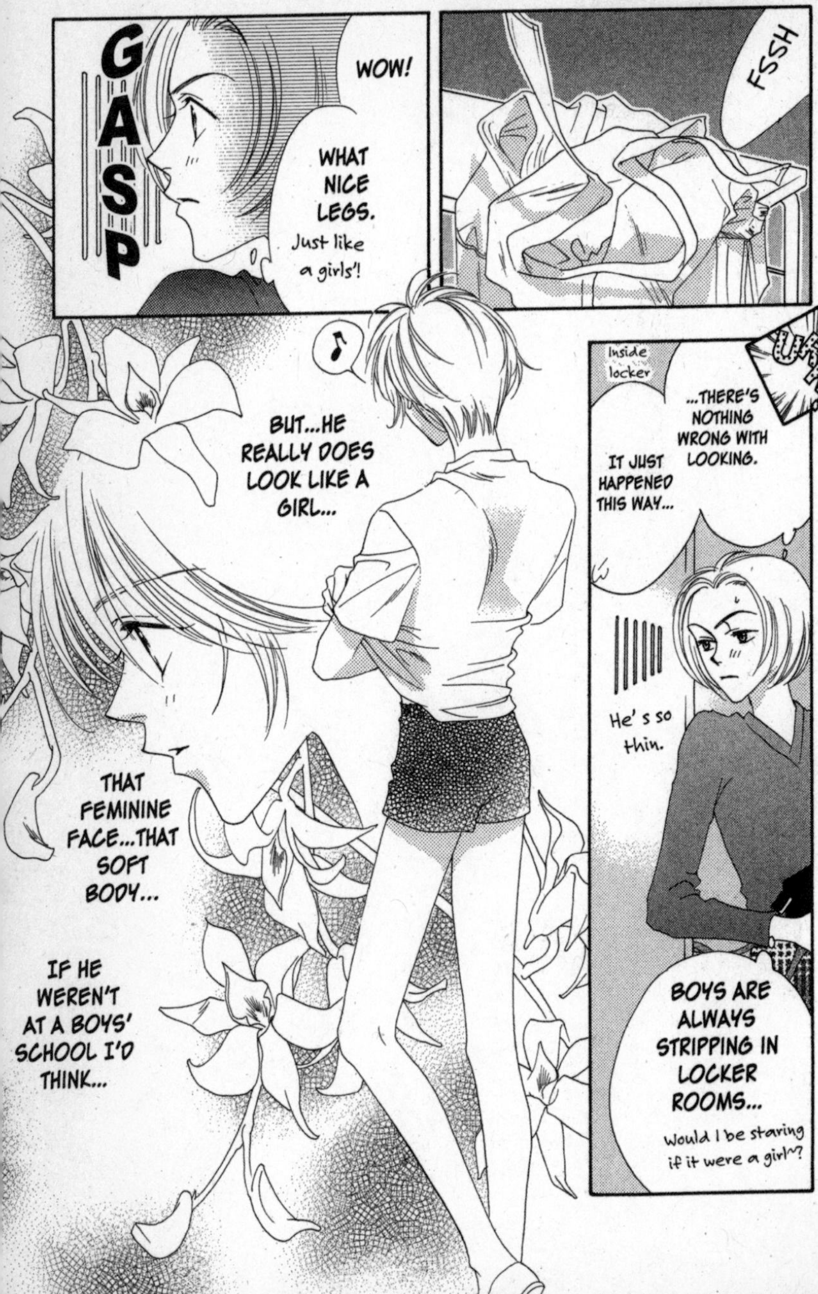
FSSH
GASP
WOW!
WHAT NICE LEGS.
Just like a girls'!
Inside locker
URK
...THERE'S NOTHING WRONG WITH LOOKING.
IT JUST HAPPENED THIS WAY...
He's so thin.
BOYS ARE ALWAYS STRIPPING IN LOCKER ROOMS...
Would I be staring if it were a girl~?
♪
BUT...HE REALLY DOES LOOK LIKE A GIRL...
THAT FEMININE FACE...THAT SOFT BODY...
IF HE WEREN'T AT A BOYS' SCHOOL I'D THINK...

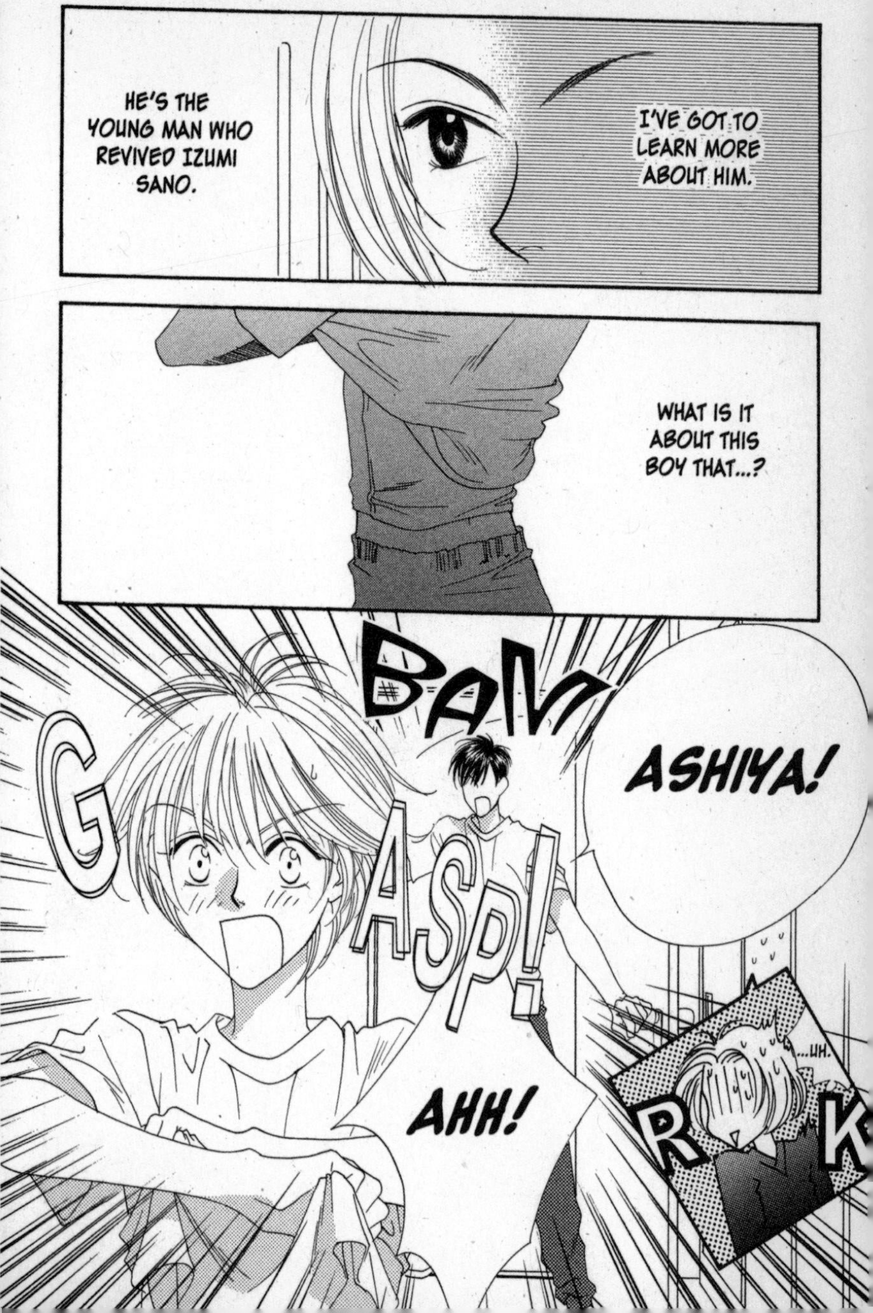
I'VE GOT TO LEARN MORE ABOUT HIM.
HE'S THE YOUNG MAN WHO REVIVED IZUMI SANO.
WHAT IS IT ABOUT THIS BOY THAT...?
BAM
ASHIYA!
...UH.
RK
GASP!
AHH!

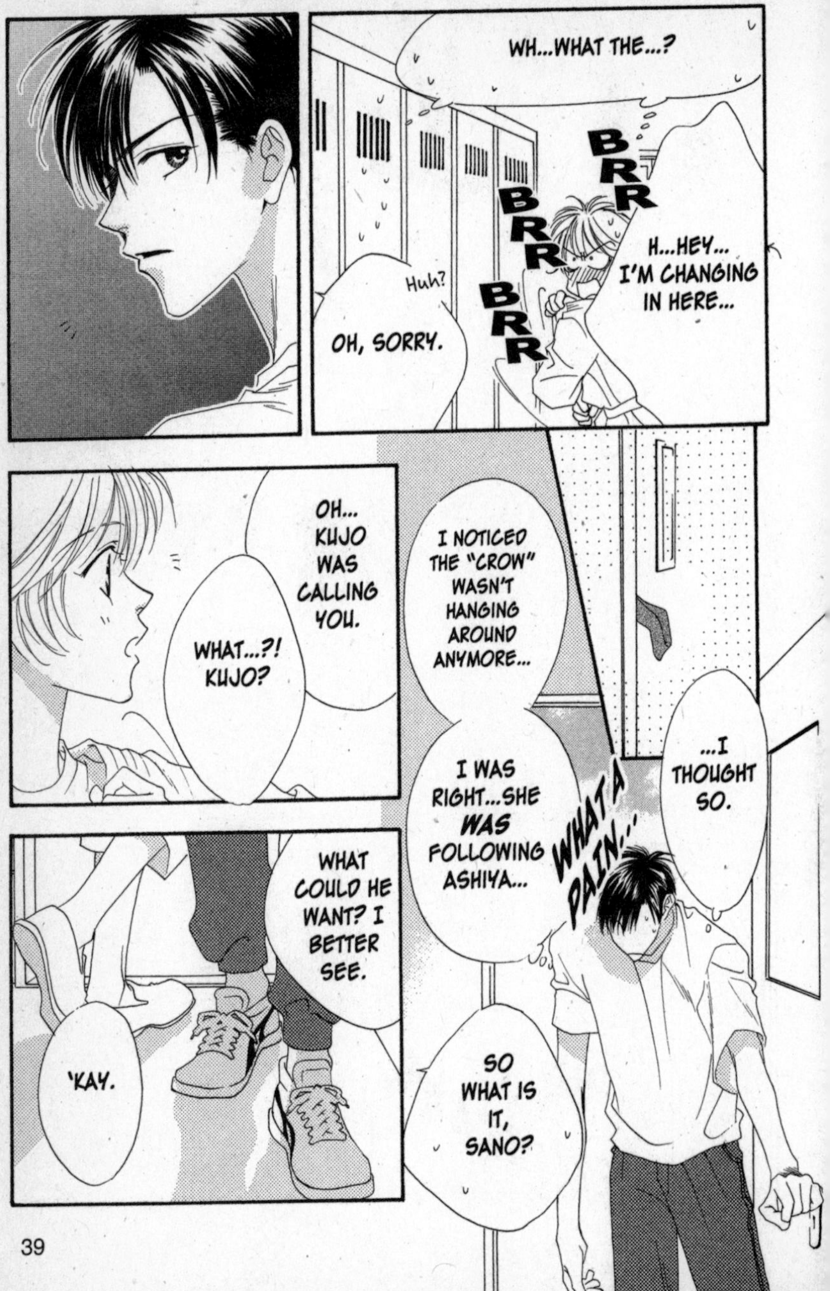
WH...WHAT THE...?
BRRR BRRR BRRR
H...HEY... I'M CHANGING IN HERE...
Huh?
OH, SORRY.
I NOTICED THE "CROW" WASN'T HANGING AROUND ANYMORE...
I WAS RIGHT...SHE *WAS* FOLLOWING ASHIYA...
...I THOUGHT SO.
WHAT A PAIN..
SO WHAT IS IT, SANO?
OH... KUJO WAS CALLING YOU.
WHAT...?! KUJO?
WHAT COULD HE WANT? I BETTER SEE.
'KAY.

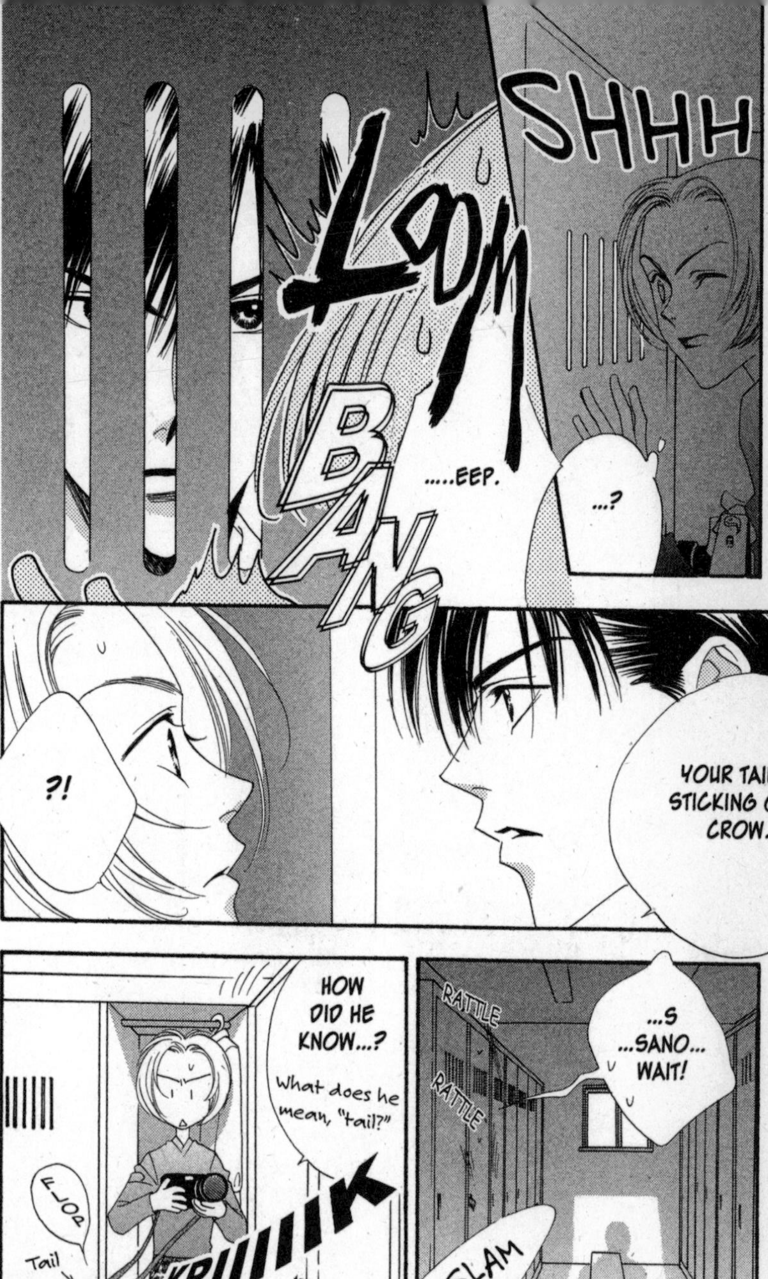
SHHH
...?
Loom
.....EEP.
BANG
YOUR TAIL'S STICKING OUT, CROW.
?!
RATTLE
RATTLE
...S ...SANO... WAIT!
SLAM
HOW DID HE KNOW...?
What does he mean, "tail?"
KRIIIIIK
FLOP
Tail

* Osaka High School

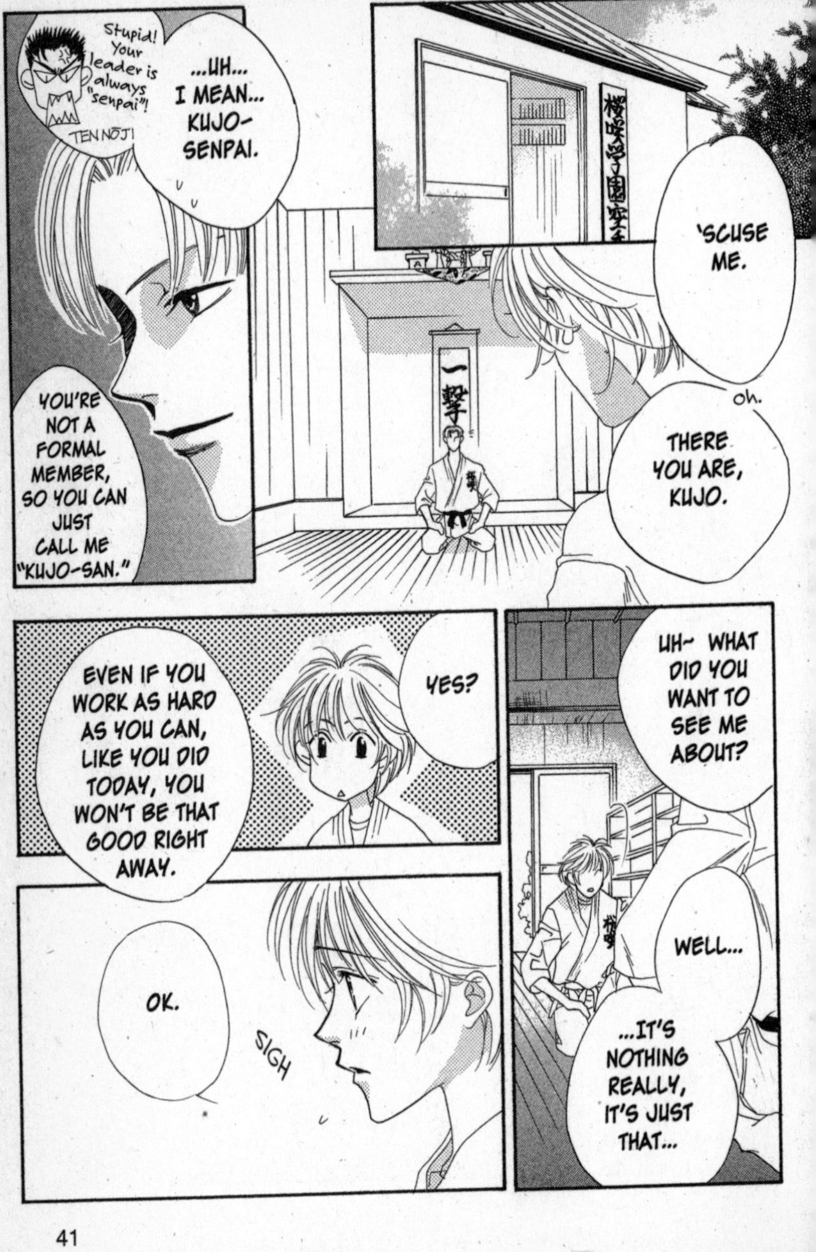
桜咲学園空手
'SCUSE ME.
oh.
THERE YOU ARE, KUJO.
一撃
...UH... I MEAN... KUJO-SENPAI.
Stupid! Your leader is always "senpai"!!
TEN NŌJI
YOU'RE NOT A FORMAL MEMBER, SO YOU CAN JUST CALL ME "KUJO-SAN."
UH~ WHAT DID YOU WANT TO SEE ME ABOUT?
WELL...
...IT'S NOTHING REALLY, IT'S JUST THAT...
YES?
EVEN IF YOU WORK AS HARD AS YOU CAN, LIKE YOU DID TODAY, YOU WON'T BE THAT GOOD RIGHT AWAY.
OK.
SIGH

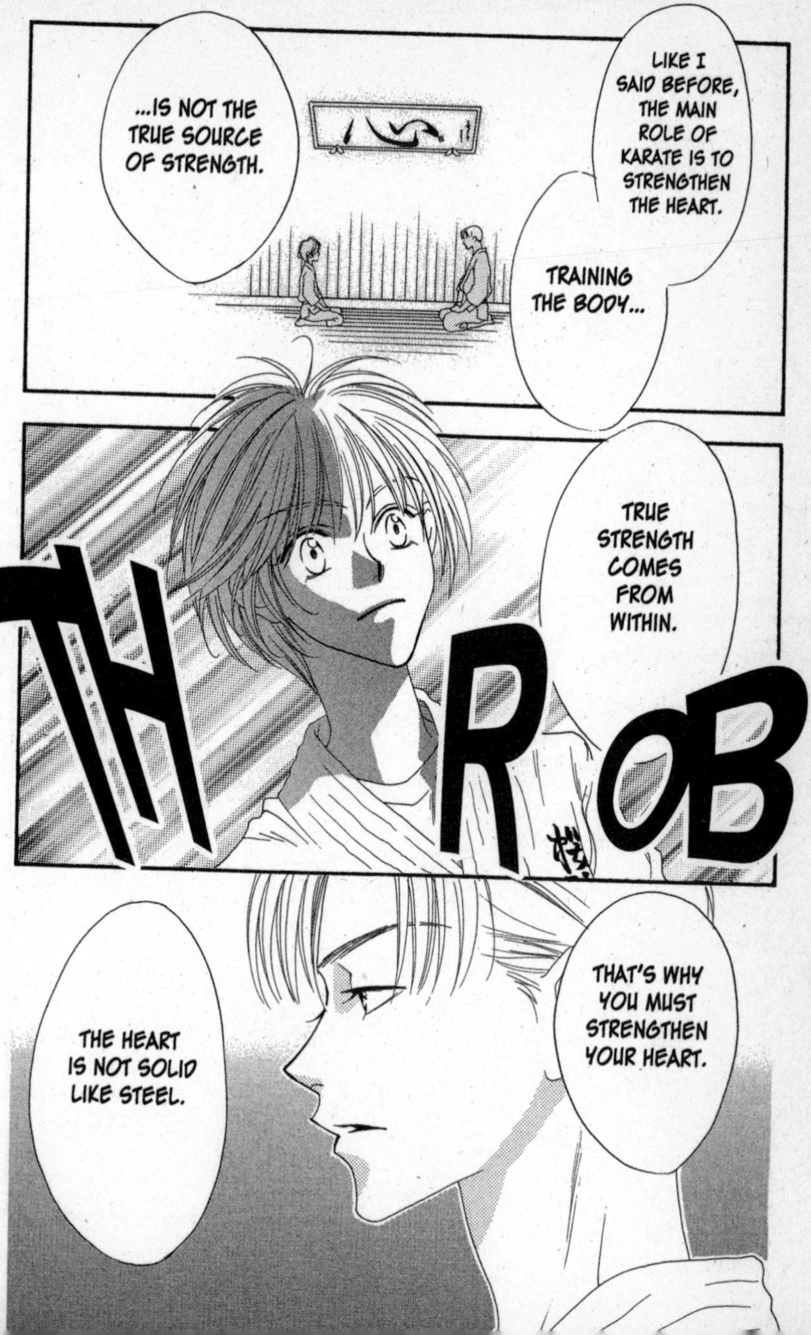
LIKE I SAID BEFORE, THE MAIN ROLE OF KARATE IS TO STRENGTHEN THE HEART.
TRAINING THE BODY...
...IS NOT THE TRUE SOURCE OF STRENGTH.
TRUE STRENGTH COMES FROM WITHIN.
THROB
THAT'S WHY YOU MUST STRENGTHEN YOUR HEART.
THE HEART IS NOT SOLID LIKE STEEL.

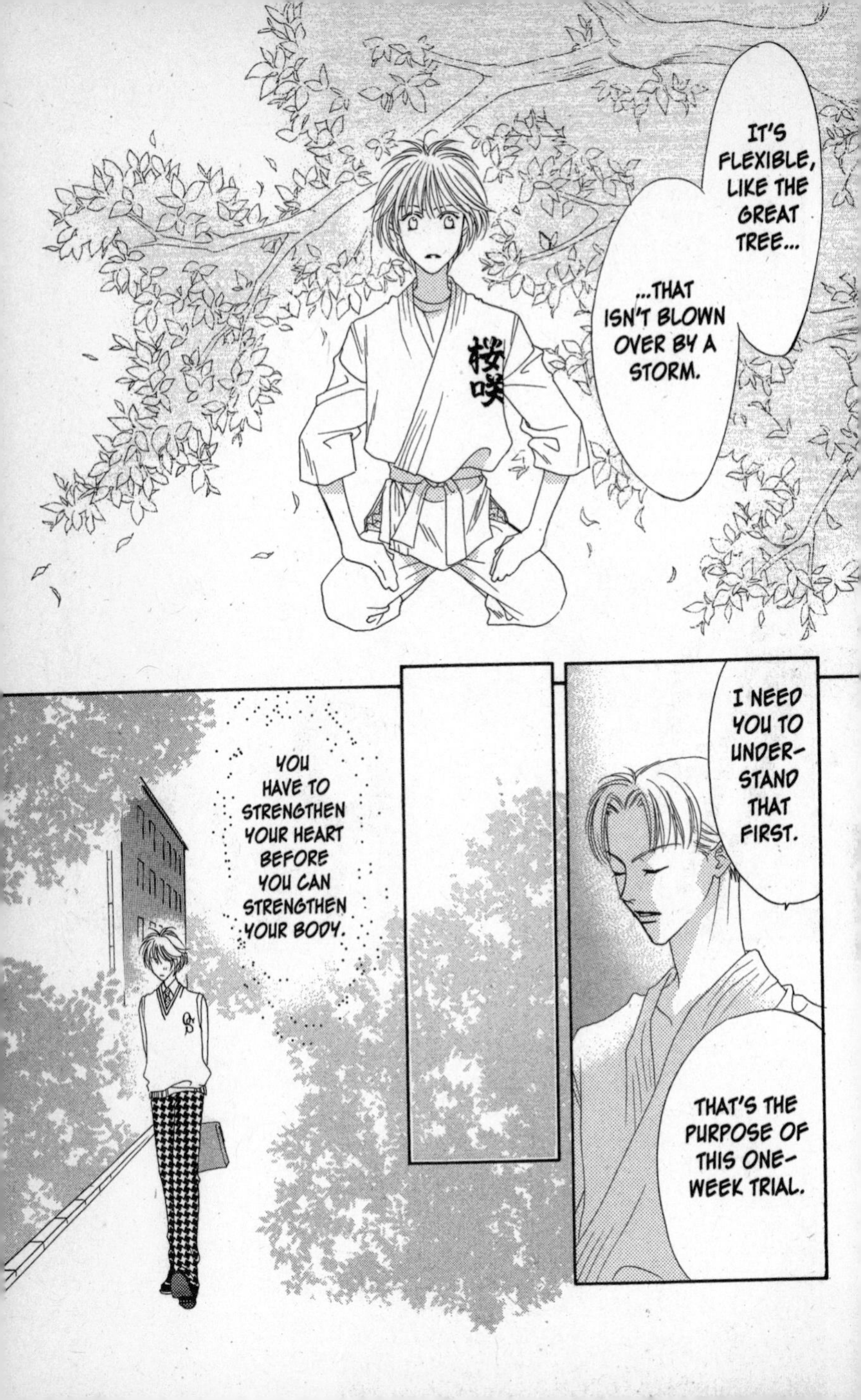
IT'S FLEXIBLE, LIKE THE GREAT TREE...
...THAT ISN'T BLOWN OVER BY A STORM.
桜咲
I NEED YOU TO UNDER-STAND THAT FIRST.
THAT'S THE PURPOSE OF THIS ONE-WEEK TRIAL.
YOU HAVE TO STRENGTHEN YOUR HEART BEFORE YOU CAN STRENGTHEN YOUR BODY.

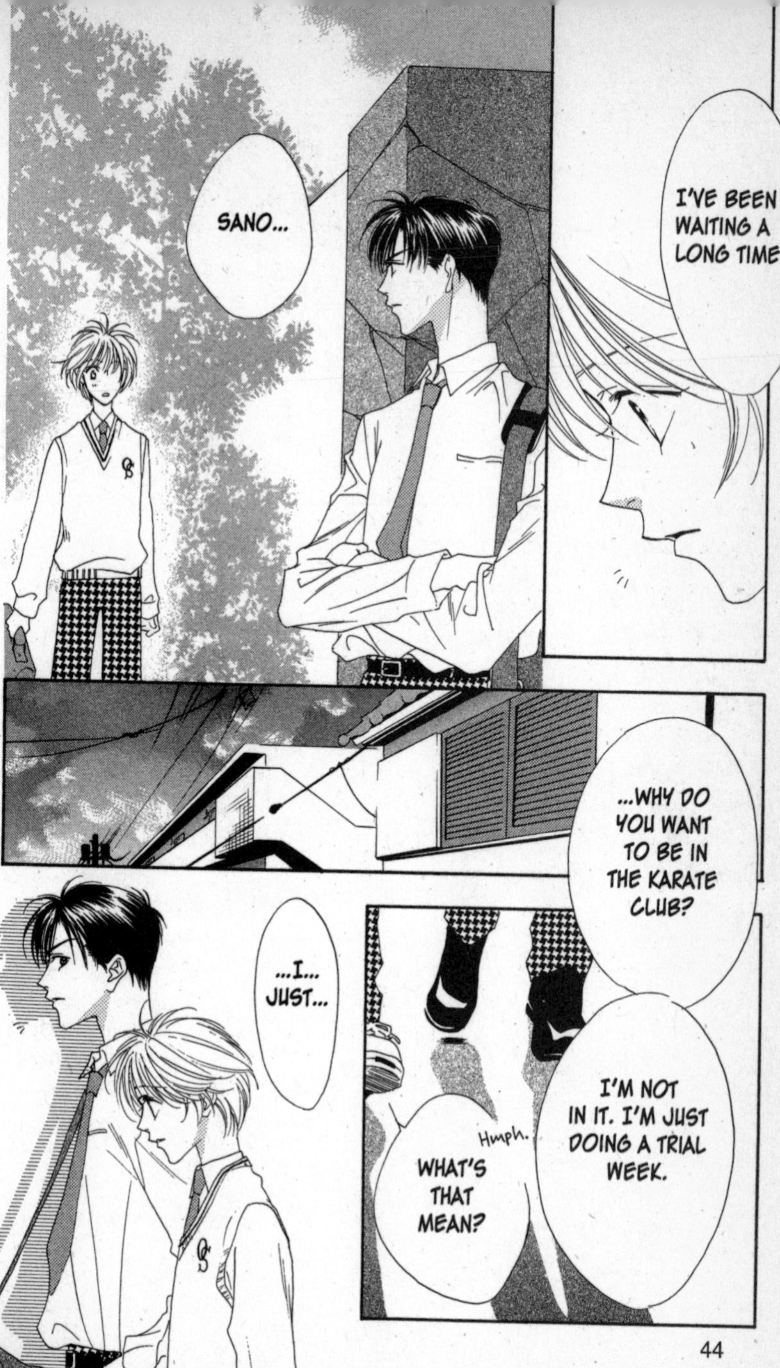
I'VE BEEN WAITING A LONG TIME.
SANO...
...WHY DO YOU WANT TO BE IN THE KARATE CLUB?
I'M NOT IN IT. I'M JUST DOING A TRIAL WEEK.
Hmph.
WHAT'S THAT MEAN?
...I... JUST...

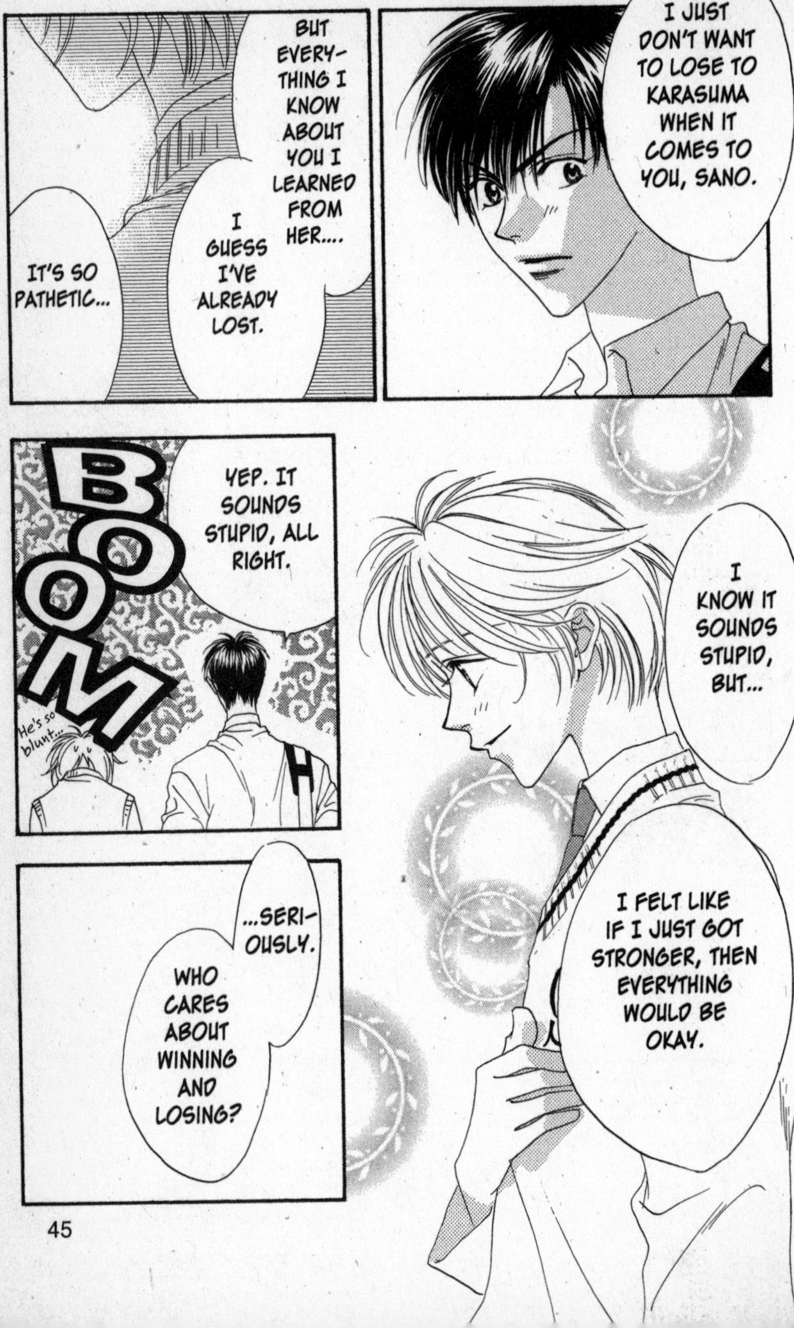
I JUST DON'T WANT TO LOSE TO KARASUMA WHEN IT COMES TO YOU, SANO.
BUT EVERYTHING I KNOW ABOUT YOU I LEARNED FROM HER....
I GUESS I'VE ALREADY LOST.
IT'S SO PATHETIC...
I KNOW IT SOUNDS STUPID, BUT...
I FELT LIKE IF I JUST GOT STRONGER, THEN EVERYTHING WOULD BE OKAY.
YEP. IT SOUNDS STUPID, ALL RIGHT.
BOOM
He's so blunt...
...SERIOUSLY.
WHO CARES ABOUT WINNING AND LOSING?

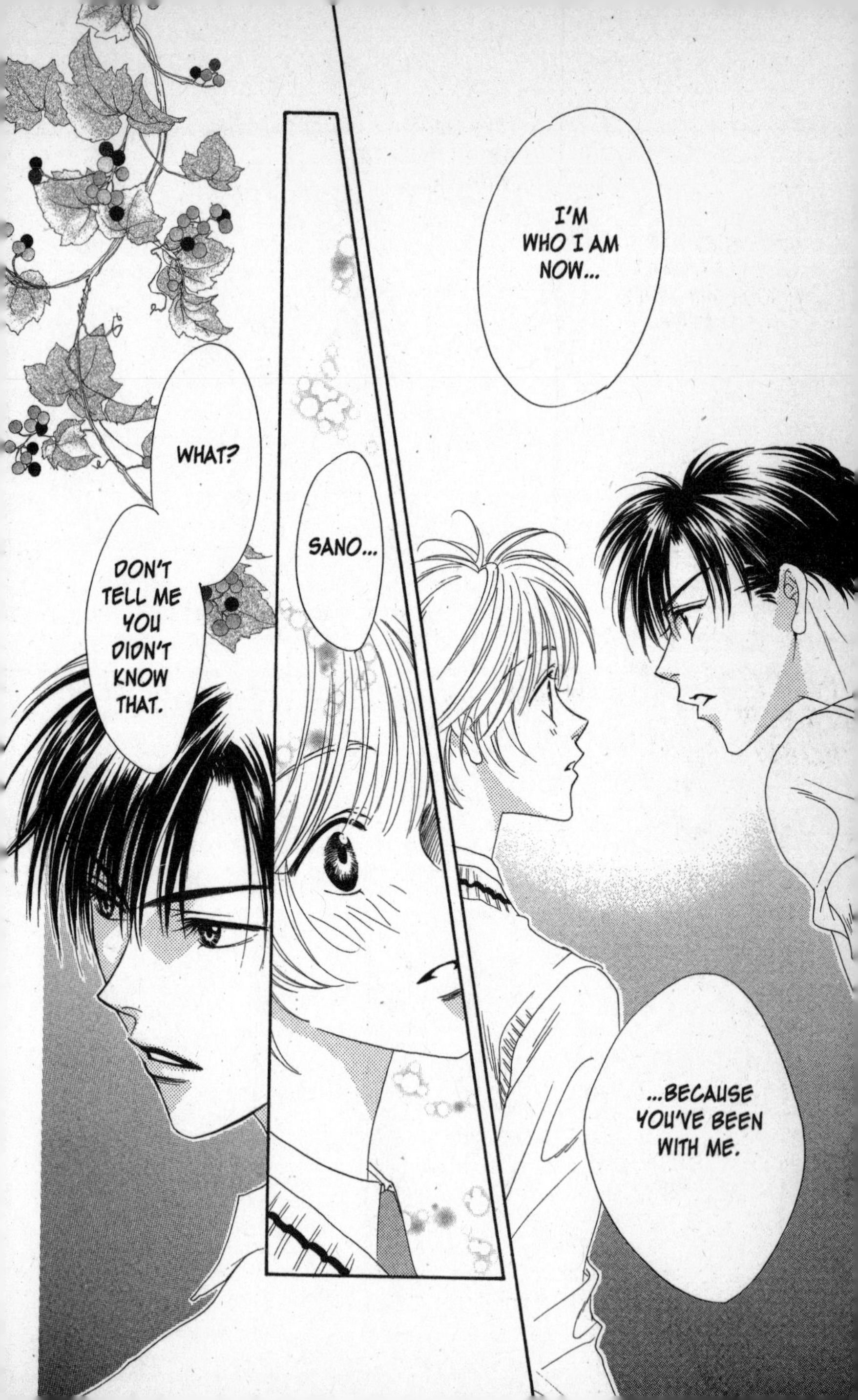
I'M WHO I AM NOW...
...BECAUSE YOU'VE BEEN WITH ME.
SANO...
WHAT?
DON'T TELL ME YOU DIDN'T KNOW THAT.

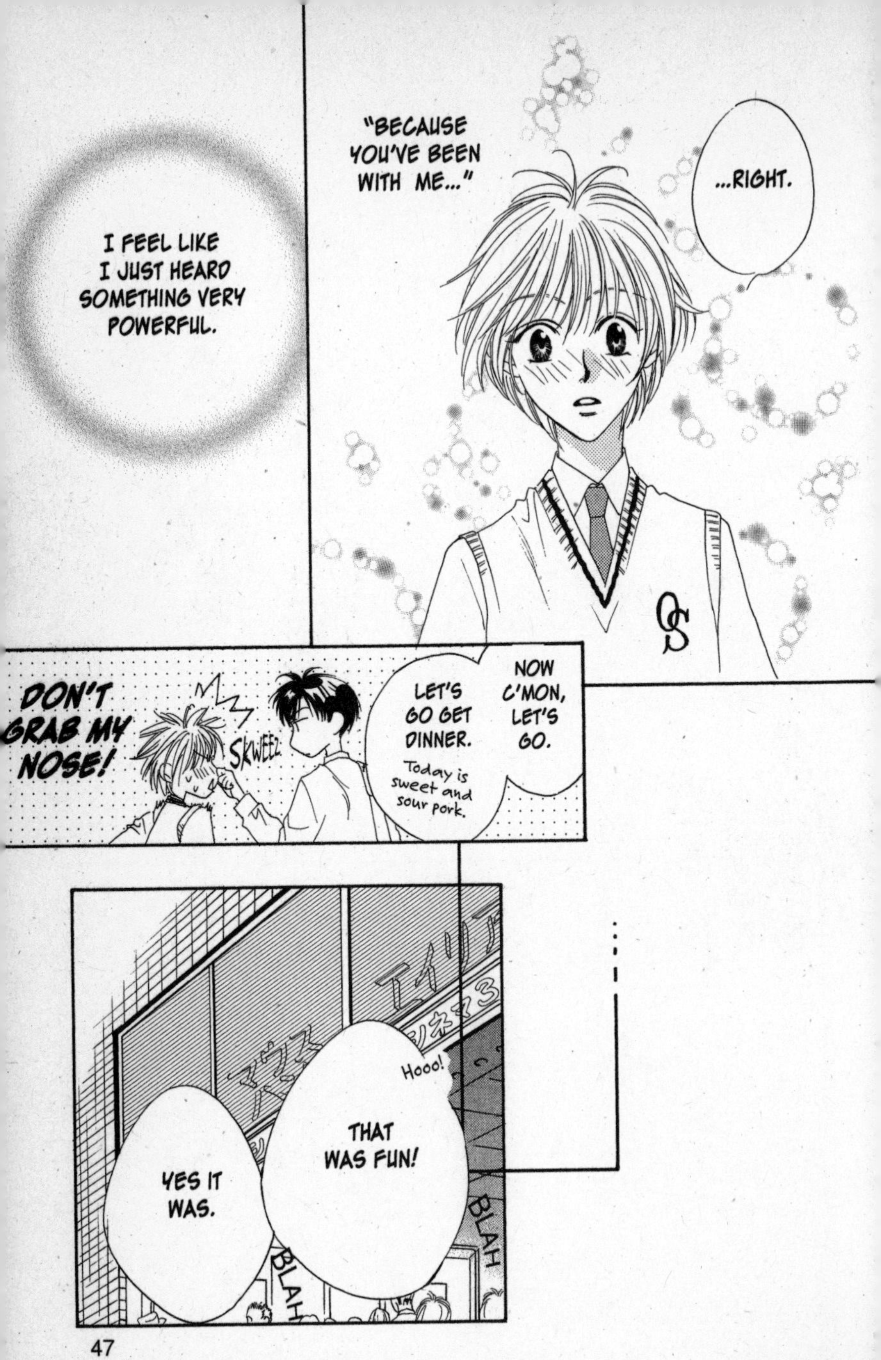
...RIGHT.
"BECAUSE YOU'VE BEEN WITH ME..."
I FEEL LIKE I JUST HEARD SOMETHING VERY POWERFUL.
NOW C'MON, LET'S GO.
LET'S GO GET DINNER.
Today is sweet and sour pork.
SKWEEZ
DON'T GRAB MY NOSE!
Hooo!
THAT WAS FUN!
YES IT WAS.
BLAH
BLAH

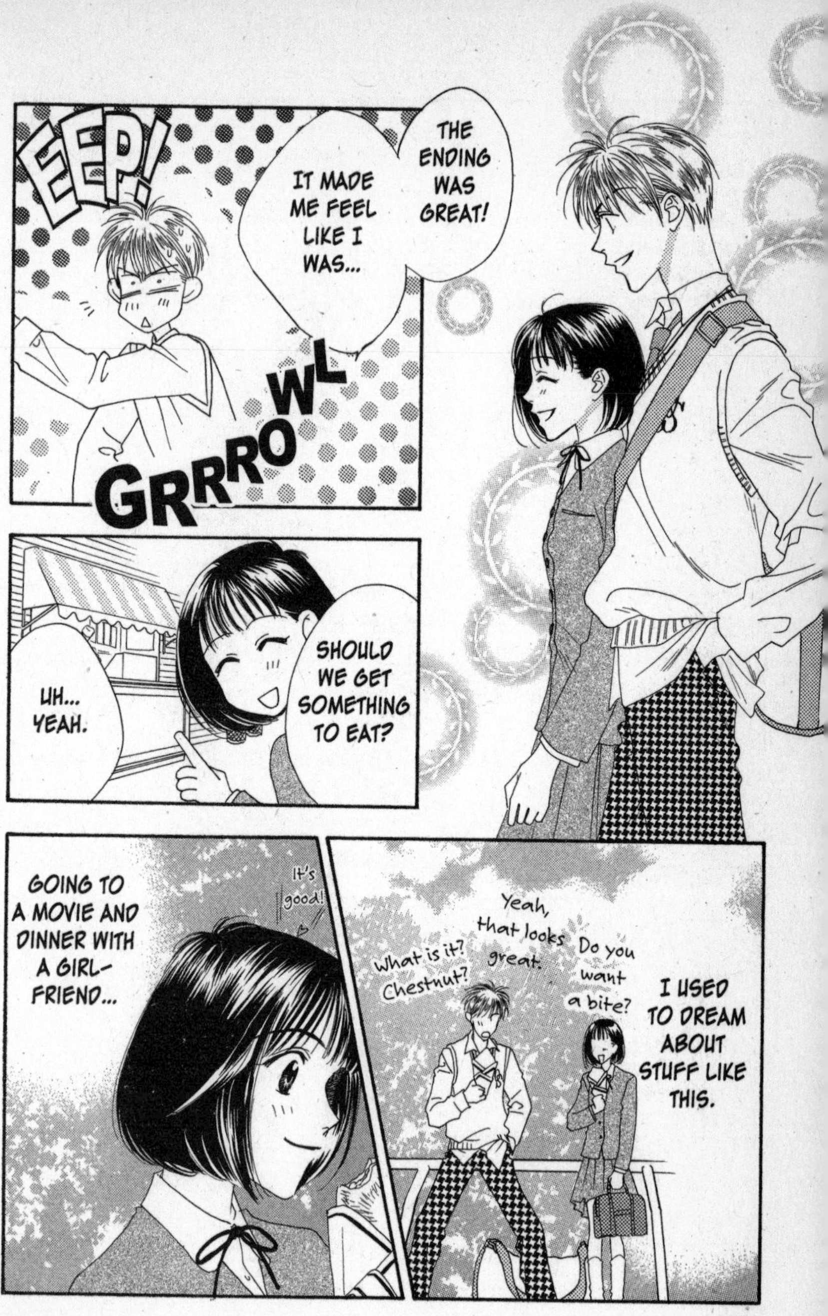
THE ENDING WAS GREAT!
IT MADE ME FEEL LIKE I WAS...
EEP!
GRRROWL
SHOULD WE GET SOMETHING TO EAT?
UH... YEAH.
I USED TO DREAM ABOUT STUFF LIKE THIS.
Do you want a bite?
Yeah, that looks great.
What is it? Chestnut?
It's good!
GOING TO A MOVIE AND DINNER WITH A GIRL-FRIEND...

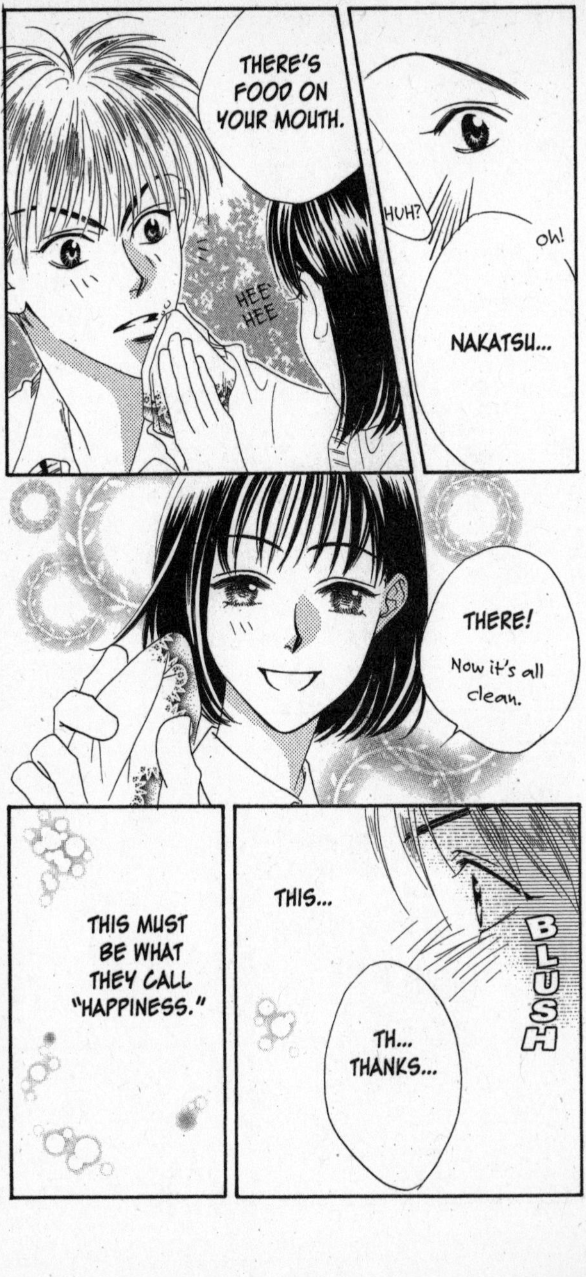
HUH?
Oh!
NAKATSU...
THERE'S FOOD ON YOUR MOUTH.
HEE HEE
THERE!
Now it's all clean.
THIS...
BLUSH
TH... THANKS...
THIS MUST BE WHAT THEY CALL "HAPPINESS."

WHISPERED SECRETS

FIGURE SKATING

MIZUKI'S OUTFIT IN CHAPTER 26 IS FROM THE FIGURE SKATER PHILIPPE CANDELORO, WHO WAS AT THE NAGANO WINTER OLYMPICS!♥ FOR HIS PROGRAM HE WORE A COSTUME BASED ON "THE THREE MUSKETEERS." THE MUSIC THEY PLAYED HAD THE SOUNDS OF SWORDS CLASHING AND HE MIMICKED FENCING MOVES AS HE SKATED. IT WAS SO COOL!! HE ALSO LOOKED REALLY COOL ON THE NHK SPECIAL YEARS AGO WHEN HE WORE ALL BLACK (AND THE MUSIC WAS THE "GODFATHER" THEME)!! I LIKE THE FACT THAT HE DOESN'T WEAR THE FRILLY STUFF THAT'S POPULAR WITH OTHER SKATERS RIGHT NOW!!

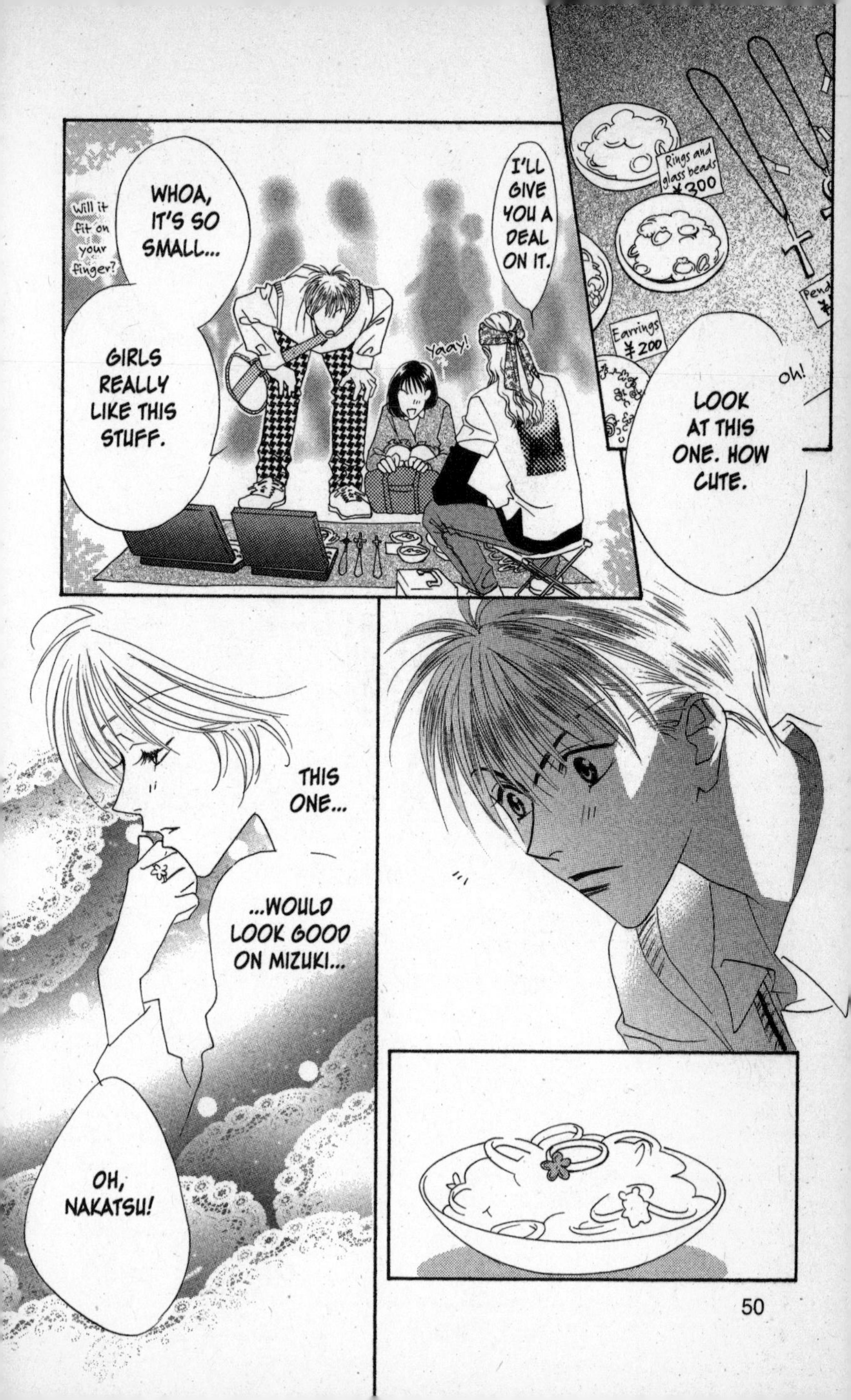
Rings and glass beads ¥300
Earrings ¥200
Oh!
LOOK AT THIS ONE. HOW CUTE.
I'LL GIVE YOU A DEAL ON IT.
Yaay!
WHOA, IT'S SO SMALL...
Will it fit on your finger?
GIRLS REALLY LIKE THIS STUFF.
THIS ONE...
...WOULD LOOK GOOD ON MIZUKI...
OH, NAKATSU!

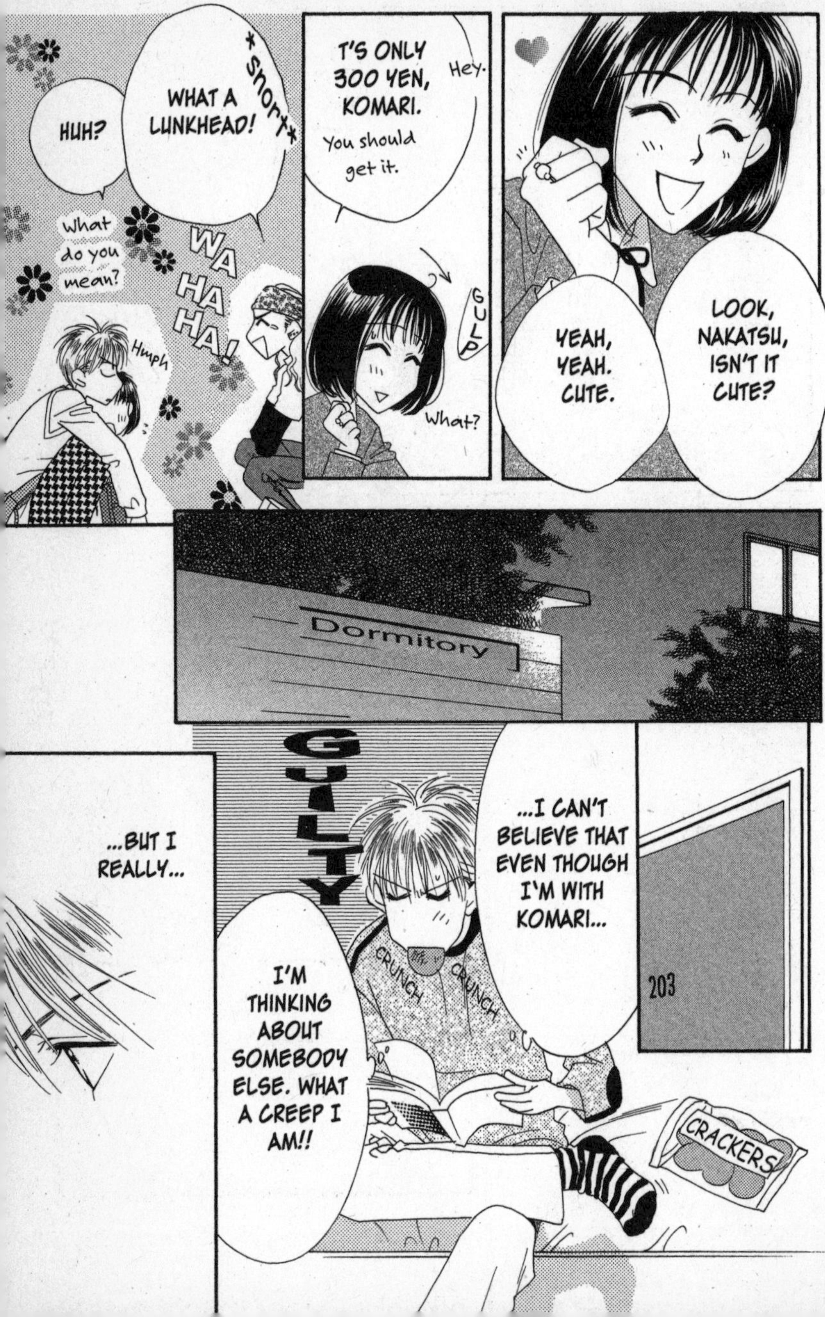
LOOK, NAKATSU, ISN'T IT CUTE?
YEAH, YEAH. CUTE.
Hey.
T'S ONLY 300 YEN, KOMARI.
You should get it.
GULP
What?
snort
WHAT A LUNKHEAD!
HUH?
WA HA HA HA!
What do you mean?
Hmph
Dormitory
GUILTY
...I CAN'T BELIEVE THAT EVEN THOUGH I'M WITH KOMARI...
203
CRUNCH
CRUNCH
I'M THINKING ABOUT SOMEBODY ELSE. WHAT A CREEP I AM!!
CRACKERS
...BUT I REALLY...

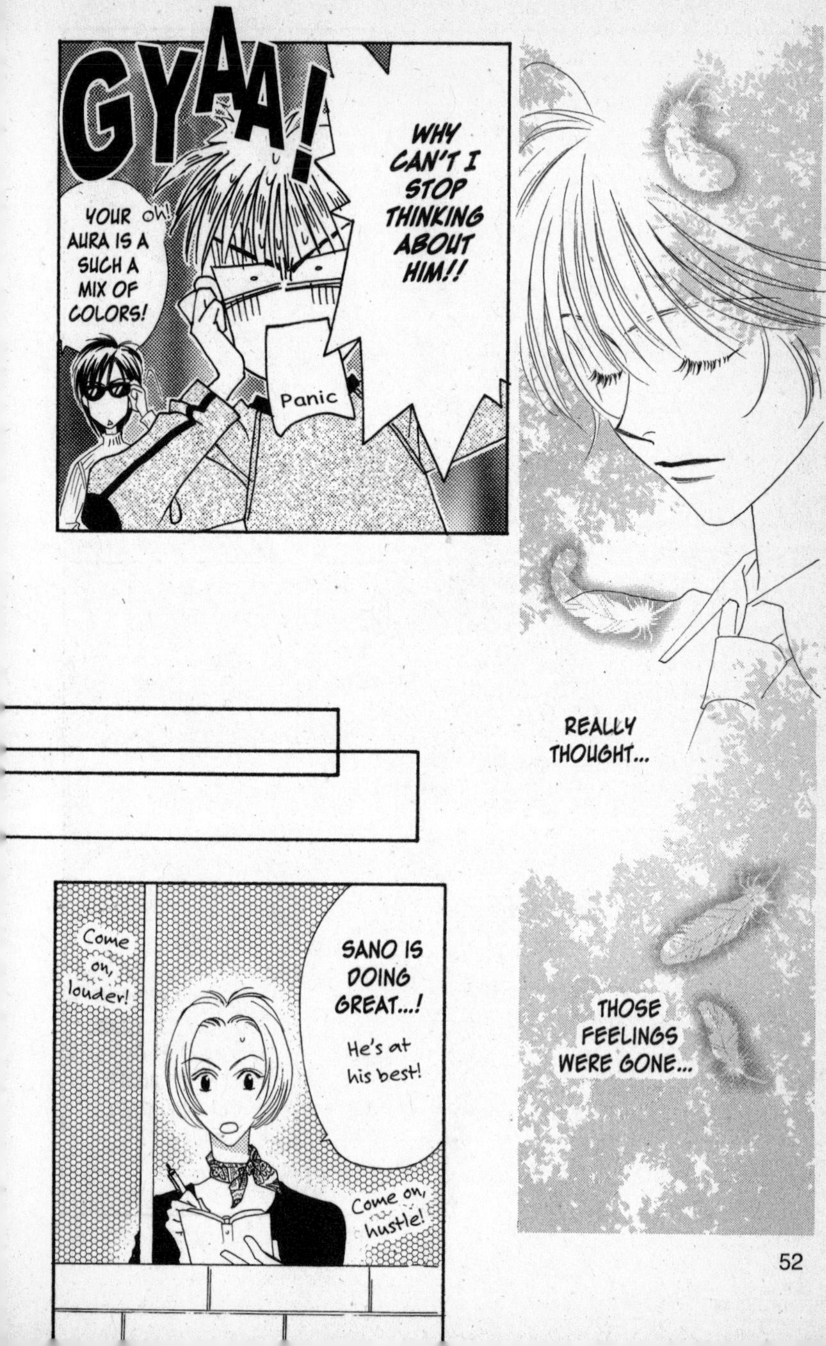
REALLY THOUGHT...
THOSE FEELINGS WERE GONE...
GYAA!
WHY CAN'T I STOP THINKING ABOUT HIM!!
Panic
YOUR AURA IS A SUCH A MIX OF COLORS!
oh!
SANO IS DOING GREAT...!
He's at his best!
Come on, louder!
Come on, hustle!

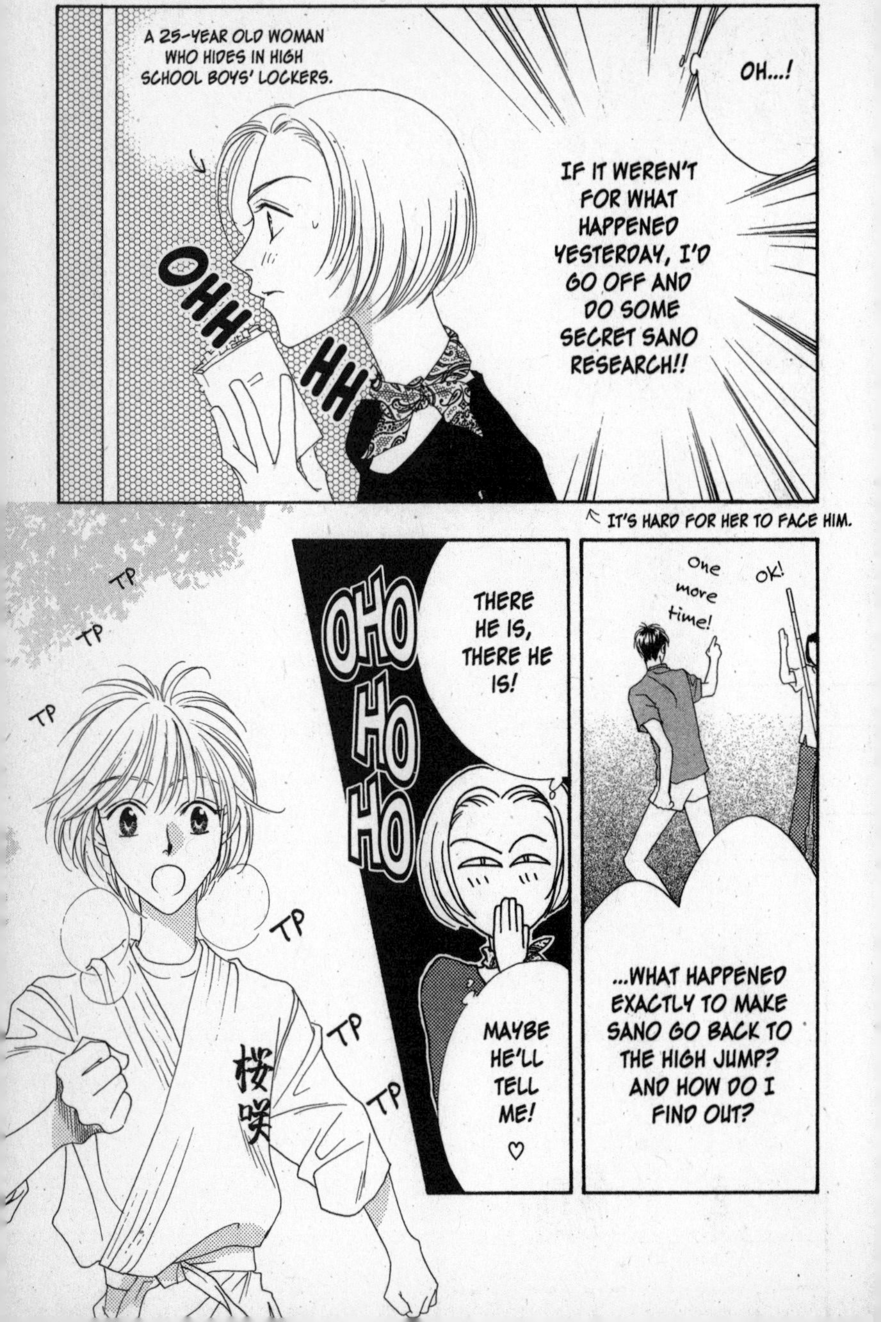
OH...!
IF IT WEREN'T FOR WHAT HAPPENED YESTERDAY, I'D GO OFF AND DO SOME SECRET SANO RESEARCH!!
OHHHH
A 25-YEAR OLD WOMAN WHO HIDES IN HIGH SCHOOL BOYS' LOCKERS.
IT'S HARD FOR HER TO FACE HIM.
OK!
One more time!
...WHAT HAPPENED EXACTLY TO MAKE SANO GO BACK TO THE HIGH JUMP? AND HOW DO I FIND OUT?
THERE HE IS, THERE HE IS!
OHOHOHO
MAYBE HE'LL TELL ME! ♡
TP
TP
TP
TP
TP
TP
桜咲

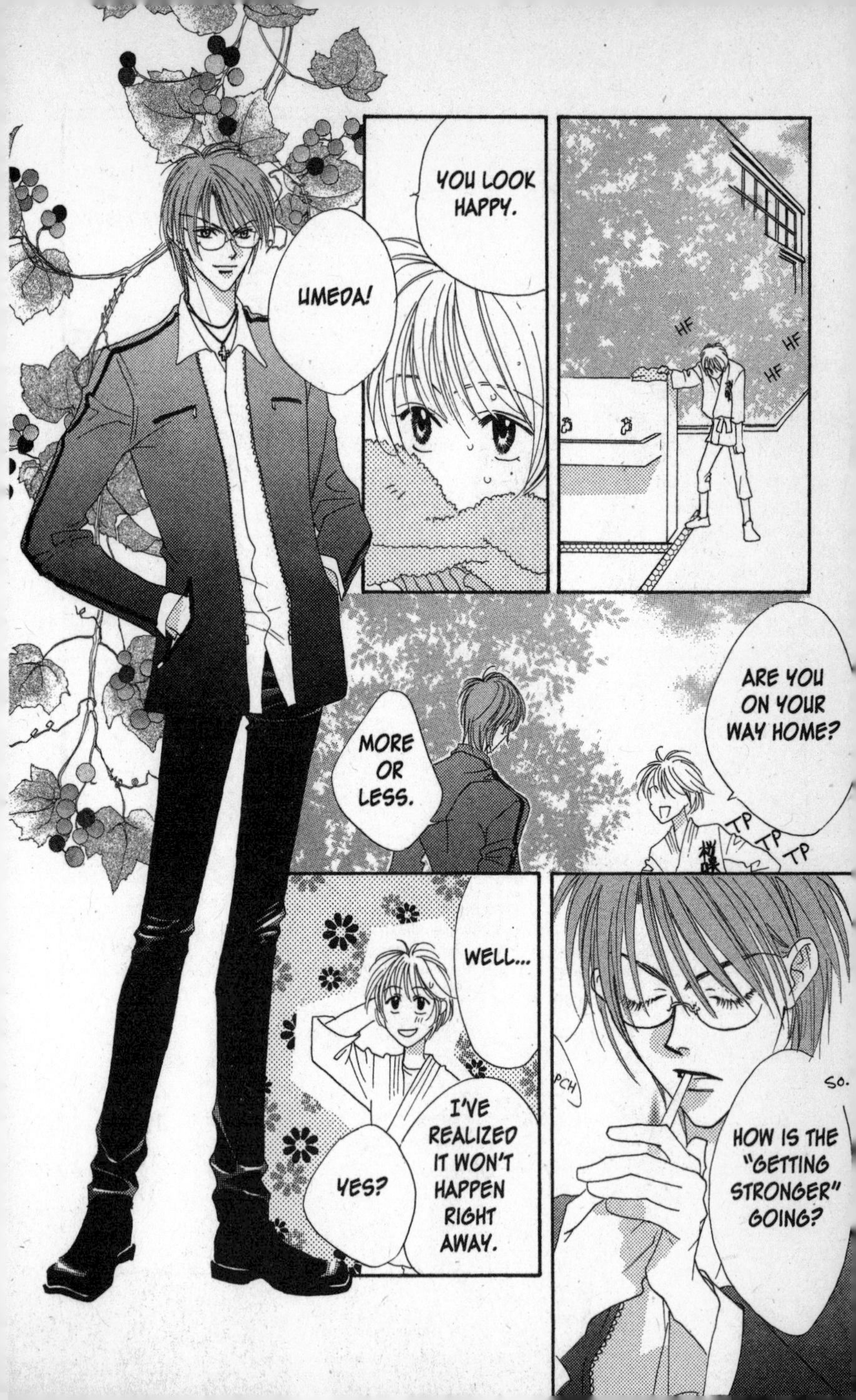
HF
HF
HF
YOU LOOK HAPPY.
UMEDA!
ARE YOU ON YOUR WAY HOME?
TP
TP
TP
MORE OR LESS.
SO.
PCH
HOW IS THE "GETTING STRONGER" GOING?
WELL...
I'VE REALIZED IT WON'T HAPPEN RIGHT AWAY.
YES?

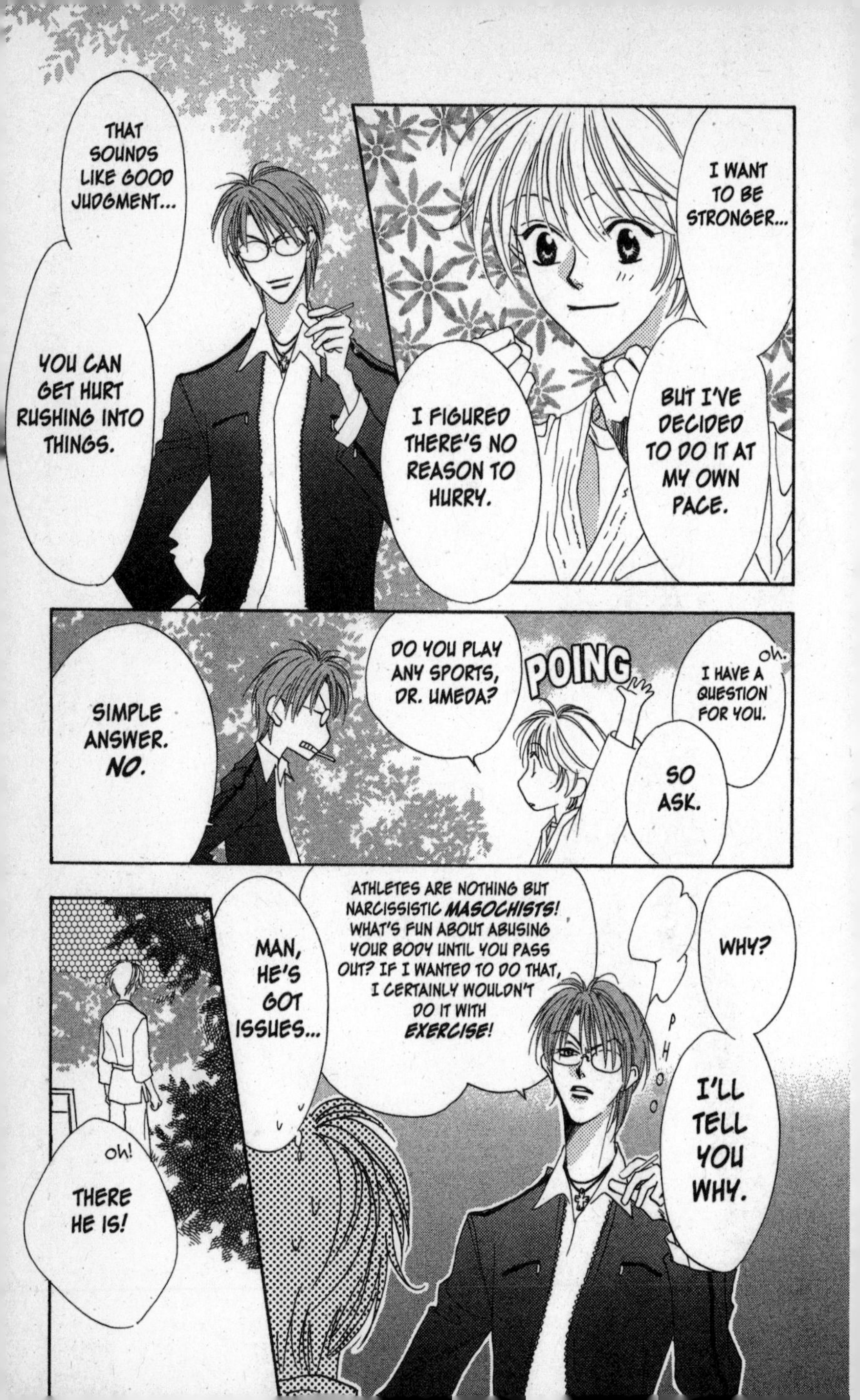
I WANT TO BE STRONGER...
BUT I'VE DECIDED TO DO IT AT MY OWN PACE.
I FIGURED THERE'S NO REASON TO HURRY.
THAT SOUNDS LIKE GOOD JUDGMENT...
YOU CAN GET HURT RUSHING INTO THINGS.
oh.
I HAVE A QUESTION FOR YOU.
SO ASK.
POING
DO YOU PLAY ANY SPORTS, DR. UMEDA?
SIMPLE ANSWER. *NO.*
WHY?
I'LL TELL YOU WHY.
PHOO
ATHLETES ARE NOTHING BUT NARCISSISTIC *MASOCHISTS*! WHAT'S FUN ABOUT ABUSING YOUR BODY UNTIL YOU PASS OUT? IF I WANTED TO DO THAT, I CERTAINLY WOULDN'T DO IT WITH *EXERCISE*!
MAN, HE'S GOT ISSUES...
oh!
THERE HE IS!

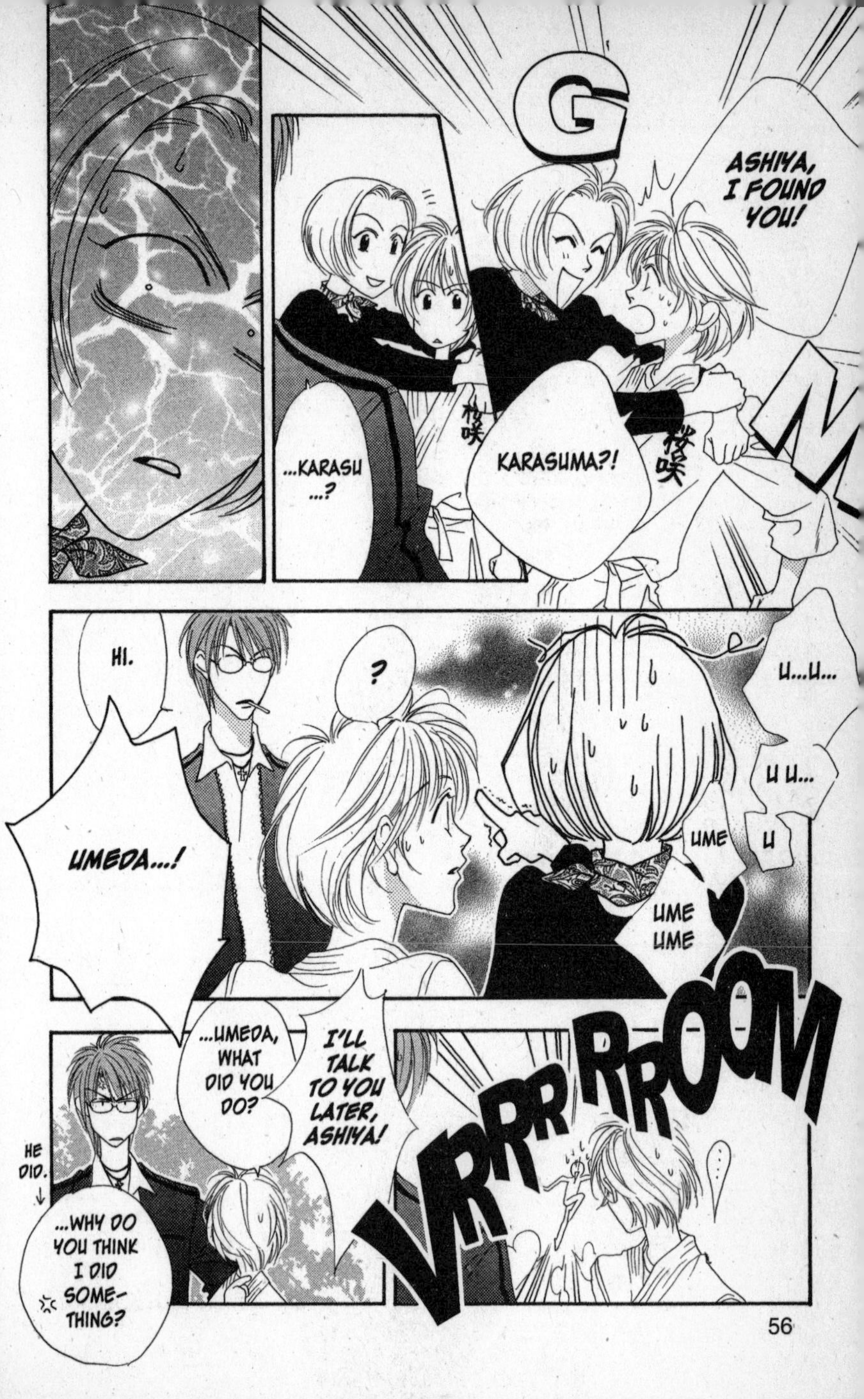

G
ASHIYA, I FOUND YOU!
M
KARASUMA?!
...KARASU ...?
U...U...
U U...
U
UME
UME UME
?
HI.
UMEDA...!
VRRRRROOM
I'LL TALK TO YOU LATER, ASHIYA!
...UMEDA, WHAT DID YOU DO?
HE DID.
...WHY DO YOU THINK I DID SOME-THING?

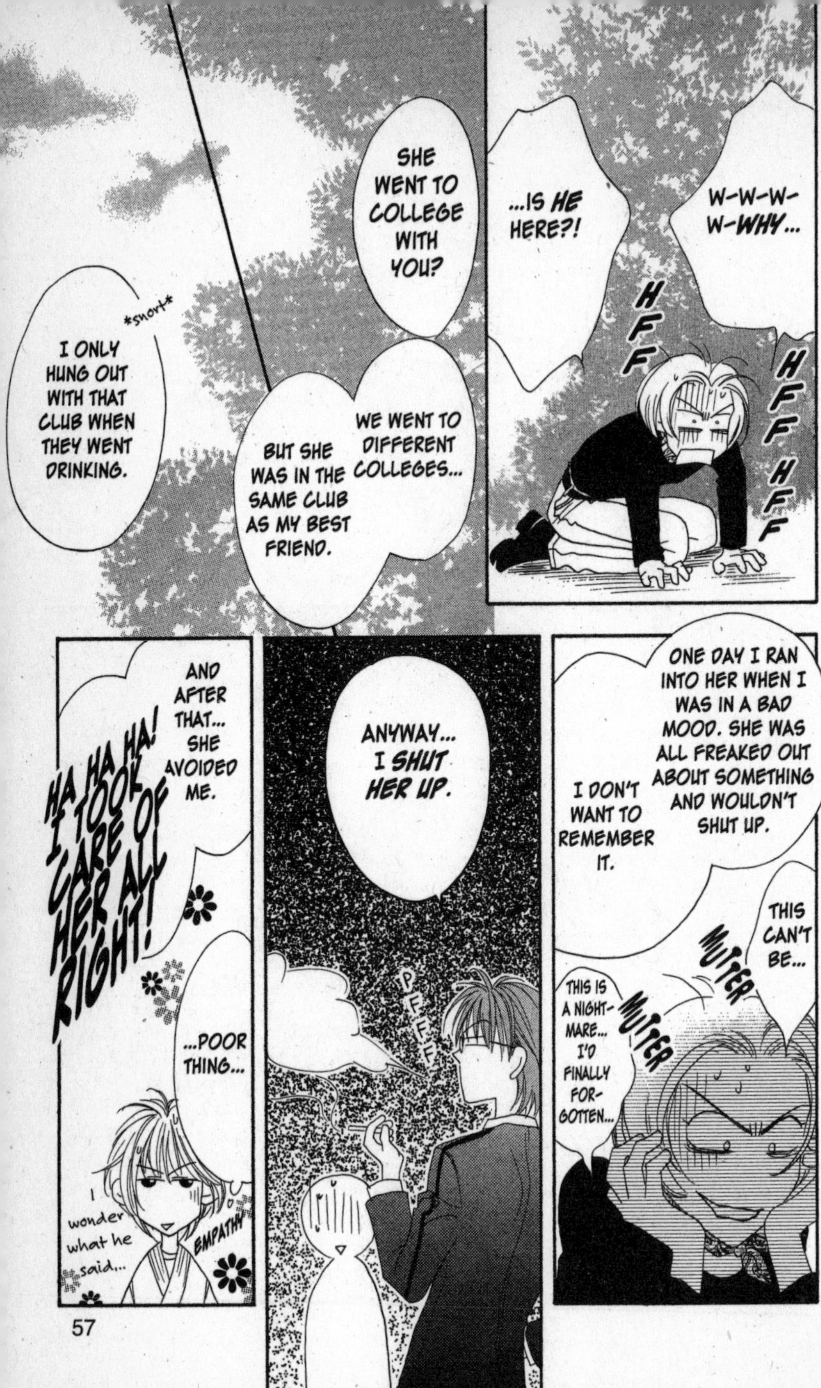
W-W-W-W-WHY...
...IS HE HERE?!
HFF
HFF HFF
SHE WENT TO COLLEGE WITH YOU?
WE WENT TO DIFFERENT COLLEGES...
BUT SHE WAS IN THE SAME CLUB AS MY BEST FRIEND.
snort
I ONLY HUNG OUT WITH THAT CLUB WHEN THEY WENT DRINKING.
ONE DAY I RAN INTO HER WHEN I WAS IN A BAD MOOD. SHE WAS ALL FREAKED OUT ABOUT SOMETHING AND WOULDN'T SHUT UP.
I DON'T WANT TO REMEMBER IT.
THIS CAN'T BE...
MUTTER
MUTTER
THIS IS A NIGHTMARE... I'D FINALLY FORGOTTEN...
ANYWAY... I SHUT HER UP.
PFFF
AND AFTER THAT... SHE AVOIDED ME.
HA HA HA! I TOOK CARE OF HER ALL RIGHT!
...POOR THING...
I wonder what he said...
EMPATHY

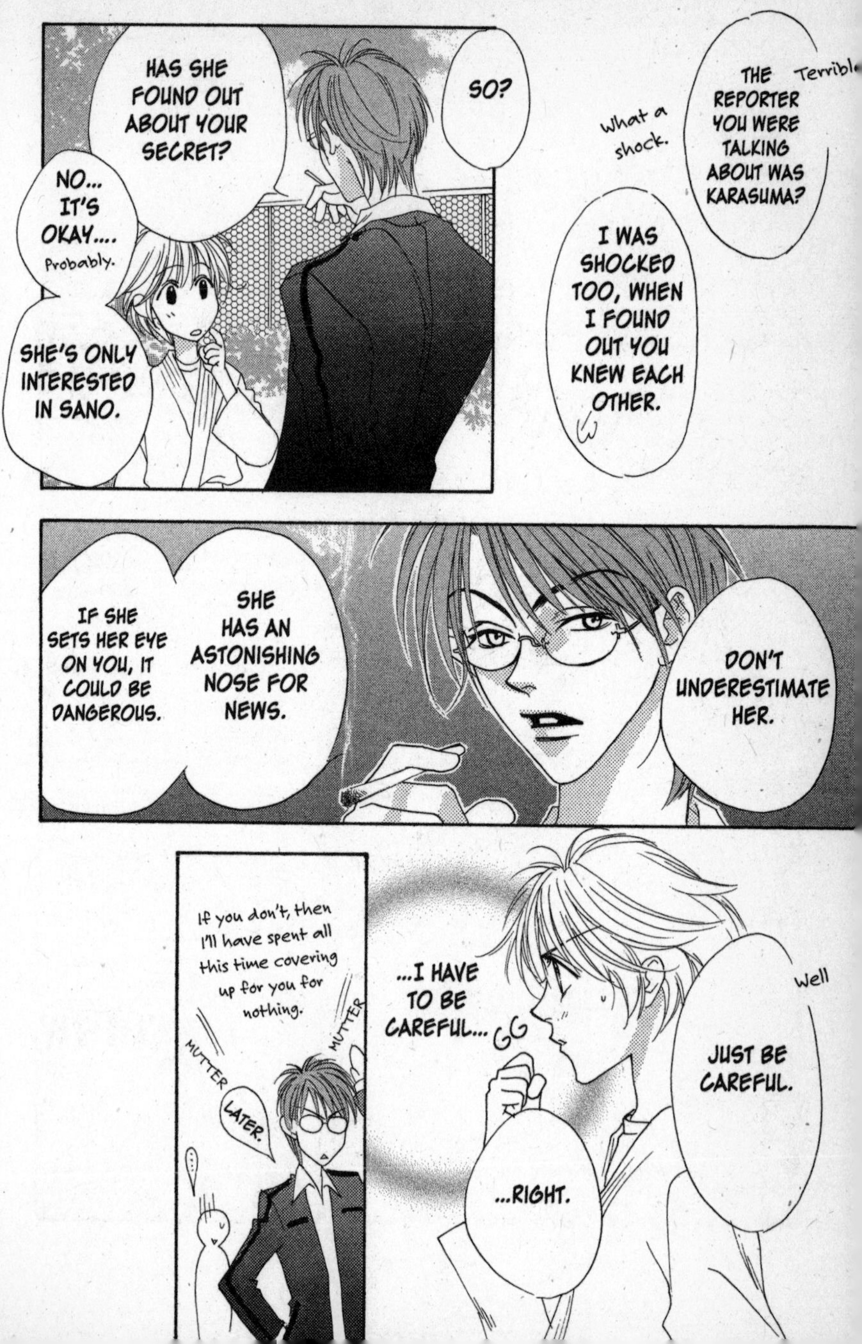
THE REPORTER YOU WERE TALKING ABOUT WAS KARASUMA?
Terrible
What a shock.
I WAS SHOCKED TOO, WHEN I FOUND OUT YOU KNEW EACH OTHER.
SO?
HAS SHE FOUND OUT ABOUT YOUR SECRET?
NO... IT'S OKAY....
Probably.
SHE'S ONLY INTERESTED IN SANO.
DON'T UNDERESTIMATE HER.
SHE HAS AN ASTONISHING NOSE FOR NEWS.
IF SHE SETS HER EYE ON YOU, IT COULD BE DANGEROUS.
Well
JUST BE CAREFUL.
...RIGHT.
...I HAVE TO BE CAREFUL...
GG
If you don't, then I'll have spent all this time covering up for you for nothing.
MUTTER
MUTTER
LATER.
...

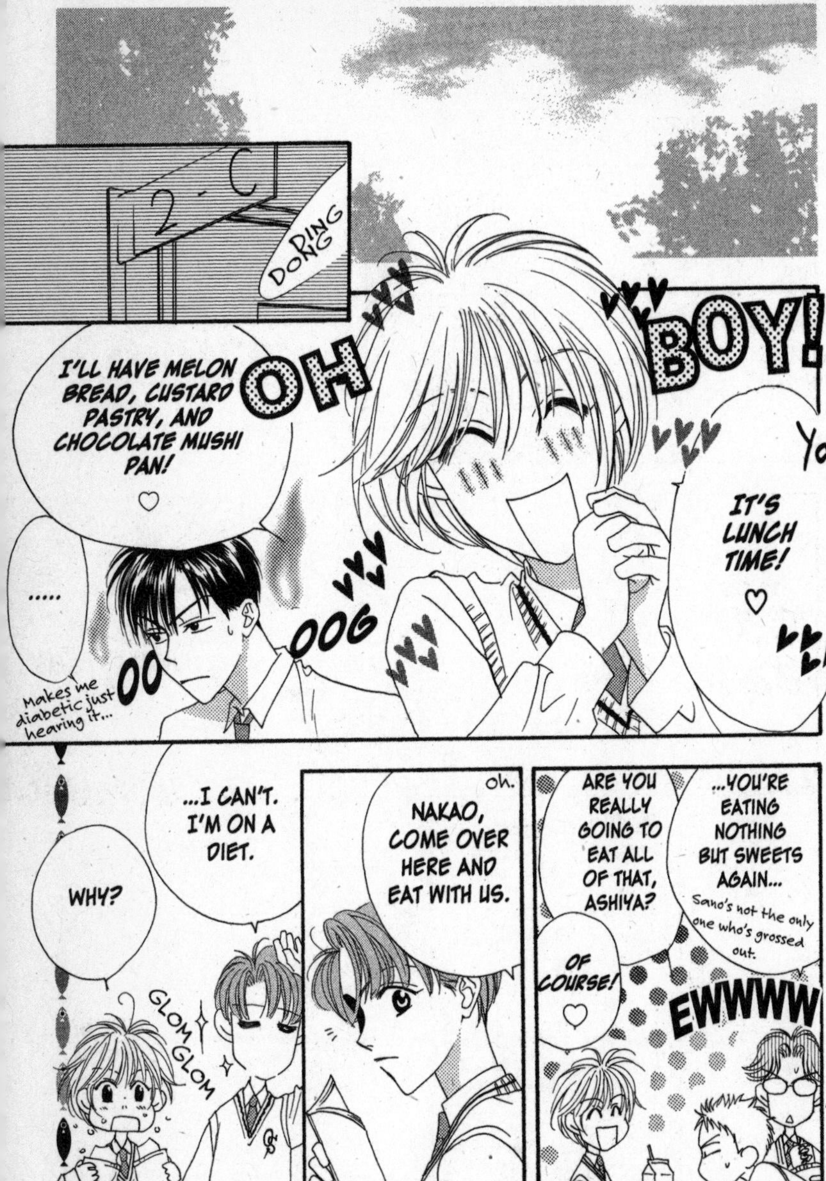

2-C
DING DONG
OH BOY!
Yay!
IT'S LUNCH TIME! ♡
I'LL HAVE MELON BREAD, CUSTARD PASTRY, AND CHOCOLATE MUSHI PAN! ♡
.....
OOOOG
Makes me diabetic just hearing it...
...YOU'RE EATING NOTHING BUT SWEETS AGAIN...
Sano's not the only one who's grossed out.
ARE YOU REALLY GOING TO EAT ALL OF THAT, ASHIYA?
OF COURSE! ♡
EWWWW
oh.
NAKAO, COME OVER HERE AND EAT WITH US.
...I CAN'T. I'M ON A DIET.
WHY?
GLOM GLOM

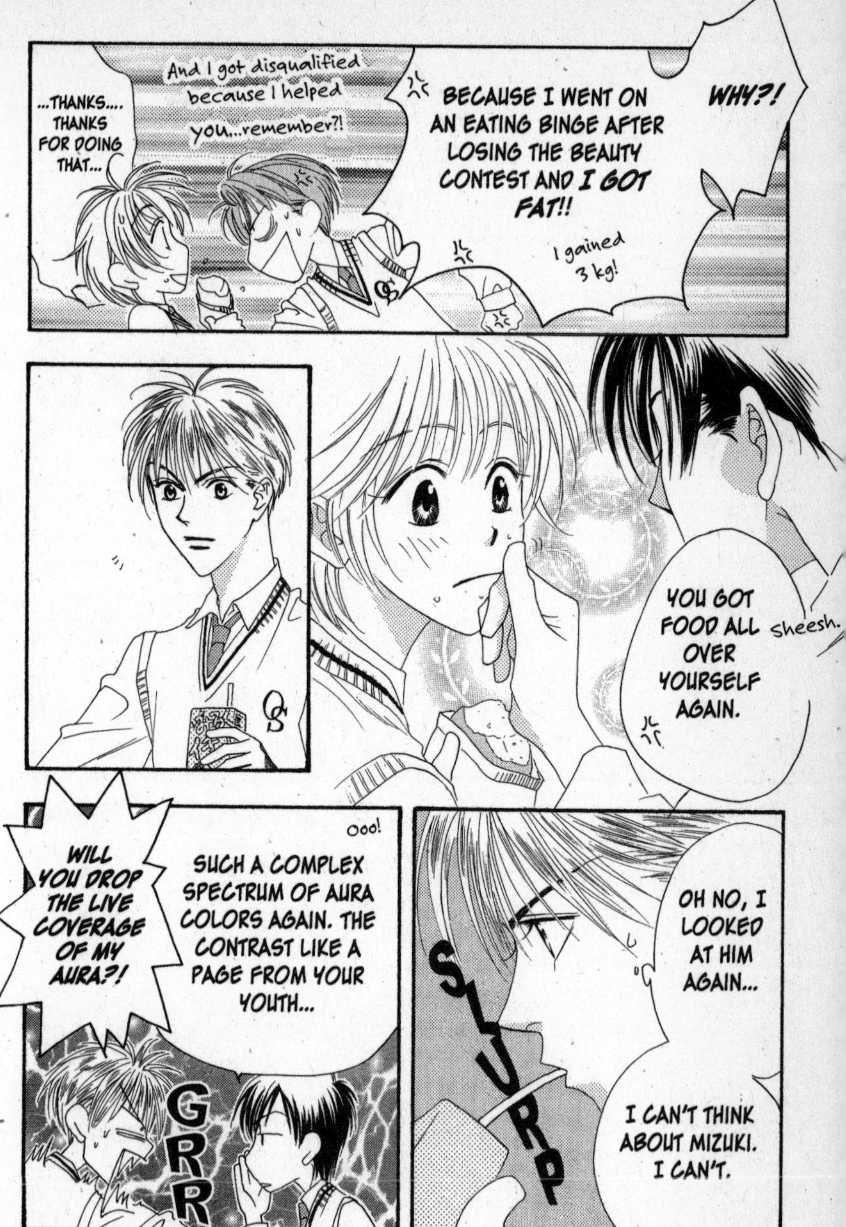

WHY?!
BECAUSE I WENT ON AN EATING BINGE AFTER LOSING THE BEAUTY CONTEST AND I GOT FAT!!
I gained 3 kg!
And I got disqualified because I helped you...remember?!
...THANKS.... THANKS FOR DOING THAT...
Sheesh.
YOU GOT FOOD ALL OVER YOURSELF AGAIN.
OH NO, I LOOKED AT HIM AGAIN...
SLURP
I CAN'T THINK ABOUT MIZUKI. I CAN'T.
Ooo!
SUCH A COMPLEX SPECTRUM OF AURA COLORS AGAIN. THE CONTRAST LIKE A PAGE FROM YOUR YOUTH...
WILL YOU DROP THE LIVE COVERAGE OF MY AURA?!
GRR

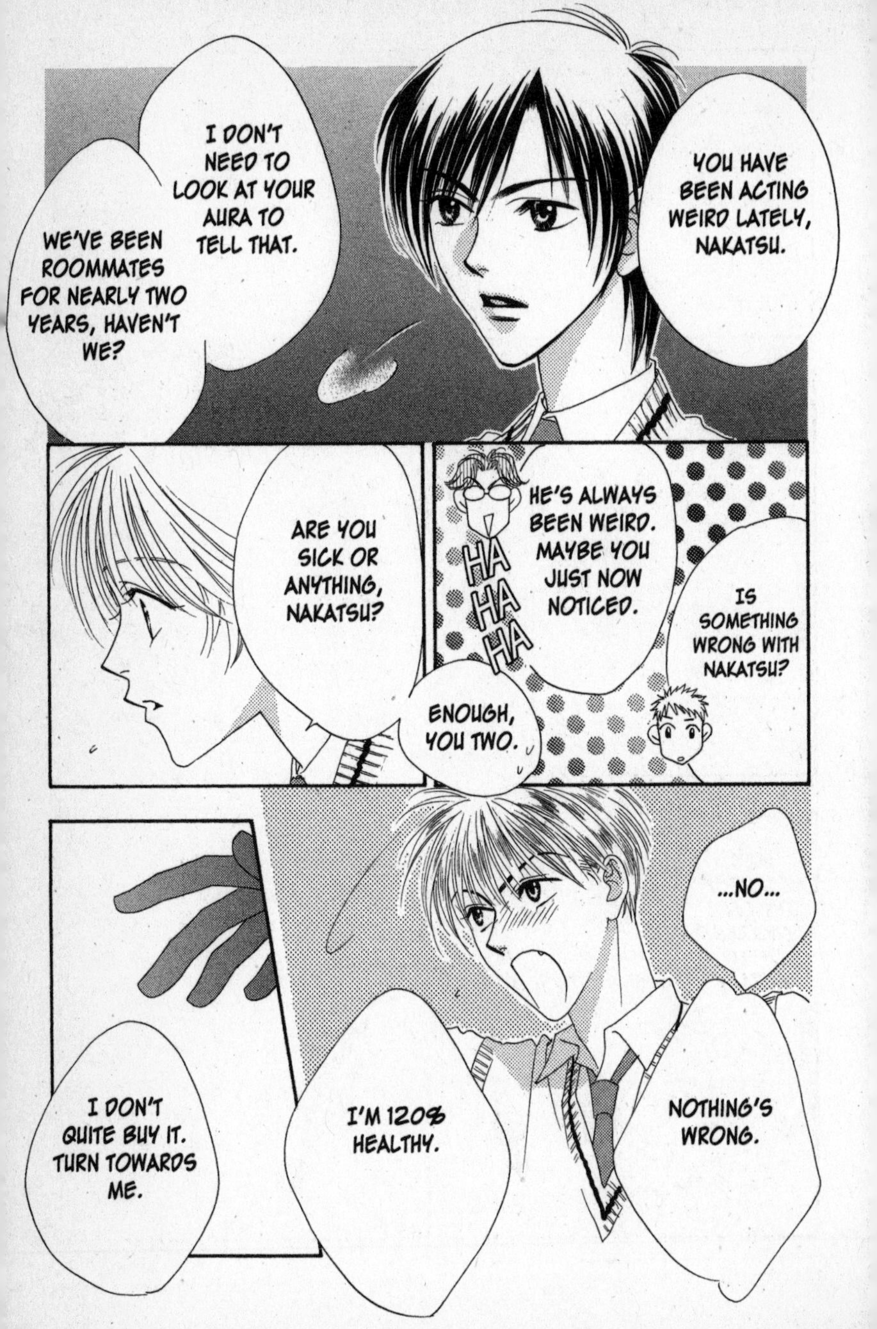
YOU HAVE BEEN ACTING WEIRD LATELY, NAKATSU.
I DON'T NEED TO LOOK AT YOUR AURA TO TELL THAT.
WE'VE BEEN ROOMMATES FOR NEARLY TWO YEARS, HAVEN'T WE?
IS SOMETHING WRONG WITH NAKATSU?
HE'S ALWAYS BEEN WEIRD. MAYBE YOU JUST NOW NOTICED.
HA HA HA
ENOUGH, YOU TWO.
ARE YOU SICK OR ANYTHING, NAKATSU?
...NO...
NOTHING'S WRONG.
I'M 120% HEALTHY.
I DON'T QUITE BUY IT. TURN TOWARDS ME.

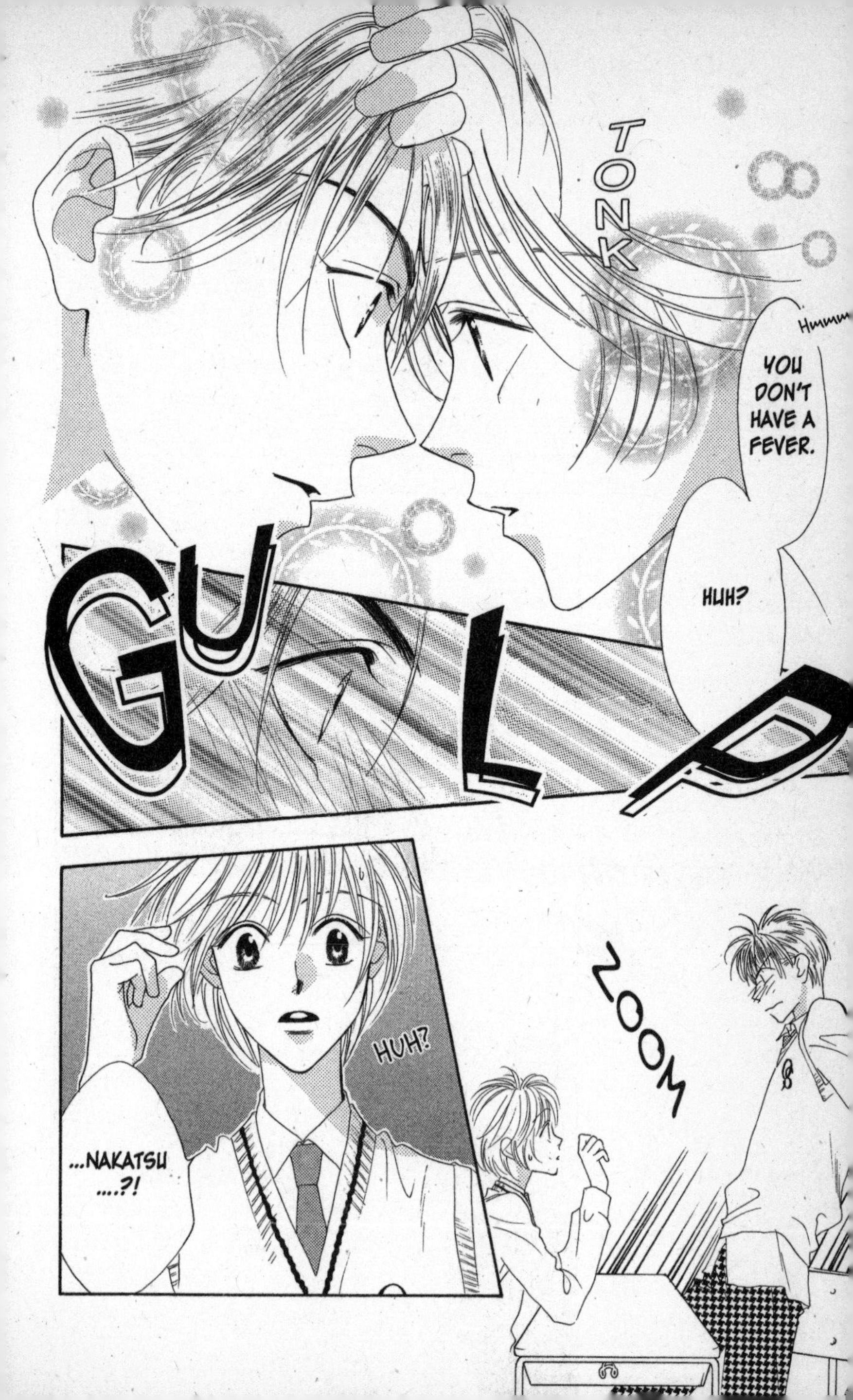
TONK
Hmmm
YOU DON'T HAVE A FEVER.
HUH?
GULP
ZOOM
HUH?
...NAKATSU ....?!

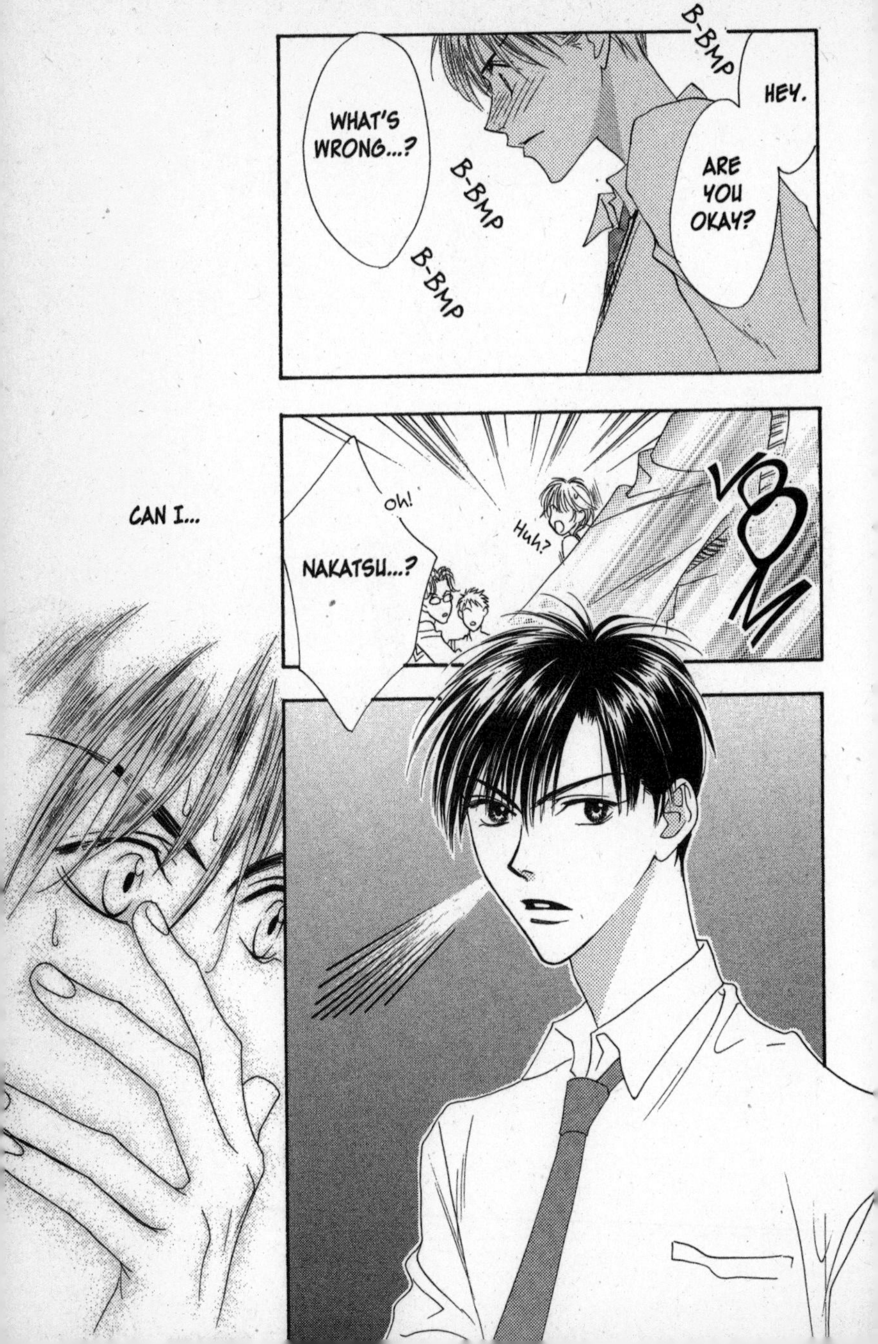
B-BMP
HEY.
ARE YOU OKAY?
WHAT'S WRONG...?
B-BMP
B-BMP
VOOM
Huh?
Oh!
NAKATSU...?
CAN I...

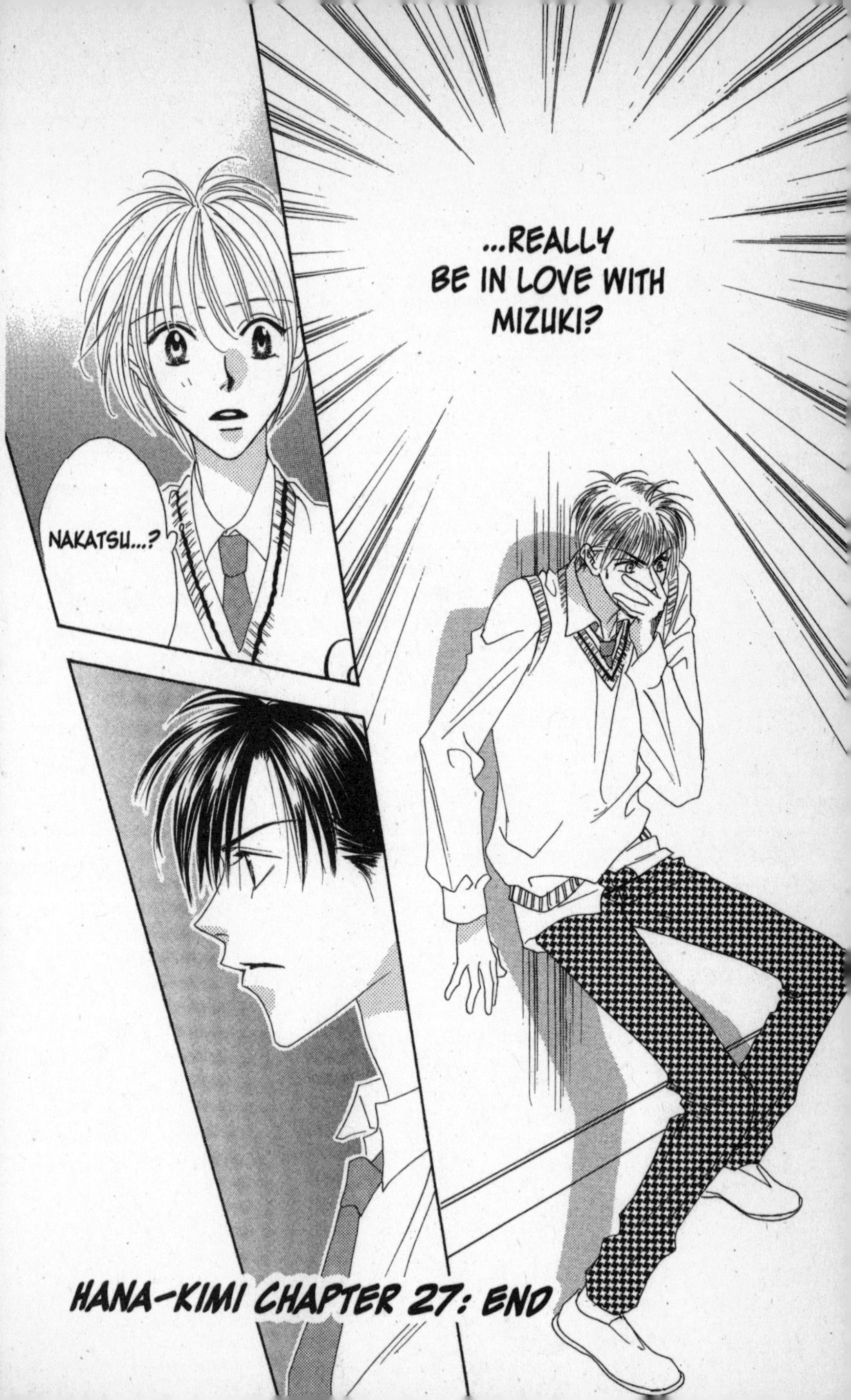
...REALLY BE IN LOVE WITH MIZUKI?
NAKATSU...?
HANA-KIMI CHAPTER 27: END

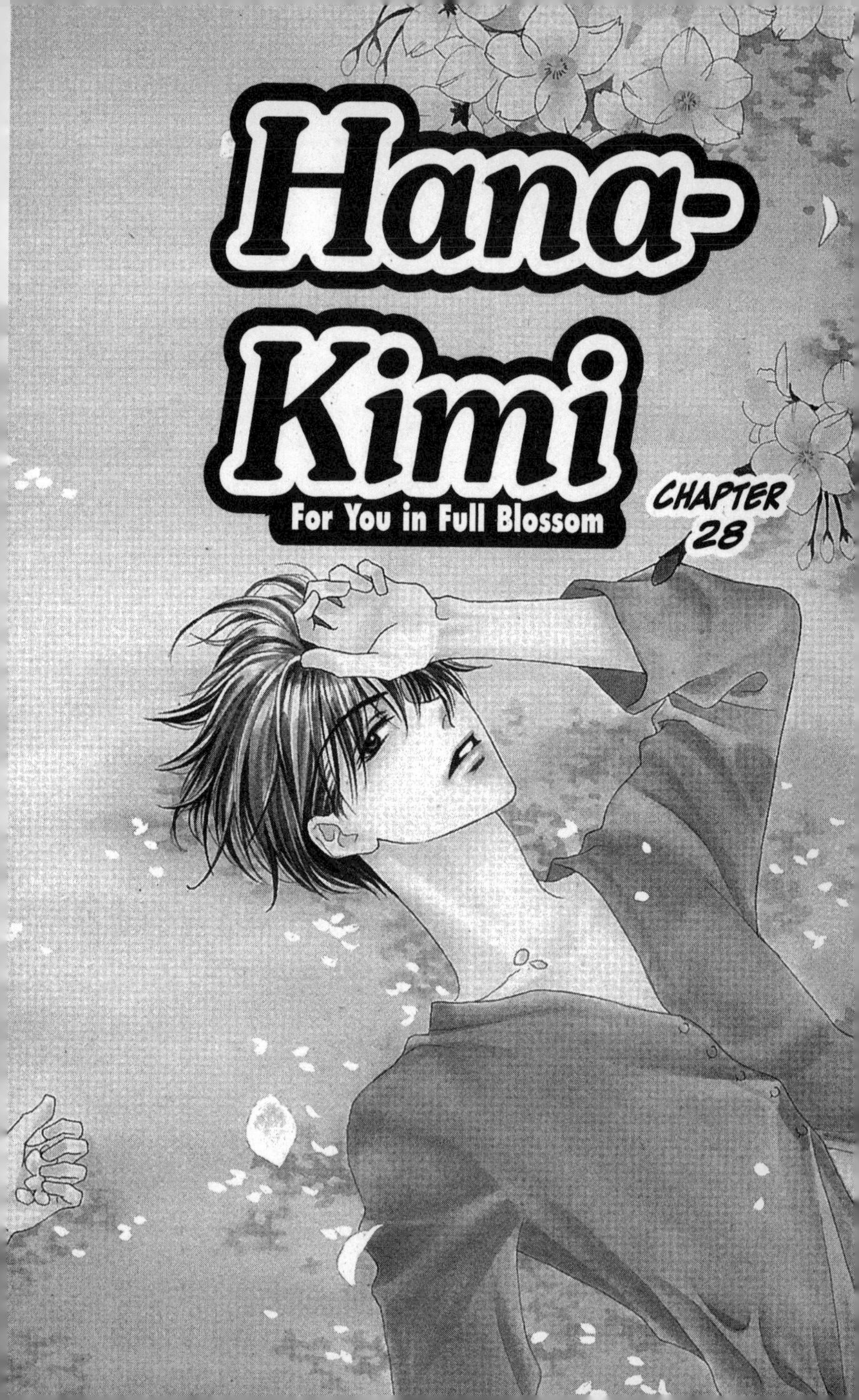
Hana-Kimi
For You in Full Blossom
CHAPTER 28

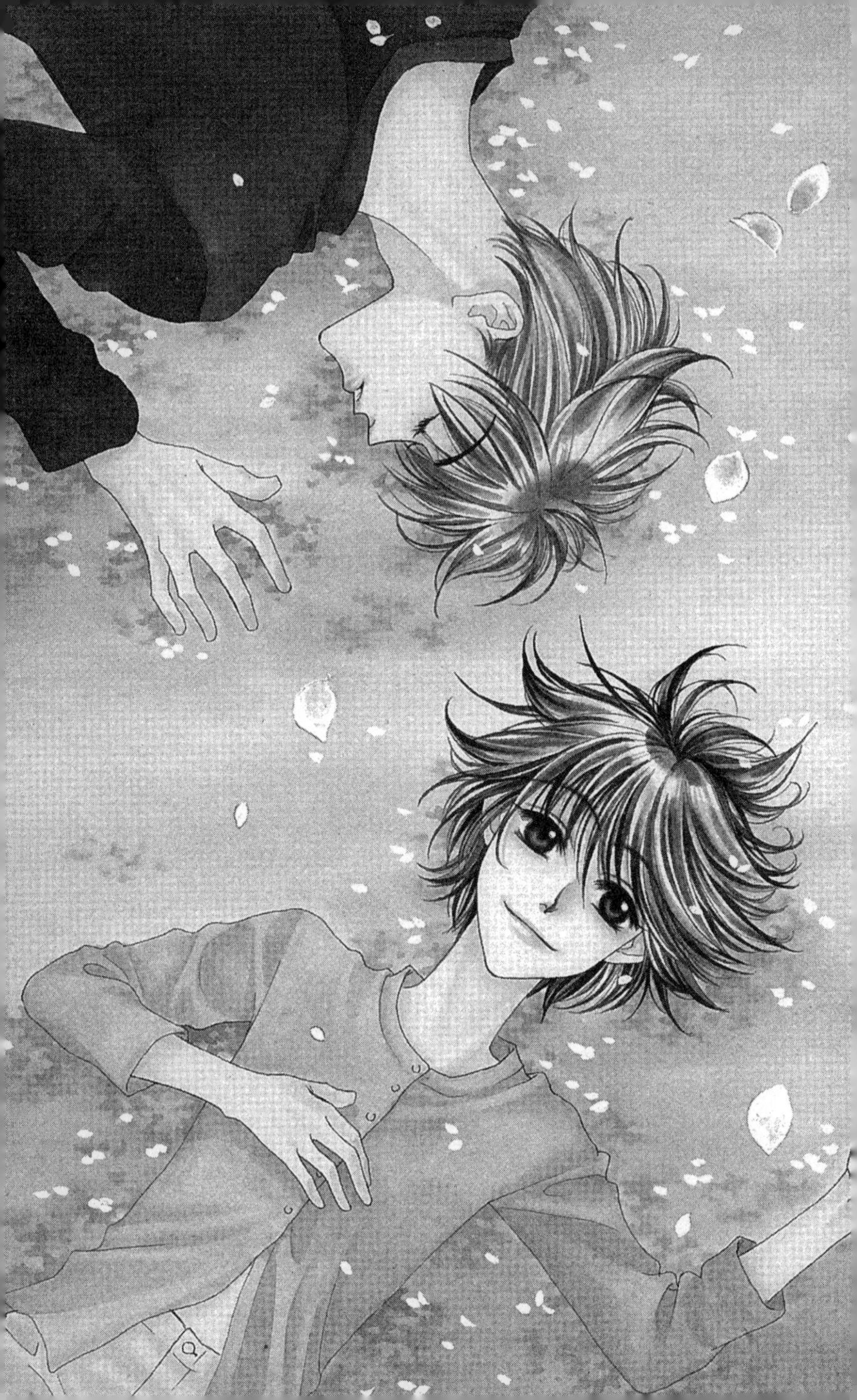

DO I...

...REALLY LOVE MIZUKI...?

STUFF I LOVE Part 3

「 DOLLS 」

I LOVE TEDDY BEARS!!! WHEN IT COMES TO STUFFED ANIMALS, IT'S ALL ABOUT BEARS!! NOTHING BUT BEARS!! (HA HA!) EVEN AT MY AGE, I STILL LIKE STUFFED ANIMALS (AND THERE'S NOTHING WRONG WITH THAT! REALLY!) I'D LIKE TO GET A STEIFF TEDDY BEAR. I LIKE SOME CATS, TOO, BUT ONLY REALLY WELL-DESIGNED ONES. I ALSO HAVE A FROG.

A stuffed cat that plays music and is the size of my palm... I've been looking for it for four years. (Its face, hands and paws are porcelain).

Pink!!

I have a matching watch!! It's so cute!

I named this one Majorica.

69

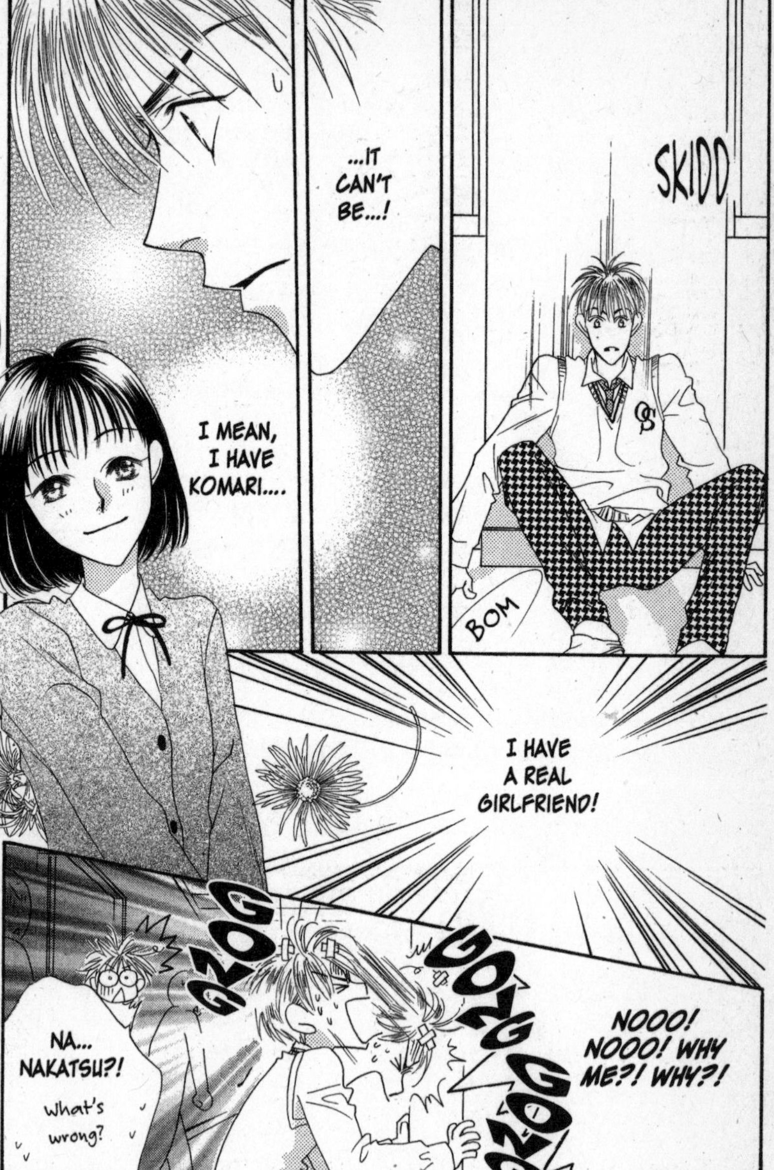
SKIDD
BOM
...IT CAN'T BE...!
I MEAN, I HAVE KOMARI....
I HAVE A REAL GIRLFRIEND!
NOOO! NOOO! WHY ME?! WHY?!
GONG GONG
GONG
NA... NAKATSU?!
what's wrong?

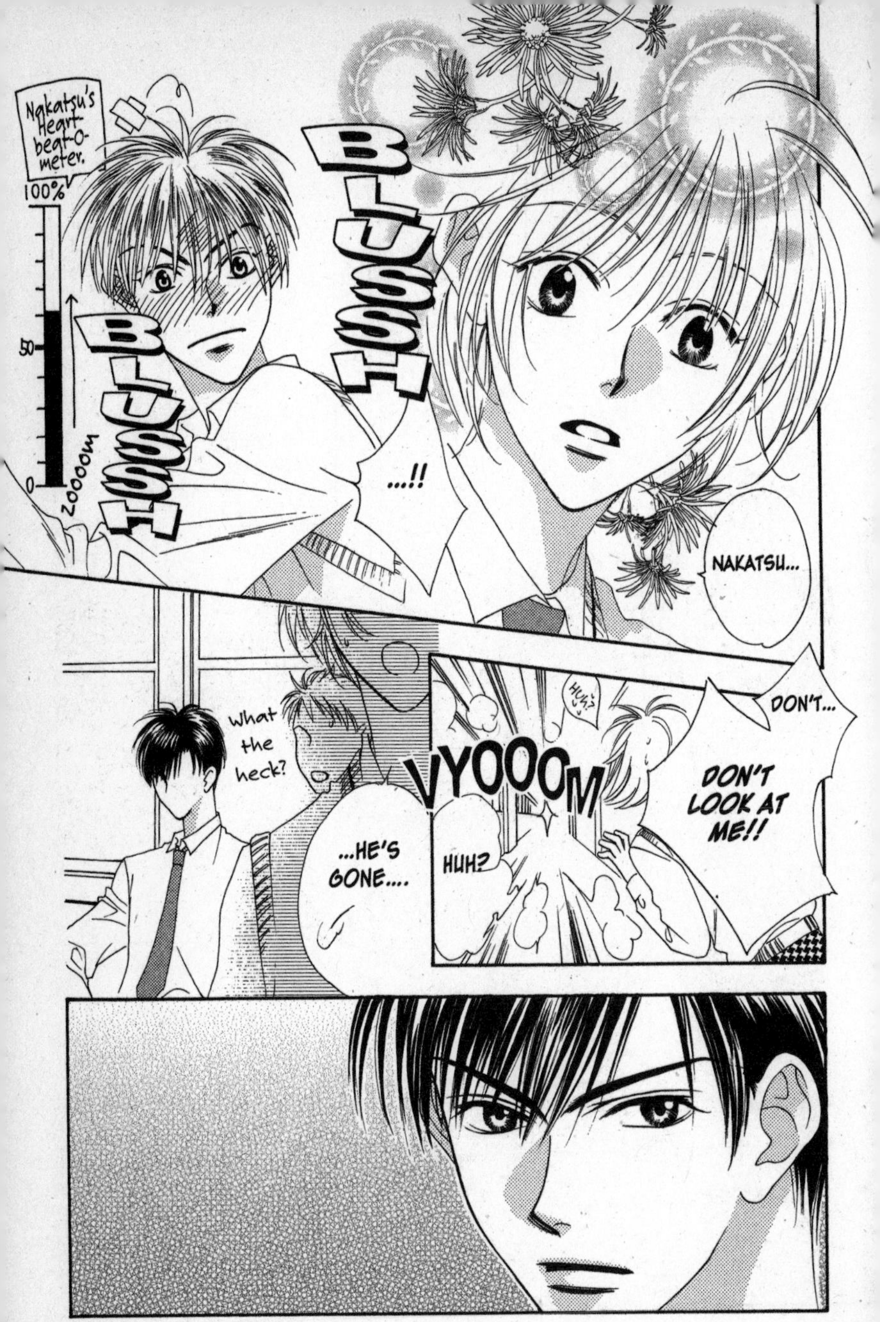
NAKATSU...
...!!
BLUSSH
BLUSSH
Nakatsu's Heart-beat-o-meter.
100%
50
0
zoooom
DON'T...
DON'T LOOK AT ME!!
HUH?
VYOOOM
HUH?
...HE'S GONE....
What the heck?

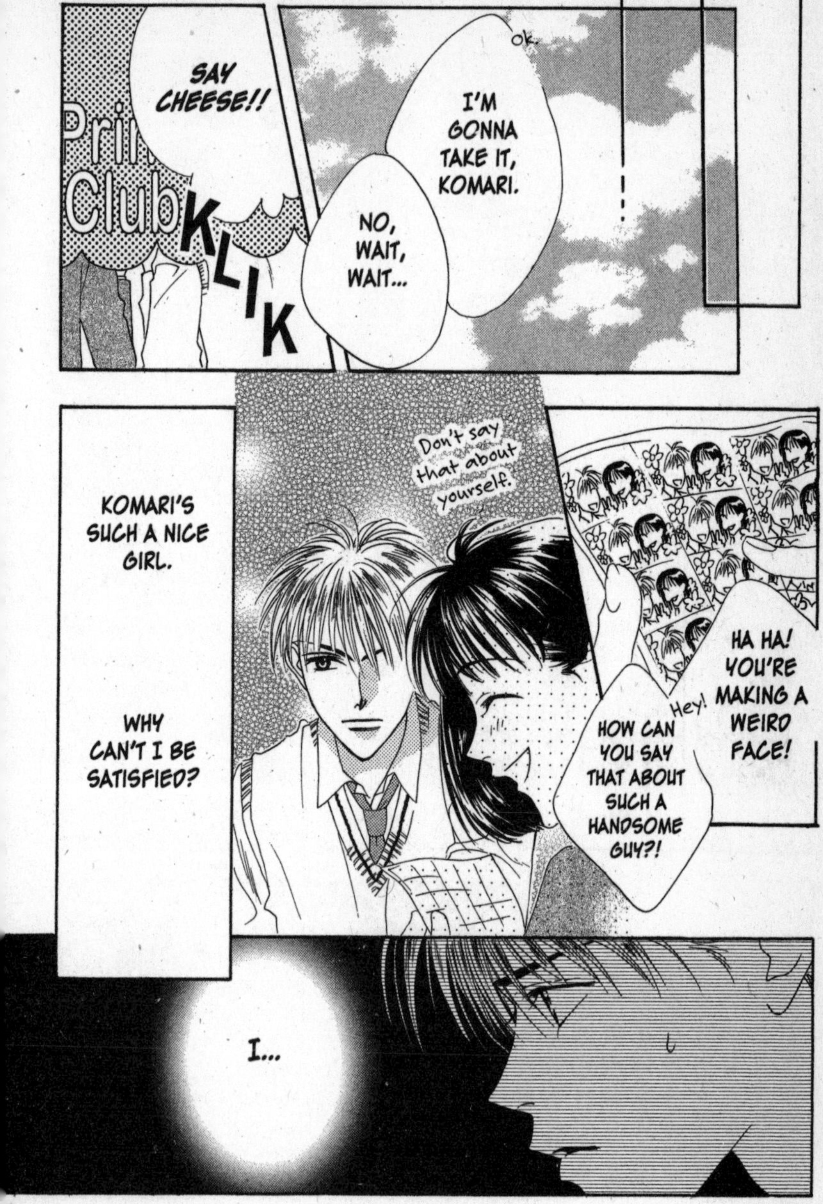
ok.
I'M GONNA TAKE IT, KOMARI.
NO, WAIT, WAIT...
SAY CHEESE!!
Club
KLIK
HA HA! YOU'RE MAKING A WEIRD FACE!
Hey!
HOW CAN YOU SAY THAT ABOUT SUCH A HANDSOME GUY?!
Don't say that about yourself.
KOMARI'S SUCH A NICE GIRL.
WHY CAN'T I BE SATISFIED?
I...

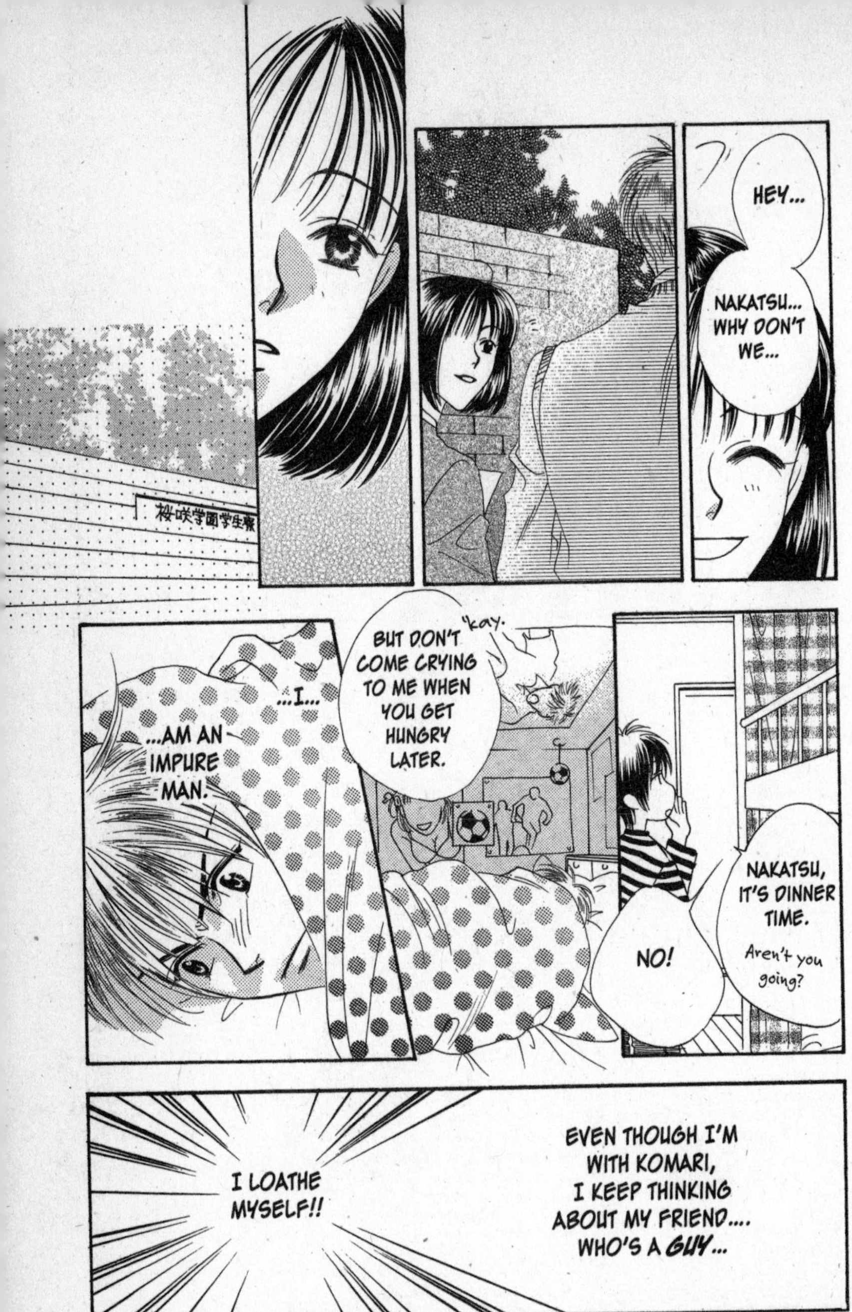
HEY...
NAKATSU... WHY DON'T WE...
桜咲学園学生寮
NAKATSU, IT'S DINNER TIME.
Aren't you going?
NO!
BUT DON'T COME CRYING TO ME WHEN YOU GET HUNGRY LATER.
'kay.
...I...
...AM AN IMPURE MAN.
EVEN THOUGH I'M WITH KOMARI, I KEEP THINKING ABOUT MY FRIEND.... WHO'S A GUY...
I LOATHE MYSELF!!

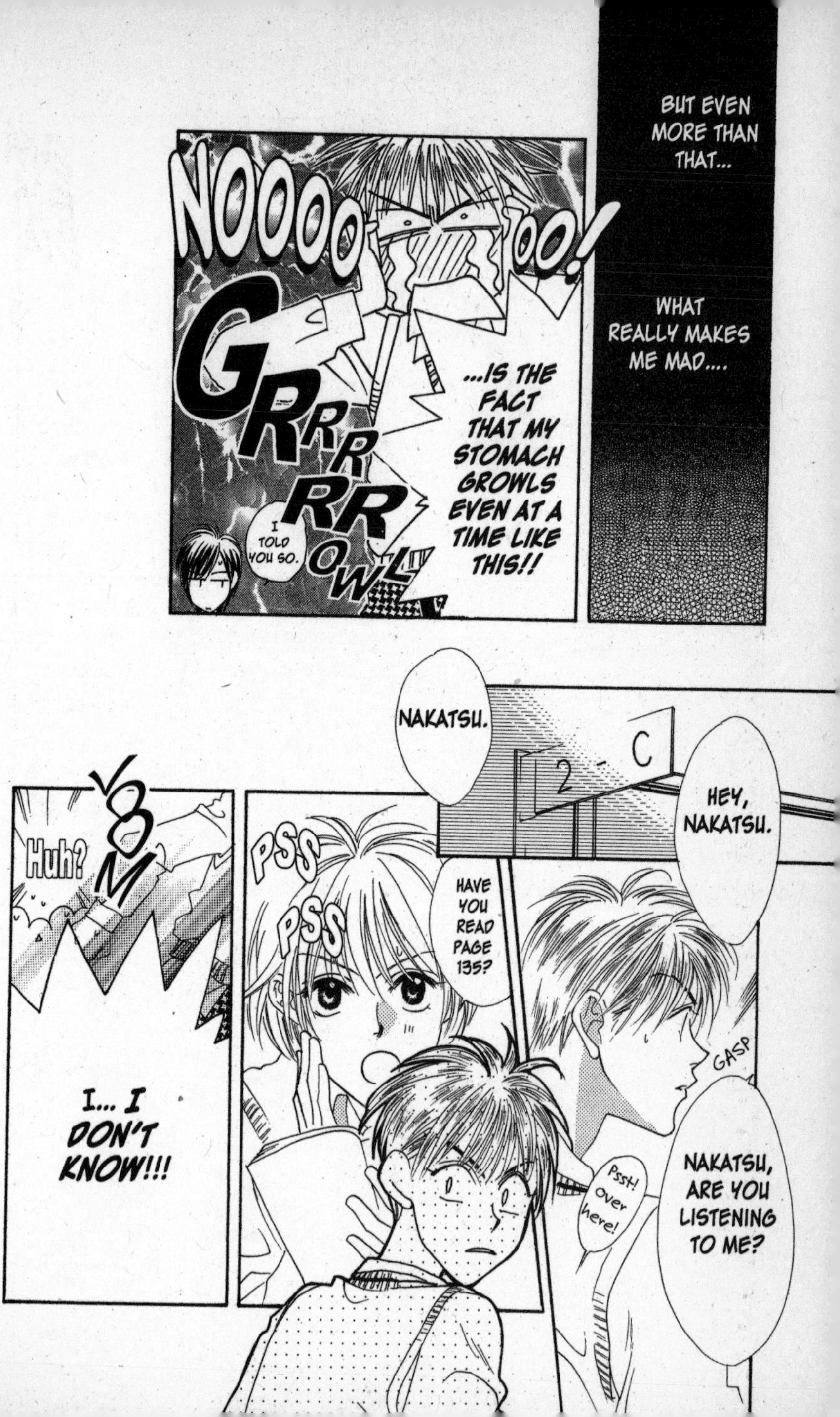
BUT EVEN MORE THAN THAT...
WHAT REALLY MAKES ME MAD....
NOOOOOOO!
GRRRRROWL
...IS THE FACT THAT MY STOMACH GROWLS EVEN AT A TIME LIKE THIS!!
I TOLD YOU SO.
NAKATSU.
HEY, NAKATSU.
GASP
NAKATSU, ARE YOU LISTENING TO ME?
Psst! Over here!
HAVE YOU READ PAGE 135?
PSS
PSS
VOOM
Huh?
I... I DON'T KNOW!!!

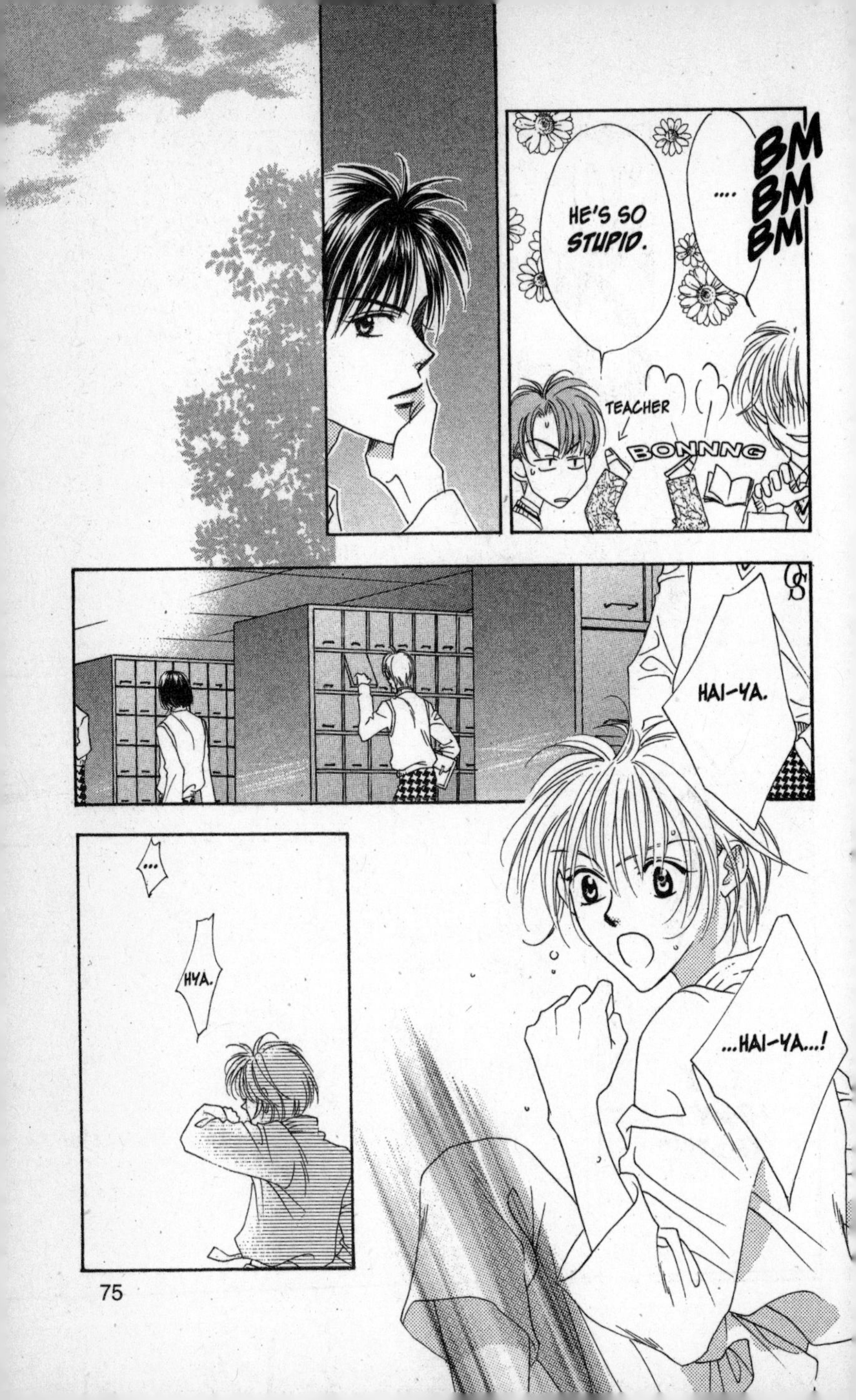
....
BM BM BM
HE'S SO STUPID.
TEACHER
BONNNG
HAI-YA.
...HAI-YA...!
...
HYA.

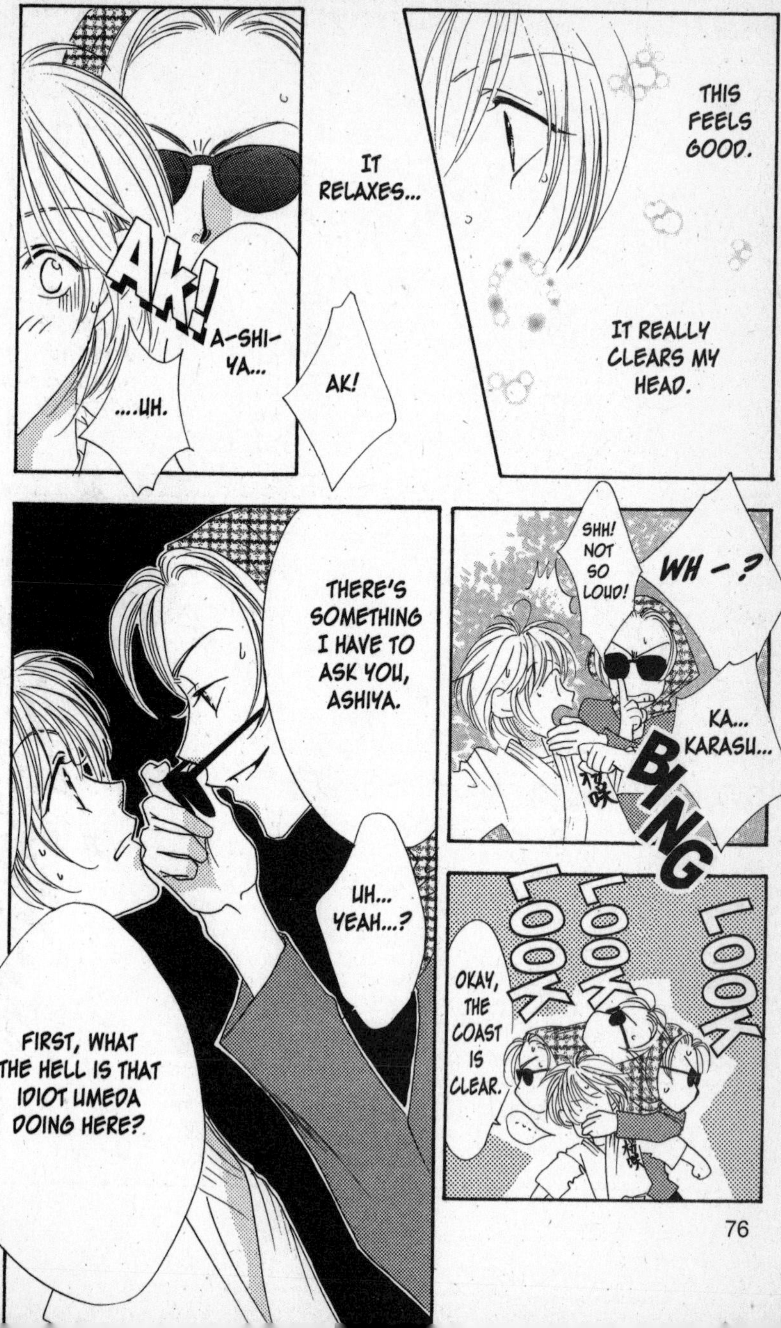
THIS FEELS GOOD.
IT REALLY CLEARS MY HEAD.
IT RELAXES...
AK!
AK!
A-SHI-YA...
....UH.
WH - ?
SHH! NOT SO LOUD!
KA... KARASU...
BING
LOOK LOOK LOOK
OKAY, THE COAST IS CLEAR.
THERE'S SOMETHING I HAVE TO ASK YOU, ASHIYA.
UH... YEAH...?
FIRST, WHAT THE HELL IS THAT IDIOT UMEDA DOING HERE?

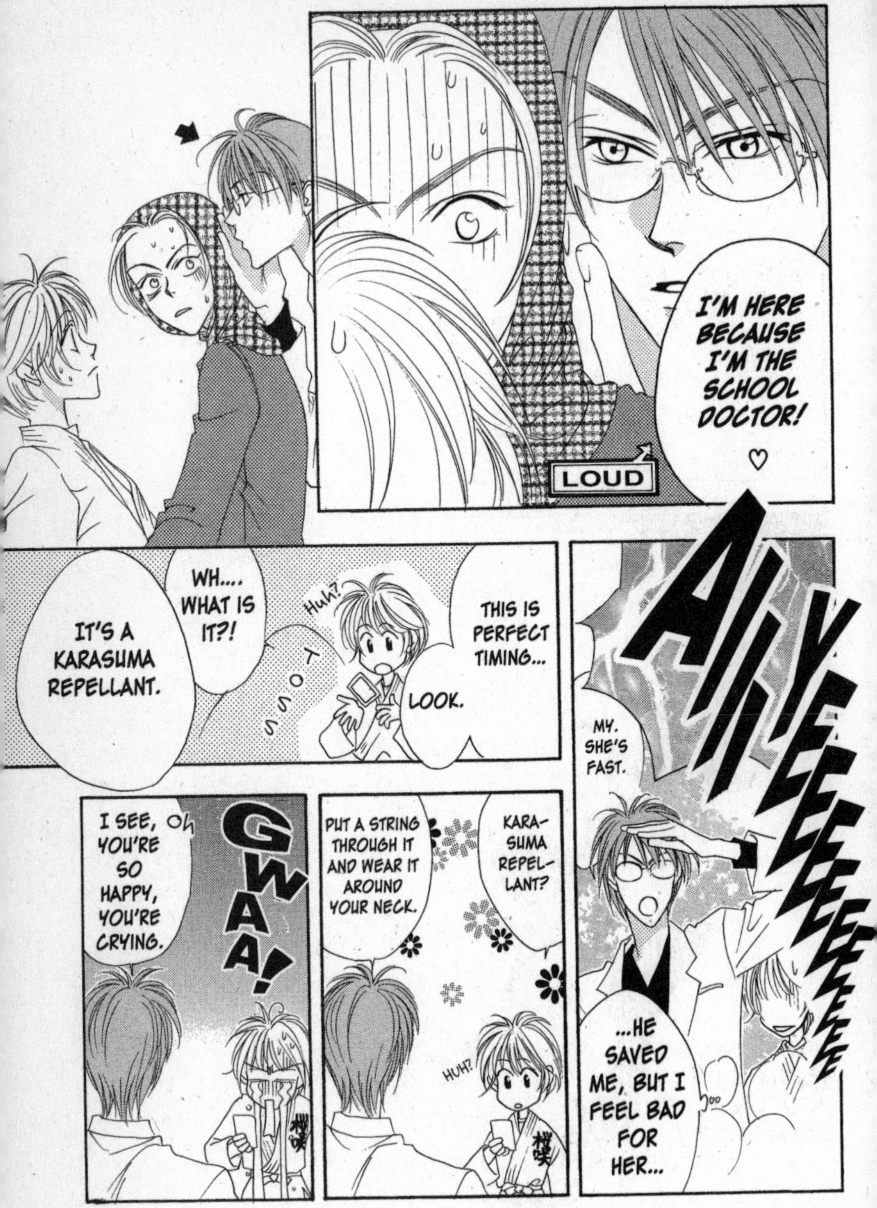
I'M HERE BECAUSE I'M THE SCHOOL DOCTOR! ♡
LOUD
AIIYEEEEEEEEEE
MY. SHE'S FAST.
...HE SAVED ME, BUT I FEEL BAD FOR HER...
THIS IS PERFECT TIMING...
LOOK.
Huh?
TOSS
WH.... WHAT IS IT?!
IT'S A KARASUMA REPELLANT.
KARA-SUMA REPEL-LANT?
PUT A STRING THROUGH IT AND WEAR IT AROUND YOUR NECK.
HUH?
GWAA!
I SEE, YOU'RE SO HAPPY, YOU'RE CRYING.
Oh

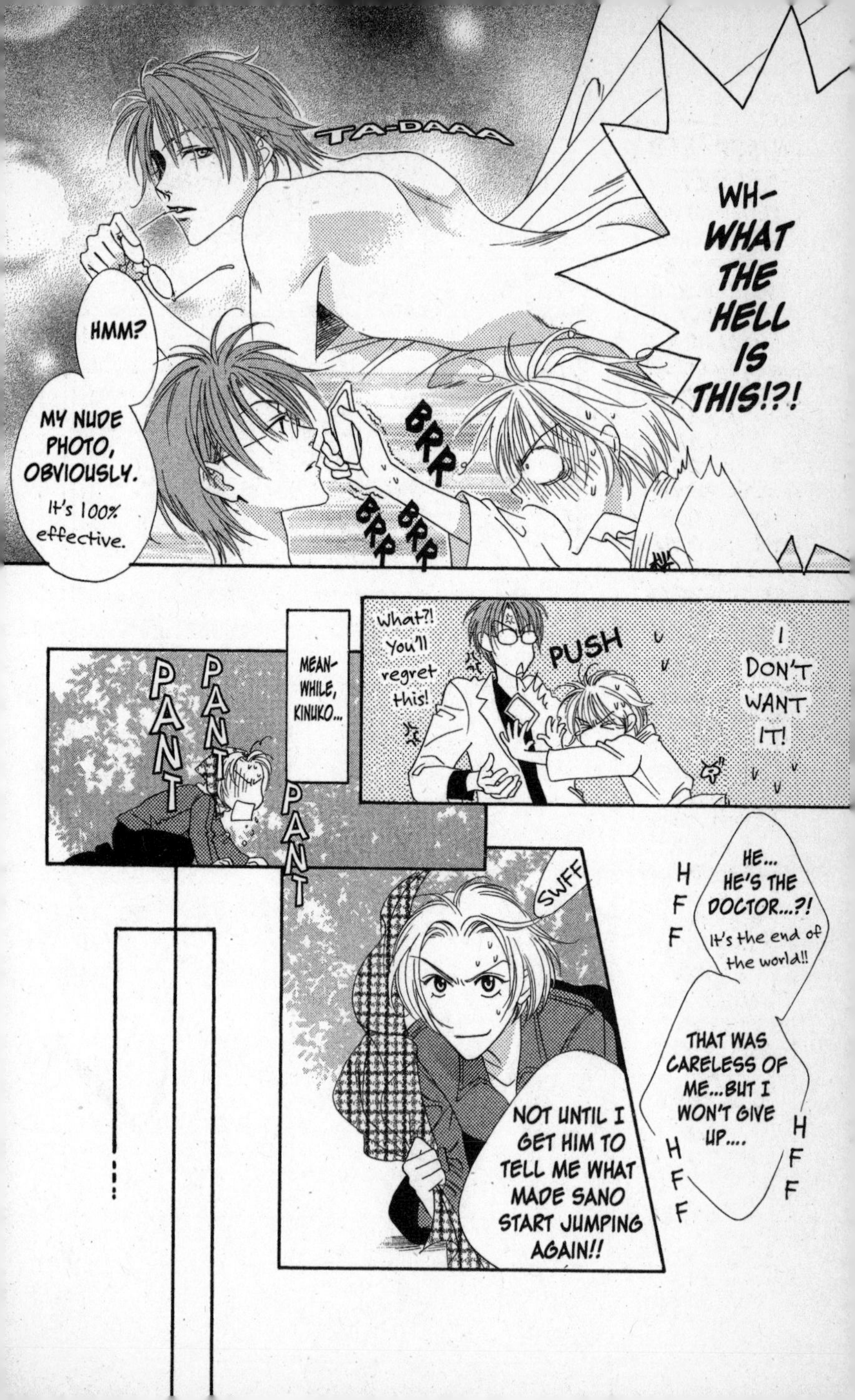
WH-WHAT THE HELL IS THIS!?!
TA-DAAA
BRR BRR BRR
HMM?
MY NUDE PHOTO, OBVIOUSLY. It's 100% effective.
I DON'T WANT IT!
PUSH
What?! You'll regret this!
MEAN-WHILE, KINUKO...
PANT PANT PANT
HE... HE'S THE DOCTOR...?! It's the end of the world!!
HFF
THAT WAS CARELESS OF ME...BUT I WON'T GIVE UP....
HFF HFF
SWFF
NOT UNTIL I GET HIM TO TELL ME WHAT MADE SANO START JUMPING AGAIN!!
...

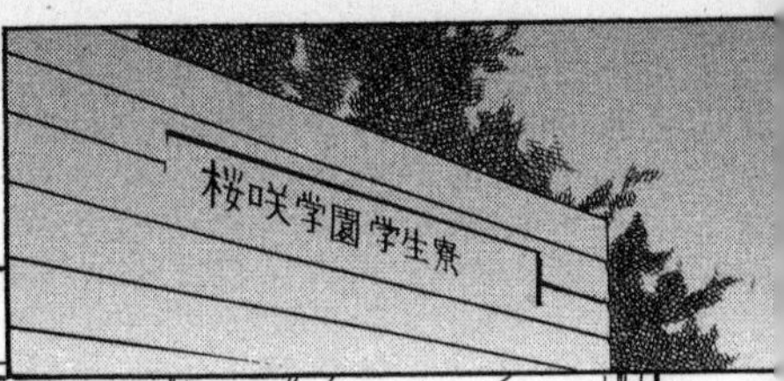
桜咲学園学生寮

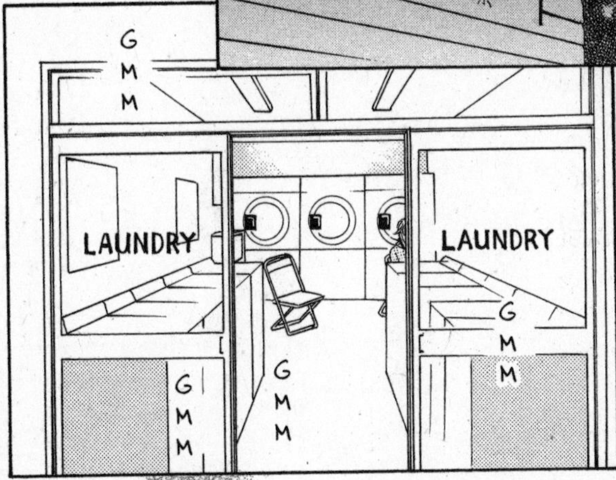
GMM
LAUNDRY
LAUNDRY
GMM
GMM
GMM

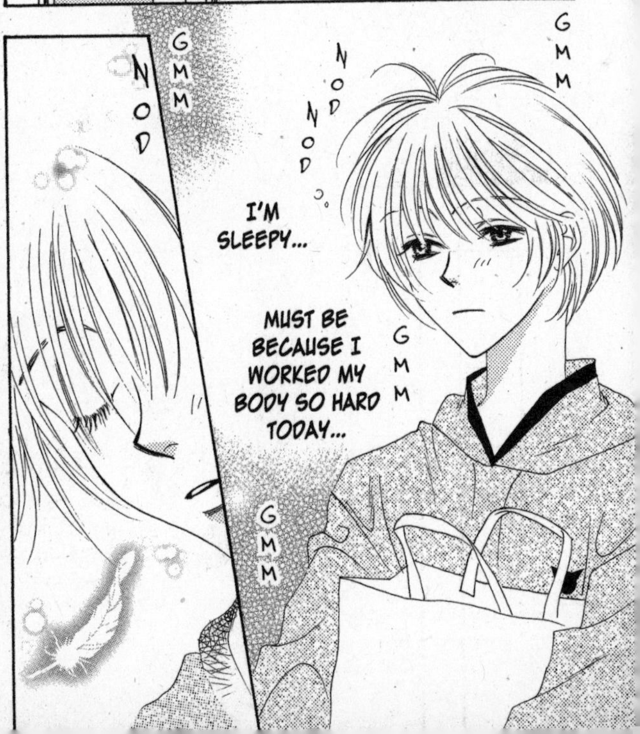
GMM
NOD
NOD
NOD
I'M SLEEPY...
MUST BE BECAUSE I WORKED MY BODY SO HARD TODAY...
GMM
GMM
NOD
GMM

WHISPERED SECRETS

LOVE AND COURAGE

I WROTE THIS STORY FOR NAKATSU. YOU FINALLY BECAME A MAN, NAKATSU! (!?) LOVE TAKES COURAGE! ...BUT POOR KOMARI! MY REPUTATION FOR PURITY WAS FINALLY DESTROYED BY THE APPEARANCE OF UMEDA'S NUDE PHOTO (SEE FACING PAGE)! HA! RIGHT NOW, I'M REALLY INTO SMAP X SMAP'S "TAKE NO ZUKA KAGEKI DAN"!♥ I MELT WHEN I HEAR THEIR THEME SONG "OTOKO" (MAN), AND KIMUTAKU'S "AI YUKI" (LOVE AND COURAGE).

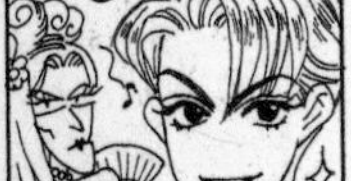
Otoko

Yosuke Saito. I love him!!

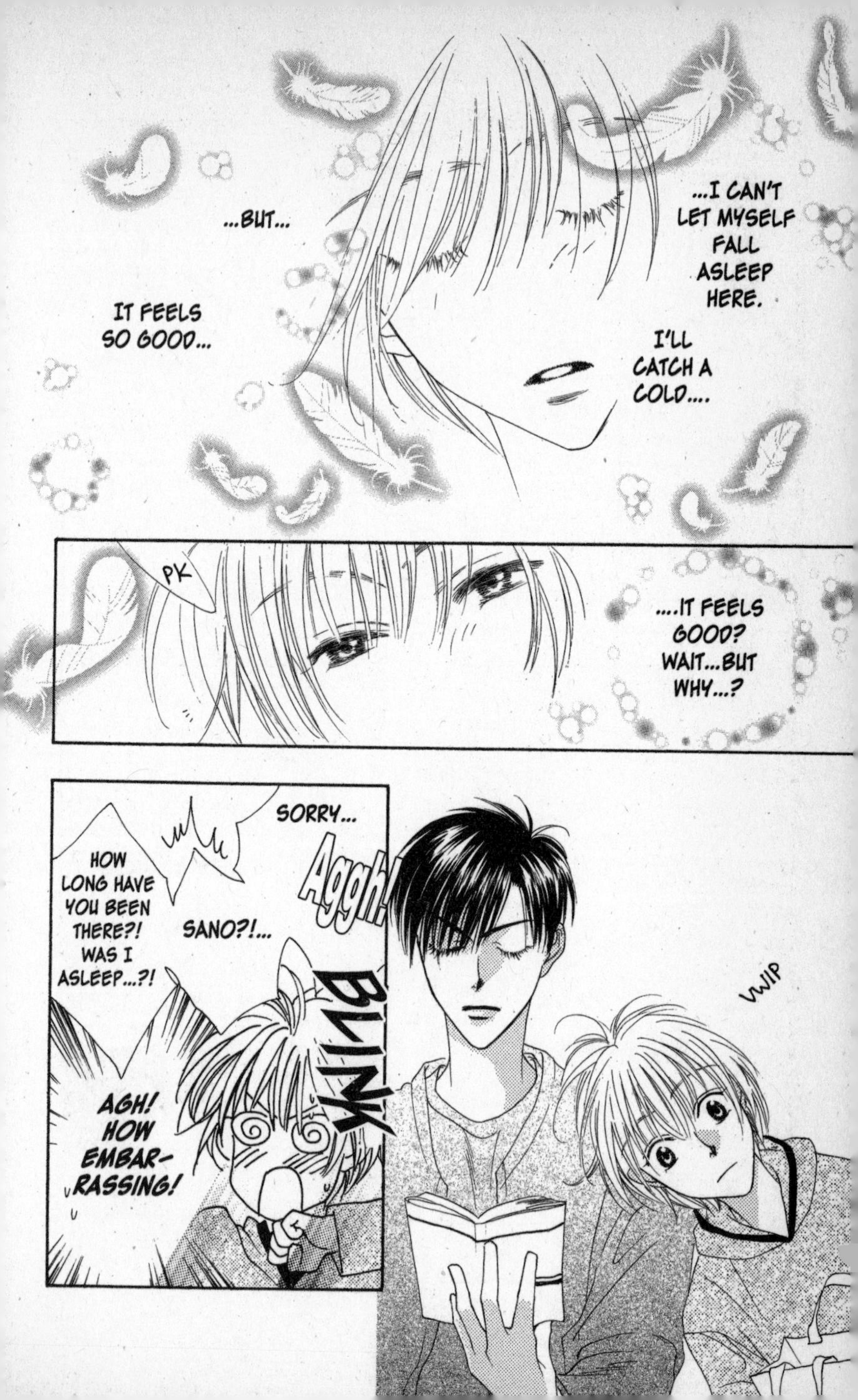
...I CAN'T LET MYSELF FALL ASLEEP HERE.
I'LL CATCH A COLD....
...BUT...
IT FEELS SO GOOD...
....IT FEELS GOOD? WAIT...BUT WHY...?
PK
VWIP
SORRY...
Agggh!
SANO?!...
HOW LONG HAVE YOU BEEN THERE?! WAS I ASLEEP...?!
BLINK
AGH! HOW EMBAR-RASSING!

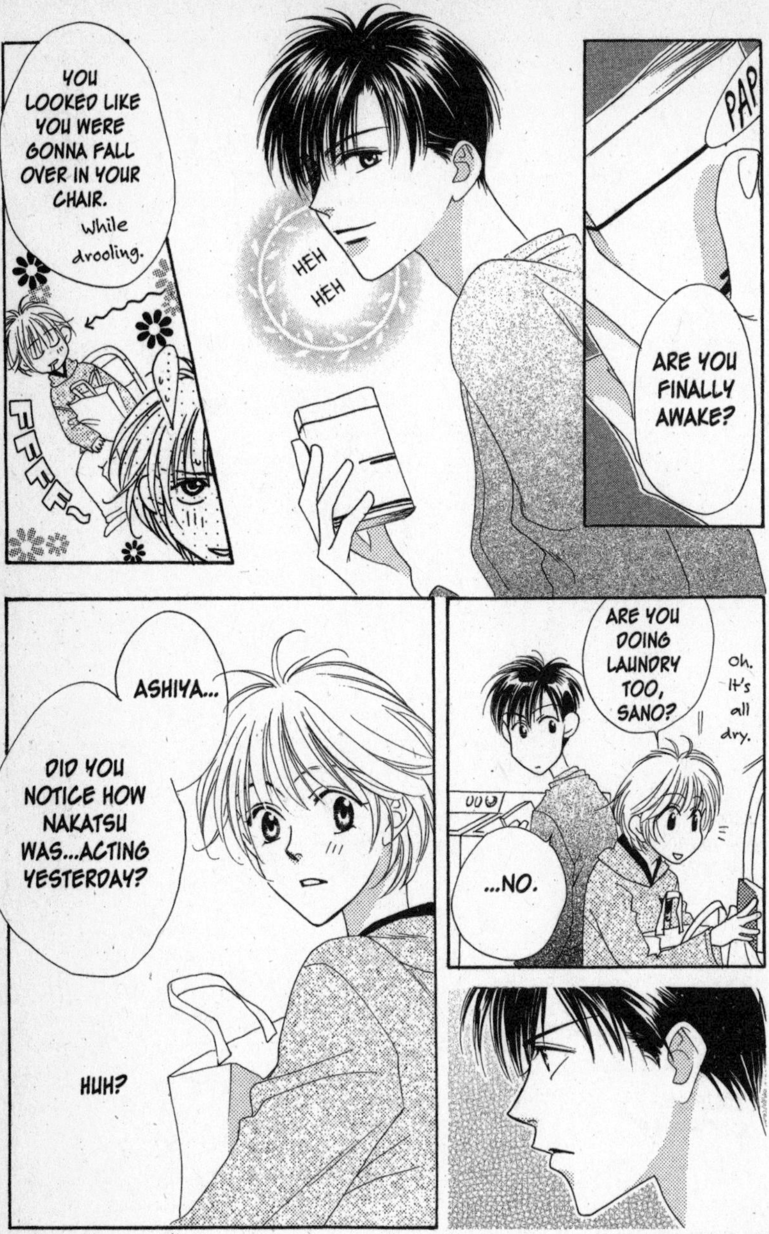
PAP
ARE YOU FINALLY AWAKE?
HEH HEH
YOU LOOKED LIKE YOU WERE GONNA FALL OVER IN YOUR CHAIR.
While drooling.
FFFF~
ARE YOU DOING LAUNDRY TOO, SANO?
Oh. It's all dry.
...NO.
ASHIYA...
DID YOU NOTICE HOW NAKATSU WAS...ACTING YESTERDAY?
HUH?

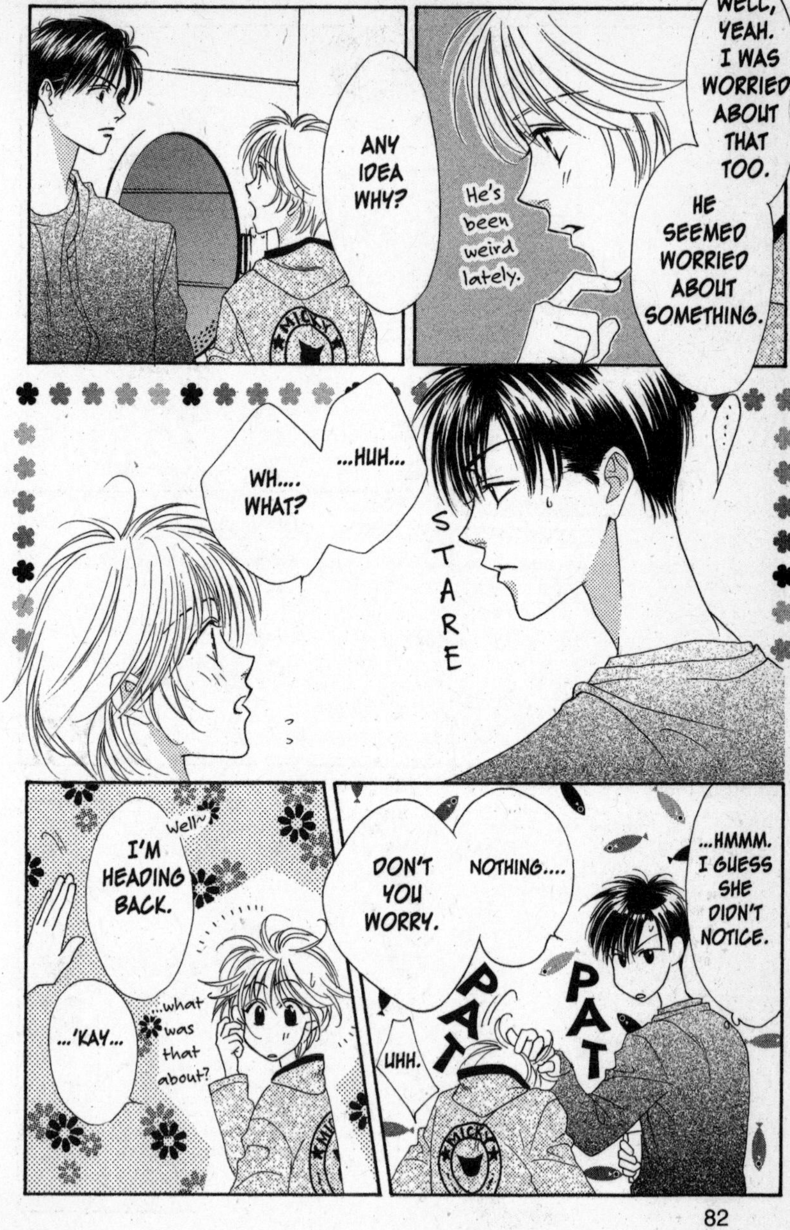
WELL, YEAH. I WAS WORRIED ABOUT THAT TOO.
HE SEEMED WORRIED ABOUT SOMETHING.
He's been weird lately.
ANY IDEA WHY?
...
...HUH...
WH.... WHAT?
STARE
...HMMM. I GUESS SHE DIDN'T NOTICE.
NOTHING....
DON'T YOU WORRY.
PAT
PAT
PAT
UHH.
Well~
I'M HEADING BACK.
...'KAY...
...what was that about?

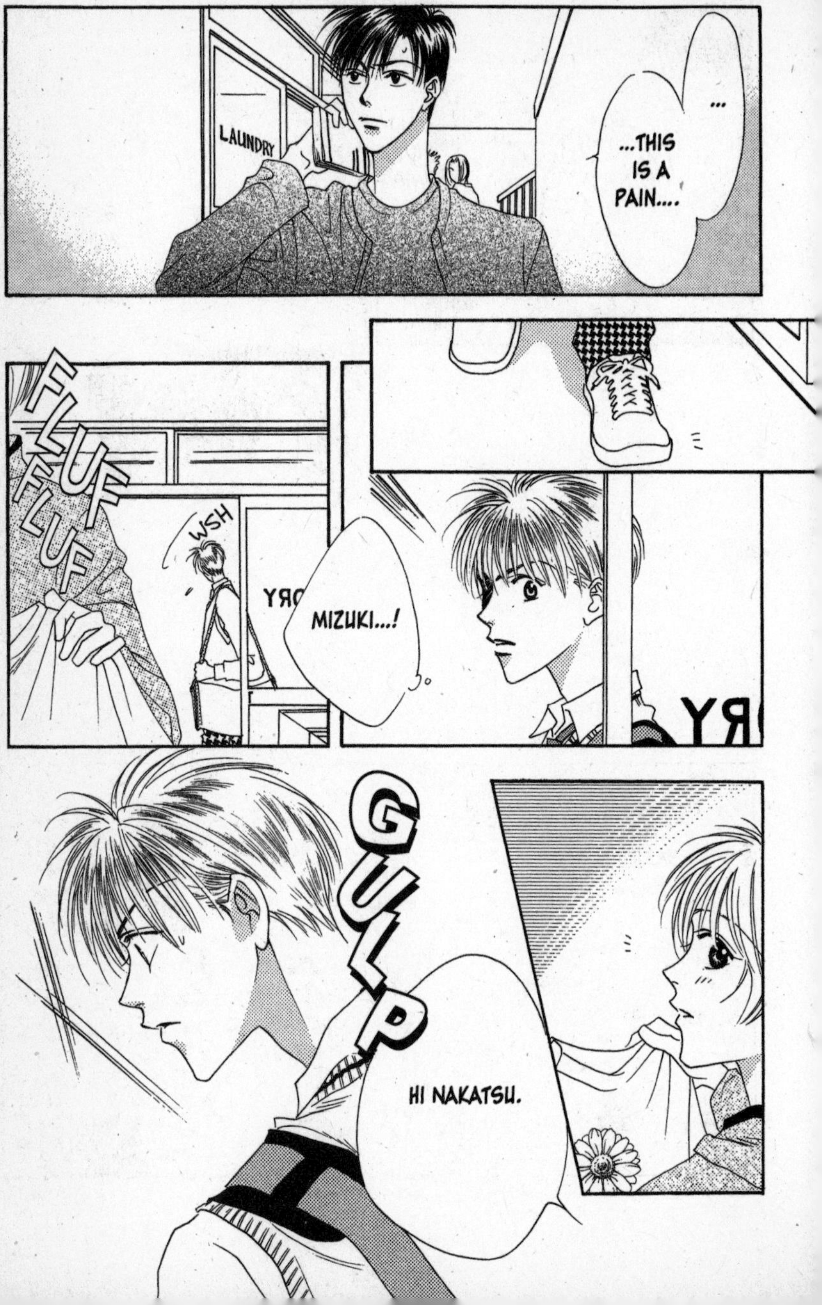
...
...THIS IS A PAIN....
LAUNDRY
MIZUKI...!
FLUF FLUF
WSH
GULP
HI NAKATSU.

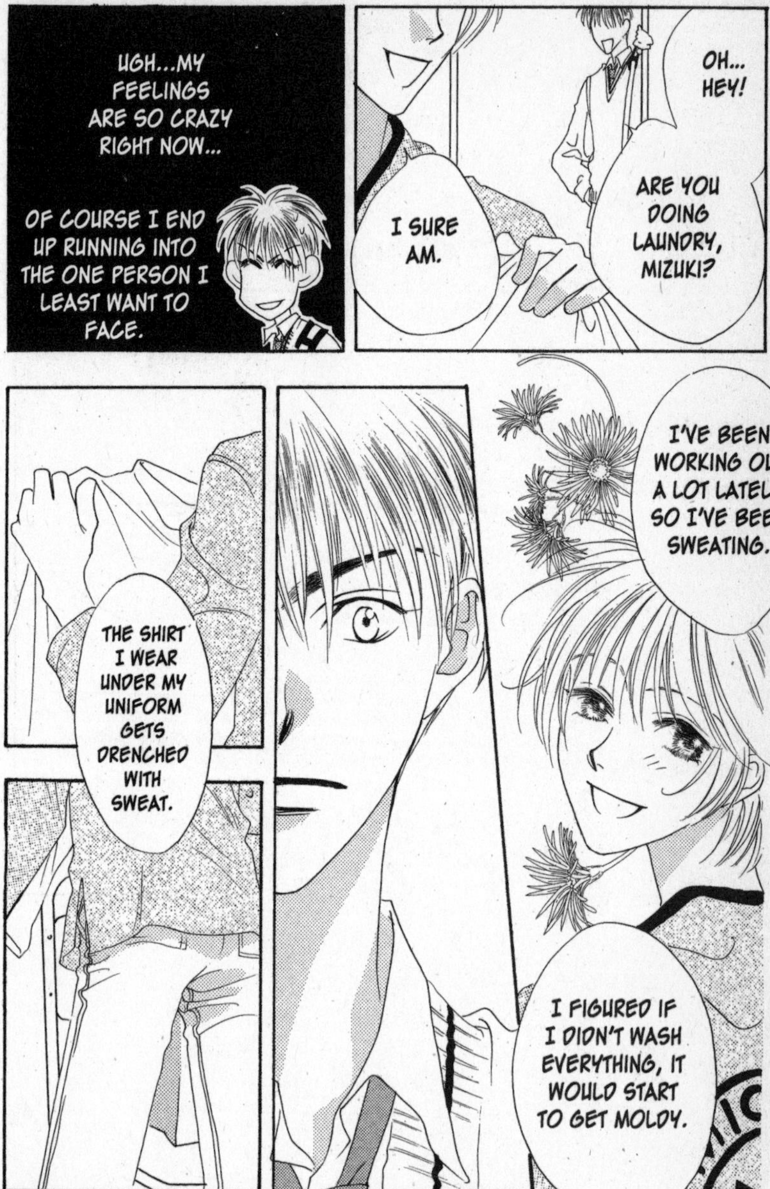
OH... HEY!
ARE YOU DOING LAUNDRY, MIZUKI?
I SURE AM.
UGH...MY FEELINGS ARE SO CRAZY RIGHT NOW...
OF COURSE I END UP RUNNING INTO THE ONE PERSON I LEAST WANT TO FACE.
I'VE BEEN WORKING OUT A LOT LATELY, SO I'VE BEEN SWEATING.
I FIGURED IF I DIDN'T WASH EVERYTHING, IT WOULD START TO GET MOLDY.
THE SHIRT I WEAR UNDER MY UNIFORM GETS DRENCHED WITH SWEAT.

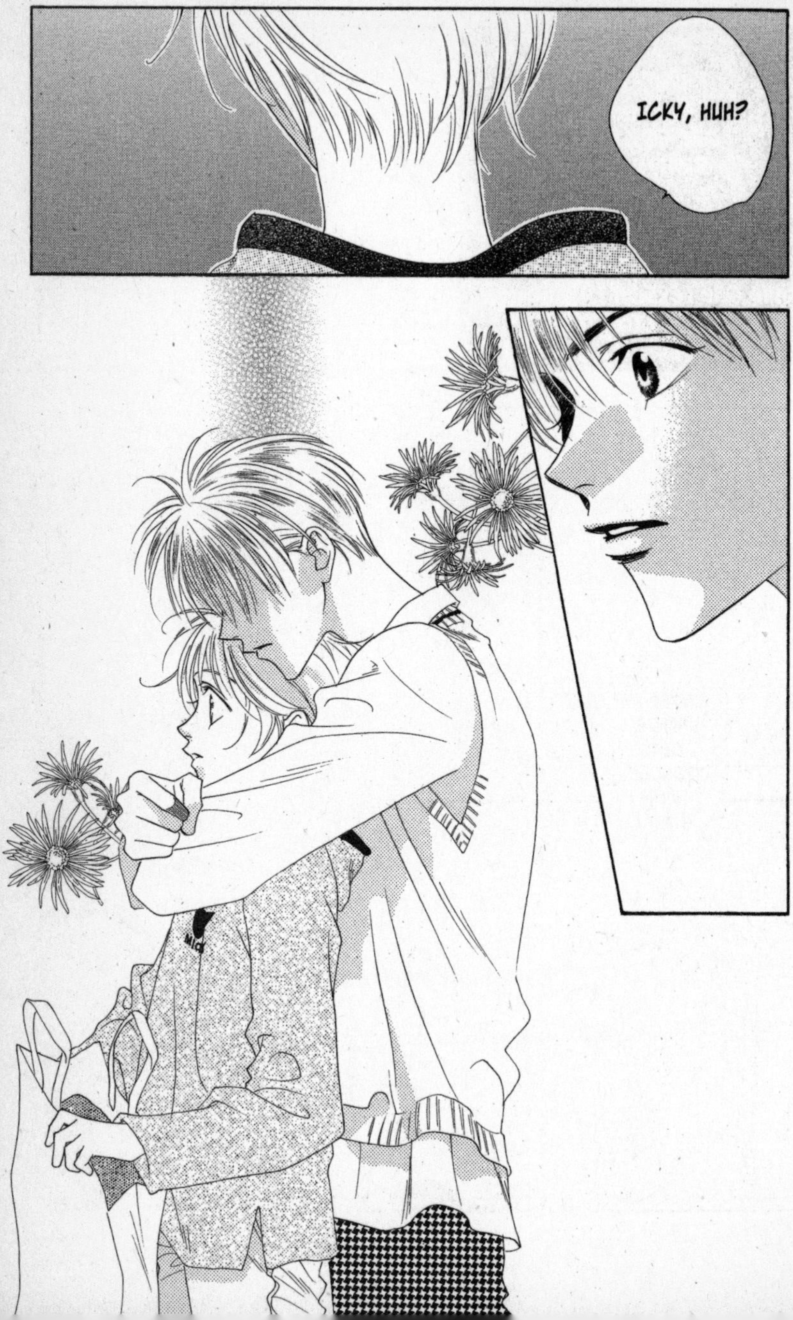
ICKY, HUH?

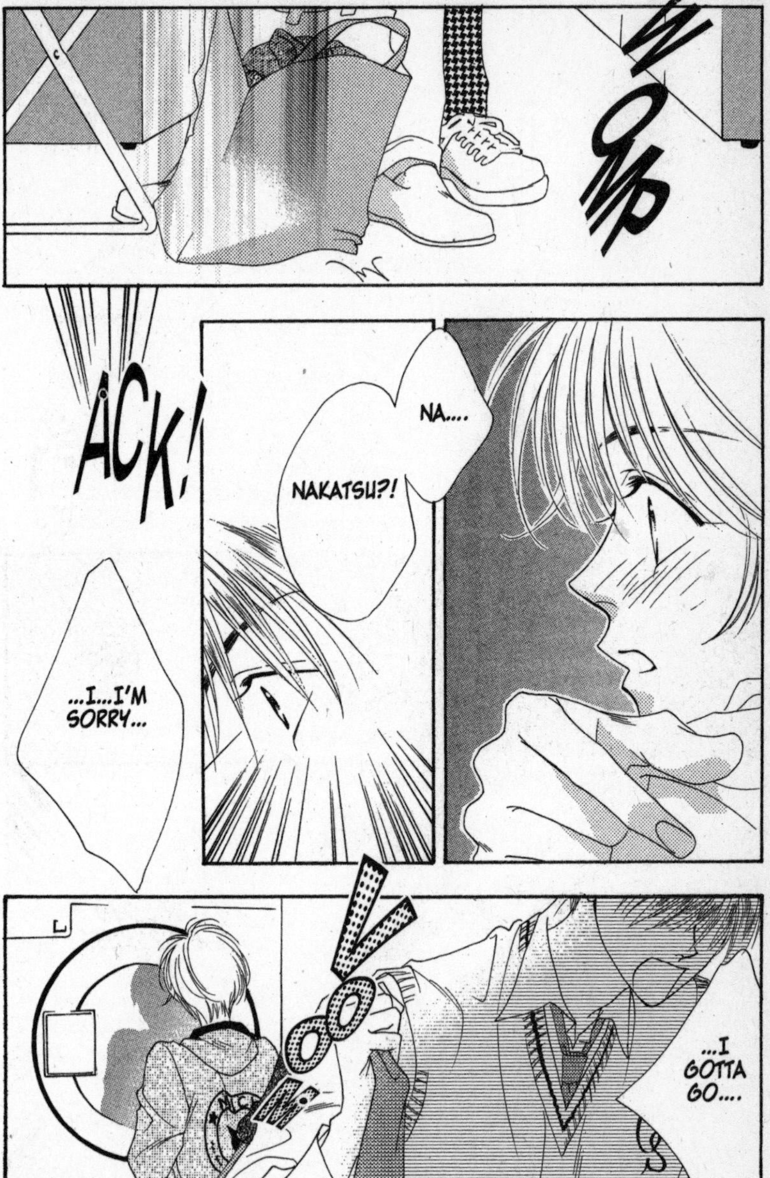
WOMP
NA....
NAKATSU?!
ACK!
...I...I'M SORRY...
...I GOTTA GO....
VOOM!

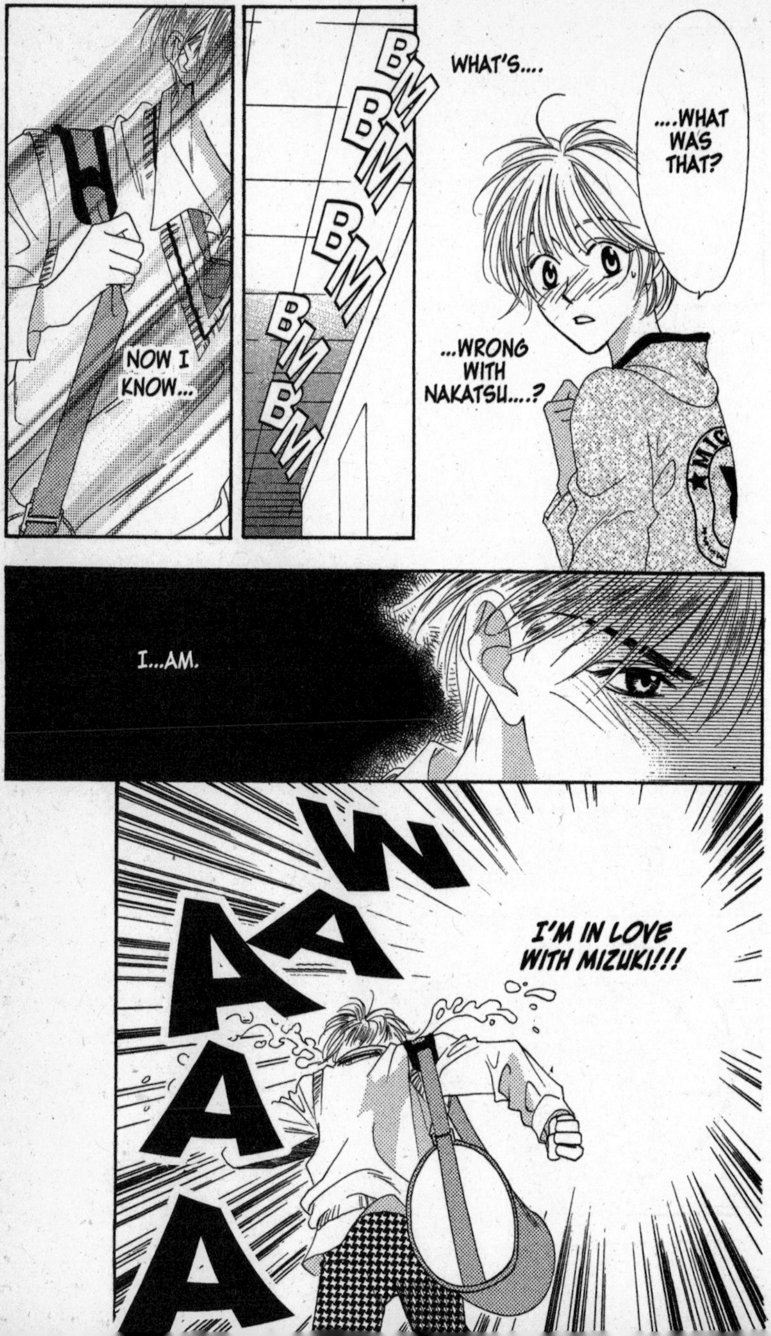
....WHAT WAS THAT?
WHAT'S....
...WRONG WITH NAKATSU....?
BMBMBMBMBM
NOW I KNOW...
I...AM.
WAAAA
I'M IN LOVE WITH MIZUKI!!!

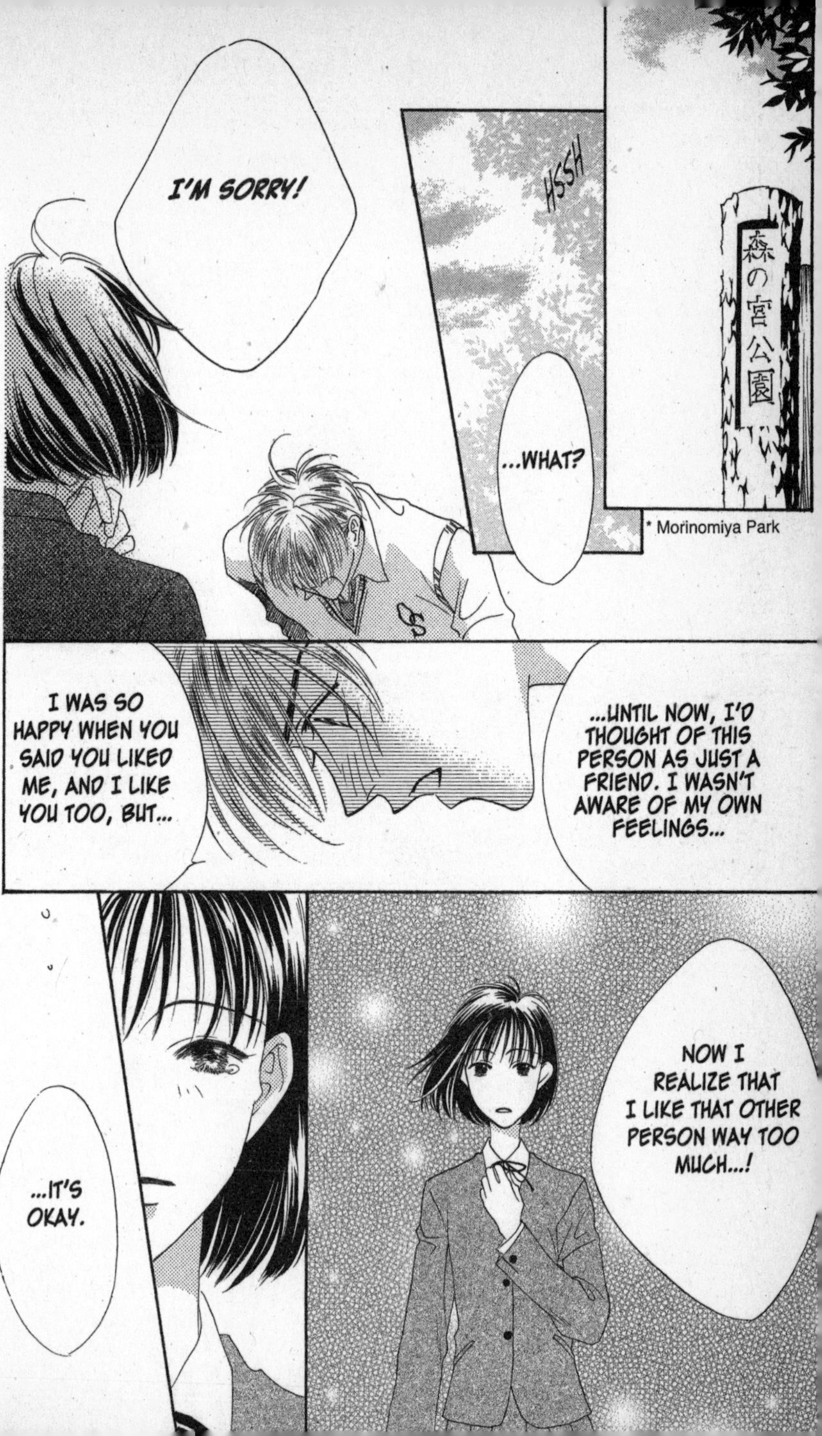
森の宮公園
* Morinomiya Park
HSSH
I'M SORRY!
...WHAT?
...UNTIL NOW, I'D THOUGHT OF THIS PERSON AS JUST A FRIEND. I WASN'T AWARE OF MY OWN FEELINGS...
I WAS SO HAPPY WHEN YOU SAID YOU LIKED ME, AND I LIKE YOU TOO, BUT...
NOW I REALIZE THAT I LIKE THAT OTHER PERSON WAY TOO MUCH...!
...IT'S OKAY.

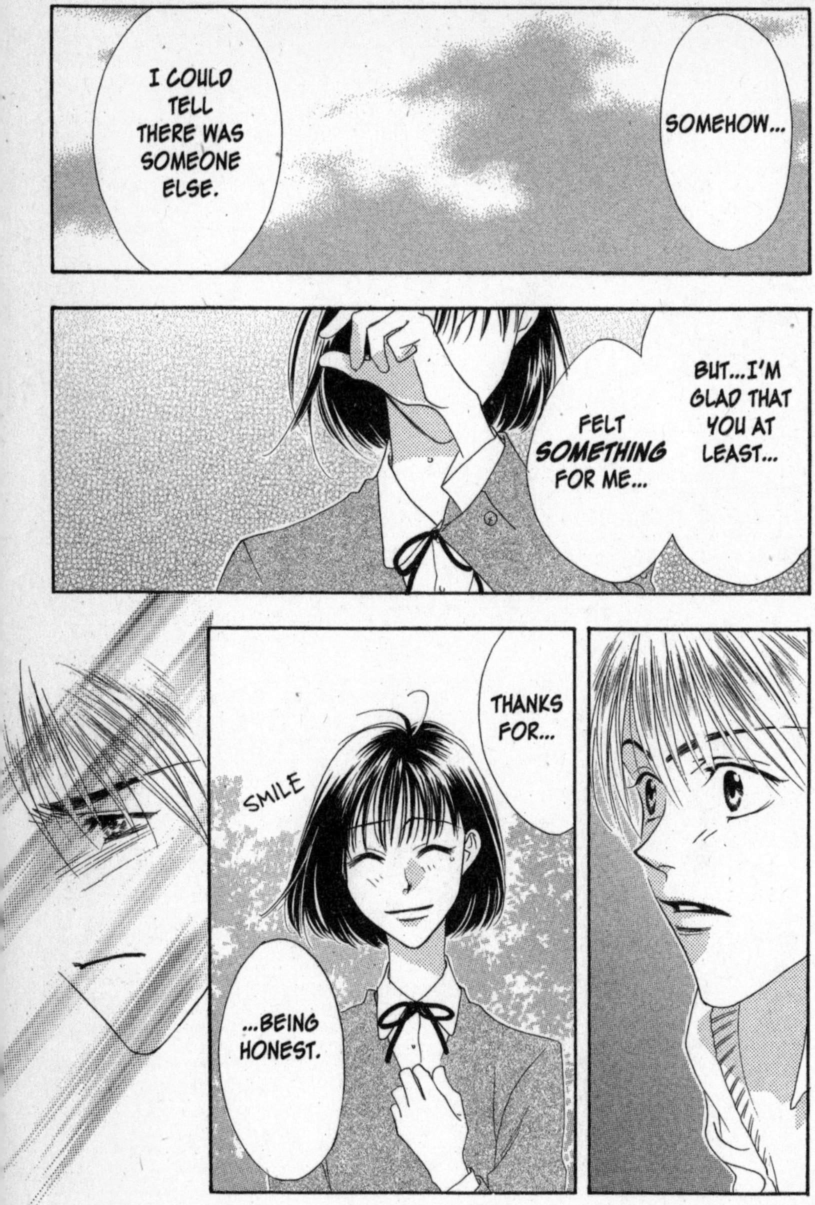
SOMEHOW...
I COULD TELL THERE WAS SOMEONE ELSE.
BUT...I'M GLAD THAT YOU AT LEAST...
FELT **SOMETHING** FOR ME...
THANKS FOR...
SMILE
...BEING HONEST.

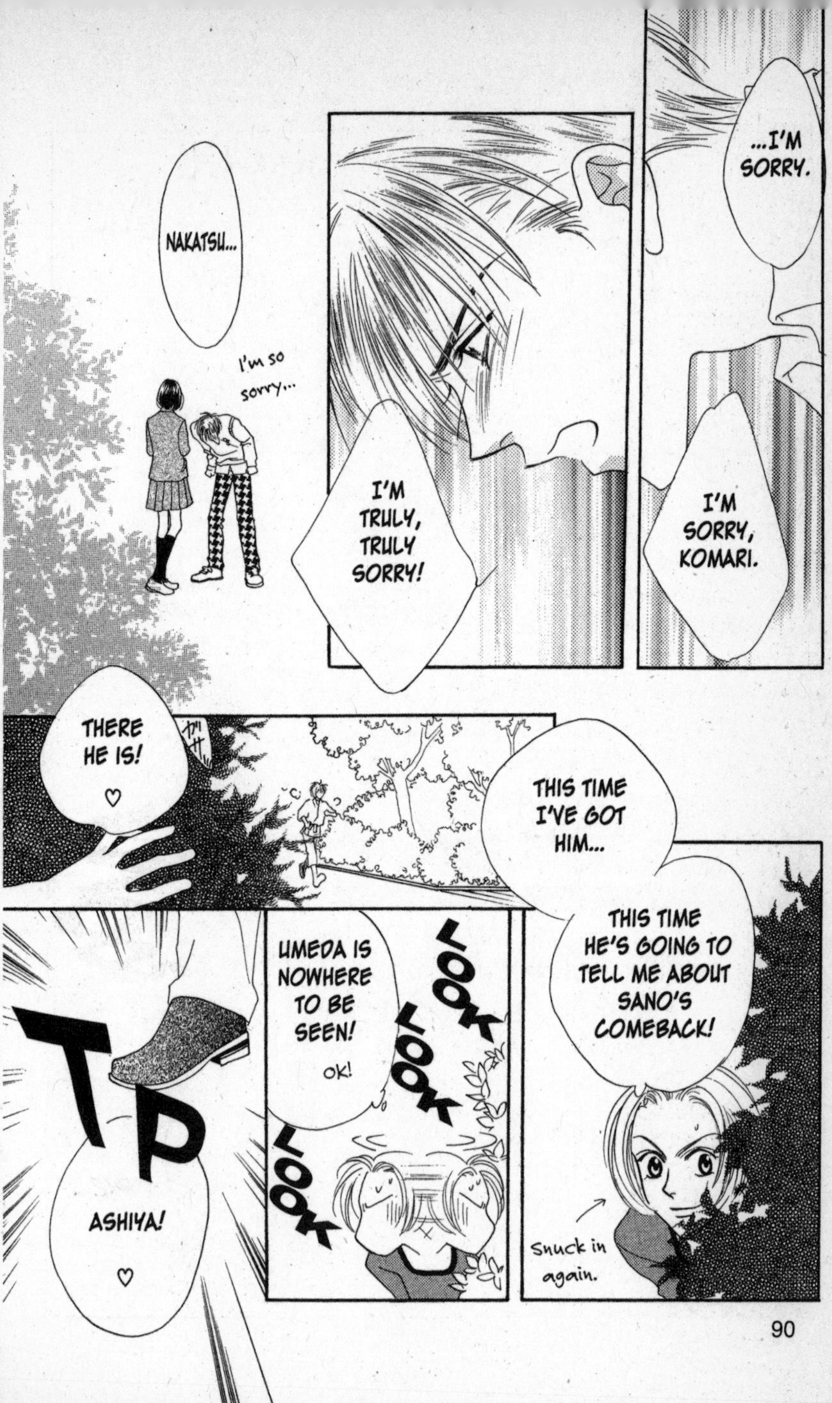
...I'M SORRY.
I'M SORRY, KOMARI.
I'M TRULY, TRULY SORRY!
NAKATSU...
I'm so sorry...
THERE HE IS! ♡
THIS TIME I'VE GOT HIM...
THIS TIME HE'S GOING TO TELL ME ABOUT SANO'S COMEBACK!
Snuck in again.
UMEDA IS NOWHERE TO BE SEEN!
OK!
LOOK
LOOK
LOOK
LOOK
TP
ASHIYA! ♡

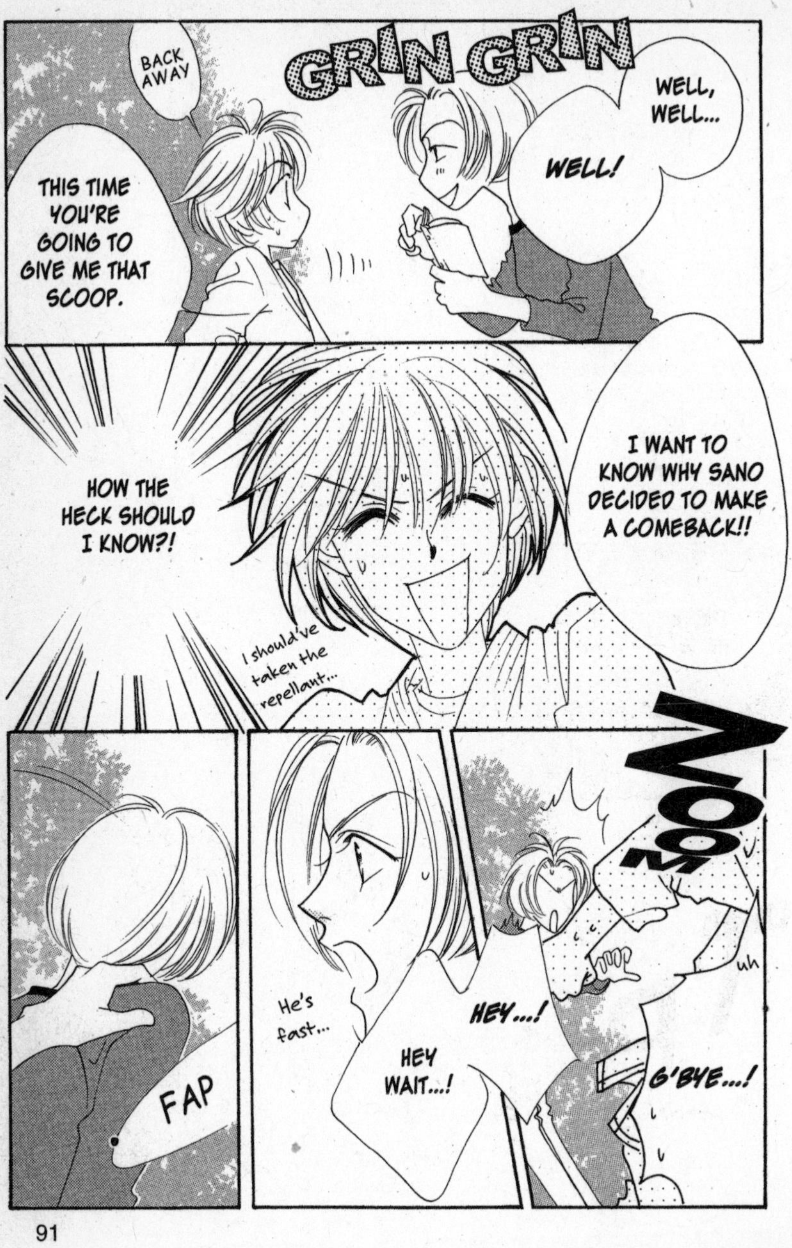
GRIN GRIN
WELL, WELL...
WELL!
BACK AWAY
THIS TIME YOU'RE GOING TO GIVE ME THAT SCOOP.
I WANT TO KNOW WHY SANO DECIDED TO MAKE A COMEBACK!!
HOW THE HECK SHOULD I KNOW?!
I should've taken the repellant...
VOOM
uh
HEY...!
G'BYE...!
He's fast...
HEY WAIT...!
FAP

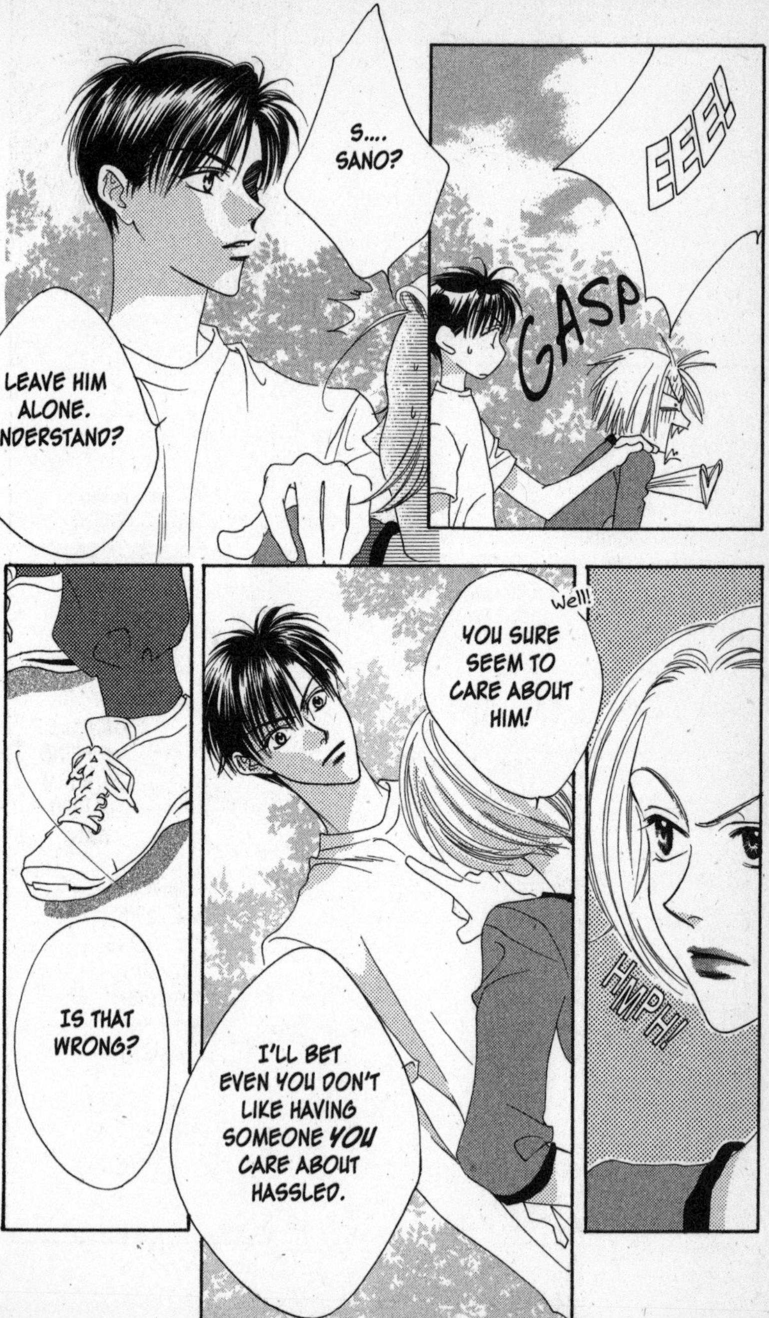
EEE!
GASP
S.... SANO?
LEAVE HIM ALONE. UNDERSTAND?
HMPH!
Well!
YOU SURE SEEM TO CARE ABOUT HIM!
I'LL BET EVEN YOU DON'T LIKE HAVING SOMEONE *YOU* CARE ABOUT HASSLED.
IS THAT WRONG?

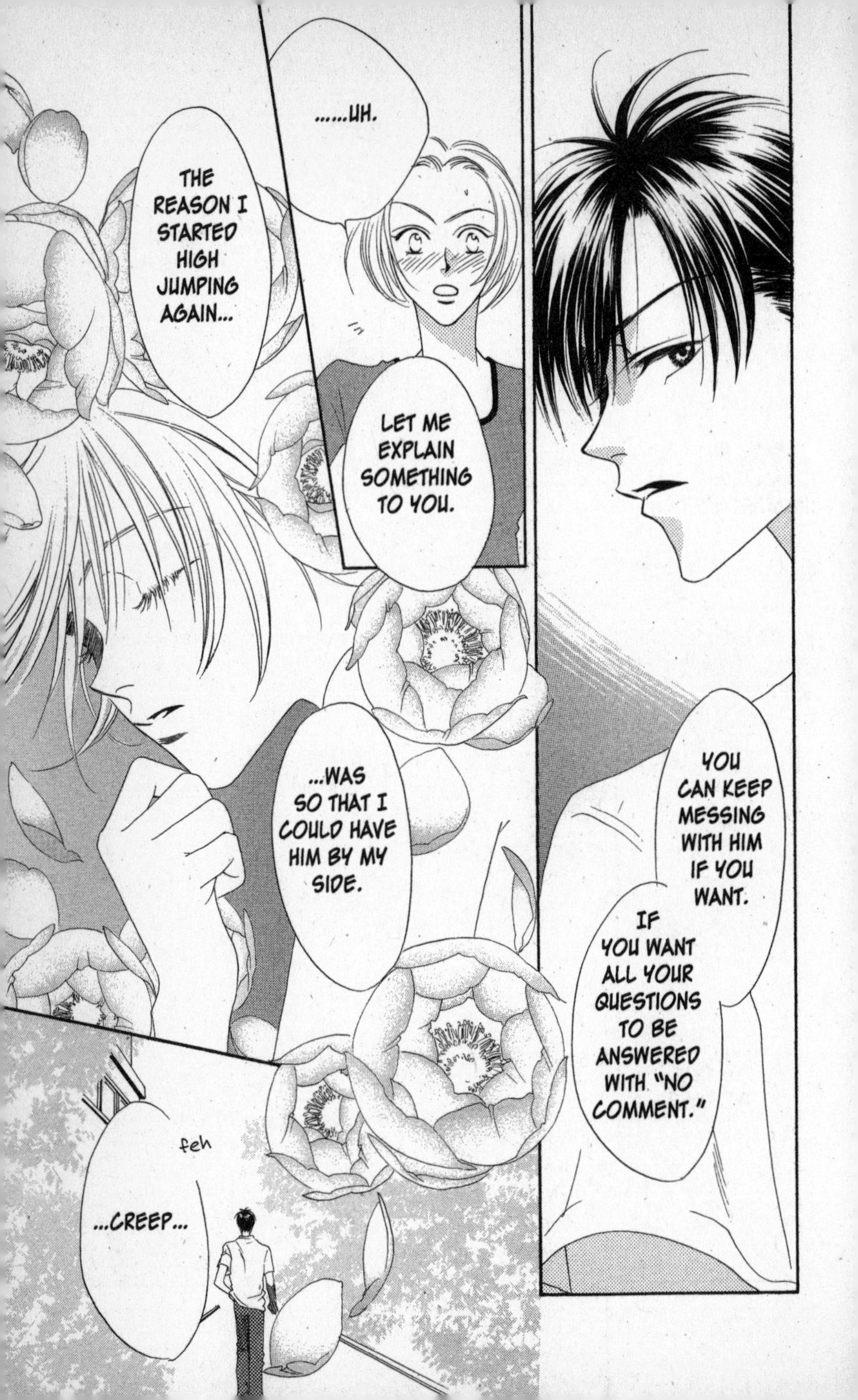
YOU CAN KEEP MESSING WITH HIM IF YOU WANT.
IF YOU WANT ALL YOUR QUESTIONS TO BE ANSWERED WITH "NO COMMENT."
......UH.
LET ME EXPLAIN SOMETHING TO YOU.
THE REASON I STARTED HIGH JUMPING AGAIN...
...WAS SO THAT I COULD HAVE HIM BY MY SIDE.
feh
...CREEP...

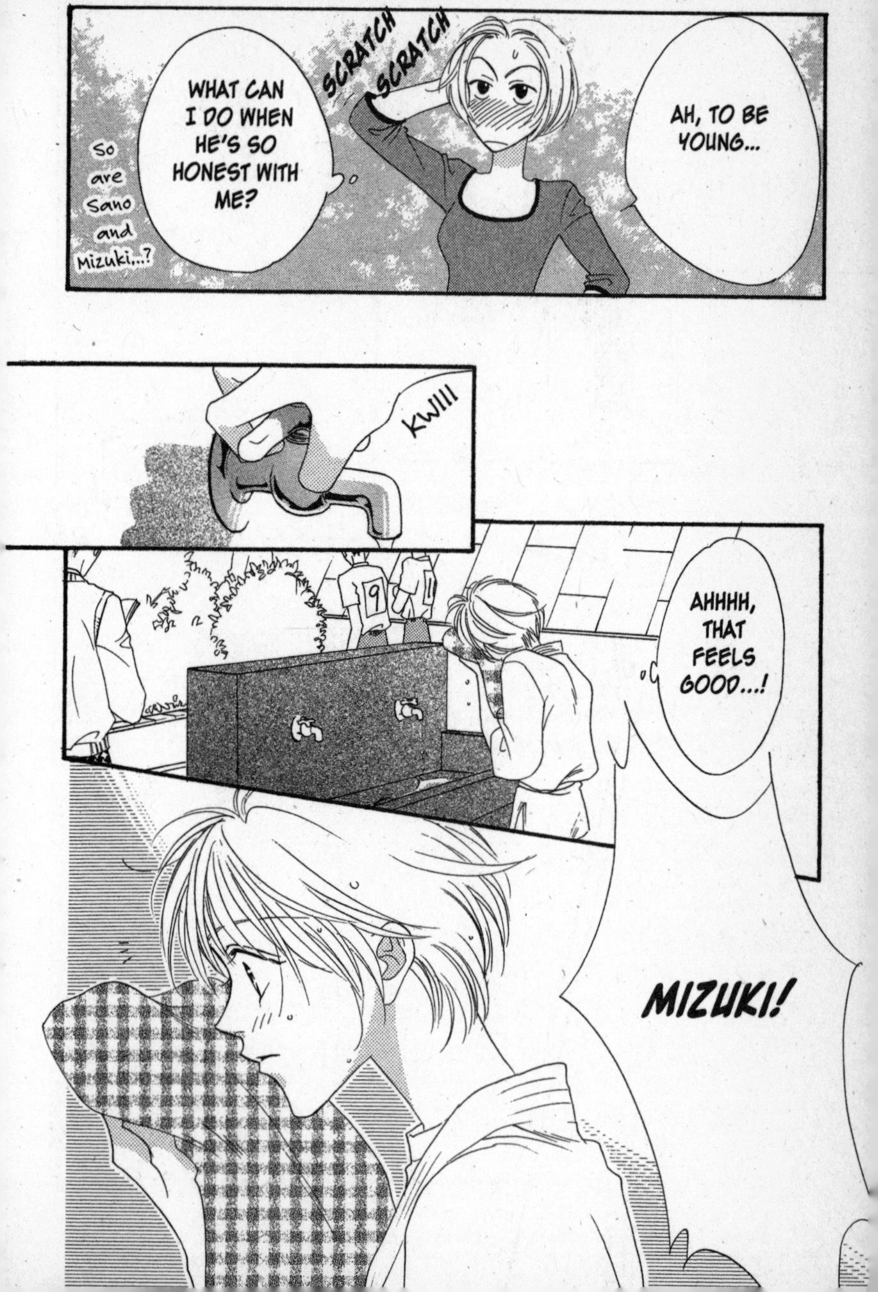
AH, TO BE YOUNG...
SCRATCH SCRATCH
WHAT CAN I DO WHEN HE'S SO HONEST WITH ME?
So are Sano and Mizuki...?
KWIII
AHHHH, THAT FEELS GOOD...!
MIZUKI!

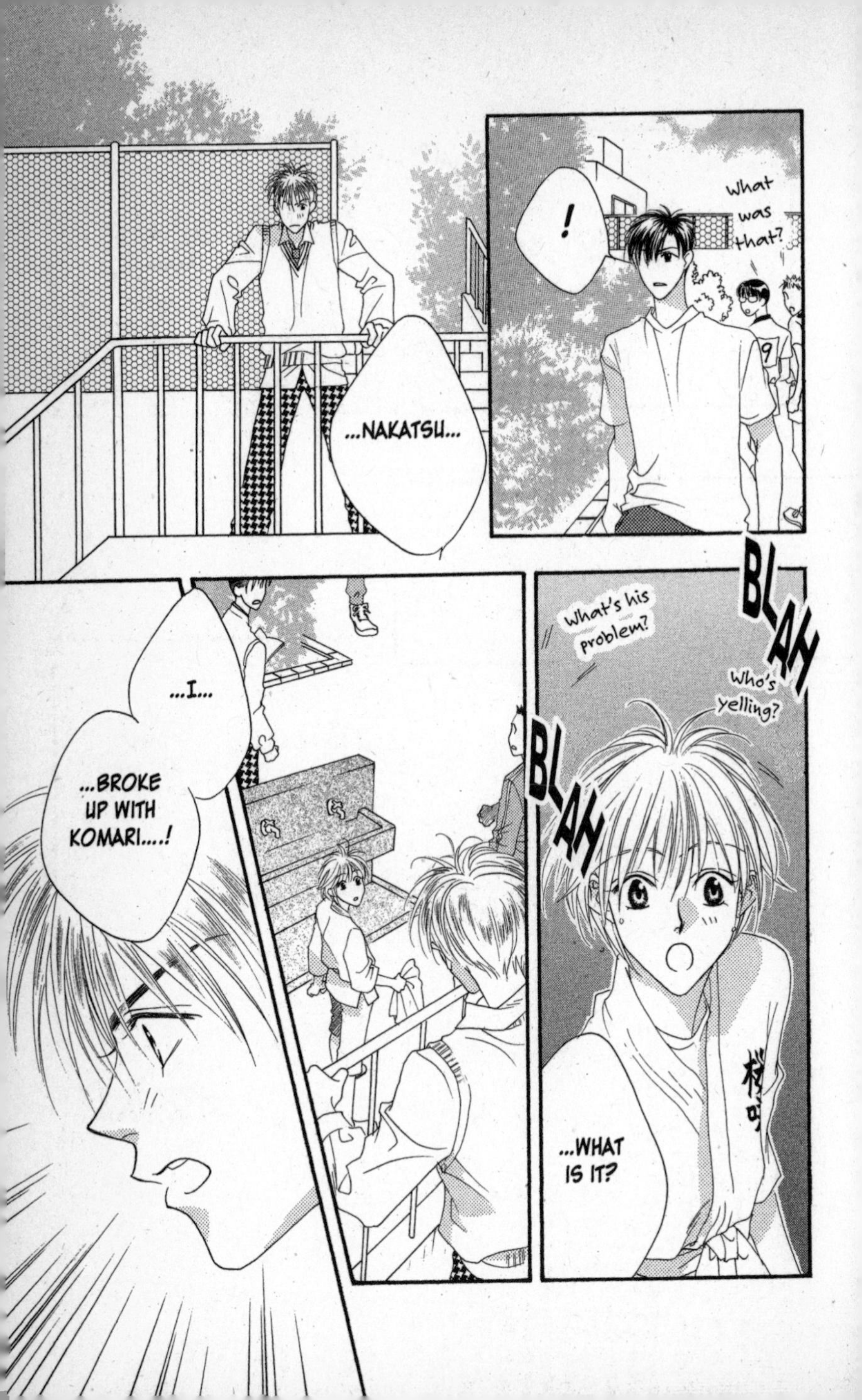
!
What was that?
...NAKATSU...
BLAH
What's his problem?
Who's yelling?
BLAH
...WHAT IS IT?
...I...
...BROKE UP WITH KOMARI....!

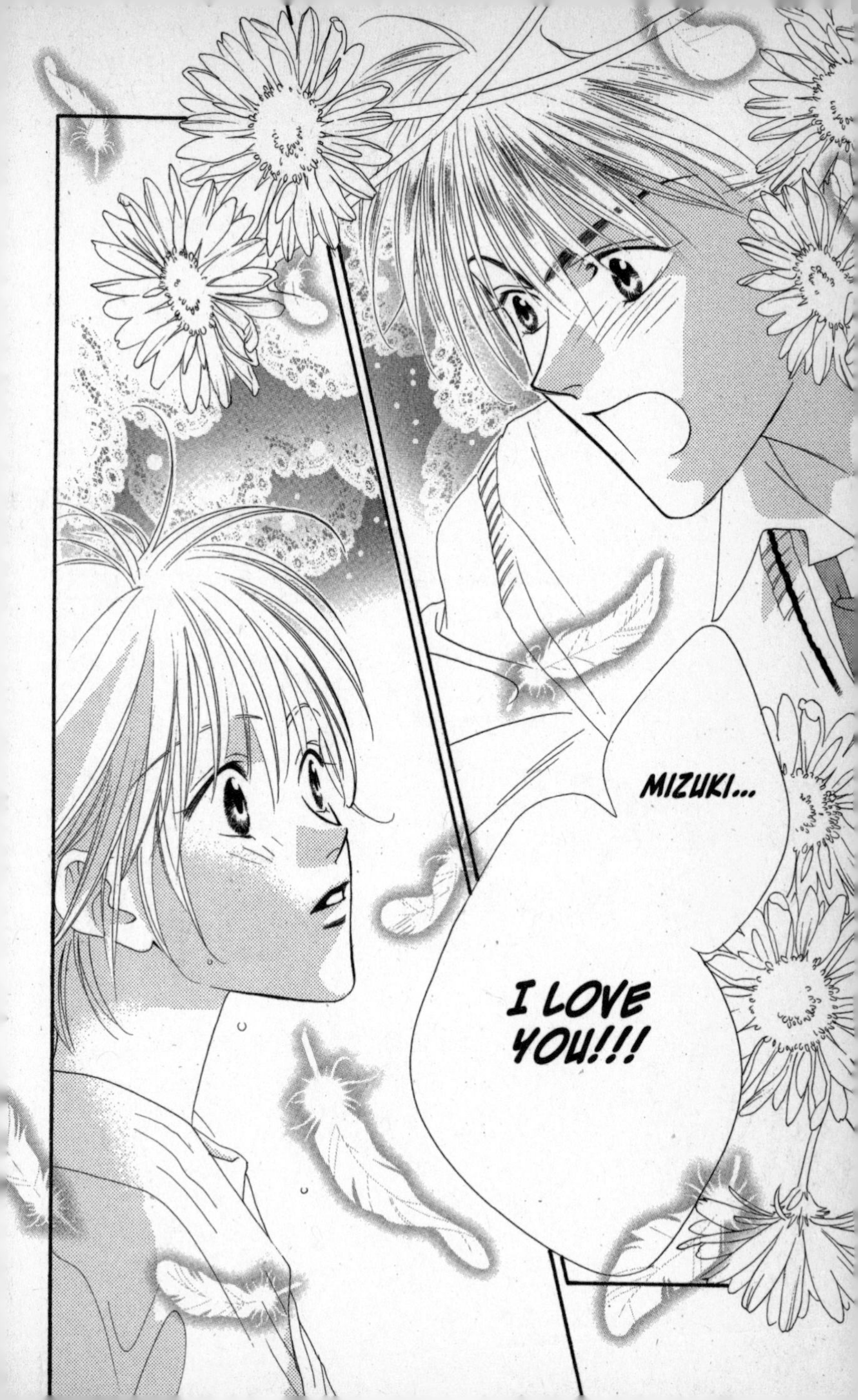
MIZUKI...
I LOVE YOU!!!

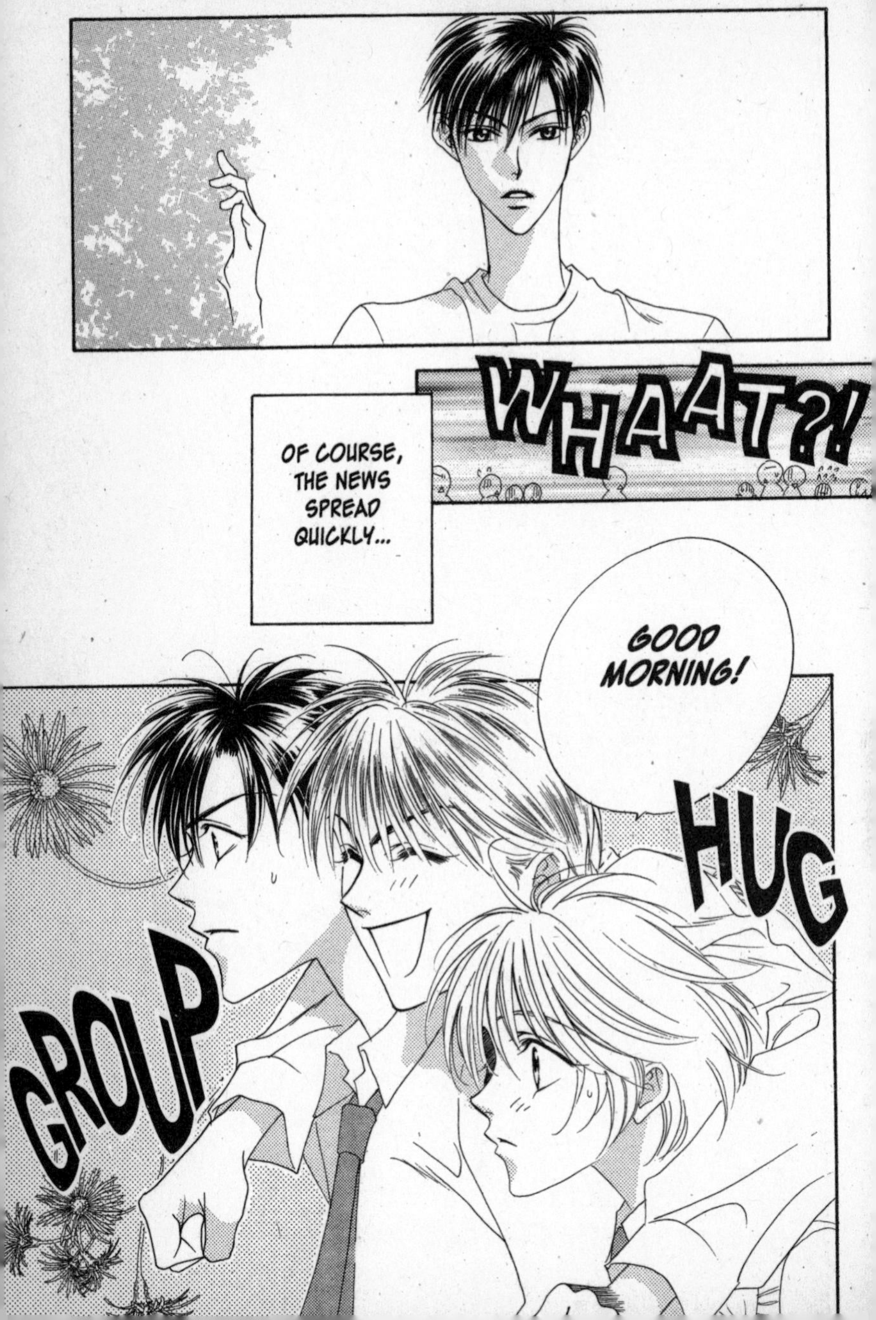
WHAAAT?!
OF COURSE, THE NEWS SPREAD QUICKLY...
GOOD MORNING!
HUG
GROUP

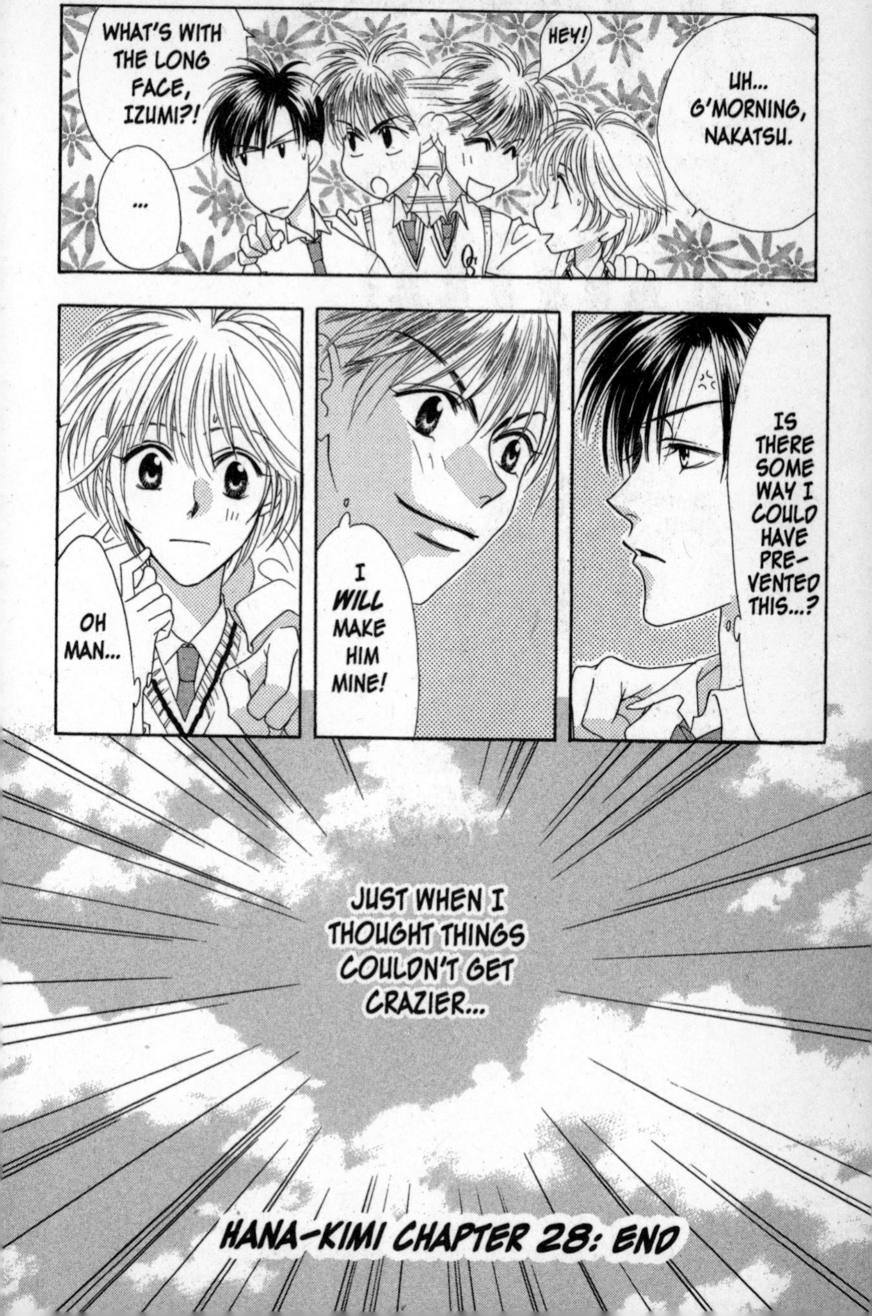
HEY!
UH... G'MORNING, NAKATSU.
WHAT'S WITH THE LONG FACE, IZUMI?!
...
IS THERE SOME WAY I COULD HAVE PRE-VENTED THIS...?
I *WILL* MAKE HIM MINE!
OH MAN...
JUST WHEN I THOUGHT THINGS COULDN'T GET CRAZIER...
HANA-KIMI CHAPTER 28: END

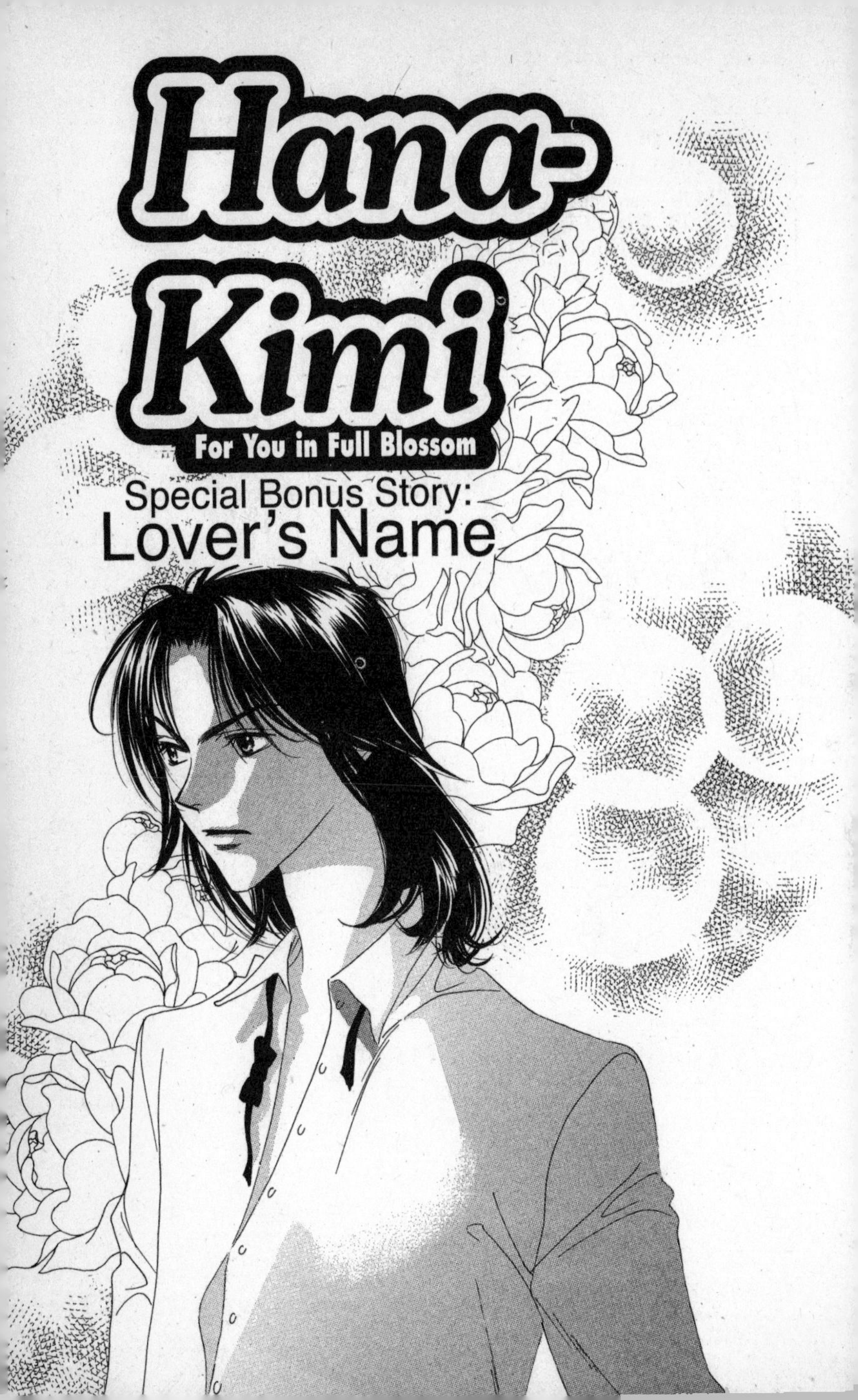
Hana-Kimi
For You in Full Blossom
Special Bonus Story:
Lover's Name

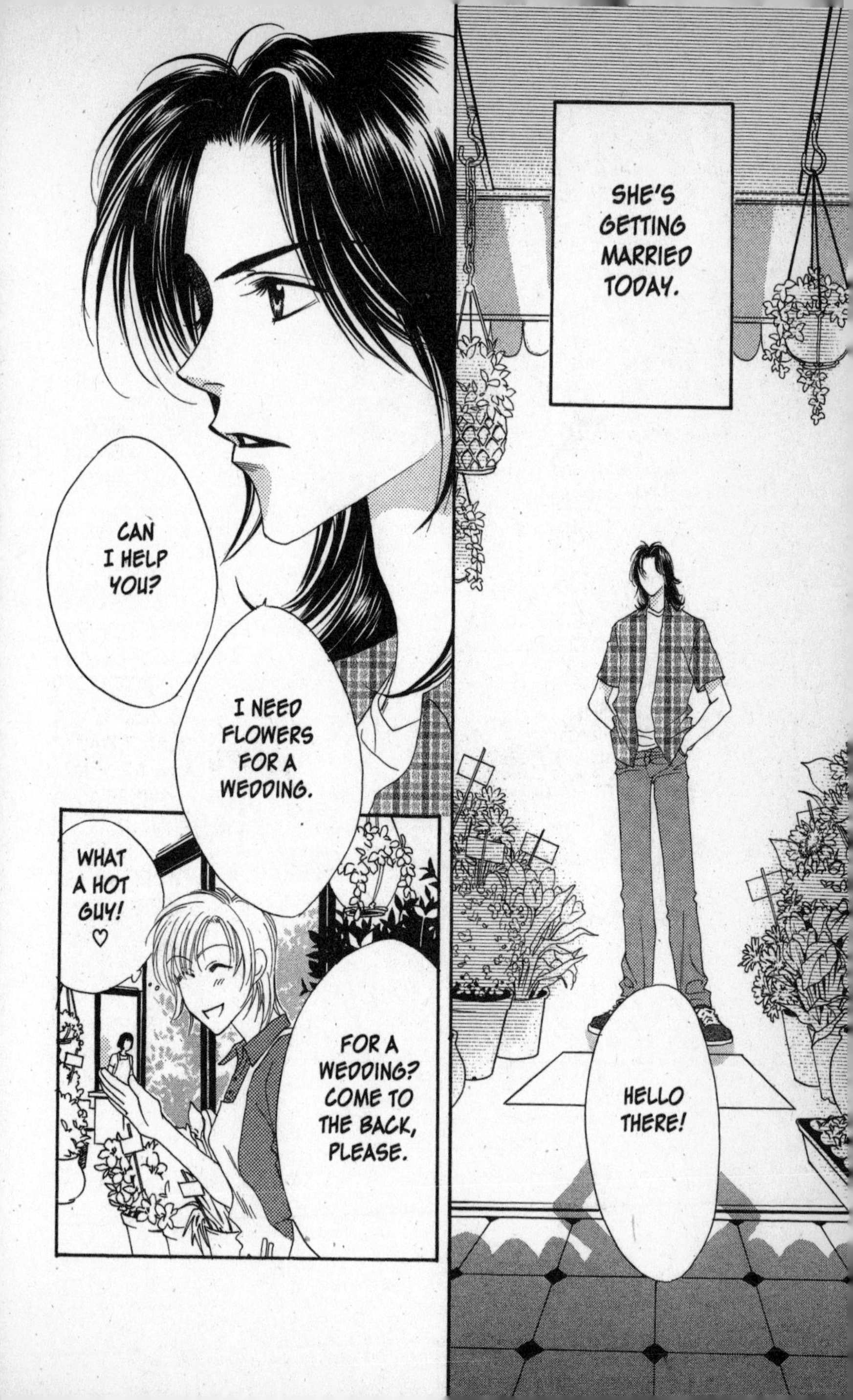
SHE'S GETTING MARRIED TODAY.
HELLO THERE!
CAN I HELP YOU?
I NEED FLOWERS FOR A WEDDING.
WHAT A HOT GUY! ♡
FOR A WEDDING? COME TO THE BACK, PLEASE.

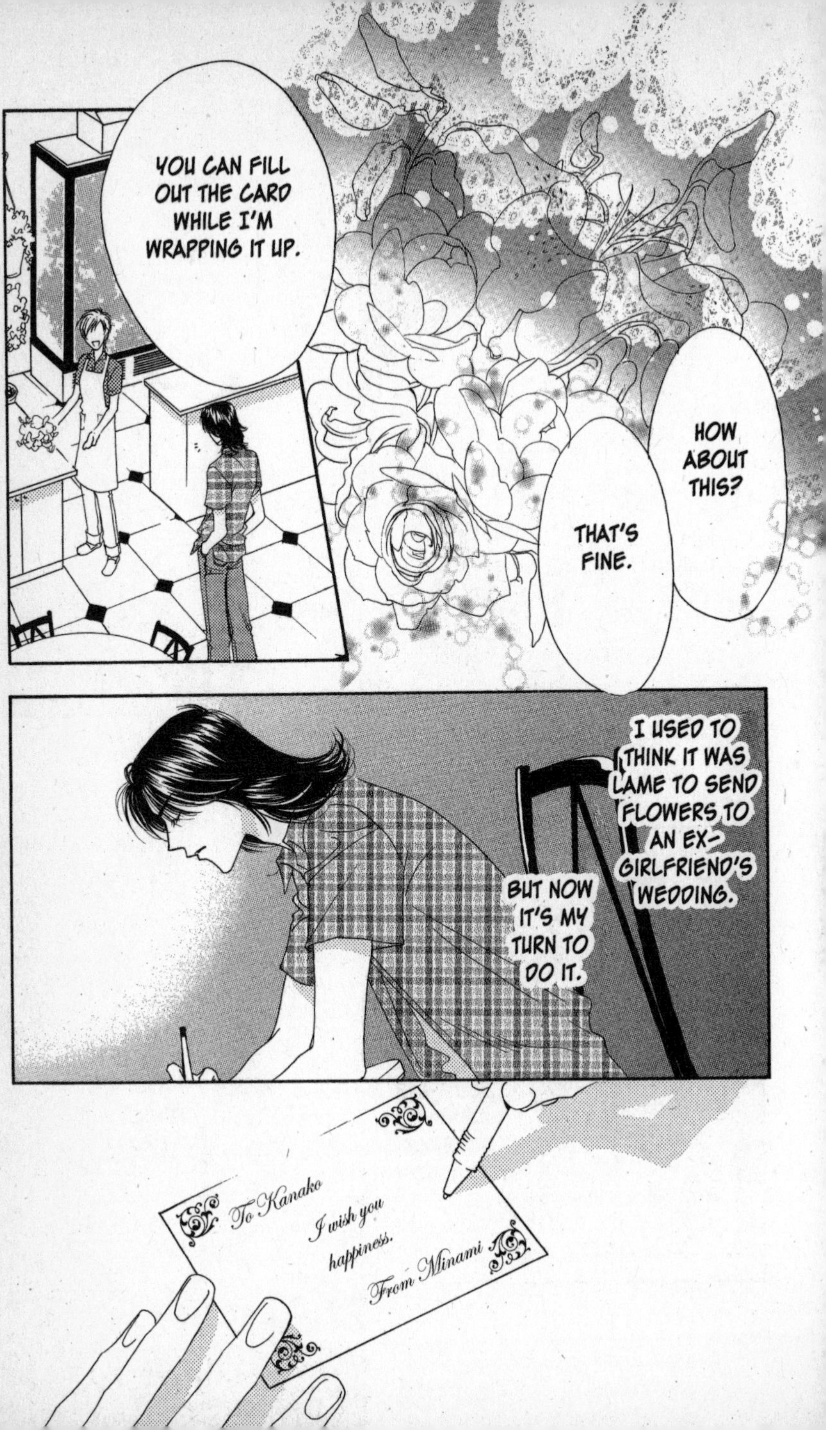
HOW ABOUT THIS?
THAT'S FINE.
YOU CAN FILL OUT THE CARD WHILE I'M WRAPPING IT UP.
I USED TO THINK IT WAS LAME TO SEND FLOWERS TO AN EX-GIRLFRIEND'S WEDDING.
BUT NOW IT'S MY TURN TO DO IT.
To Kanako
I wish you happiness.
From Minami

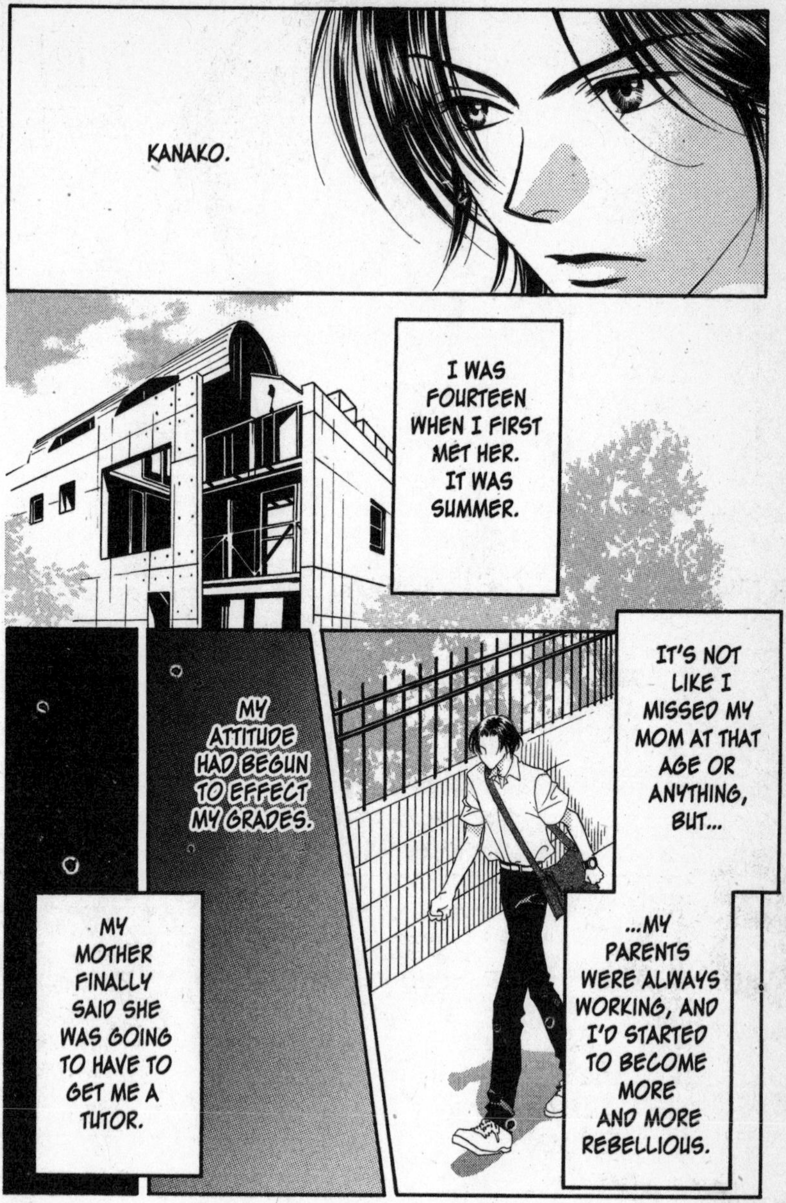
KANAKO.
I WAS FOURTEEN WHEN I FIRST MET HER. IT WAS SUMMER.
IT'S NOT LIKE I MISSED MY MOM AT THAT AGE OR ANYTHING, BUT...
...MY PARENTS WERE ALWAYS WORKING, AND I'D STARTED TO BECOME MORE AND MORE REBELLIOUS.
MY ATTITUDE HAD BEGUN TO EFFECT MY GRADES.
MY MOTHER FINALLY SAID SHE WAS GOING TO HAVE TO GET ME A TUTOR.

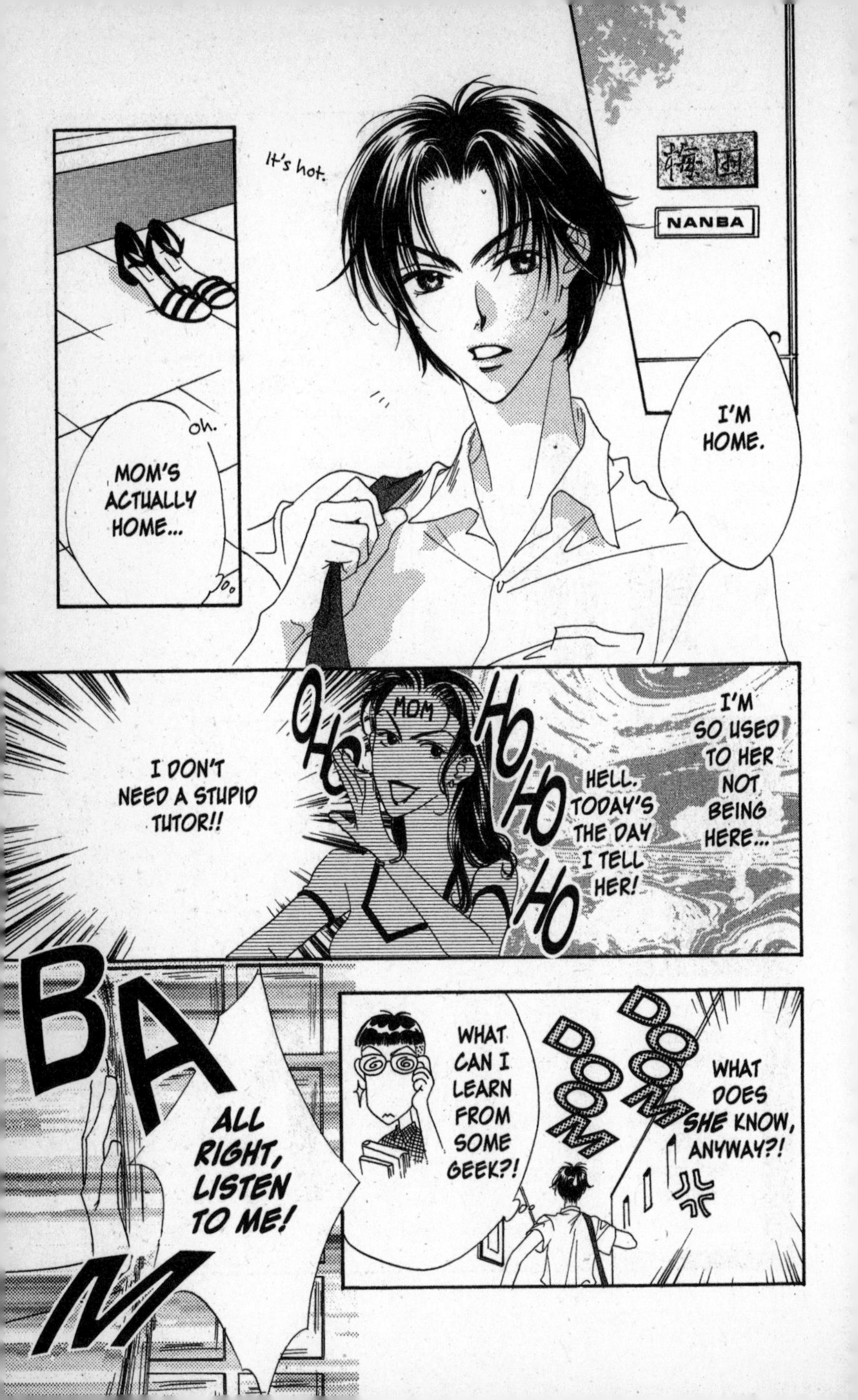
NANBA
It's hot.
I'M HOME.
oh.
MOM'S ACTUALLY HOME...
I'M SO USED TO HER NOT BEING HERE...
HELL. TODAY'S THE DAY I TELL HER!
OHO HO HO HO HO
MOM
I DON'T NEED A STUPID TUTOR!!
WHAT DOES SHE KNOW, ANYWAY?!
DOOM DOOM
WHAT CAN I LEARN FROM SOME GEEK?!
BAM
ALL RIGHT, LISTEN TO ME!

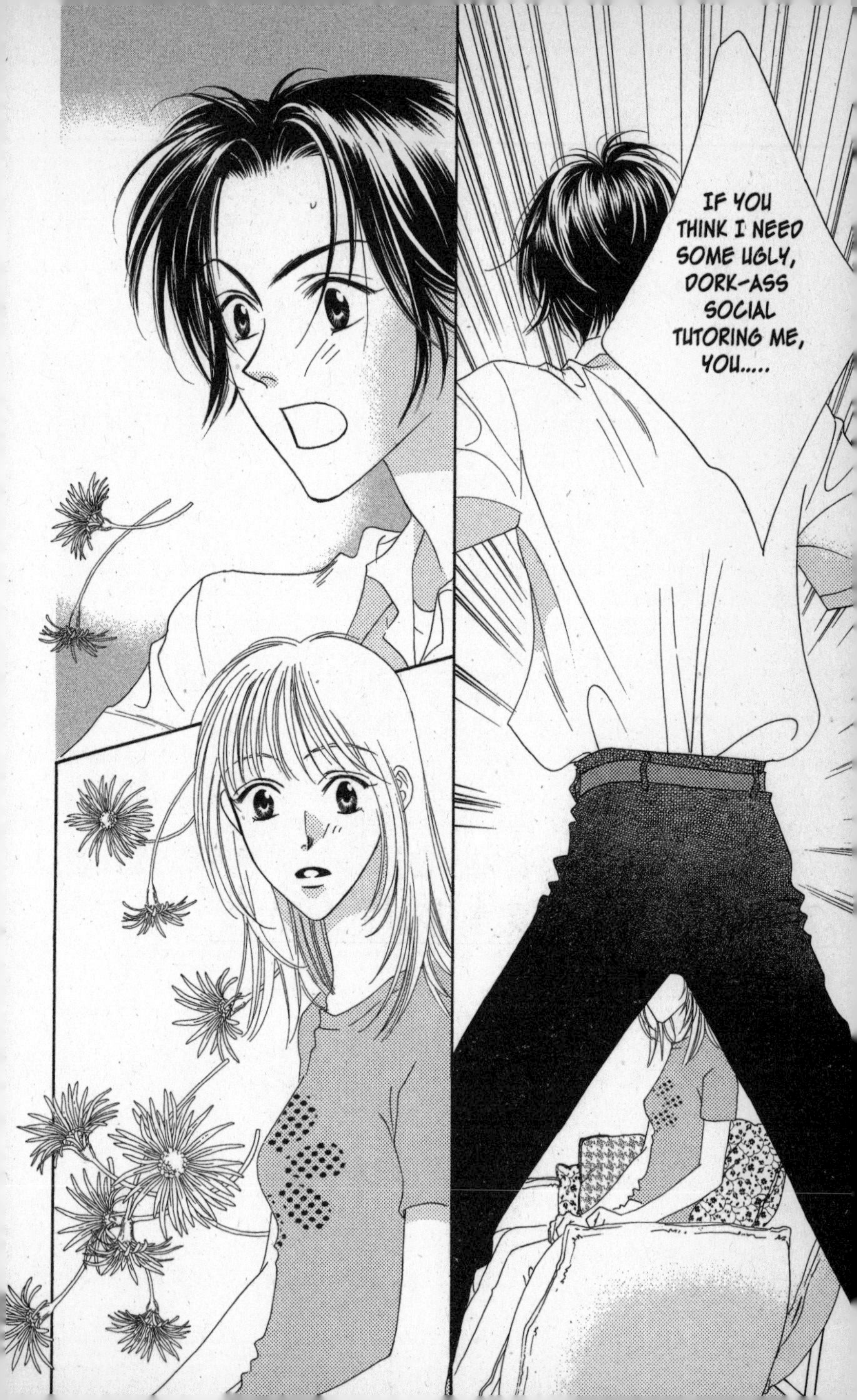
IF YOU THINK I NEED SOME UGLY, DORK-ASS SOCIAL TUTORING ME, YOU.....

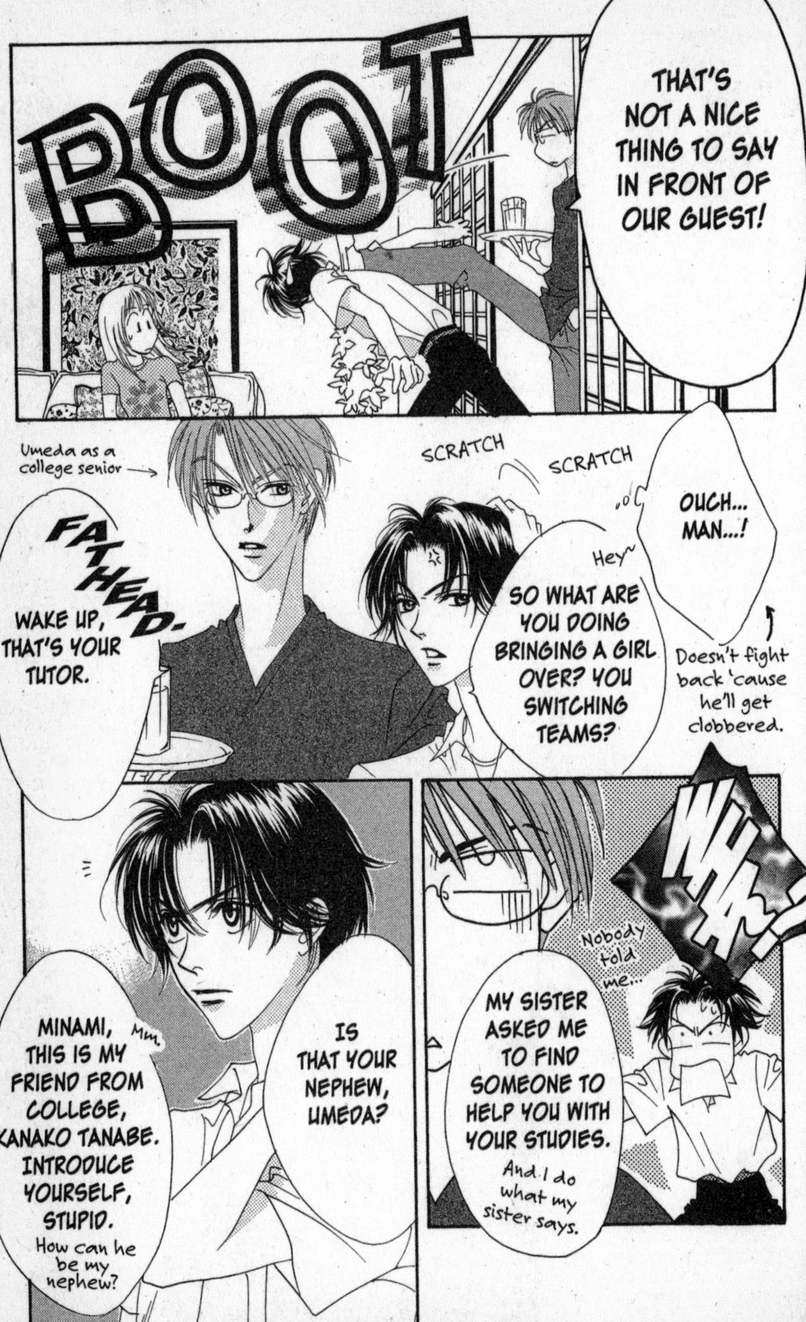
THAT'S NOT A NICE THING TO SAY IN FRONT OF OUR GUEST!
BOOT
OUCH... MAN...!
Doesn't fight back 'cause he'll get clobbered.
SCRATCH
SCRATCH
Hey~
SO WHAT ARE YOU DOING BRINGING A GIRL OVER? YOU SWITCHING TEAMS?
Umeda as a college senior
FATHEAD-
WAKE UP, THAT'S YOUR TUTOR.
Nobody told me...
MY SISTER ASKED ME TO FIND SOMEONE TO HELP YOU WITH YOUR STUDIES.
And I do what my sister says.
IS THAT YOUR NEPHEW, UMEDA?
Mm.
MINAMI, THIS IS MY FRIEND FROM COLLEGE, KANAKO TANABE. INTRODUCE YOURSELF, STUPID.
How can he be my nephew?

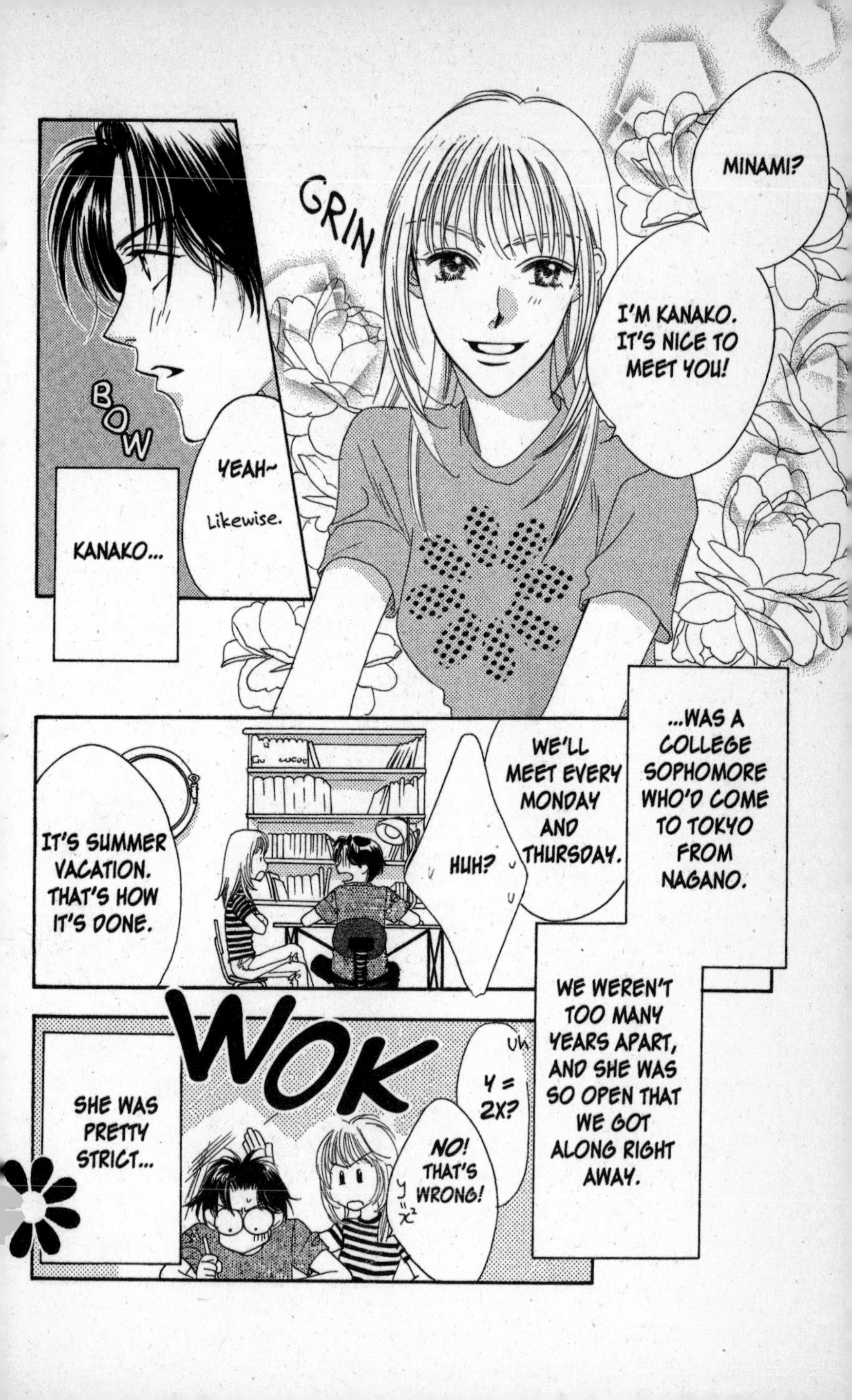
MINAMI?
I'M KANAKO. IT'S NICE TO MEET YOU!
GRIN
BOW
YEAH~
Likewise.
KANAKO...
...WAS A COLLEGE SOPHOMORE WHO'D COME TO TOKYO FROM NAGANO.
WE'LL MEET EVERY MONDAY AND THURSDAY.
HUH?
IT'S SUMMER VACATION. THAT'S HOW IT'S DONE.
WE WEREN'T TOO MANY YEARS APART, AND SHE WAS SO OPEN THAT WE GOT ALONG RIGHT AWAY.
Uh
Y = 2X?
NO! THAT'S WRONG!
$y = x^2$
WOK
SHE WAS PRETTY STRICT...

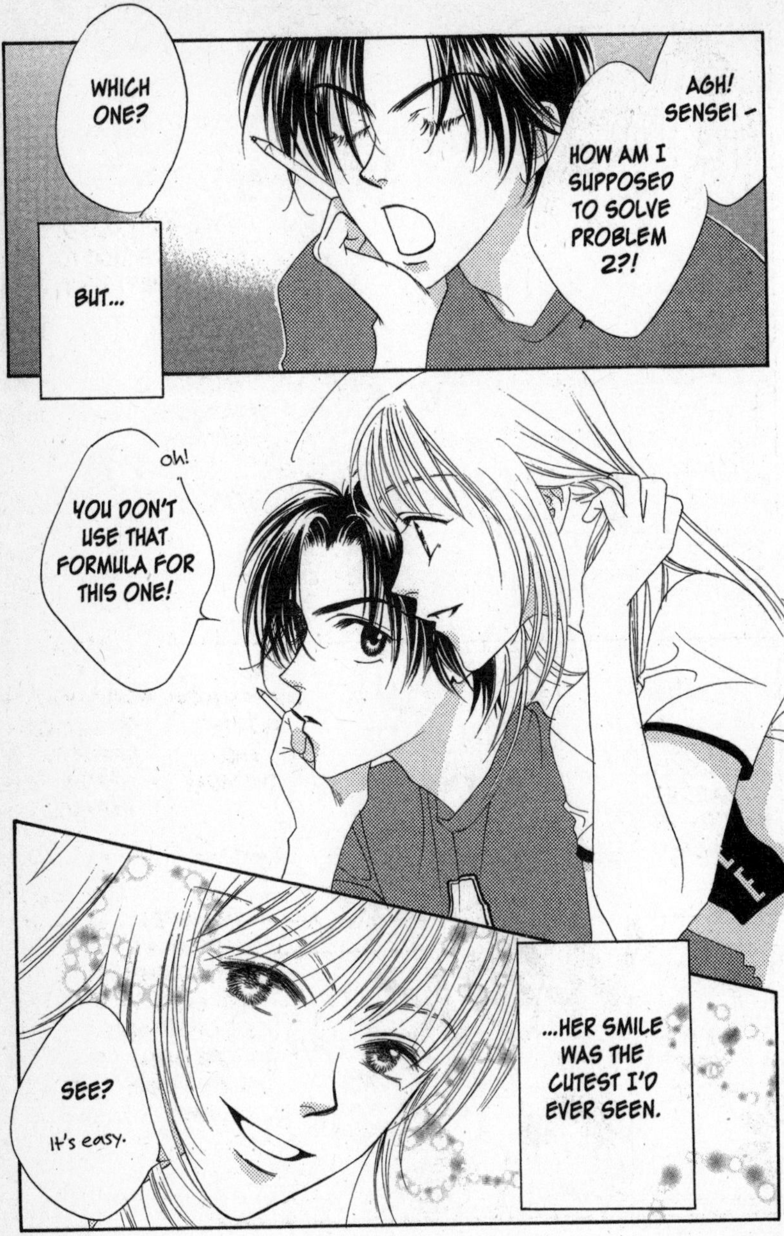
AGH! SENSEI -
HOW AM I SUPPOSED TO SOLVE PROBLEM 2?!
WHICH ONE?
BUT...
oh!
YOU DON'T USE THAT FORMULA FOR THIS ONE!
...HER SMILE WAS THE CUTEST I'D EVER SEEN.
SEE?
It's easy.

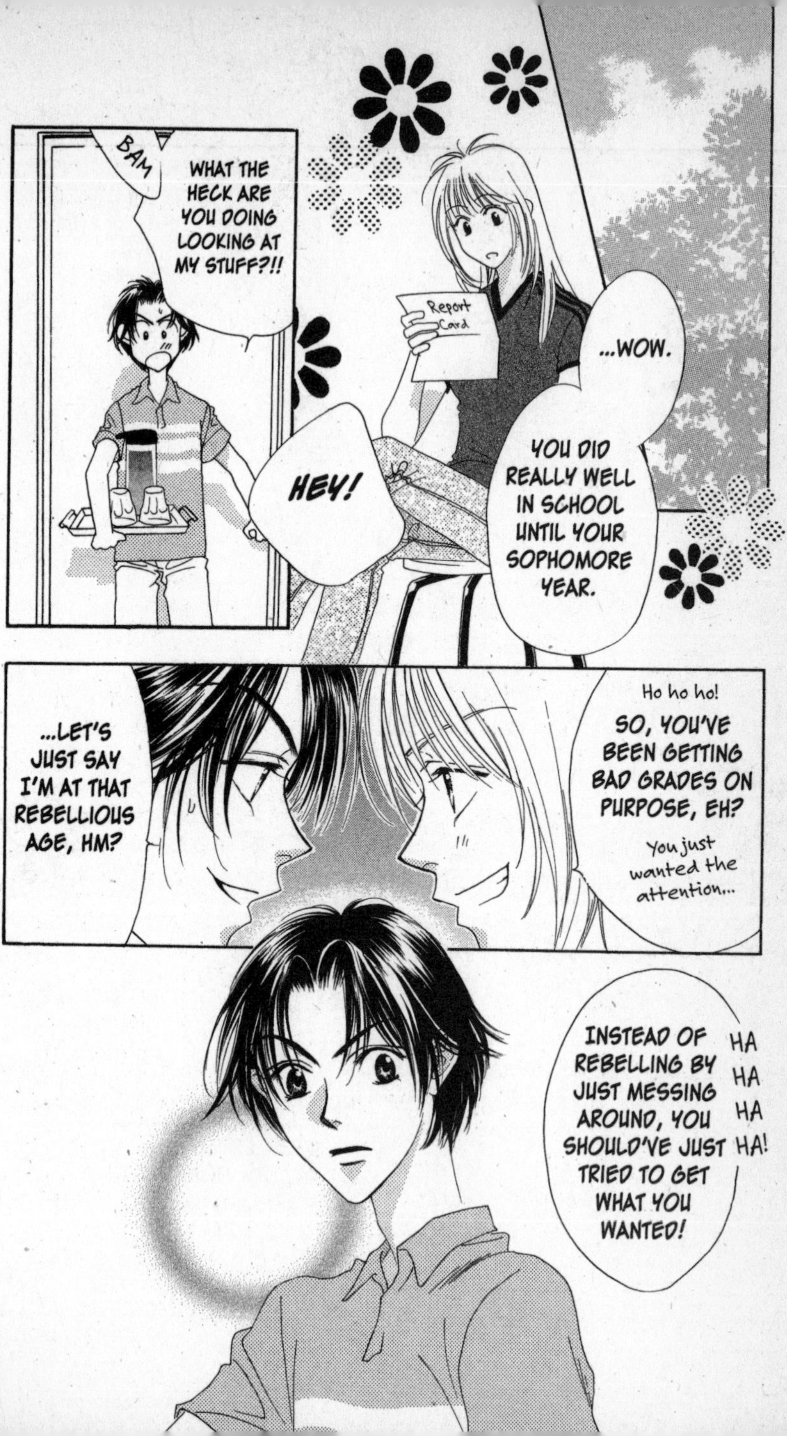
Report Card
...WOW.
YOU DID REALLY WELL IN SCHOOL UNTIL YOUR SOPHOMORE YEAR.
HEY!
BAM
WHAT THE HECK ARE YOU DOING LOOKING AT MY STUFF?!!
Ho ho ho!
SO, YOU'VE BEEN GETTING BAD GRADES ON PURPOSE, EH?
You just wanted the attention...
...LET'S JUST SAY I'M AT THAT REBELLIOUS AGE, HM?
INSTEAD OF REBELLING BY JUST MESSING AROUND, YOU SHOULD'VE JUST TRIED TO GET WHAT YOU WANTED!
HA HA HA HA!

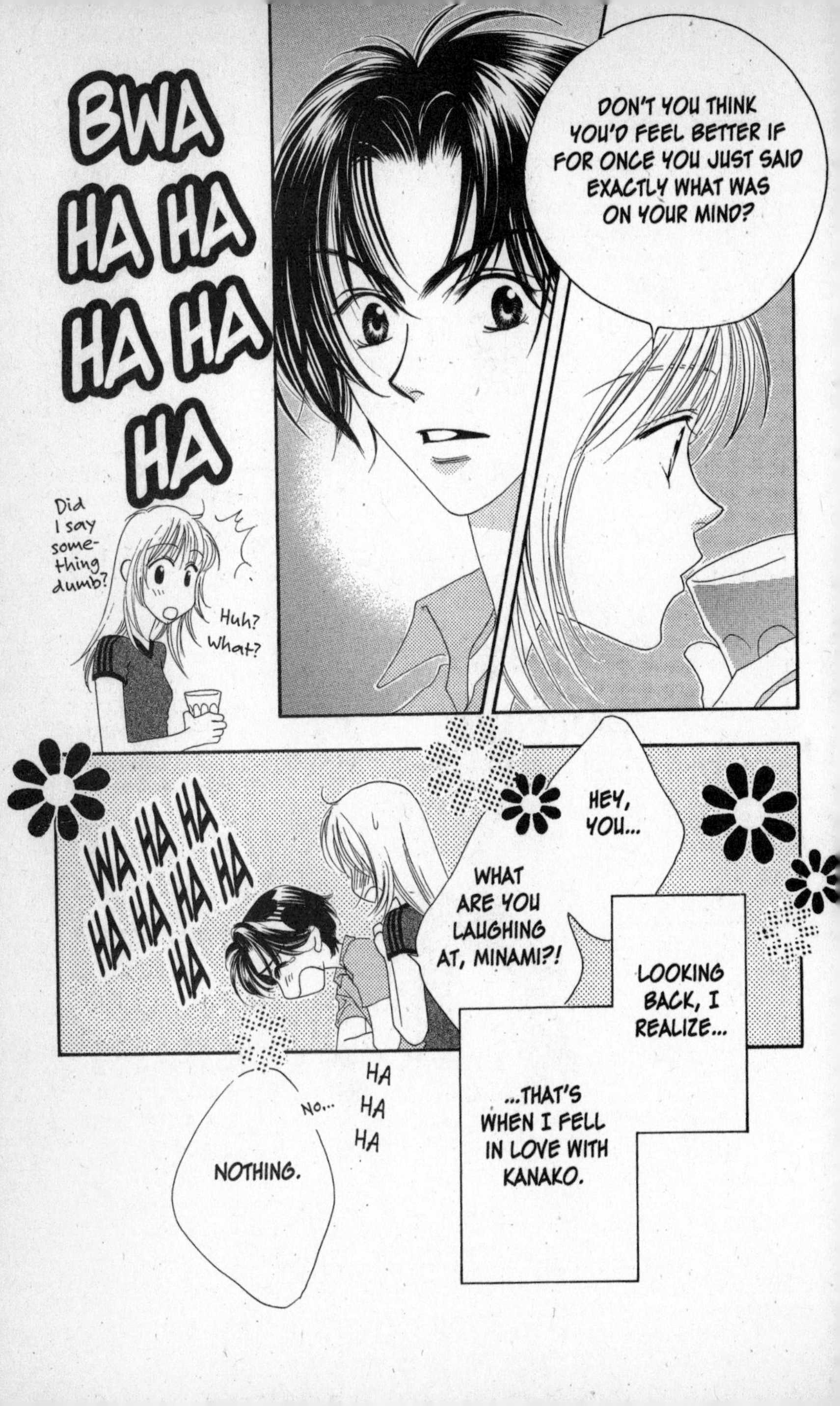
DON'T YOU THINK YOU'D FEEL BETTER IF FOR ONCE YOU JUST SAID EXACTLY WHAT WAS ON YOUR MIND?
BWA HA HA HA HA HA
Huh? What?
Did I say some-thing dumb?
HEY, YOU...
WHAT ARE YOU LAUGHING AT, MINAMI?!
WA HA HA HA HA HA HA HA
LOOKING BACK, I REALIZE...
...THAT'S WHEN I FELL IN LOVE WITH KANAKO.
HA HA HA
No...
NOTHING.

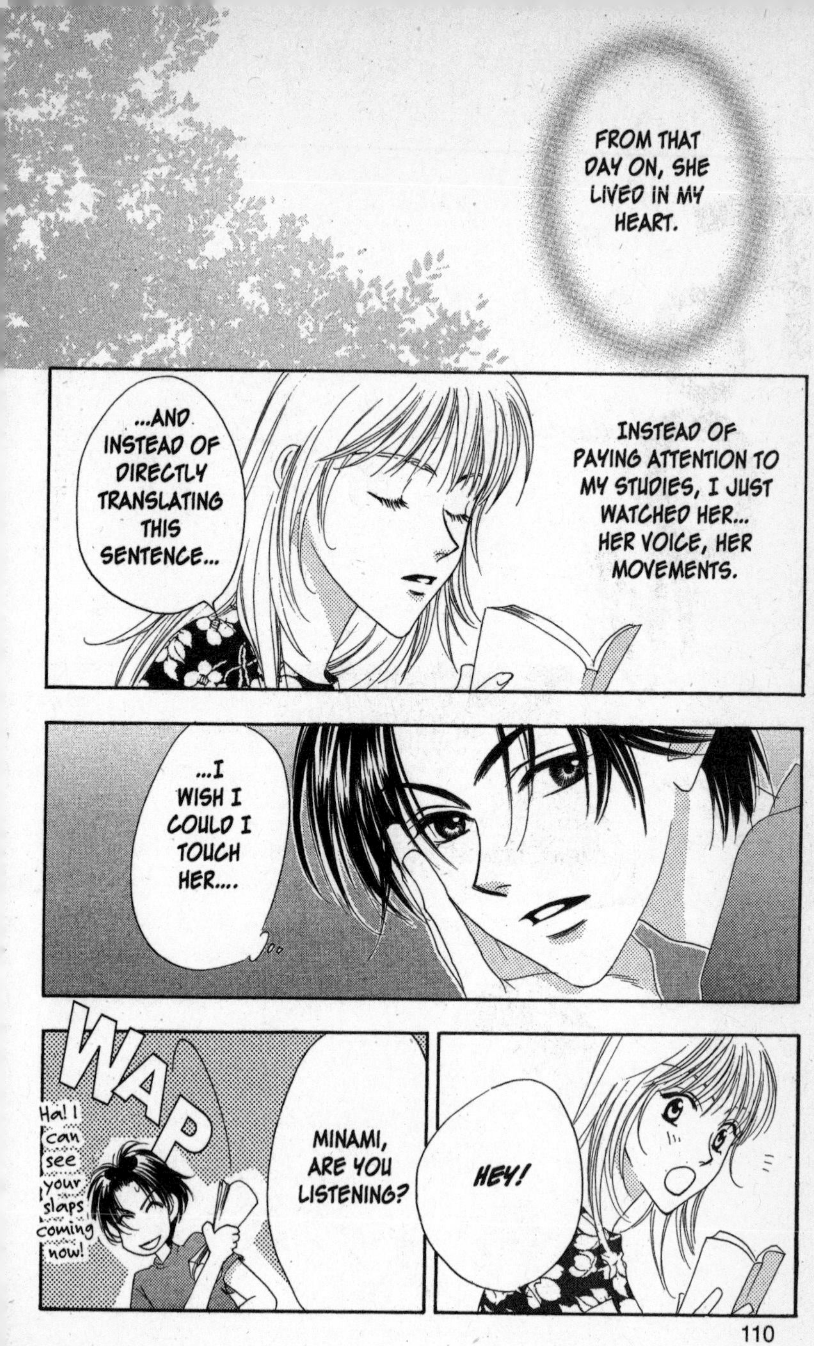
FROM THAT DAY ON, SHE LIVED IN MY HEART.
INSTEAD OF PAYING ATTENTION TO MY STUDIES, I JUST WATCHED HER... HER VOICE, HER MOVEMENTS.
...AND INSTEAD OF DIRECTLY TRANSLATING THIS SENTENCE...
...I WISH I COULD I TOUCH HER....
HEY!
MINAMI, ARE YOU LISTENING?
WAP
Ha! I can see your slaps coming now!

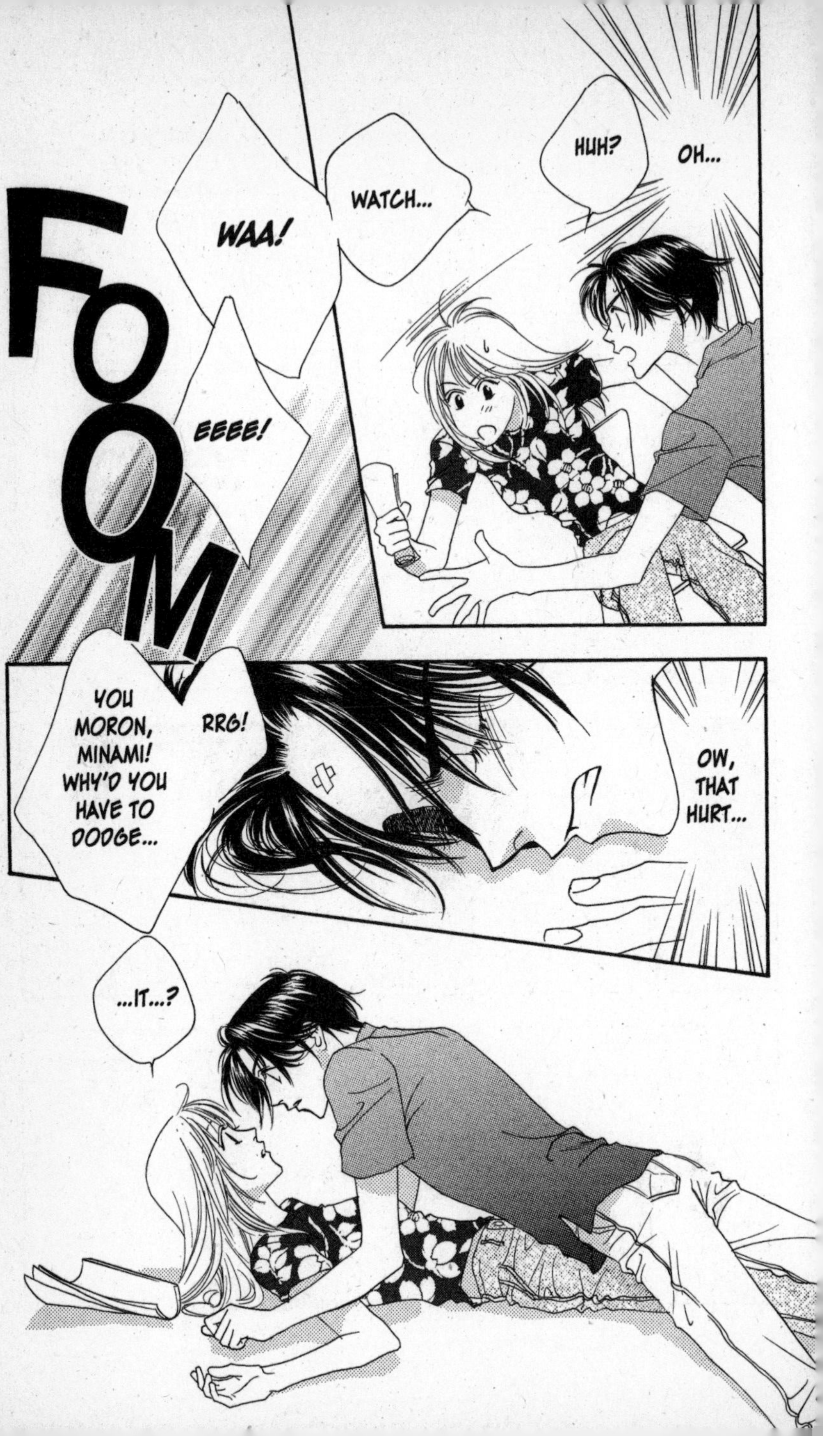
HUH?
OH...
WATCH...
WAA!
EEEE!
FOOM
OW, THAT HURT...
RRG!
YOU MORON, MINAMI! WHY'D YOU HAVE TO DODGE...
...IT...?

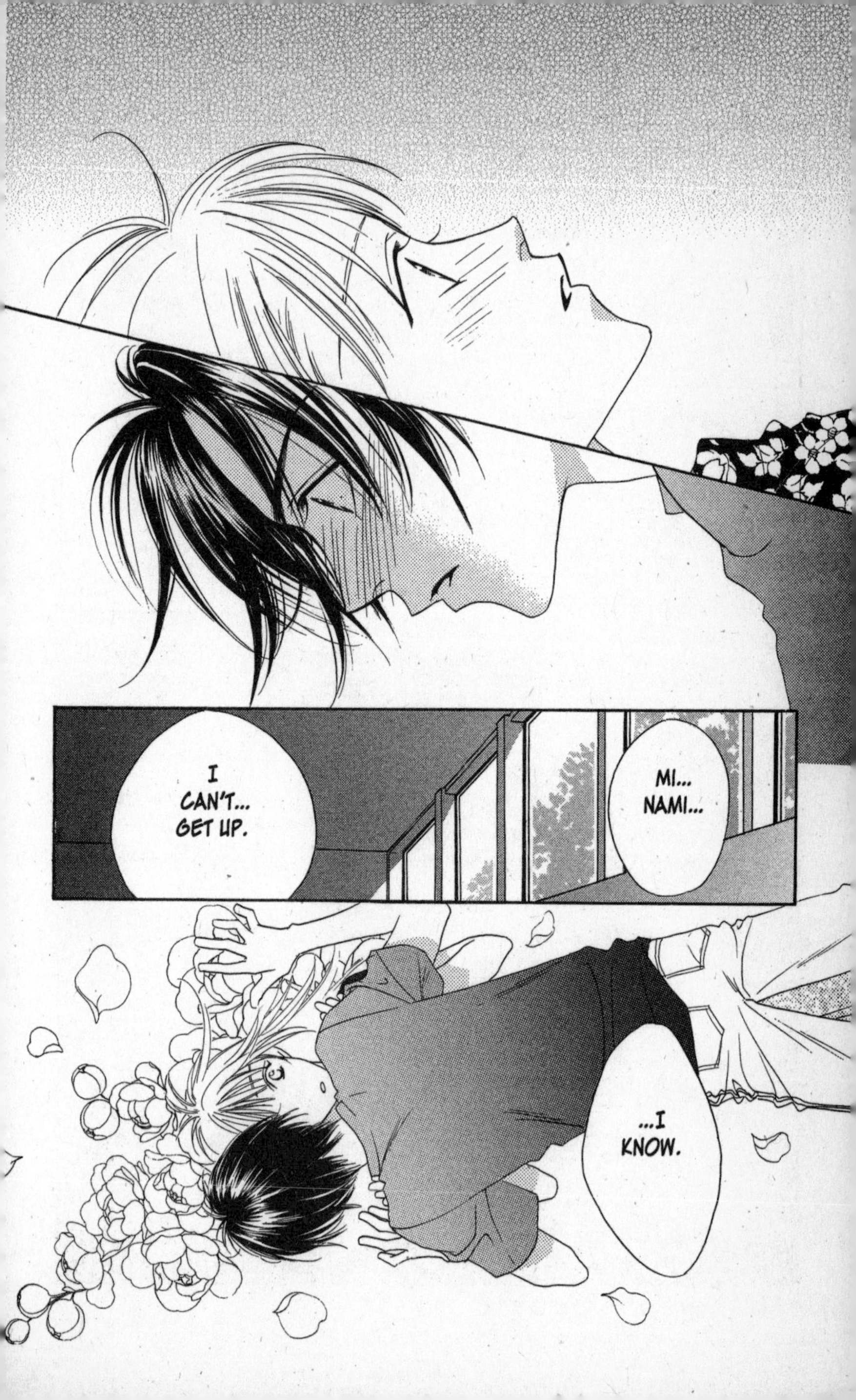
MI... NAMI...
I CAN'T... GET UP.
...I KNOW.

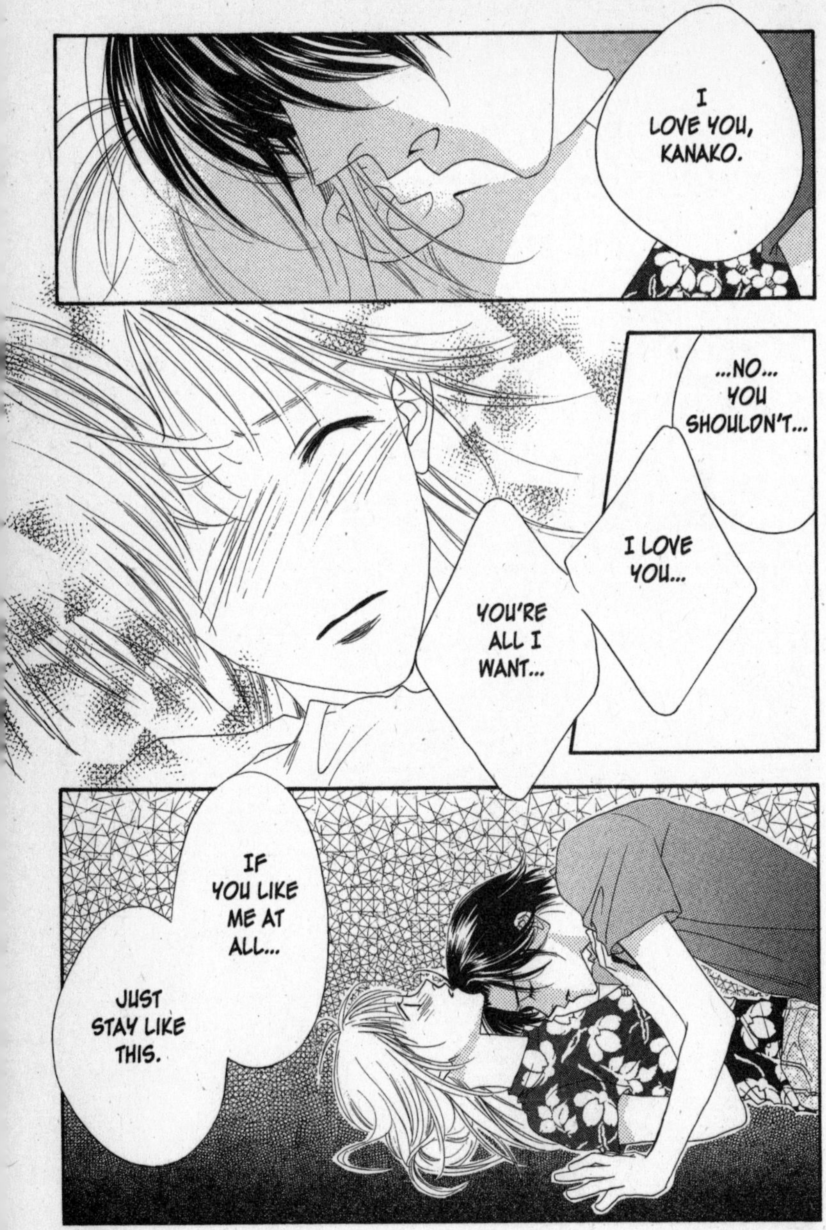
I LOVE YOU, KANAKO.
...NO... YOU SHOULDN'T...
I LOVE YOU...
YOU'RE ALL I WANT...
IF YOU LIKE ME AT ALL...
JUST STAY LIKE THIS.

...THAT'S NOT FAIR...

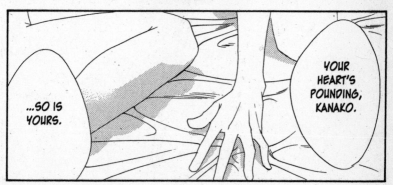

YOUR HEART'S POUNDING, KANAKO.

...SO IS YOURS.

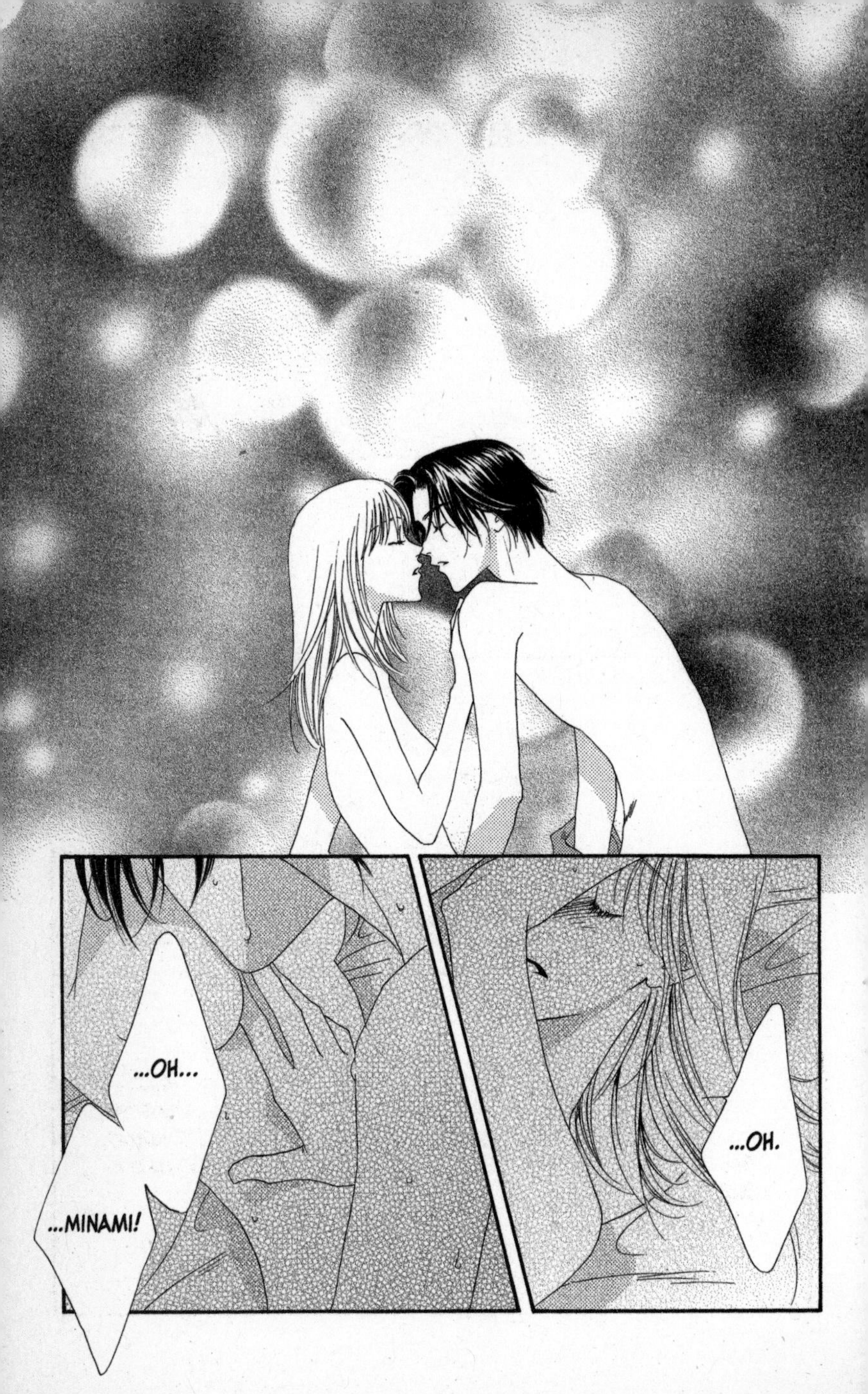
...OH.
...OH...
...MINAMI!

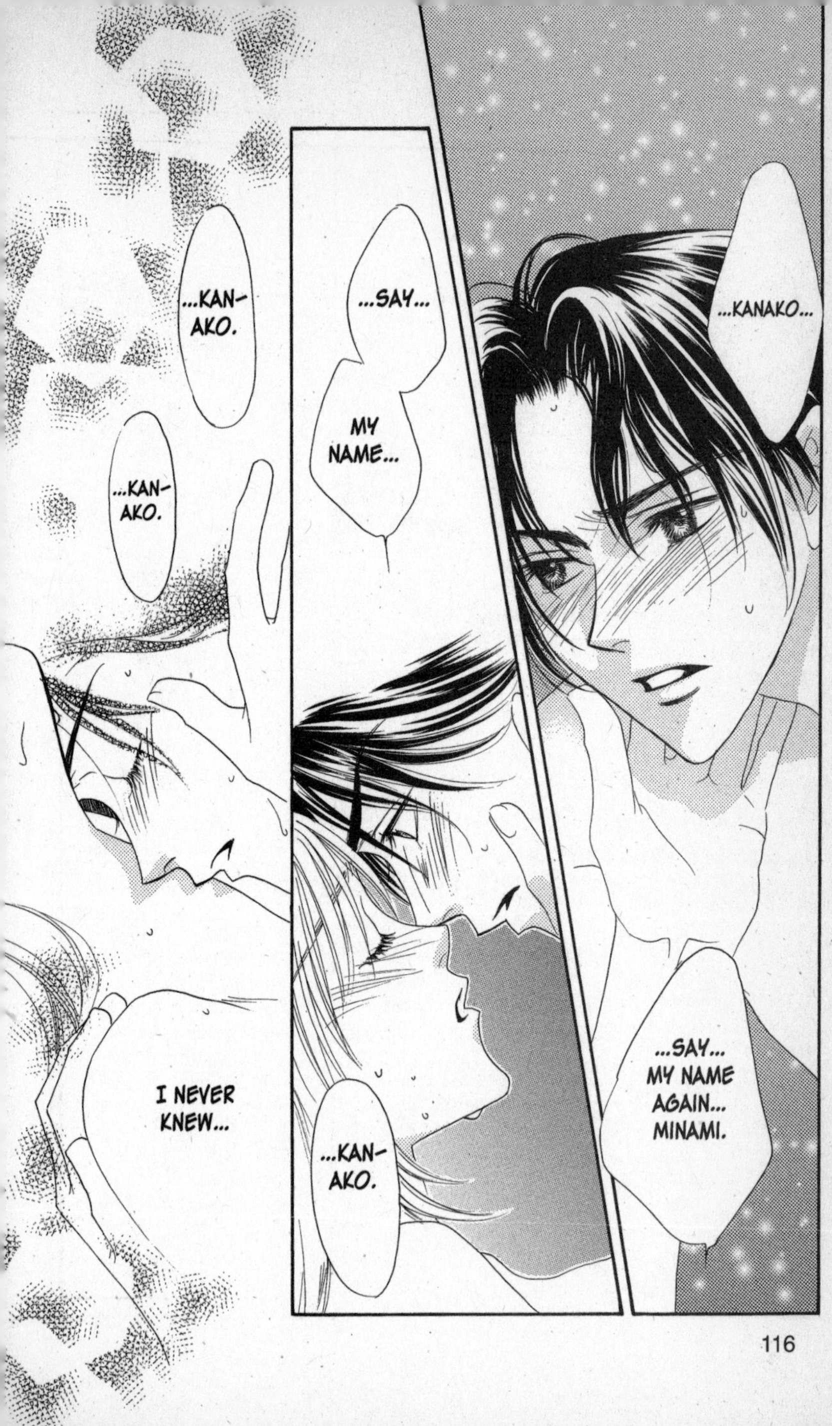
...KANAKO...
...SAY... MY NAME AGAIN... MINAMI.
...SAY...
MY NAME...
...KAN-AKO.
...KAN-AKO.
...KAN-AKO.
I NEVER KNEW...

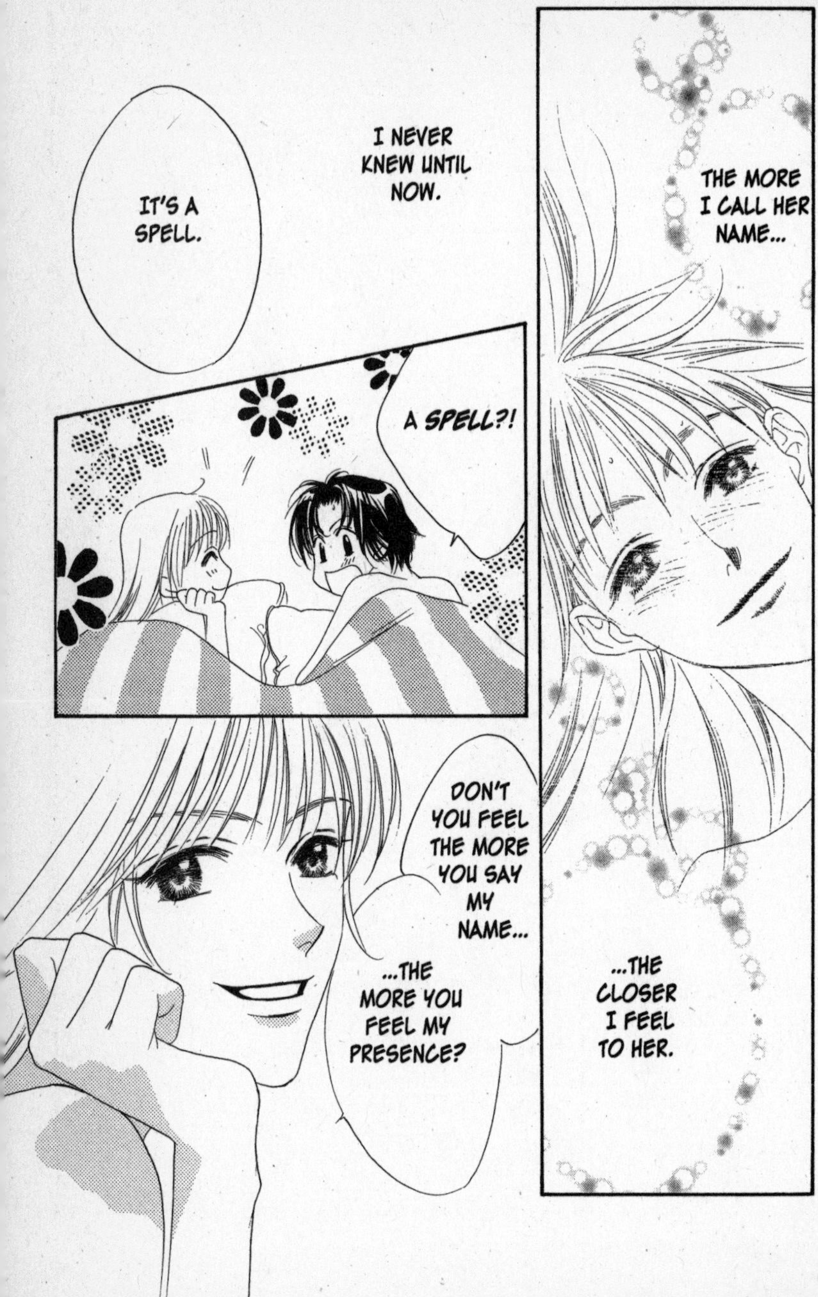
THE MORE I CALL HER NAME...
...THE CLOSER I FEEL TO HER.
I NEVER KNEW UNTIL NOW.
IT'S A SPELL.
A *SPELL?!*
DON'T YOU FEEL THE MORE YOU SAY MY NAME...
...THE MORE YOU FEEL MY PRESENCE?

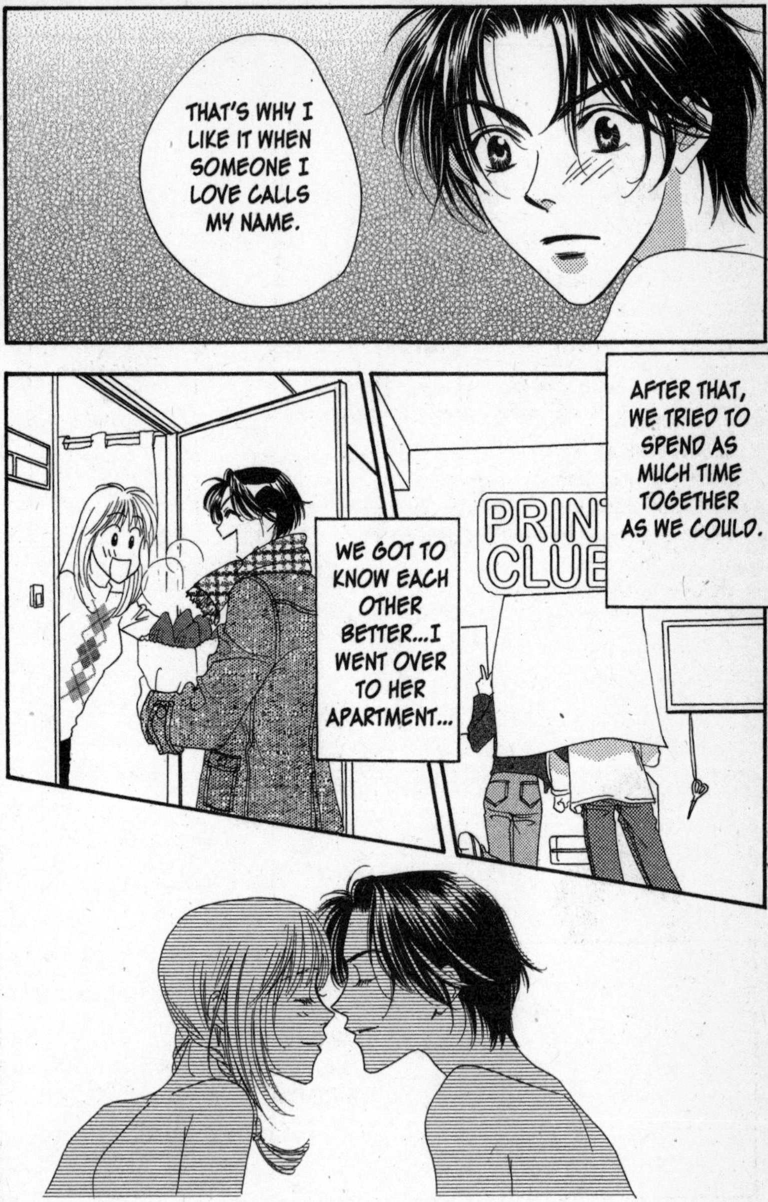
THAT'S WHY I LIKE IT WHEN SOMEONE I LOVE CALLS MY NAME.
AFTER THAT, WE TRIED TO SPEND AS MUCH TIME TOGETHER AS WE COULD.
PRINT CLUB
WE GOT TO KNOW EACH OTHER BETTER...I WENT OVER TO HER APARTMENT...

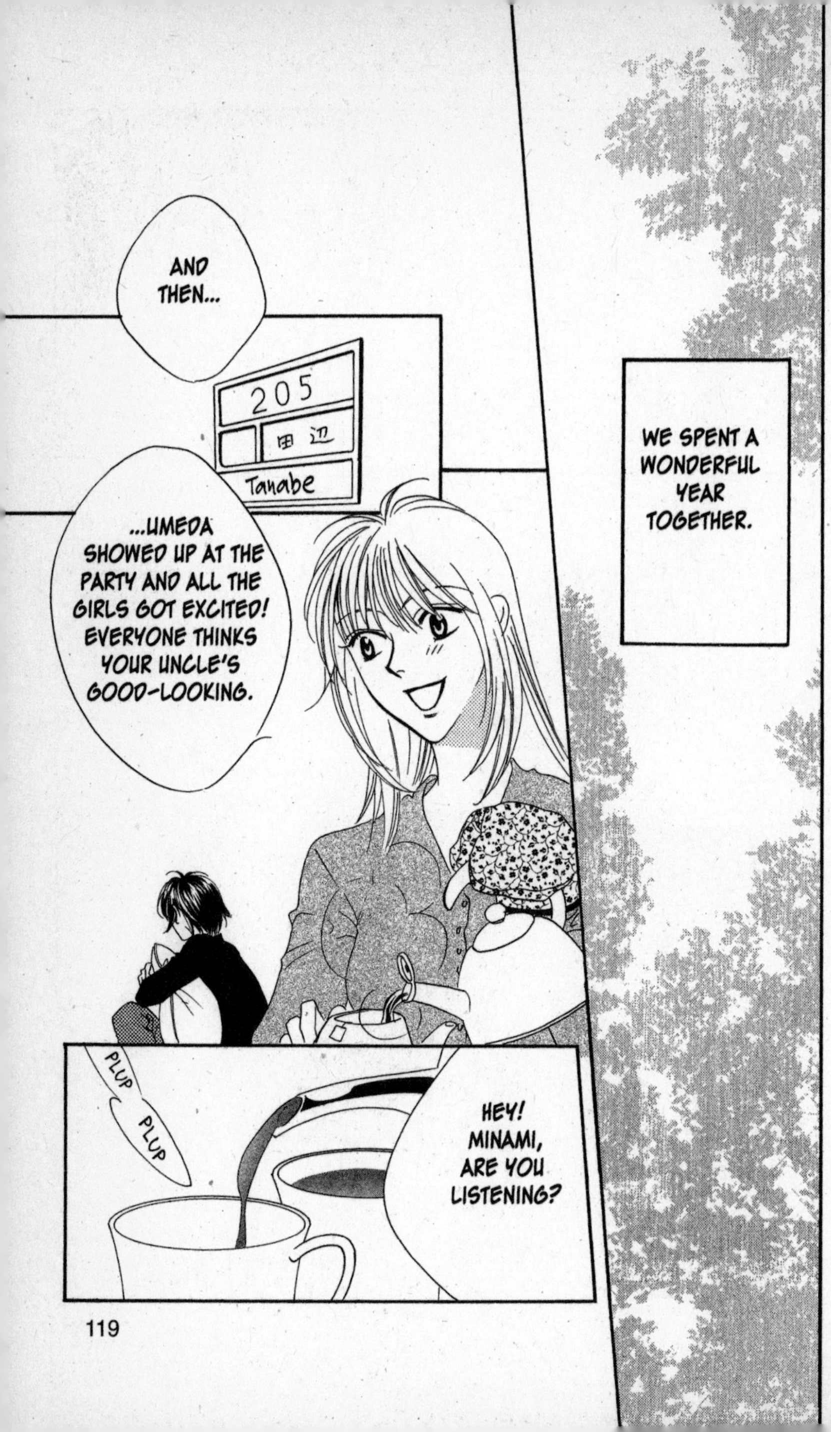
WE SPENT A WONDERFUL YEAR TOGETHER.
AND THEN...
205
田辺
Tanabe
...UMEDA SHOWED UP AT THE PARTY AND ALL THE GIRLS GOT EXCITED! EVERYONE THINKS YOUR UNCLE'S GOOD-LOOKING.
HEY! MINAMI, ARE YOU LISTENING?
PLUP PLUP

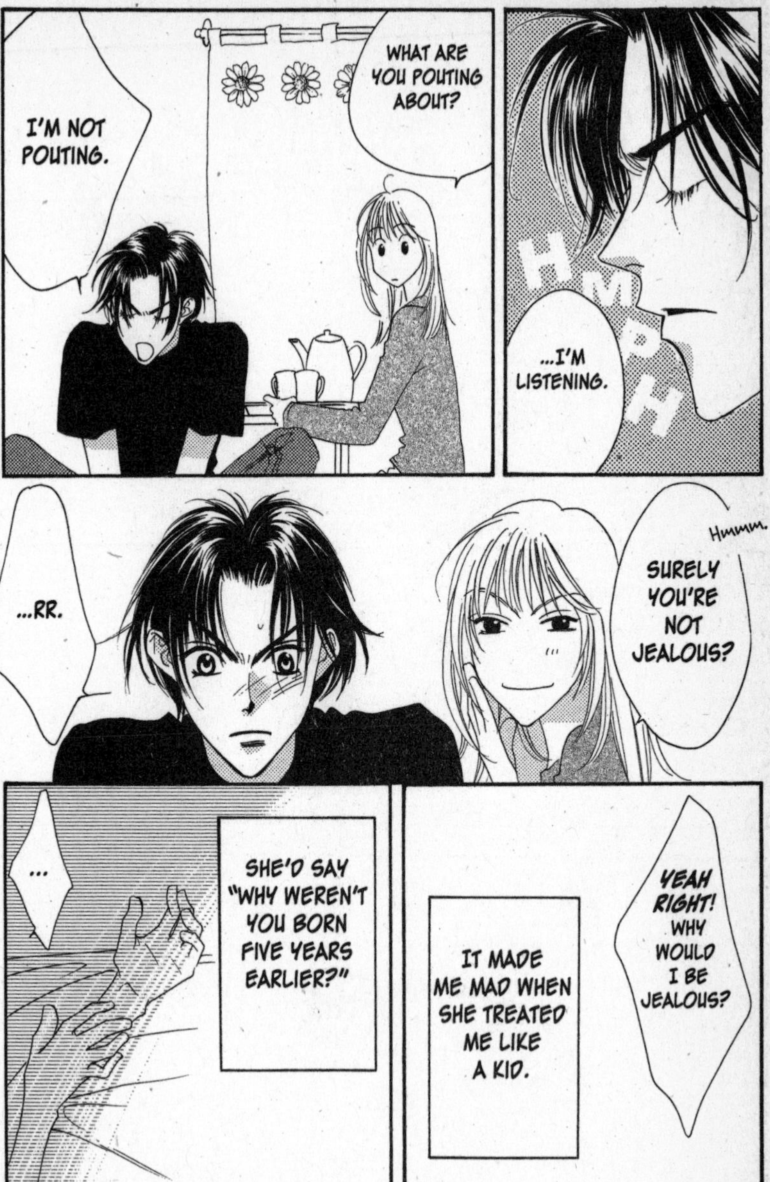
HMPH
...I'M LISTENING.
WHAT ARE YOU POUTING ABOUT?
I'M NOT POUTING.
Hmmm.
SURELY YOU'RE NOT JEALOUS?
...RR.
YEAH RIGHT! WHY WOULD I BE JEALOUS?
IT MADE ME MAD WHEN SHE TREATED ME LIKE A KID.
SHE'D SAY "WHY WEREN'T YOU BORN FIVE YEARS EARLIER?"
...

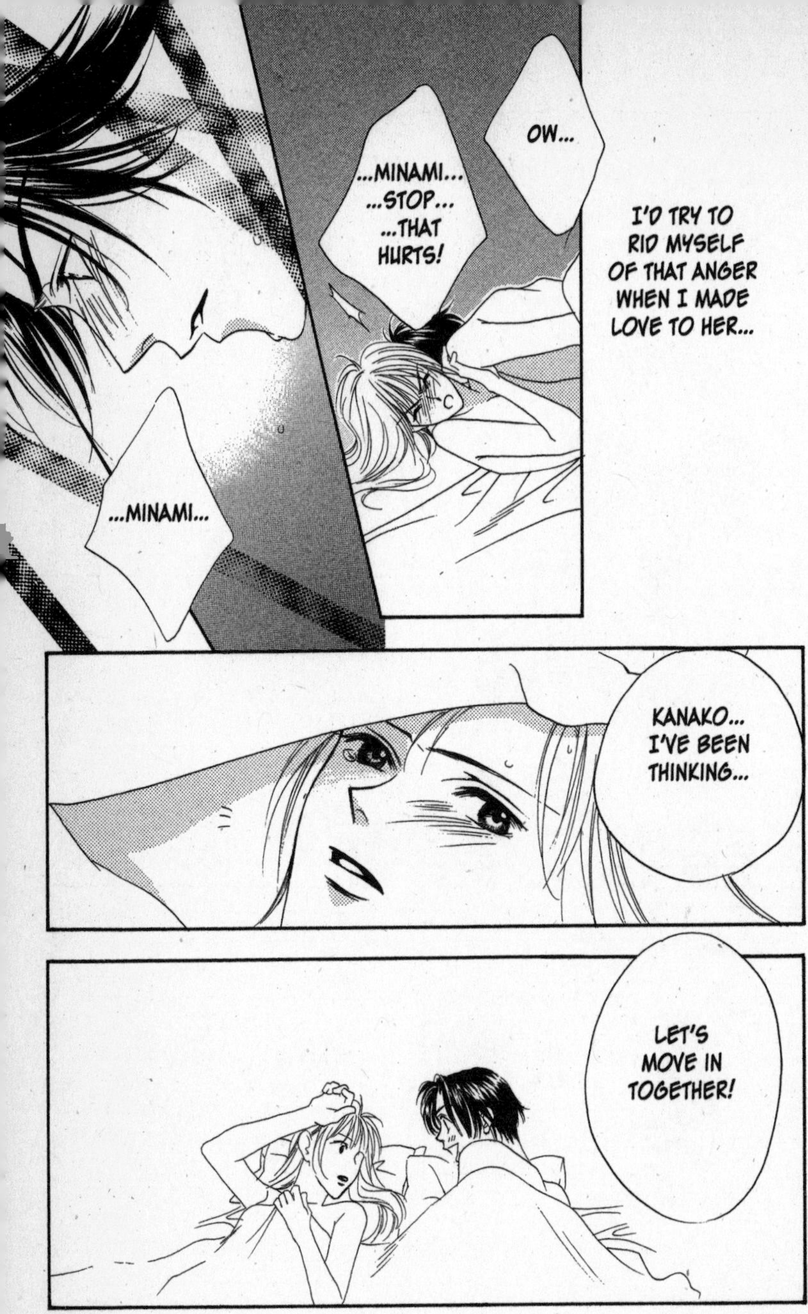
I'D TRY TO RID MYSELF OF THAT ANGER WHEN I MADE LOVE TO HER...
OW...
...MINAMI... ...STOP... ...THAT HURTS!
...MINAMI...
KANAKO... I'VE BEEN THINKING...
LET'S MOVE IN TOGETHER!

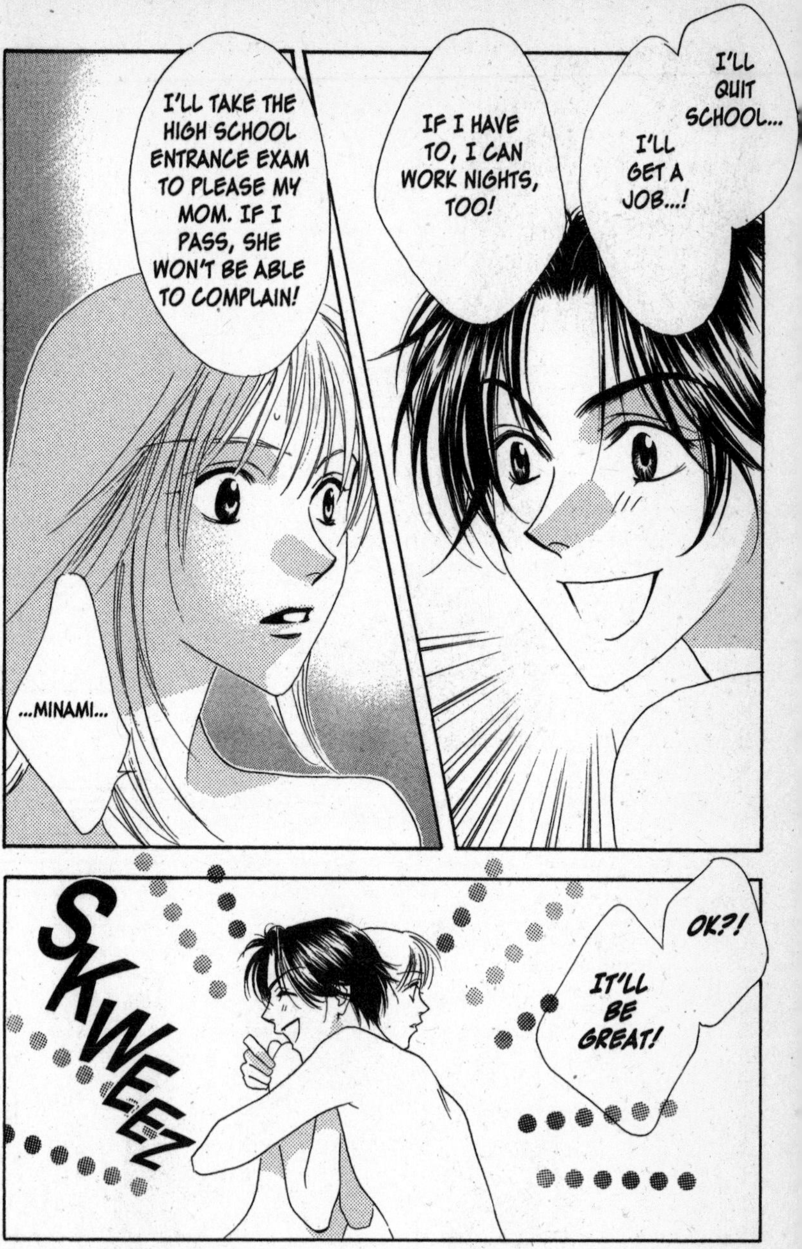
I'LL QUIT SCHOOL... I'LL GET A JOB...!
IF I HAVE TO, I CAN WORK NIGHTS, TOO!
I'LL TAKE THE HIGH SCHOOL ENTRANCE EXAM TO PLEASE MY MOM. IF I PASS, SHE WON'T BE ABLE TO COMPLAIN!
...MINAMI...
OK?! IT'LL BE GREAT!
SKWEEZ

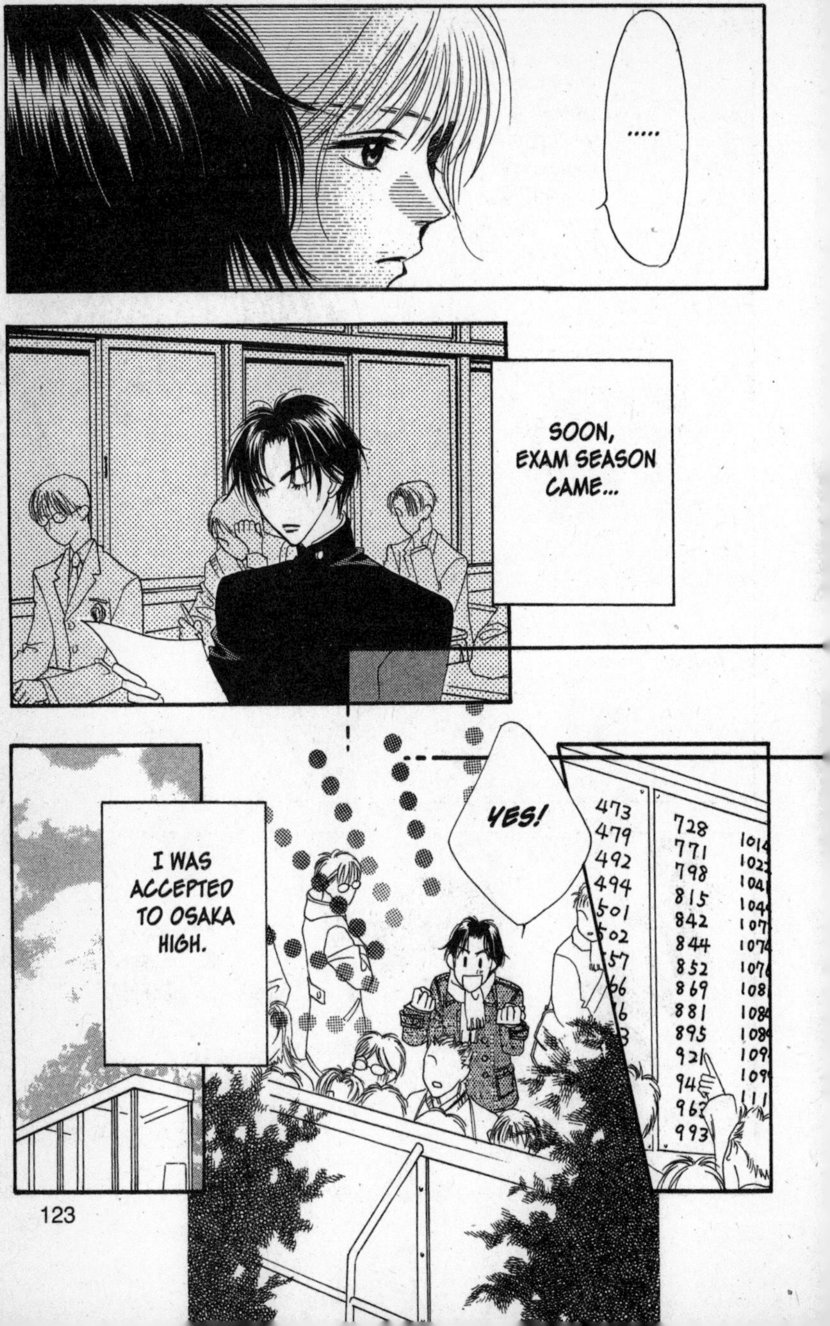
.....
SOON, EXAM SEASON CAME...
YES!
I WAS ACCEPTED TO OSAKA HIGH.

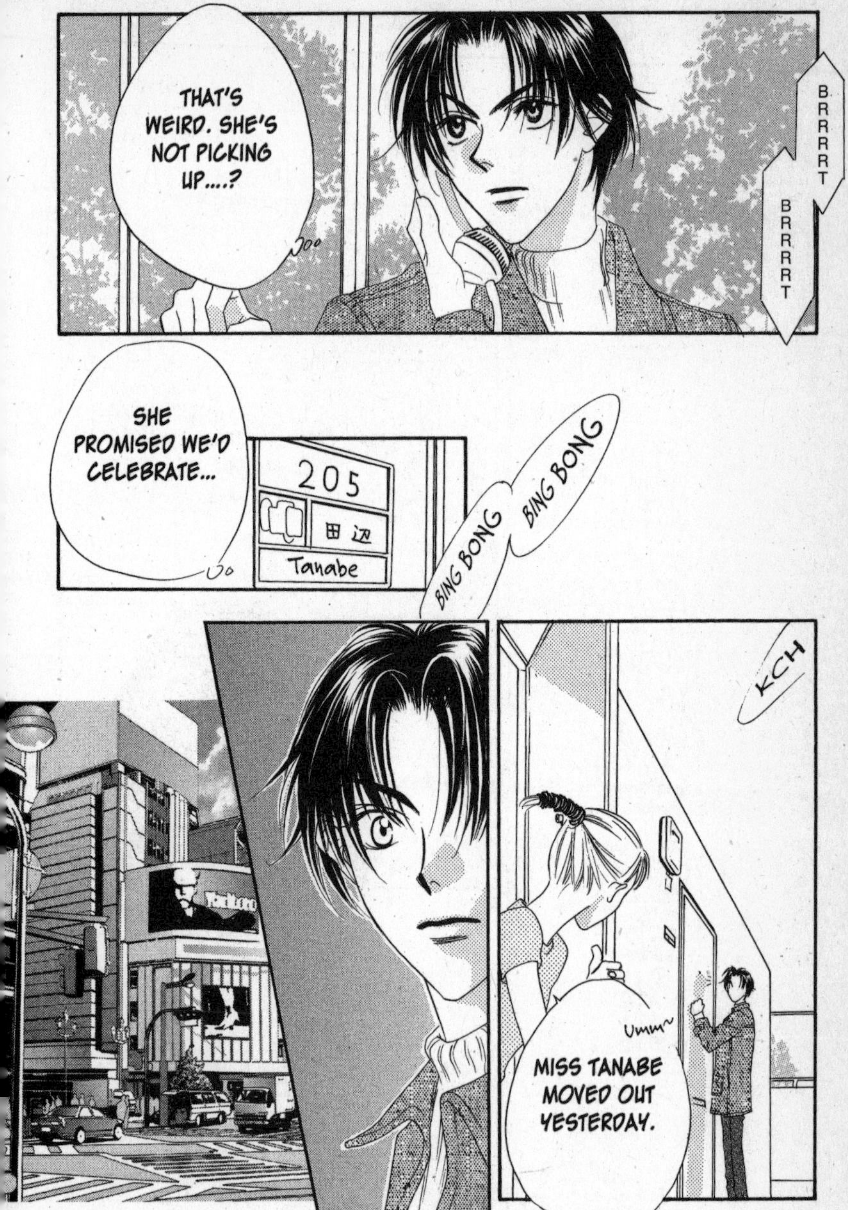
BRRRRT
BRRRRT
THAT'S WEIRD. SHE'S NOT PICKING UP....?
BING BONG
BING BONG
205
田辺
Tanabe
SHE PROMISED WE'D CELEBRATE...
KCH
Umm~
MISS TANABE MOVED OUT YESTERDAY.

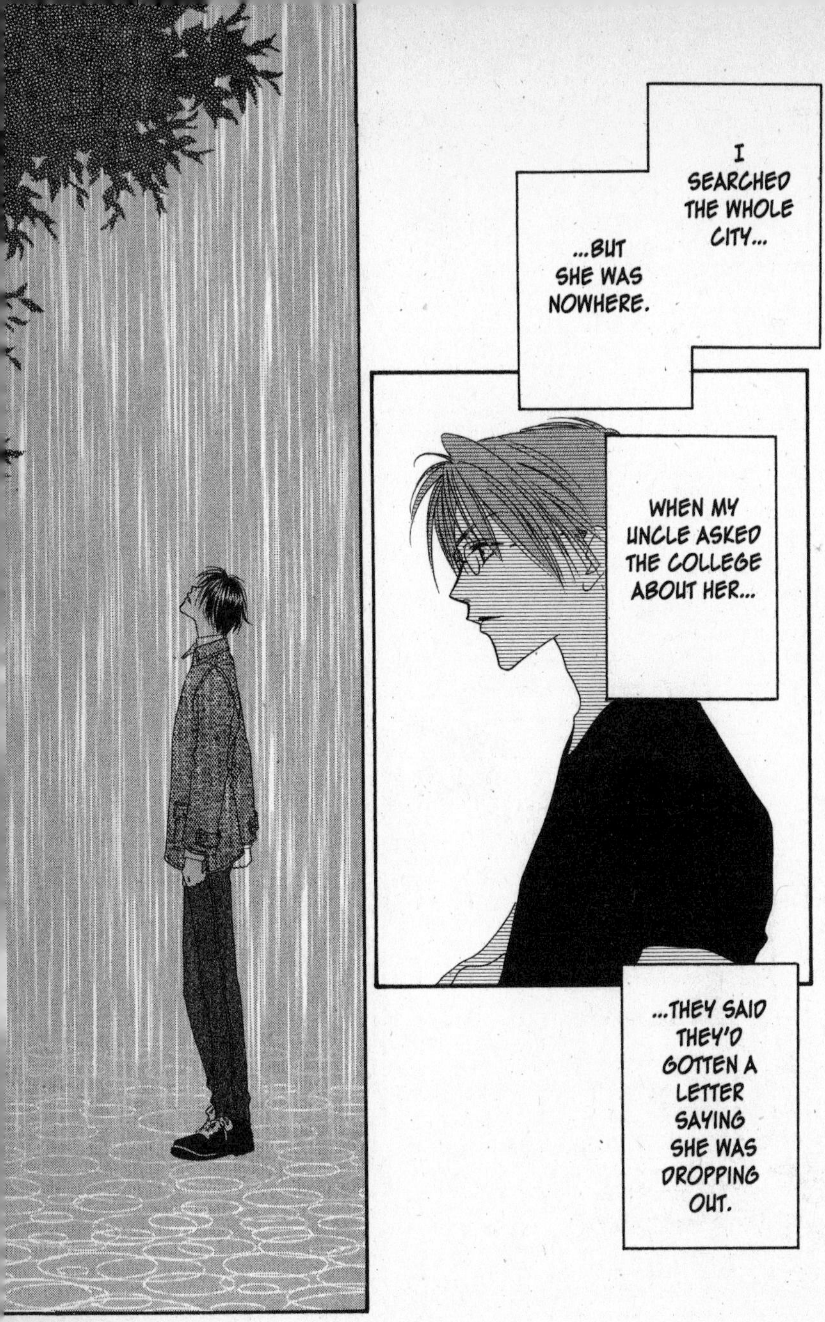
I SEARCHED THE WHOLE CITY...
...BUT SHE WAS NOWHERE.
WHEN MY UNCLE ASKED THE COLLEGE ABOUT HER...
...THEY SAID THEY'D GOTTEN A LETTER SAYING SHE WAS DROPPING OUT.

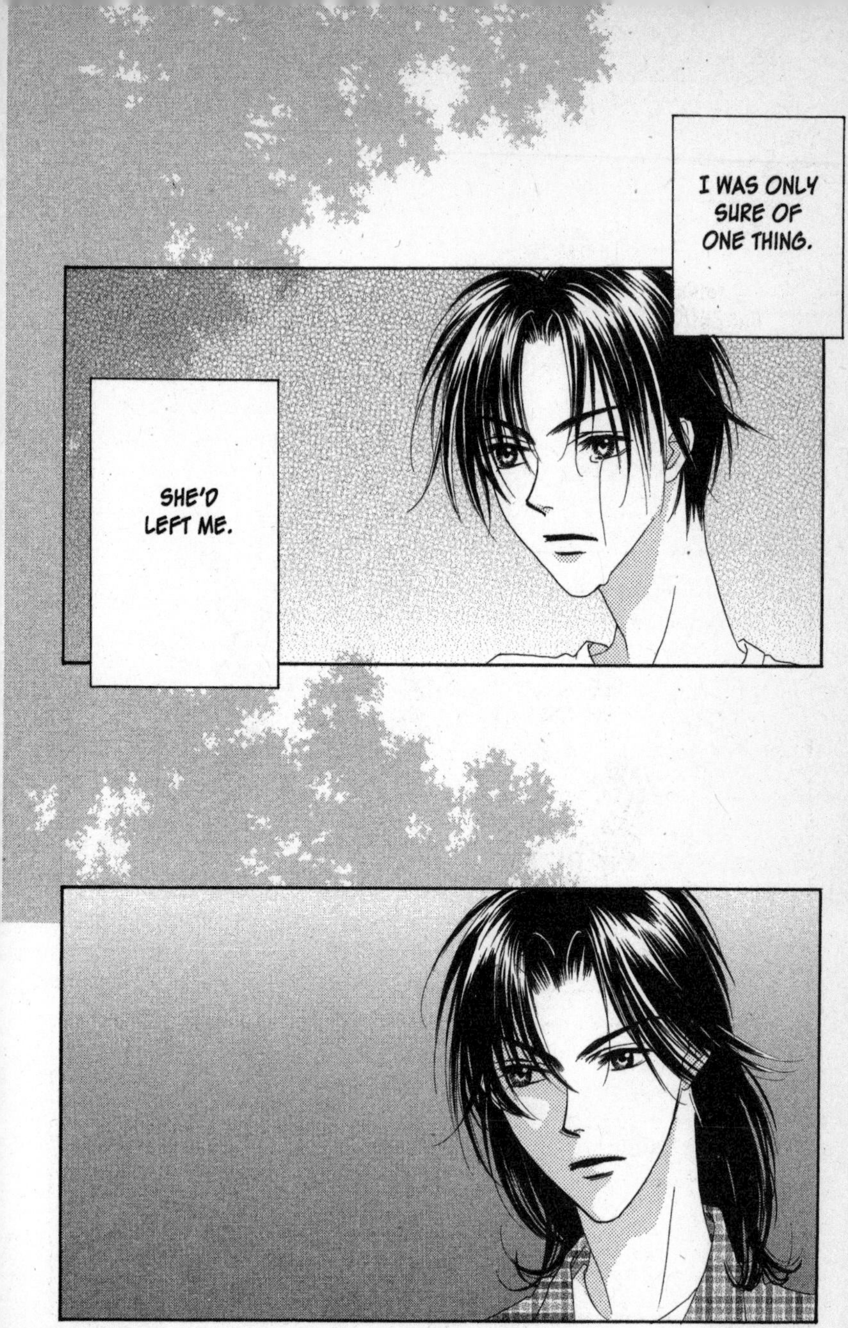
I WAS ONLY SURE OF ONE THING.
SHE'D LEFT ME.

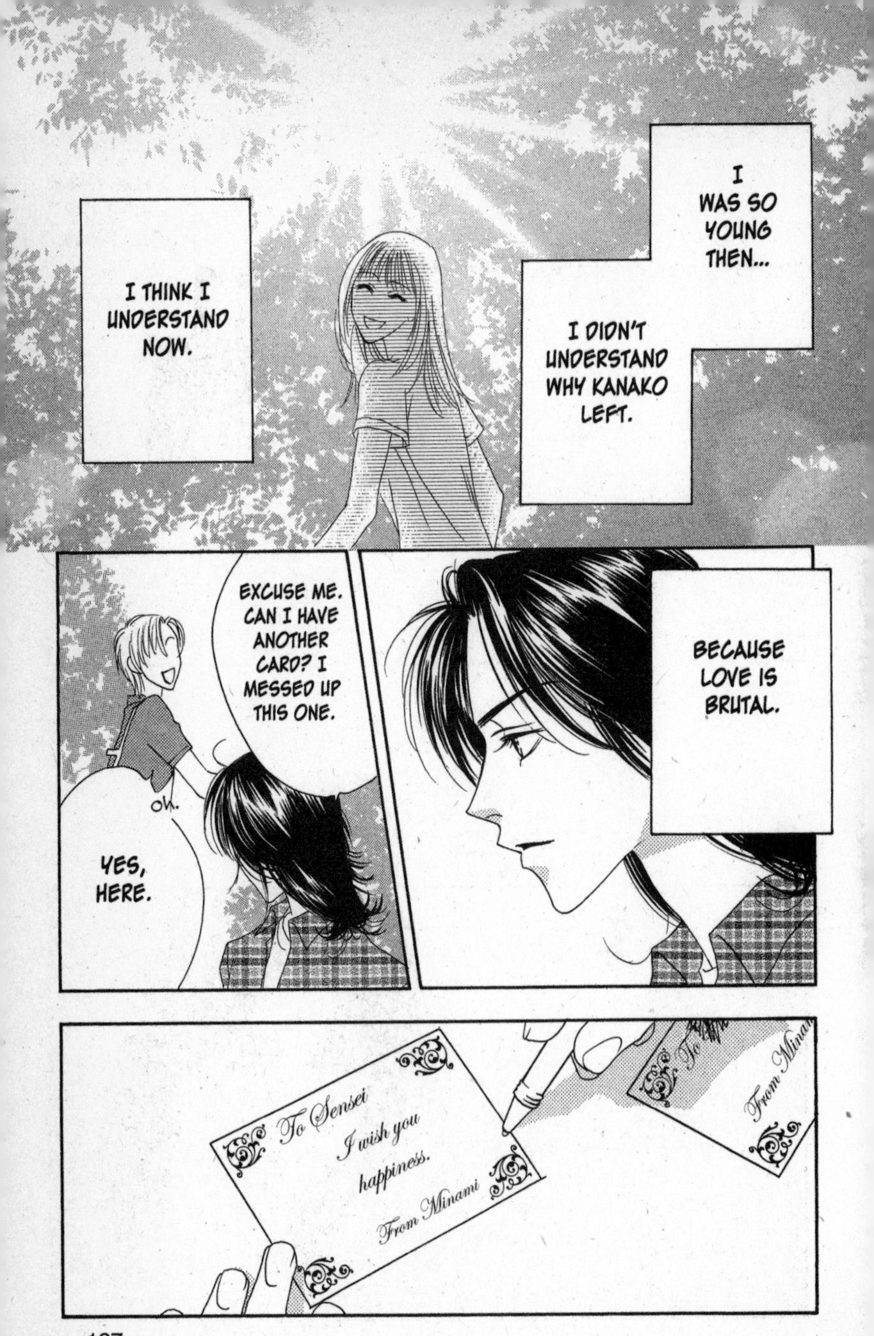
I WAS SO YOUNG THEN...
I DIDN'T UNDERSTAND WHY KANAKO LEFT.
I THINK I UNDERSTAND NOW.
BECAUSE LOVE IS BRUTAL.
EXCUSE ME. CAN I HAVE ANOTHER CARD? I MESSED UP THIS ONE.
Oh.
YES, HERE.
To Sensei
I wish you happiness.
From Minami

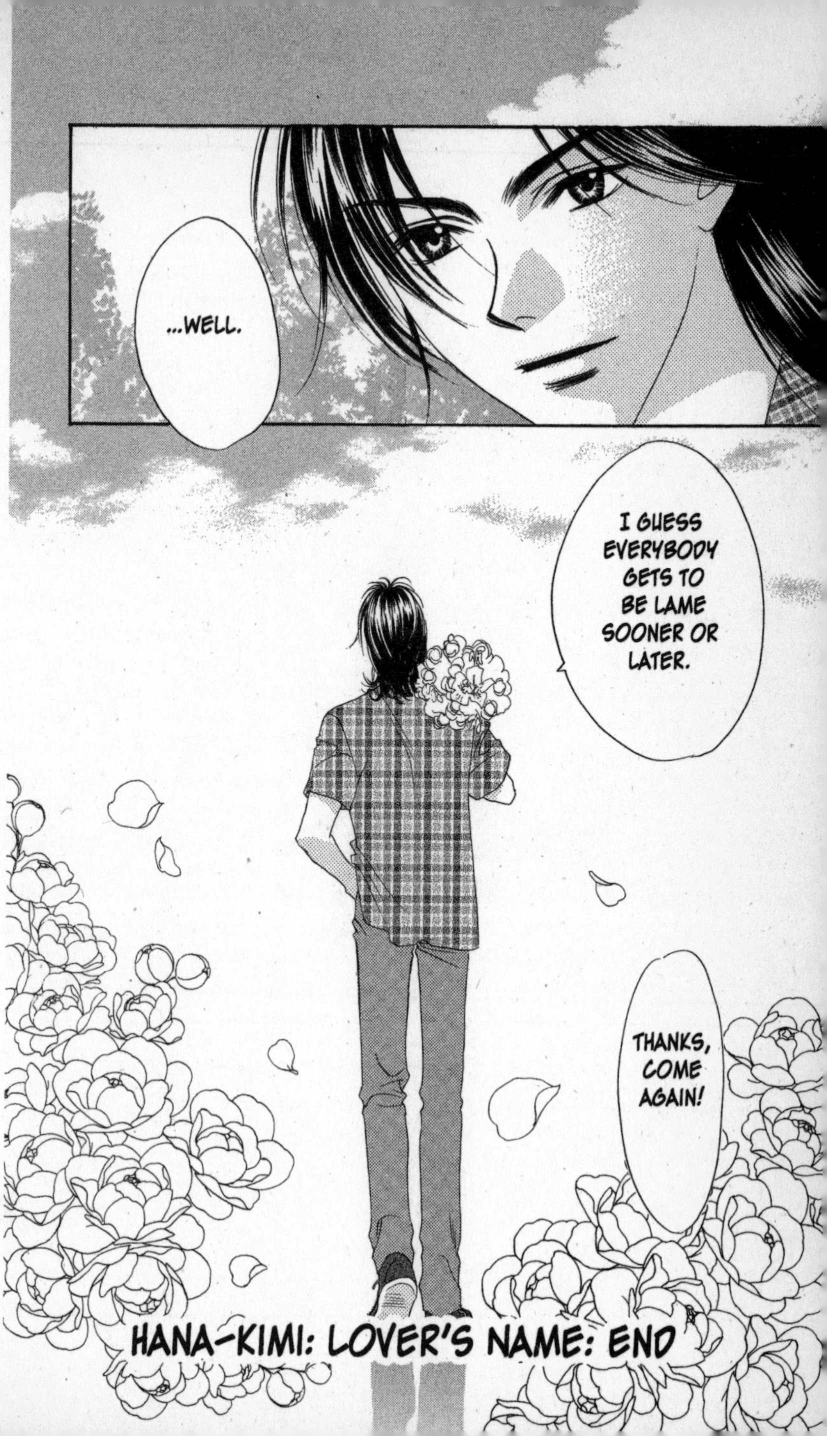
...WELL.
I GUESS EVERYBODY GETS TO BE LAME SOONER OR LATER.
THANKS, COME AGAIN!
HANA-KIMI: LOVER'S NAME: END

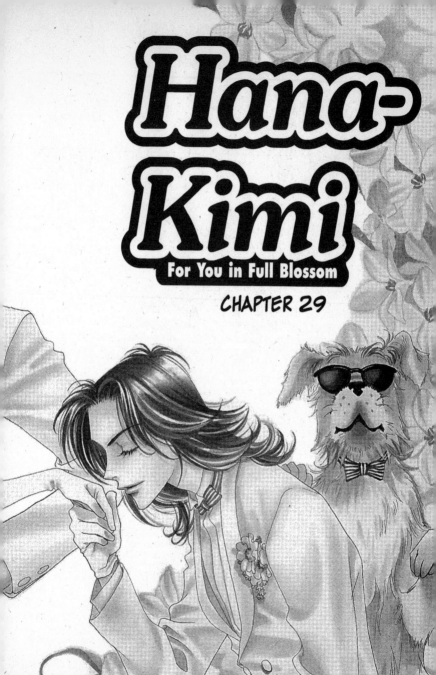

Hana-Kimi

For You in Full Blossom

CHAPTER 29

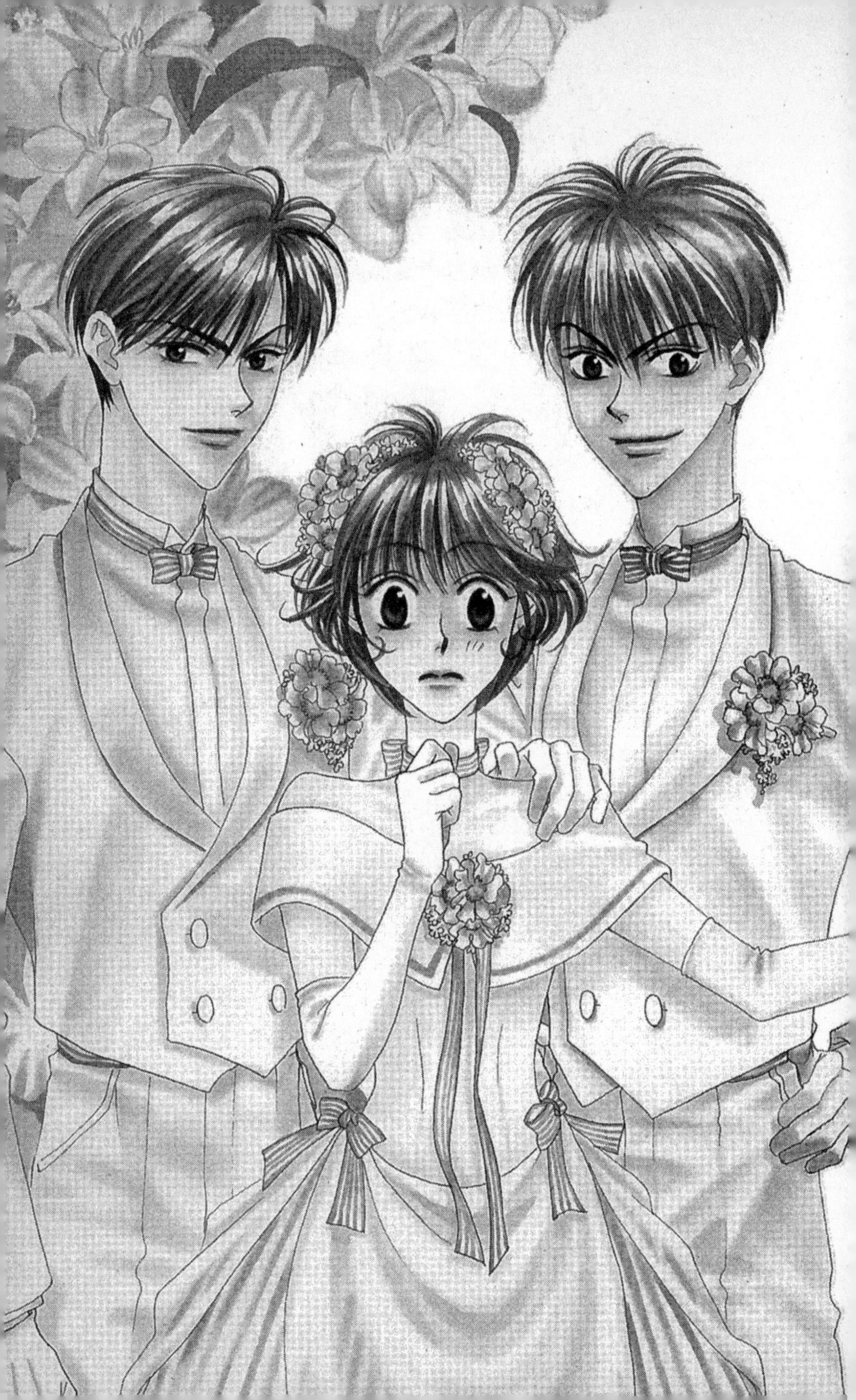

THE FAMOUS OSAKA PRIVATE SCHOOL...

...IS AN ALL-BOYS' SCHOOL, AND ALL THE STUDENTS LIVE IN DORMITORIES.

Dormitory

205

HEY, ARE YOU READY YET?

YEAH... YEAH! JUST A SEC!

oh

TUG

TUG

RG...

L'Arc~en~Ciel

[French for "Rainbow"]

YES, YES, YES! NOW THAT WE'VE DONE MALICE, IT'S TIME FOR L'ARC~EN~CIEL!! I WENT TO THEIR CONCERT IN OSAKA HALL IN 1998!! (I GOT GOOD SEATS!! YAY!!) I'VE KNOWN THE BAND L'ARC SINCE THEIR DEBUT. I EVEN DREW THEM FOR THE MAGAZINE B-PASS, BUT I WASN'T THAT INTO THEM YET. WHEN THEY GOT BACK TOGETHER AND CAME OUT WITH THE SONG "NIJI" (JAPANESE FOR "RAINBOW"), I STARTED TO REALLY GET INTO THEM. I LOVE HYDE'S VOICE AND KEN'S MUSIC. ♥ I'M GOING TO JOIN THEIR FAN CLUB!

Hyde with white hair. I was excited because he looks like Ka~ru.

I like Ken's dark melodies!! Especially "Fate!"

133

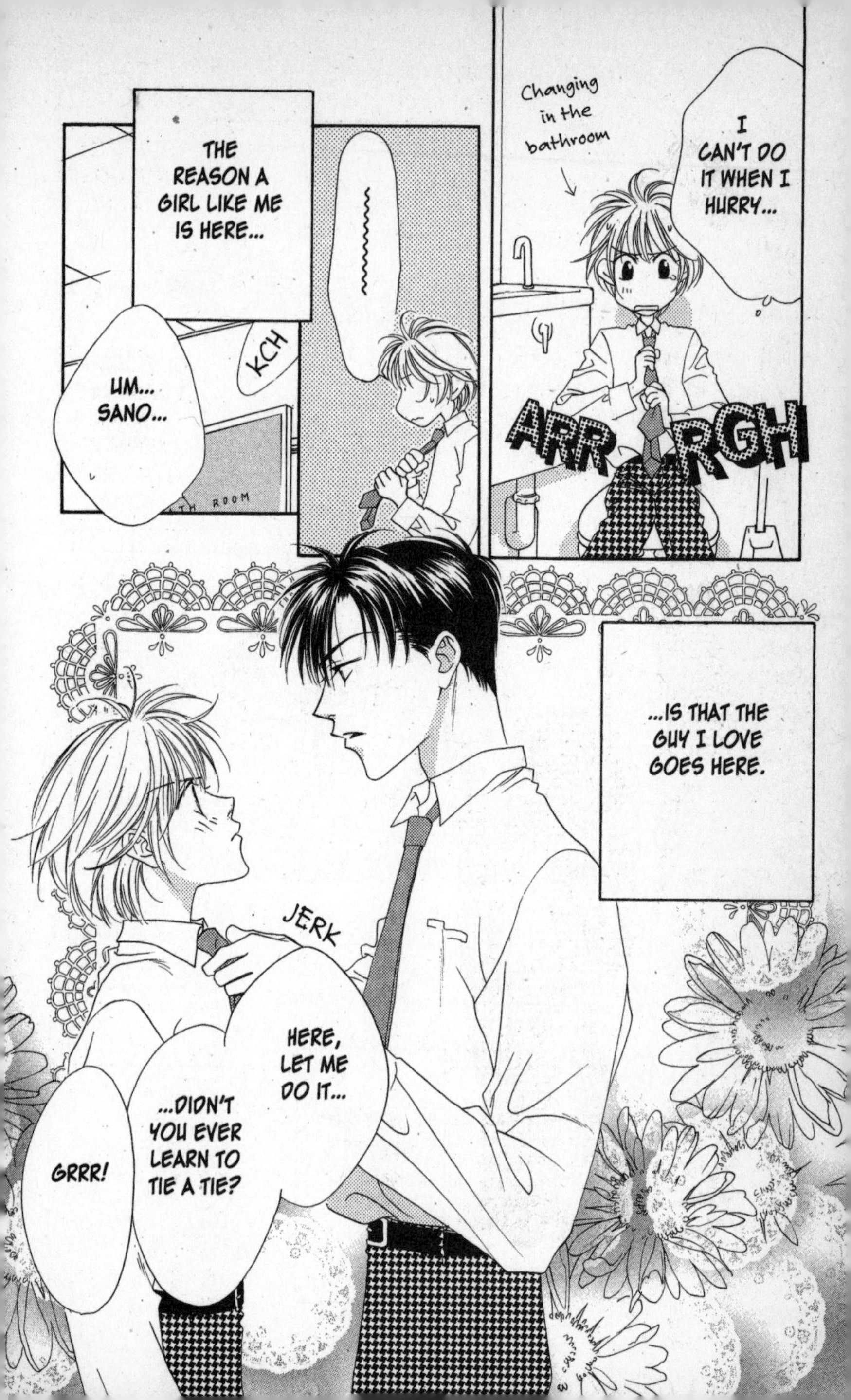

Changing in the bathroom
I CAN'T DO IT WHEN I HURRY...
ARRRGH
THE REASON A GIRL LIKE ME IS HERE...
KCH
UM... SANO...
...IS THAT THE GUY I LOVE GOES HERE.
JERK
HERE, LET ME DO IT...
...DIDN'T YOU EVER LEARN TO TIE A TIE?
GRRR!

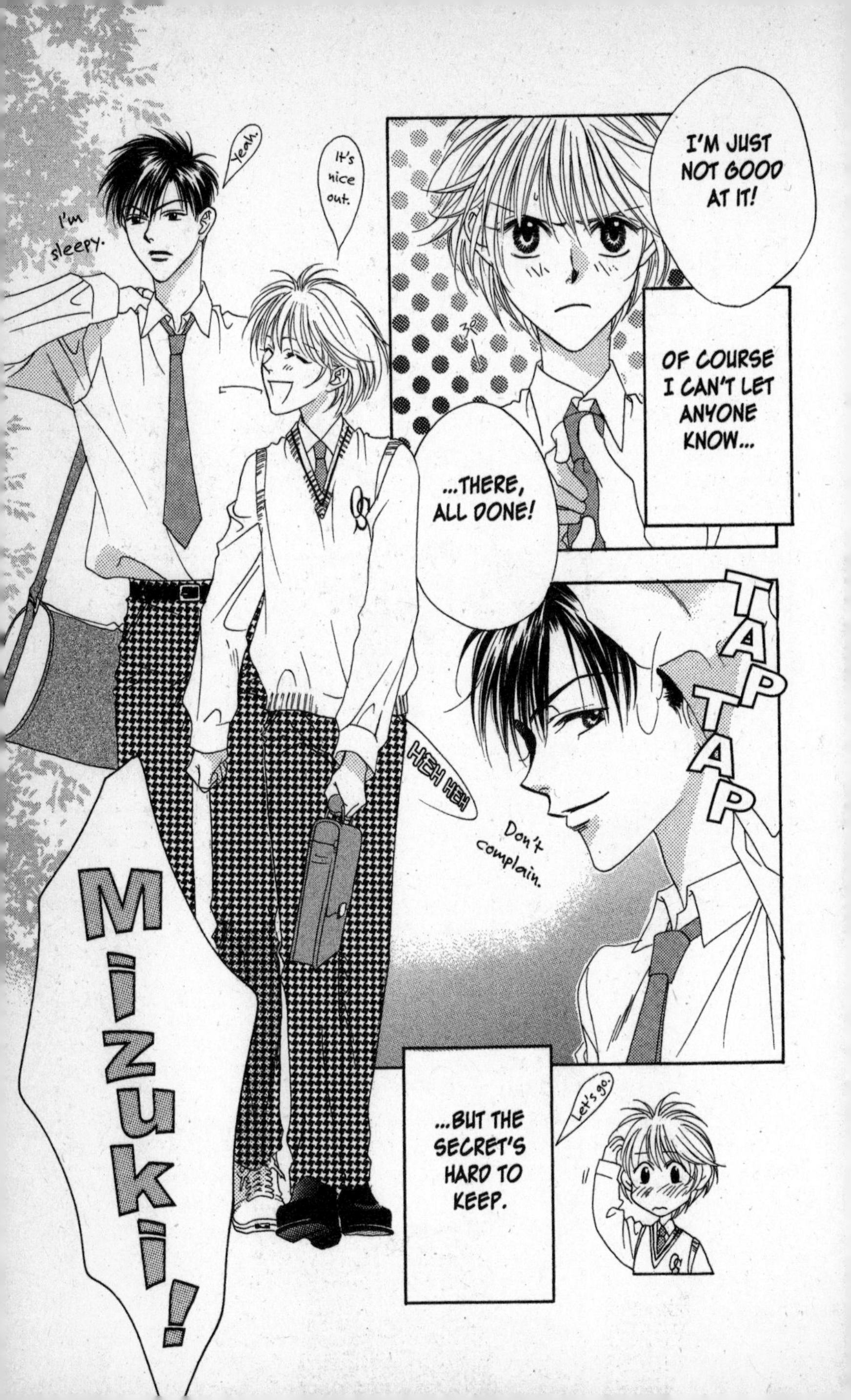
I'M JUST NOT GOOD AT IT!
OF COURSE I CAN'T LET ANYONE KNOW...
...THERE, ALL DONE!
TAP TAP
HEH HEH
Don't complain.
...BUT THE SECRET'S HARD TO KEEP.
Let's go.
It's nice out.
Yeah.
I'm sleepy.
MiZuKi!

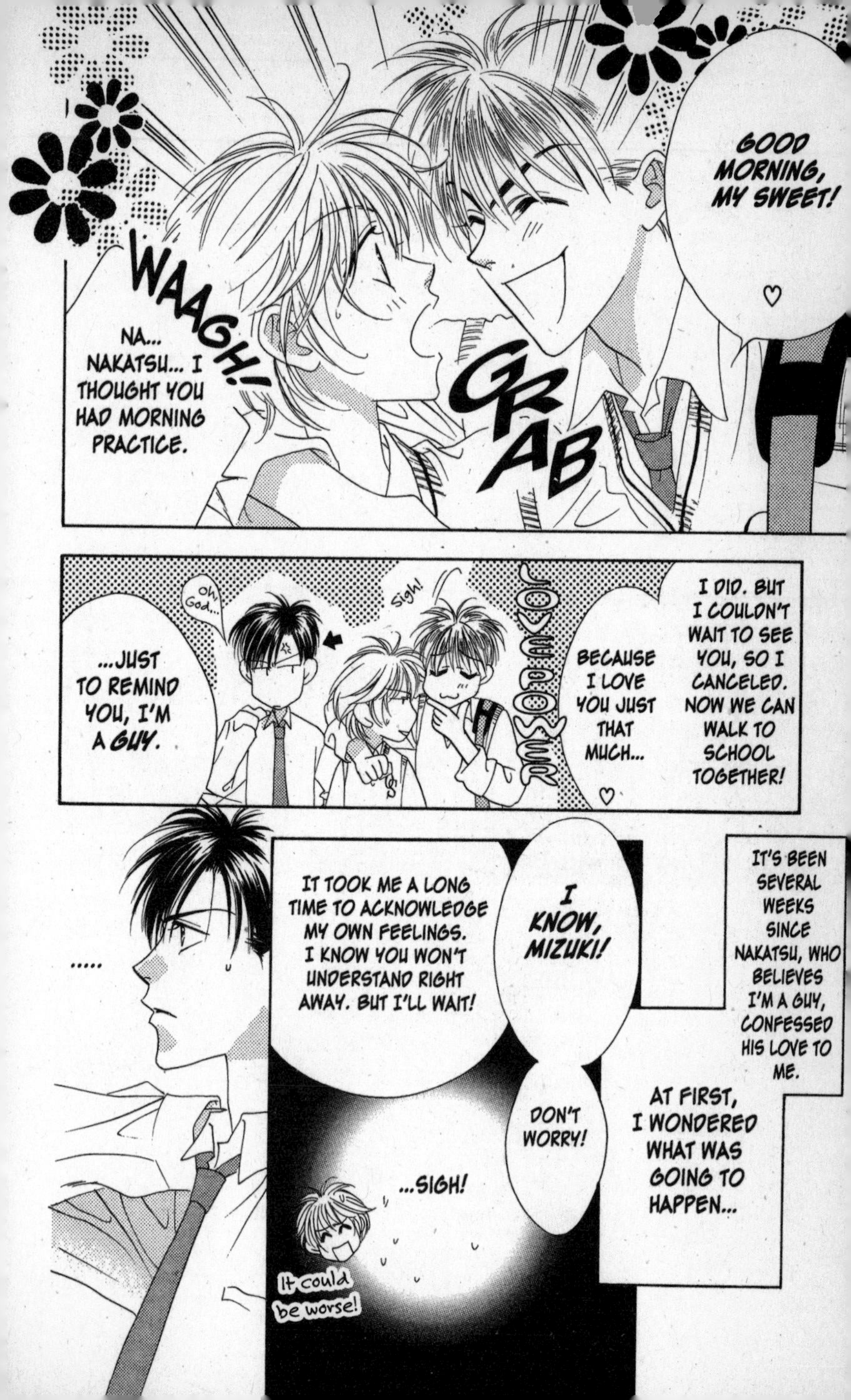
GOOD MORNING, MY SWEET! ♡
GRAB
WAAGH!
NA... NAKATSU... I THOUGHT YOU HAD MORNING PRACTICE.
I DID. BUT I COULDN'T WAIT TO SEE YOU, SO I CANCELED. NOW WE CAN WALK TO SCHOOL TOGETHER!
LOVE POWER
BECAUSE I LOVE YOU JUST THAT MUCH... ♡
Sigh!
Oh God...
...JUST TO REMIND YOU, I'M A GUY.
IT'S BEEN SEVERAL WEEKS SINCE NAKATSU, WHO BELIEVES I'M A GUY, CONFESSED HIS LOVE TO ME.
I KNOW, MIZUKI!
IT TOOK ME A LONG TIME TO ACKNOWLEDGE MY OWN FEELINGS. I KNOW YOU WON'T UNDERSTAND RIGHT AWAY. BUT I'LL WAIT!
.....
AT FIRST, I WONDERED WHAT WAS GOING TO HAPPEN...
DON'T WORRY!
...SIGH!
It could be worse!

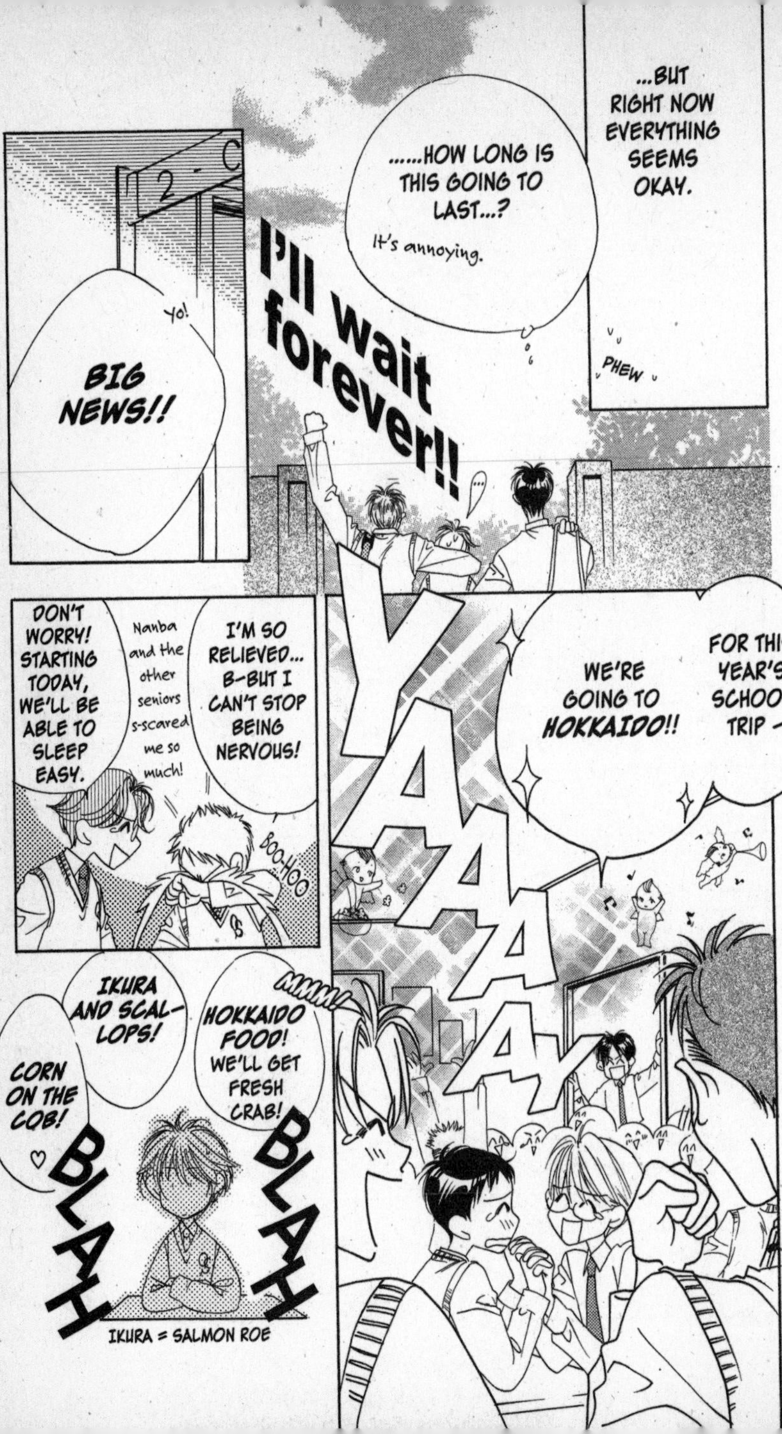
...BUT RIGHT NOW EVERYTHING SEEMS OKAY.
PHEW
......HOW LONG IS THIS GOING TO LAST...?
It's annoying.
I'll wait forever!!
Yo!
BIG NEWS!!
FOR THIS YEAR'S SCHOOL TRIP -
WE'RE GOING TO HOKKAIDO!!
YAAAAY
I'M SO RELIEVED... B-BUT I CAN'T STOP BEING NERVOUS!
Nanba and the other seniors s-scared me so much!
DON'T WORRY! STARTING TODAY, WE'LL BE ABLE TO SLEEP EASY.
BOO-HOO
MMM!
HOKKAIDO FOOD! WE'LL GET FRESH CRAB!
IKURA AND SCAL-LOPS!
CORN ON THE COB! ♡
BLAH
BLAH
IKURA = SALMON ROE

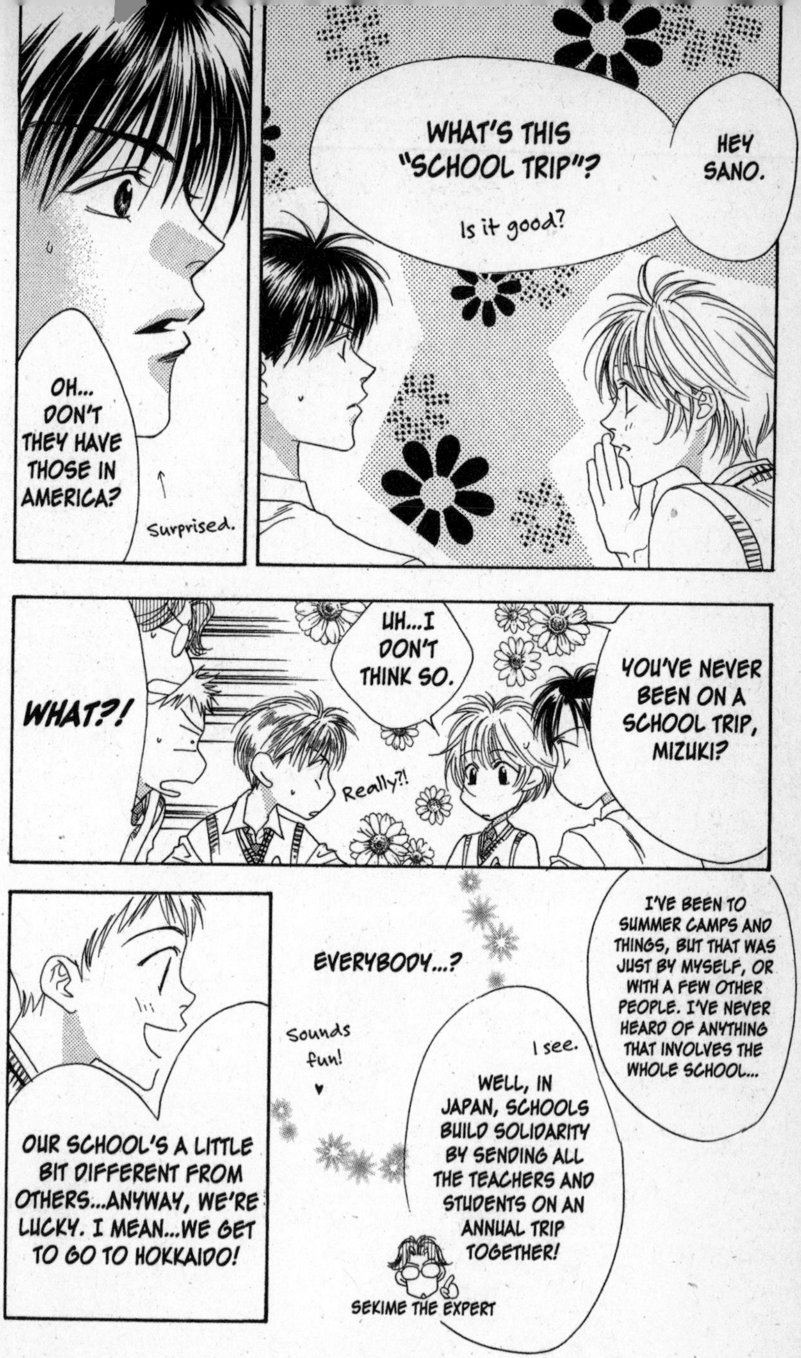
HEY SANO.
WHAT'S THIS "SCHOOL TRIP"?
Is it good?
OH... DON'T THEY HAVE THOSE IN AMERICA?
Surprised.
YOU'VE NEVER BEEN ON A SCHOOL TRIP, MIZUKI?
UH...I DON'T THINK SO.
Really?!
WHAT?!
I'VE BEEN TO SUMMER CAMPS AND THINGS, BUT THAT WAS JUST BY MYSELF, OR WITH A FEW OTHER PEOPLE. I'VE NEVER HEARD OF ANYTHING THAT INVOLVES THE WHOLE SCHOOL...
EVERYBODY...?
I see.
WELL, IN JAPAN, SCHOOLS BUILD SOLIDARITY BY SENDING ALL THE TEACHERS AND STUDENTS ON AN ANNUAL TRIP TOGETHER!
SEKIME THE EXPERT
Sounds fun! ♥
OUR SCHOOL'S A LITTLE BIT DIFFERENT FROM OTHERS...ANYWAY, WE'RE LUCKY. I MEAN...WE GET TO GO TO HOKKAIDO!

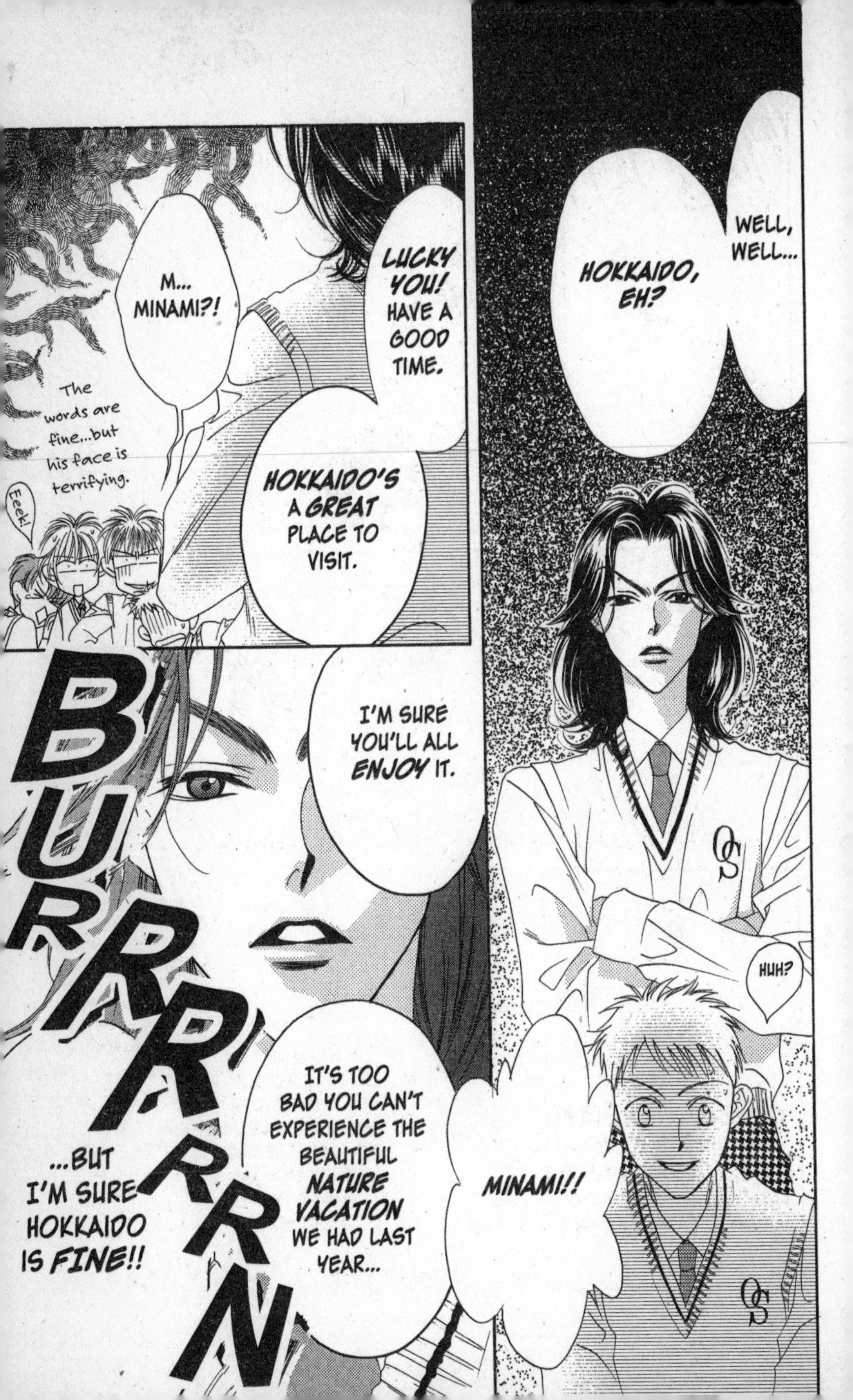
WELL, WELL...
HOKKAIDO, EH?
HUH?
MINAMI!!
LUCKY YOU! HAVE A GOOD TIME.
HOKKAIDO'S A GREAT PLACE TO VISIT.
M... MINAMI?!
The words are fine...but his face is terrifying.
Eeek!
I'M SURE YOU'LL ALL ENJOY IT.
IT'S TOO BAD YOU CAN'T EXPERIENCE THE BEAUTIFUL NATURE VACATION WE HAD LAST YEAR...
...BUT I'M SURE HOKKAIDO IS FINE!!
BURRRRN

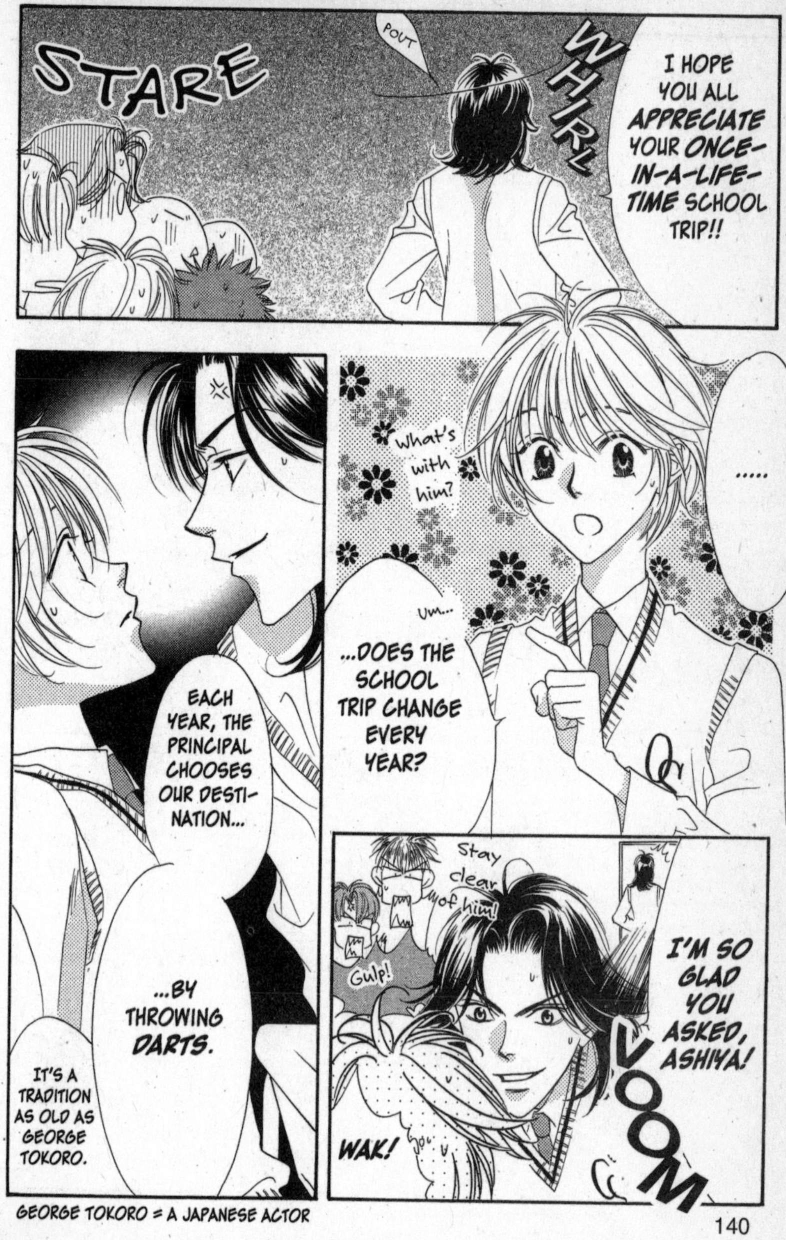
I HOPE YOU ALL APPRECIATE YOUR ONCE-IN-A-LIFE-TIME SCHOOL TRIP!!
WHIRL
POUT
STARE
.....
what's with him?
Um...
...DOES THE SCHOOL TRIP CHANGE EVERY YEAR?
I'M SO GLAD YOU ASKED, ASHIYA!
VOOM
Stay clear of him!
Gulp!
WAK!
EACH YEAR, THE PRINCIPAL CHOOSES OUR DESTI-NATION...
...BY THROWING DARTS.
IT'S A TRADITION AS OLD AS GEORGE TOKORO.

GEORGE TOKORO = A JAPANESE ACTOR

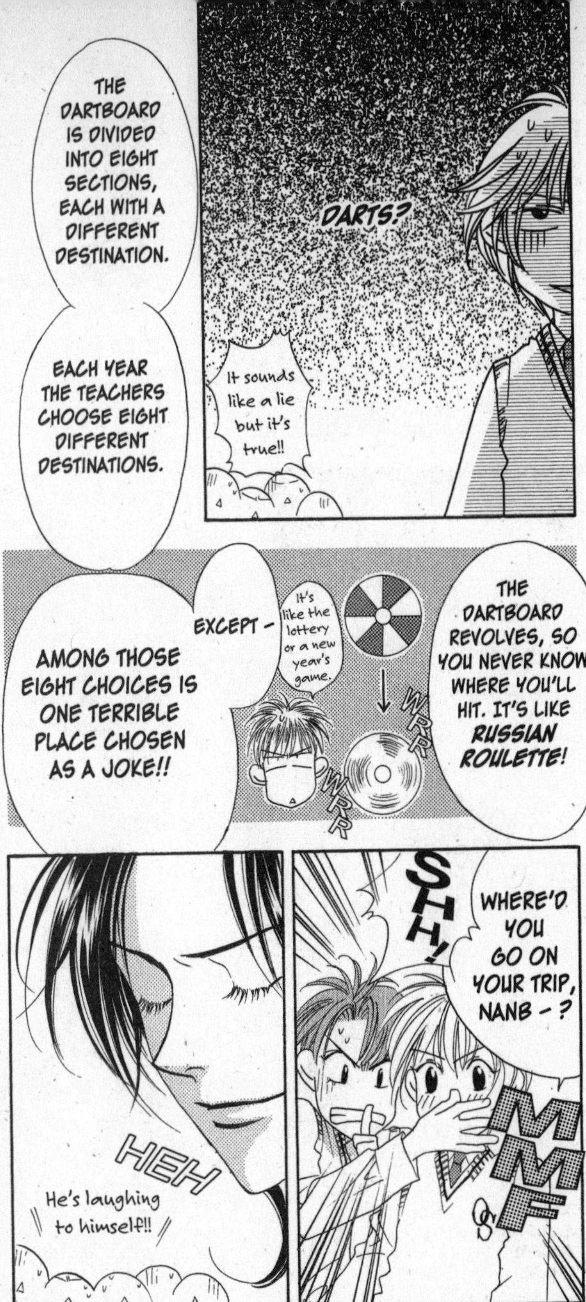
DARTS?
It sounds like a lie but it's true!!
THE DARTBOARD IS DIVIDED INTO EIGHT SECTIONS, EACH WITH A DIFFERENT DESTINATION.
EACH YEAR THE TEACHERS CHOOSE EIGHT DIFFERENT DESTINATIONS.
THE DARTBOARD REVOLVES, SO YOU NEVER KNOW WHERE YOU'LL HIT. IT'S LIKE RUSSIAN ROULETTE!
WRR
WRR
It's like the lottery or a new year's game.
EXCEPT -
AMONG THOSE EIGHT CHOICES IS ONE TERRIBLE PLACE CHOSEN AS A JOKE!!
WHERE'D YOU GO ON YOUR TRIP, NANB - ?
SHH!
MMF
HEH
He's laughing to himself!!

Whispered Secrets

FIGURE SKATING AGAIN

ALONG WITH CANDELORO, I'M ALSO WATCHING RUSSIA'S ILIA KULIK!! ILIA'S REALLY CUTE. IF CANDELORO IS A "GIGOLO ON ICE," THEN HE'S A "PRINCE ON ICE." (THAT'S WHAT NHK TV CALLS THEM.) THE WAY HE SKATES IS REALLY ARISTO-CRATIC!! YEAH!! WHEN HE STAYS IN THE RINK TOO LONG, HIS CHEEKS GET RED AND IT'S SO CUTE! ♥ HE LOOKS REALLY GOOD IN FLOWING, FRILLY COS-TUMES. AND HIS SKATING TECHNIQUE IS PERFECT!! HE LOOKS SO COOL WHEN HE DOES THOSE GRACEFUL MOVES WITH SO LITTLE EFFORT!! I LOVE HIM!!

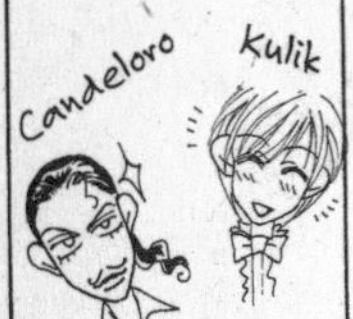
Candeloro
Kulik

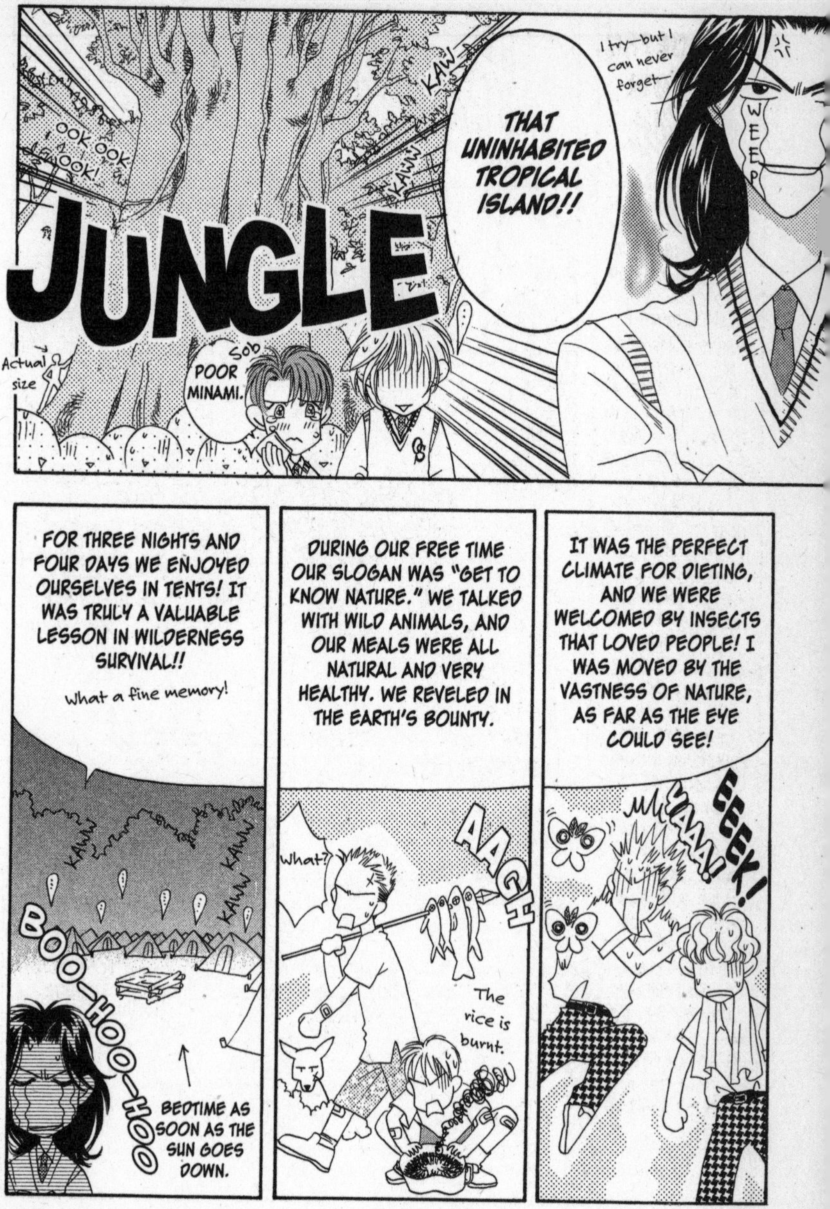
I try—but I can never forget—
WEEP
THAT UNINHABITED TROPICAL ISLAND!!
KAW
KAWW
OOK OOK OOK!
JUNGLE
Sob
POOR MINAMI.
Actual size
IT WAS THE PERFECT CLIMATE FOR DIETING, AND WE WERE WELCOMED BY INSECTS THAT LOVED PEOPLE! I WAS MOVED BY THE VASTNESS OF NATURE, AS FAR AS THE EYE COULD SEE!
EEEEK!
YAAAA!
DURING OUR FREE TIME OUR SLOGAN WAS "GET TO KNOW NATURE." WE TALKED WITH WILD ANIMALS, AND OUR MEALS WERE ALL NATURAL AND VERY HEALTHY. WE REVELED IN THE EARTH'S BOUNTY.
AAGH
What?
The rice is burnt.
FOR THREE NIGHTS AND FOUR DAYS WE ENJOYED OURSELVES IN TENTS! IT WAS TRULY A VALUABLE LESSON IN WILDERNESS SURVIVAL!!
What a fine memory!
KAWW
KAWW
BOO-HOO-HOO-HOO
BEDTIME AS SOON AS THE SUN GOES DOWN.

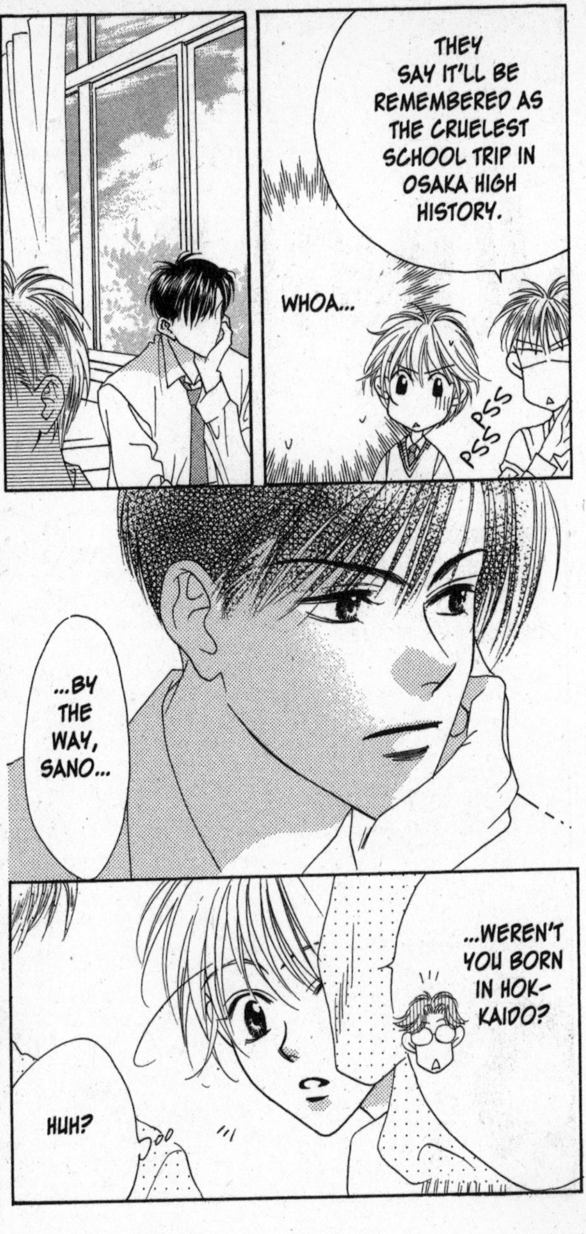
THEY SAY IT'LL BE REMEMBERED AS THE CRUELEST SCHOOL TRIP IN OSAKA HIGH HISTORY.
WHOA...
PSS PSS
...BY THE WAY, SANO...
...WEREN'T YOU BORN IN HOK-KAIDO?
HUH?

Whispered Secrets

ARRIVING IN TAIWAN

HANA-KIMI JUST CAME OUT IN TAIWAN! ✿ IN TAIWAN, THE TITLE OF "HANA-KIMI" IS "TO TO AI JA NI." APPARENTLY IT MEANS SOMETHING LIKE "I LOVE YOU FROM THE BOTTOM OF MY HEART" (I'M NOT REALLY SURE). IT FEELS DIFFERENT AND NEW TO SEE "HANA-KIMI" IN ANOTHER LANGUAGE!! IT'S WRITTEN IN KANJI, SO I CAN SORT OF GUESS THE MEANING, WHICH IS FUN. ✿ WHAT I REALLY NOTICED WAS THE SOUND EFFECTS. SOUND EFFECTS ARE DIFFERENT IN EVERY LANGUAGE. IN TAIWAN, "GOSO" (THE SOUND OF RUSTLING) IS "MO SA KU" AND "SHIIN" (THE SOUND OF SILENCE) IS "SEI." "PORO PORO," THE SOUND OF TEARS, IS "RIU RUI RIU RUI." APPARENTLY, THE KANJI THEY USE FOR THE SOUND EFFECTS HAVE SOME INHERENT MEANING.

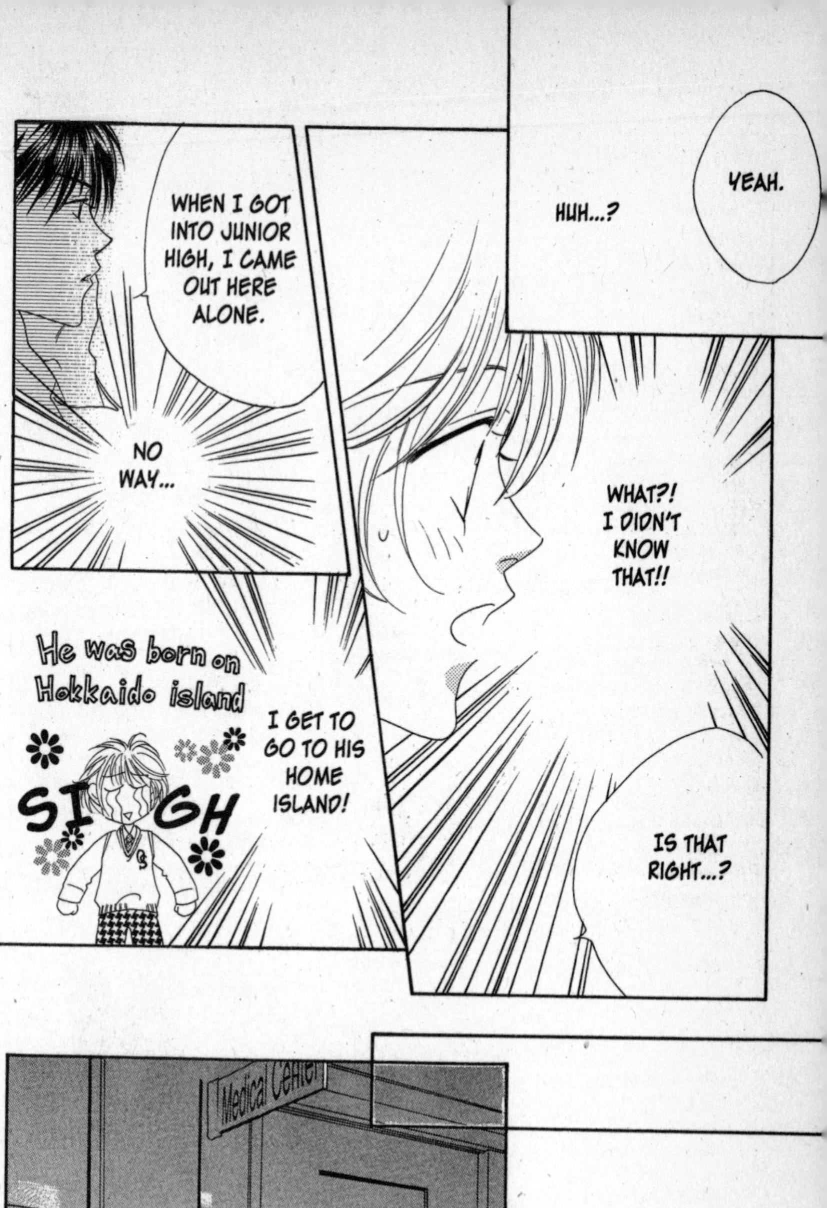
YEAH.
HUH...?
WHAT?! I DIDN'T KNOW THAT!!
IS THAT RIGHT...?
WHEN I GOT INTO JUNIOR HIGH, I CAME OUT HERE ALONE.
NO WAY...
He was born on Hokkaido island
SIGH
I GET TO GO TO HIS HOME ISLAND!
Medical Center

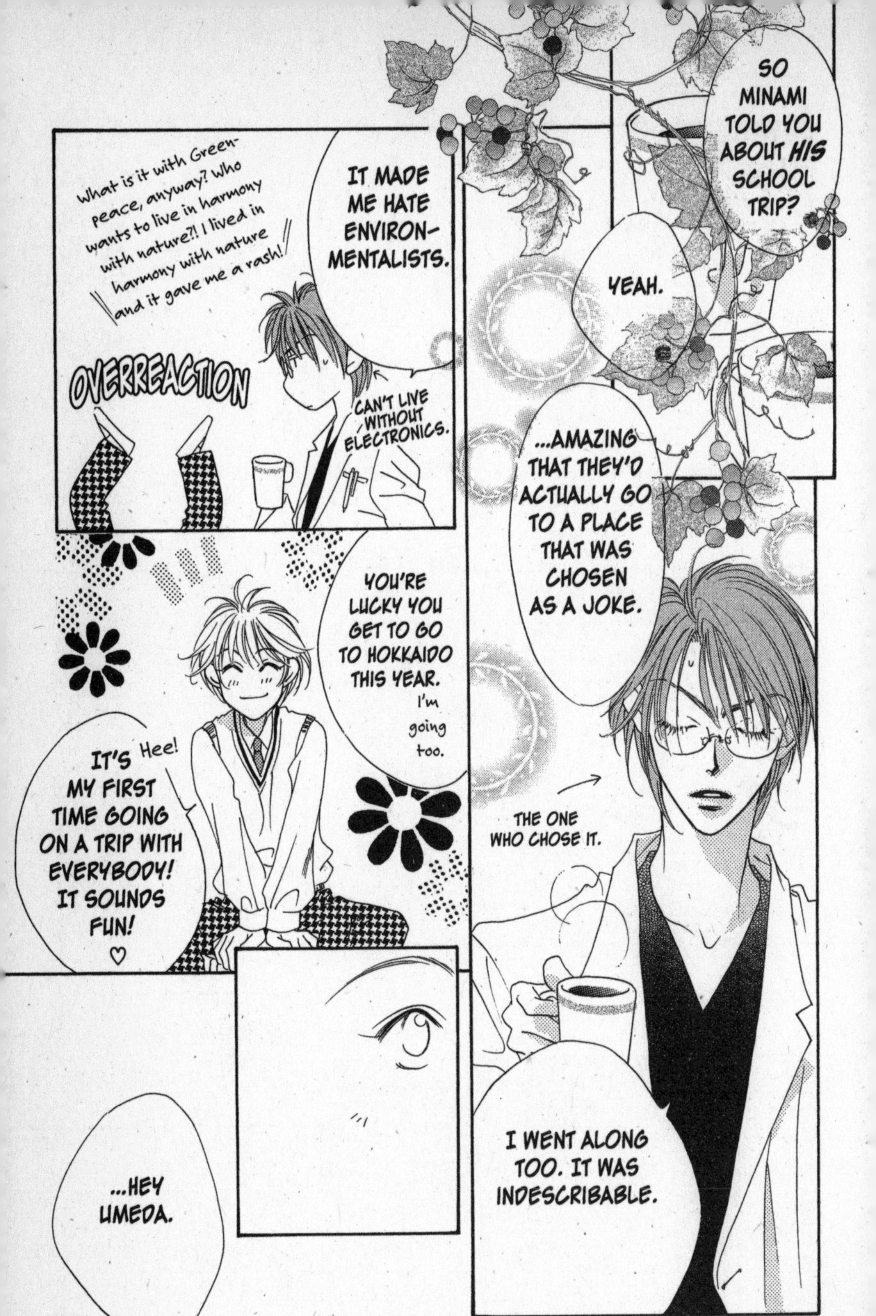
SO MINAMI TOLD YOU ABOUT HIS SCHOOL TRIP?
YEAH.
...AMAZING THAT THEY'D ACTUALLY GO TO A PLACE THAT WAS CHOSEN AS A JOKE.
THE ONE WHO CHOSE IT.
I WENT ALONG TOO. IT WAS INDESCRIBABLE.
IT MADE ME HATE ENVIRONMENTALISTS.
What is it with Greenpeace, anyway? Who wants to live in harmony with nature?! I lived in harmony with nature and it gave me a rash!
OVERREACTION
CAN'T LIVE WITHOUT ELECTRONICS.
YOU'RE LUCKY YOU GET TO GO TO HOKKAIDO THIS YEAR.
I'm going too.
IT'S MY FIRST TIME GOING ON A TRIP WITH EVERYBODY! IT SOUNDS FUN! ♡
Hee!
...HEY UMEDA.

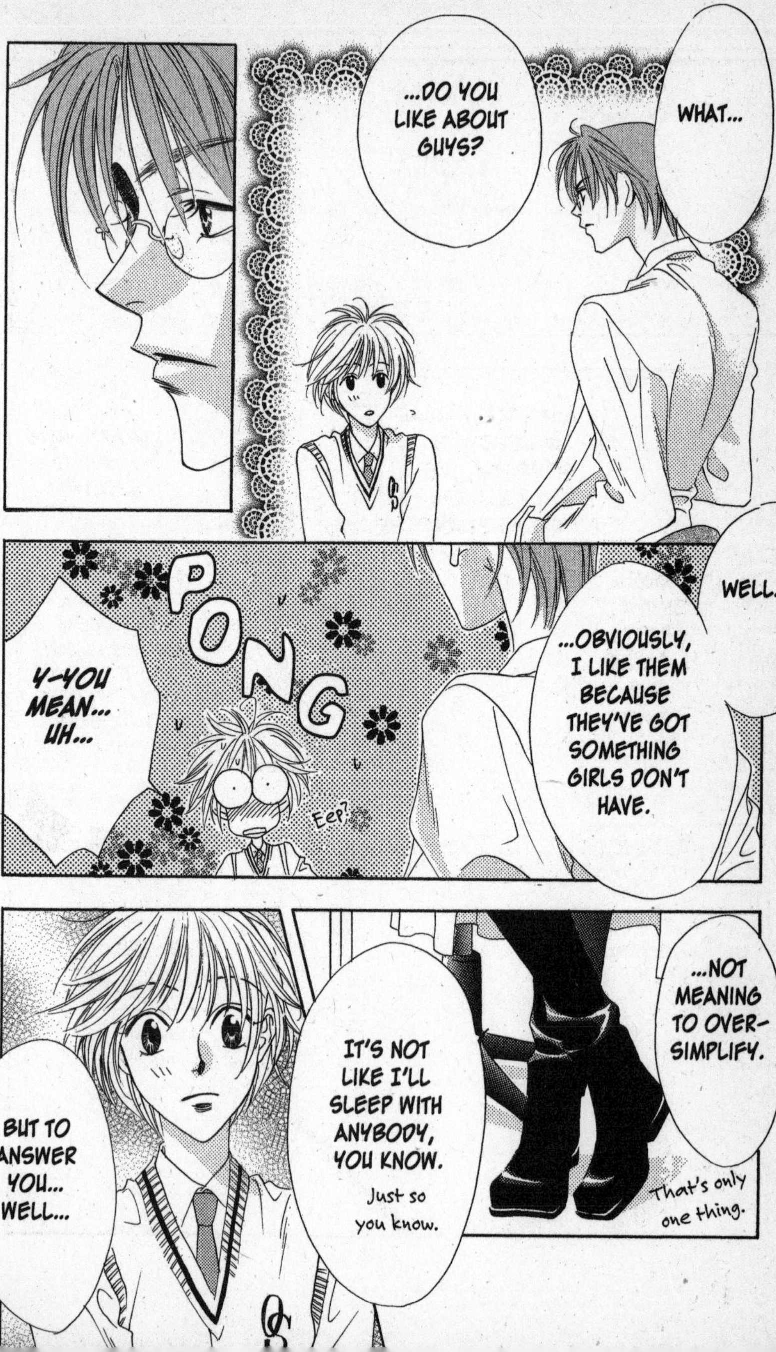
WHAT...
...DO YOU LIKE ABOUT GUYS?
WELL...
...OBVIOUSLY, I LIKE THEM BECAUSE THEY'VE GOT SOMETHING GIRLS DON'T HAVE.
PONG
Eep?
Y-YOU MEAN... UH...
...NOT MEANING TO OVER-SIMPLIFY.
That's only one thing.
IT'S NOT LIKE I'LL SLEEP WITH ANYBODY, YOU KNOW.
Just so you know.
BUT TO ANSWER YOU... WELL...

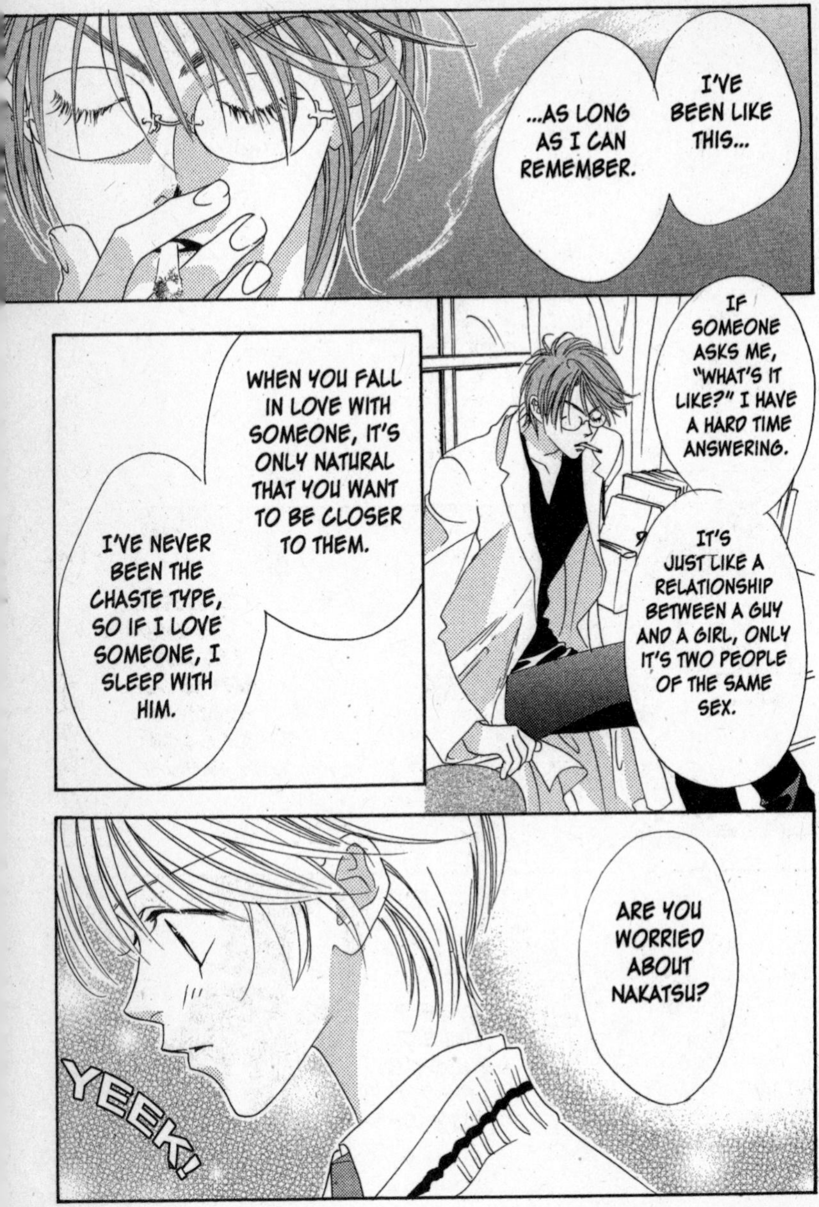
I'VE BEEN LIKE THIS...
...AS LONG AS I CAN REMEMBER.
IF SOMEONE ASKS ME, "WHAT'S IT LIKE?" I HAVE A HARD TIME ANSWERING.
IT'S JUST LIKE A RELATIONSHIP BETWEEN A GUY AND A GIRL, ONLY IT'S TWO PEOPLE OF THE SAME SEX.
WHEN YOU FALL IN LOVE WITH SOMEONE, IT'S ONLY NATURAL THAT YOU WANT TO BE CLOSER TO THEM.
I'VE NEVER BEEN THE CHASTE TYPE, SO IF I LOVE SOMEONE, I SLEEP WITH HIM.
ARE YOU WORRIED ABOUT NAKATSU?
YEEK!

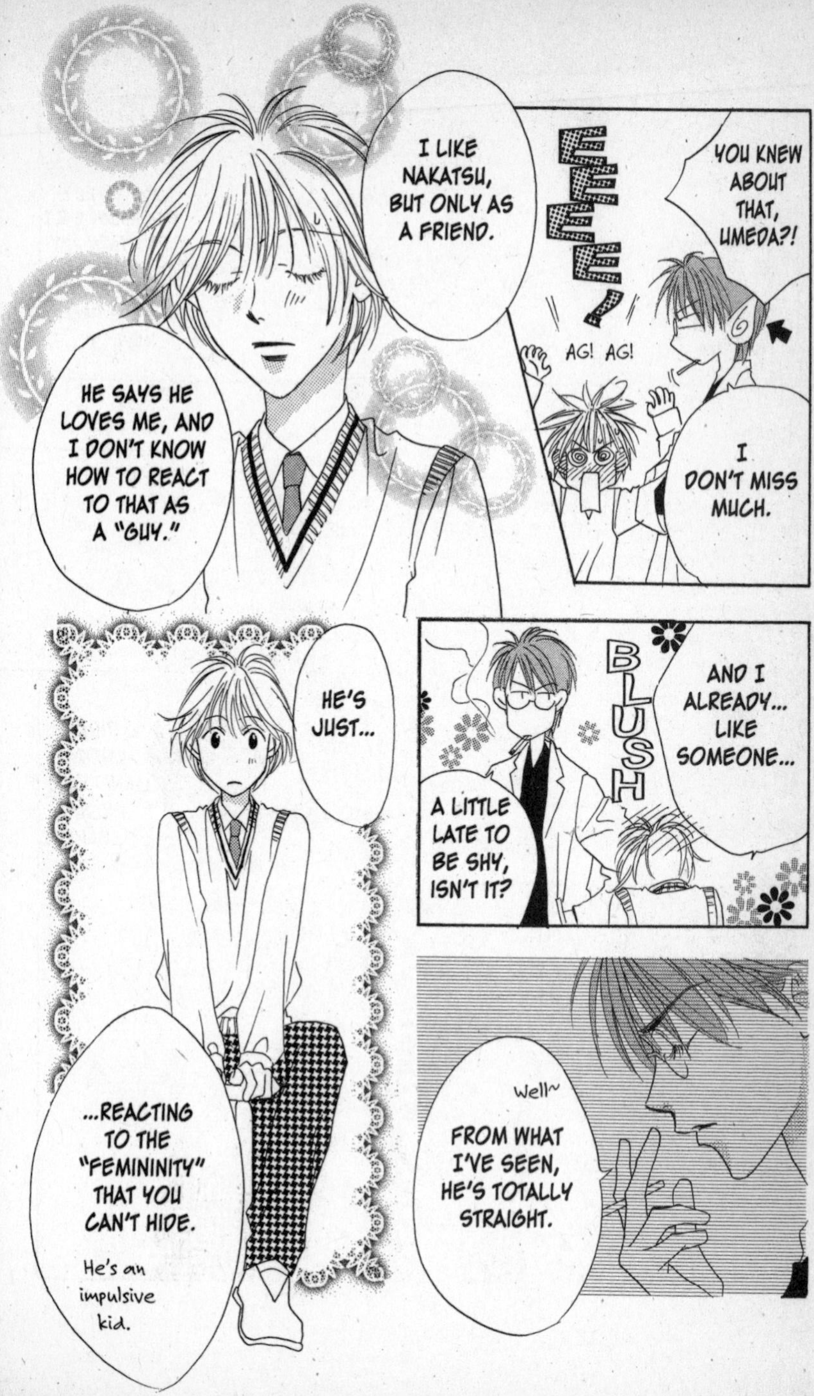
I LIKE NAKATSU, BUT ONLY AS A FRIEND.
HE SAYS HE LOVES ME, AND I DON'T KNOW HOW TO REACT TO THAT AS A "GUY."
EEEE?!
YOU KNEW ABOUT THAT, UMEDA?!
AG! AG!
I DON'T MISS MUCH.
AND I ALREADY... LIKE SOMEONE...
BLUSH
A LITTLE LATE TO BE SHY, ISN'T IT?
Well~
FROM WHAT I'VE SEEN, HE'S TOTALLY STRAIGHT.
HE'S JUST...
...REACTING TO THE "FEMININITY" THAT YOU CAN'T HIDE.
He's an impulsive kid.

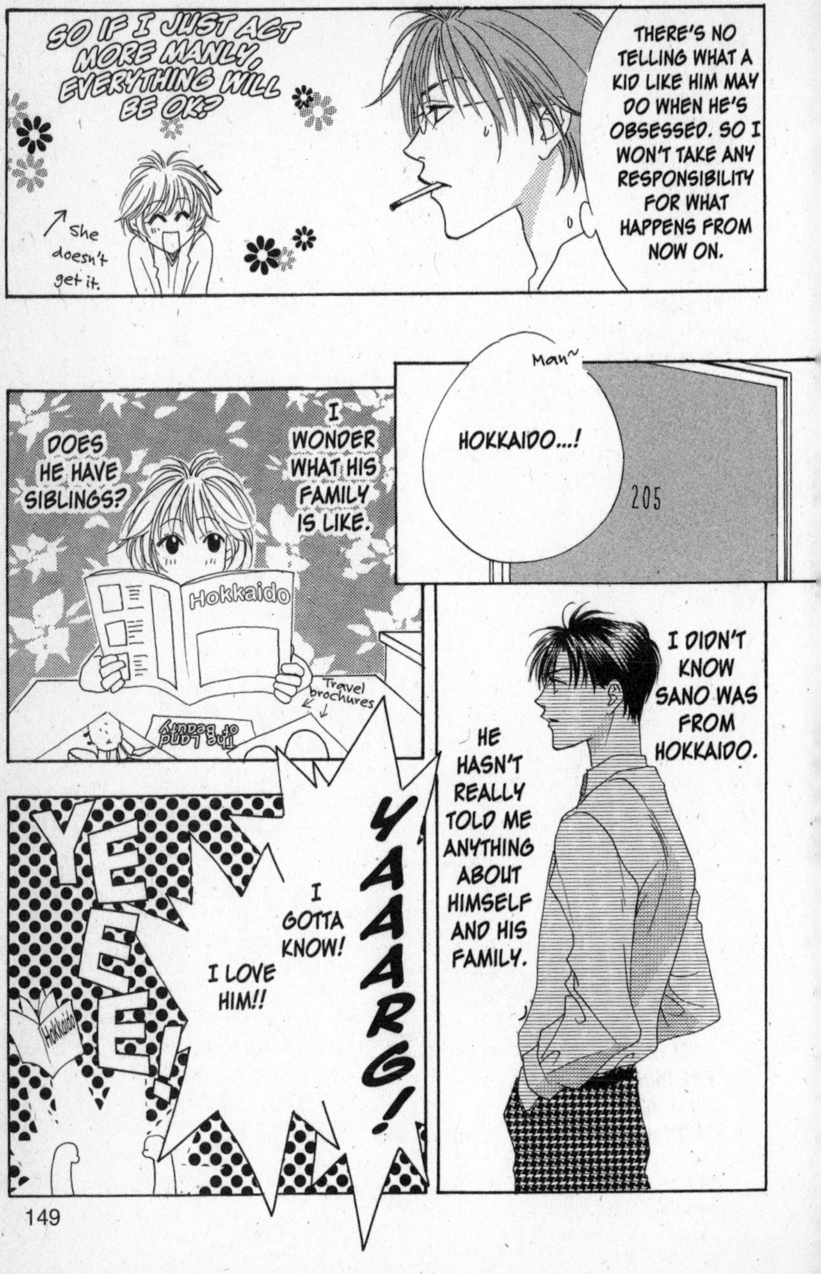
THERE'S NO TELLING WHAT A KID LIKE HIM MAY DO WHEN HE'S OBSESSED. SO I WON'T TAKE ANY RESPONSIBILITY FOR WHAT HAPPENS FROM NOW ON.
SO IF I JUST ACT MORE MANLY, EVERYTHING WILL BE OK?
She doesn't get it.
Man~
HOKKAIDO...!
205
I DIDN'T KNOW SANO WAS FROM HOKKAIDO.
HE HASN'T REALLY TOLD ME ANYTHING ABOUT HIMSELF AND HIS FAMILY.
I WONDER WHAT HIS FAMILY IS LIKE.
DOES HE HAVE SIBLINGS?
Hokkaido
Travel brochures
The Land of Beauty
YAAARG!
I GOTTA KNOW!
I LOVE HIM!!
YEEEE!
Hokkaido

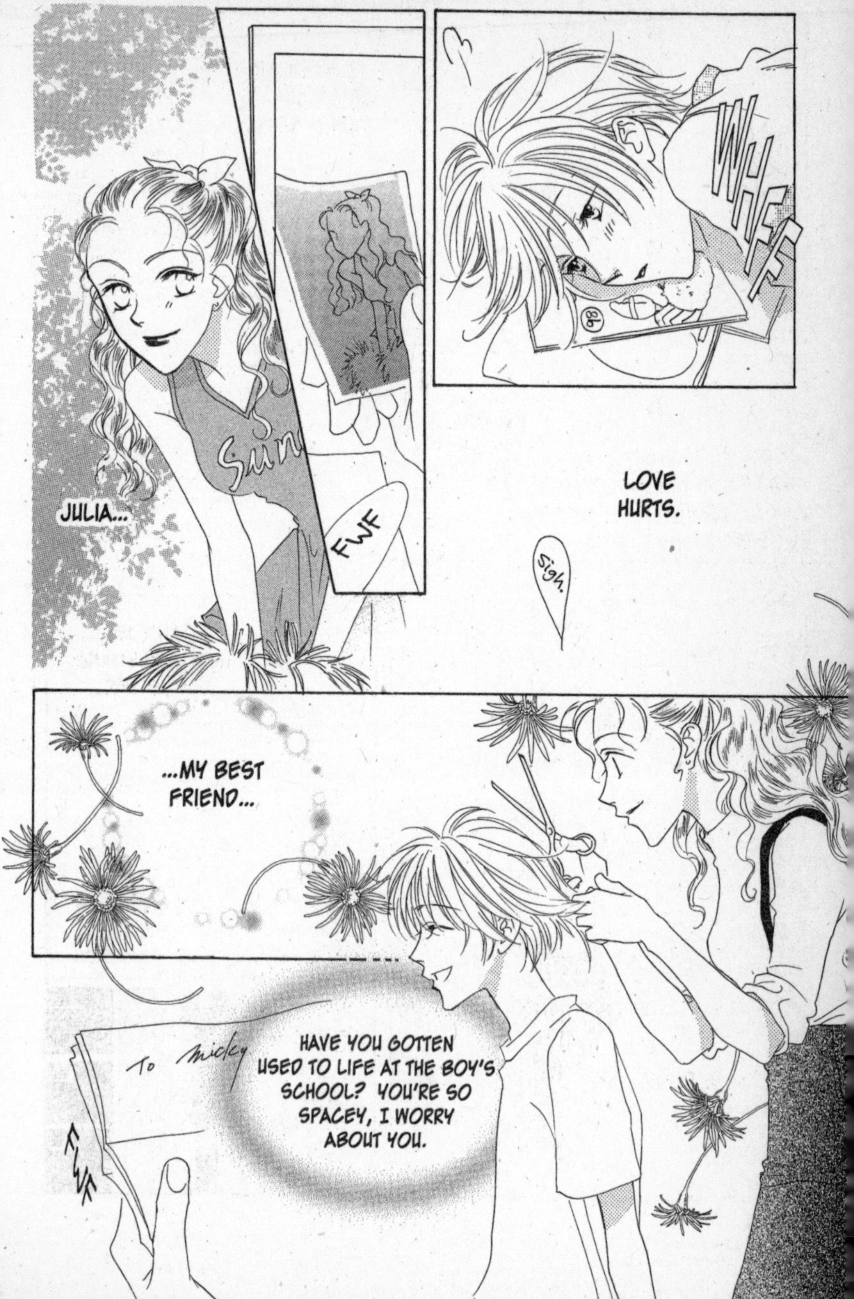
WHFF
LOVE HURTS.
Sigh.
FWF
JULIA...
...MY BEST FRIEND...
To Micky
HAVE YOU GOTTEN USED TO LIFE AT THE BOY'S SCHOOL? YOU'RE SO SPACEY, I WORRY ABOUT YOU.
FWF

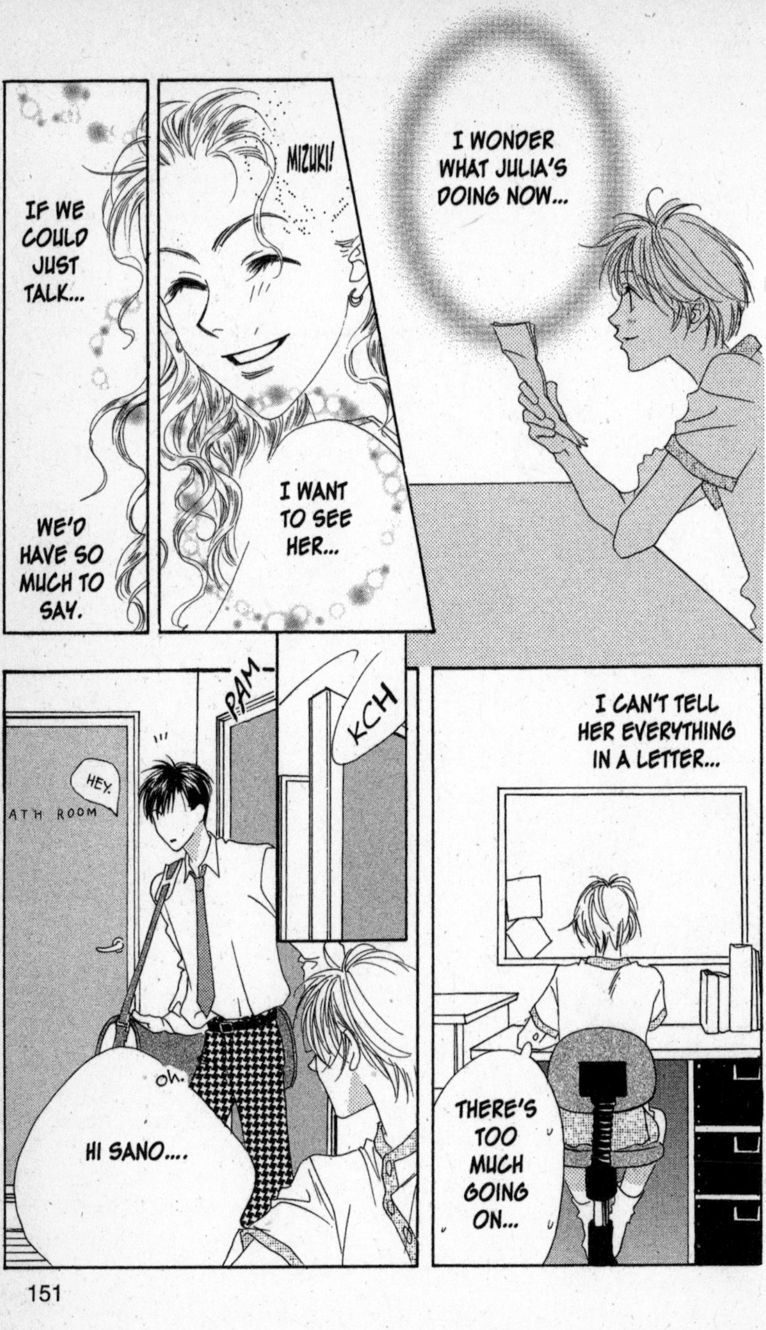
I WONDER WHAT JULIA'S DOING NOW...
MIZUKI!
I WANT TO SEE HER...
IF WE COULD JUST TALK...
WE'D HAVE SO MUCH TO SAY.
I CAN'T TELL HER EVERYTHING IN A LETTER...
THERE'S TOO MUCH GOING ON...
KCH
PAM
HEY.
ATH ROOM
oh.
HI SANO....

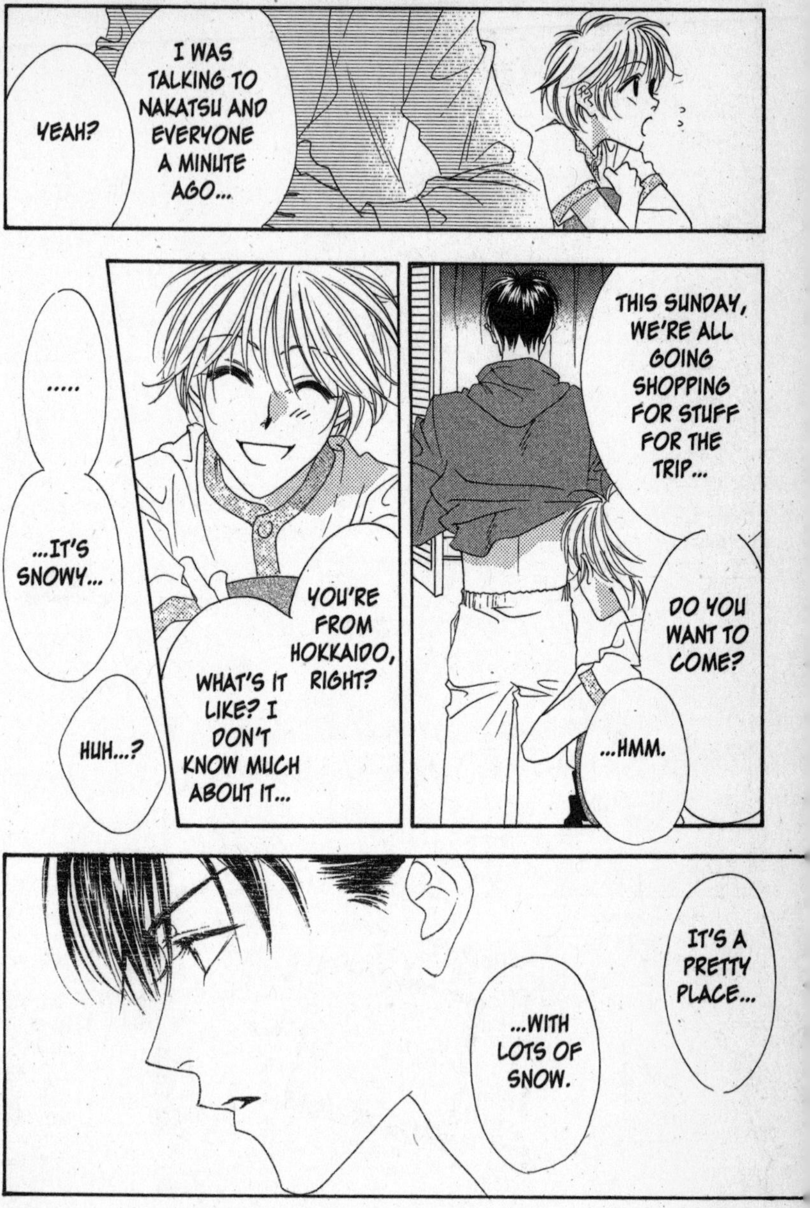
I WAS TALKING TO NAKATSU AND EVERYONE A MINUTE AGO...
YEAH?
THIS SUNDAY, WE'RE ALL GOING SHOPPING FOR STUFF FOR THE TRIP...
DO YOU WANT TO COME?
...HMM.
YOU'RE FROM HOKKAIDO, RIGHT?
WHAT'S IT LIKE? I DON'T KNOW MUCH ABOUT IT...
HUH...?
.....
...IT'S SNOWY...
IT'S A PRETTY PLACE...
...WITH LOTS OF SNOW.

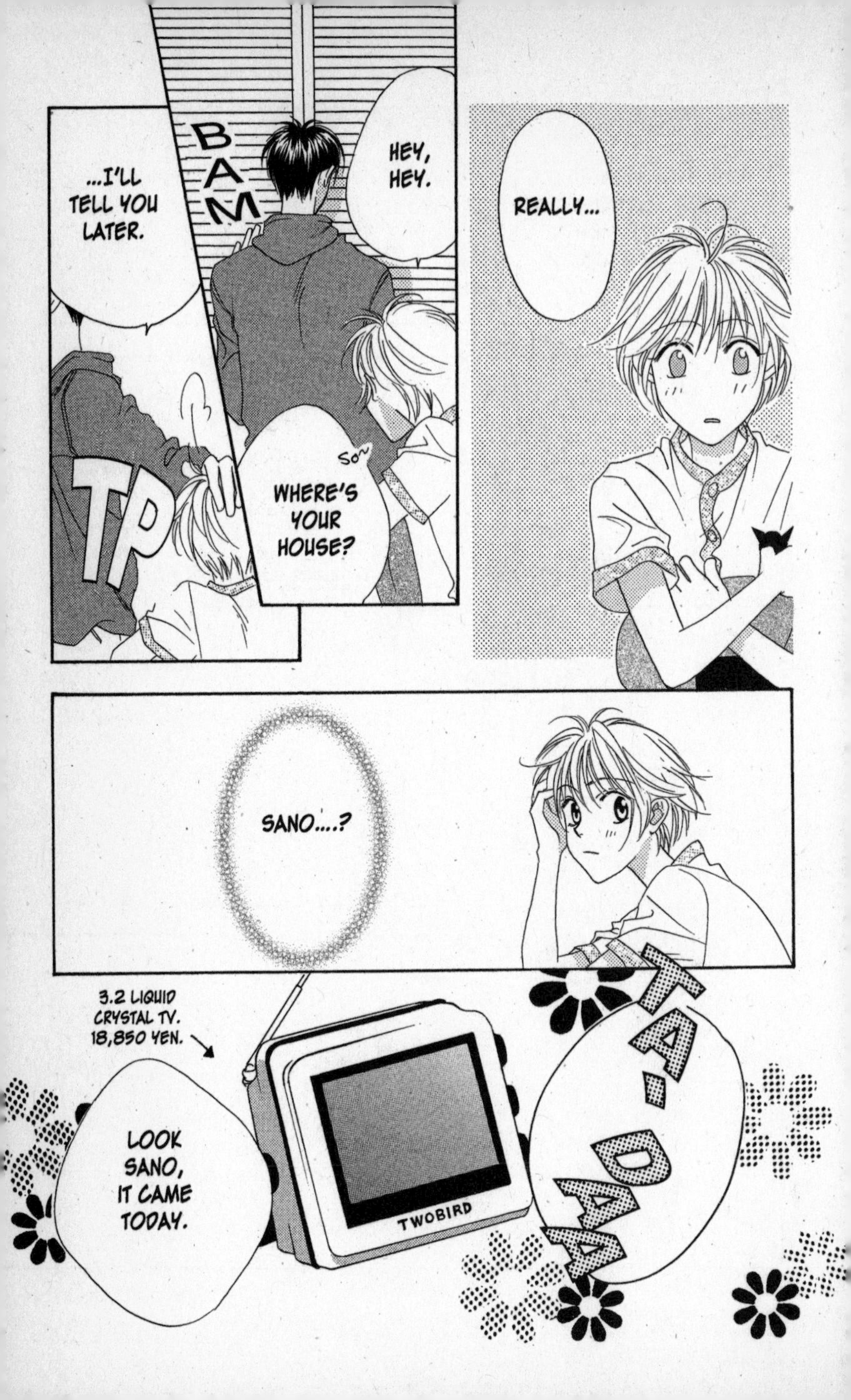
REALLY...
HEY, HEY.
BAM
SO~
WHERE'S YOUR HOUSE?
...I'LL TELL YOU LATER.
TP
SANO....?
TA-DA
3.2 LIQUID CRYSTAL TV. 18,850 YEN.
TWOBIRD
LOOK SANO, IT CAME TODAY.

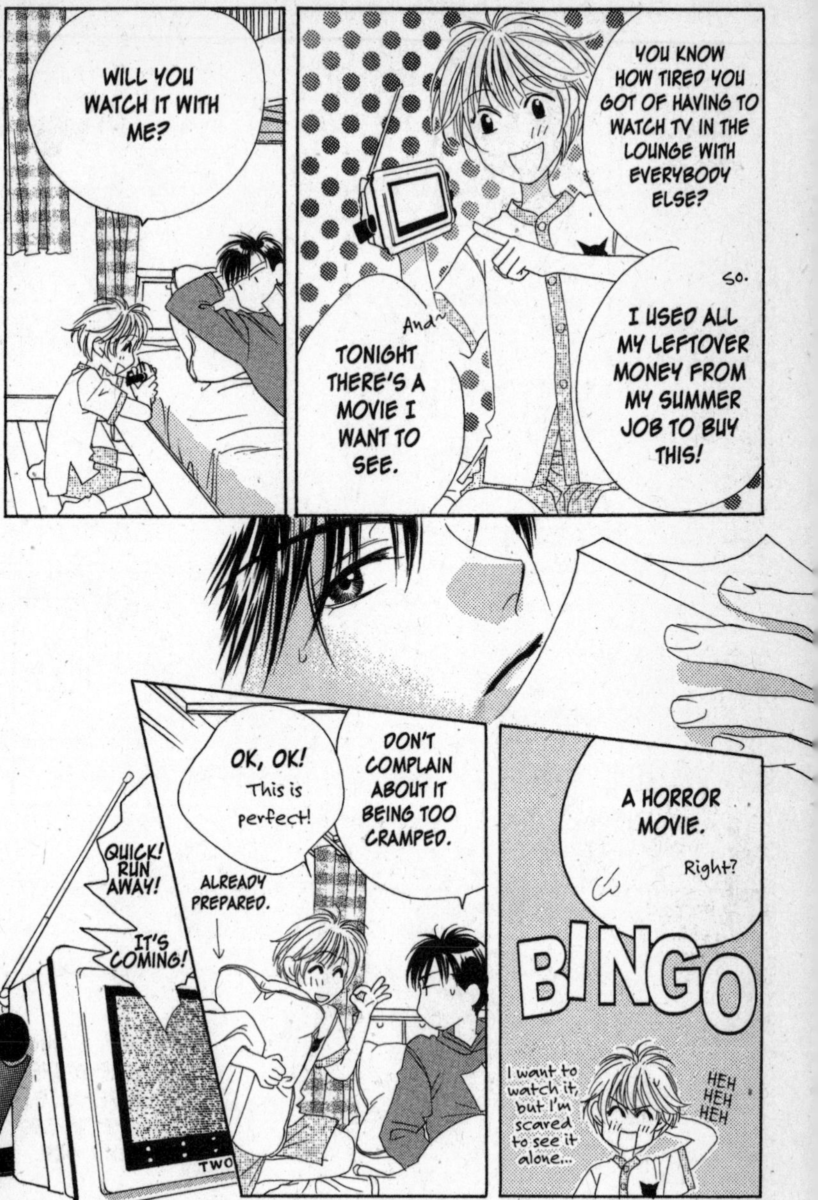
YOU KNOW HOW TIRED YOU GOT OF HAVING TO WATCH TV IN THE LOUNGE WITH EVERYBODY ELSE?
So.
I USED ALL MY LEFTOVER MONEY FROM MY SUMMER JOB TO BUY THIS!
And~
TONIGHT THERE'S A MOVIE I WANT TO SEE.
WILL YOU WATCH IT WITH ME?
A HORROR MOVIE.
Right?
BINGO
HEH HEH HEH
I want to watch it, but I'm scared to see it alone...
DON'T COMPLAIN ABOUT IT BEING TOO CRAMPED.
OK, OK!
This is perfect!
ALREADY PREPARED.
QUICK! RUN AWAY!
IT'S COMING!
TWO

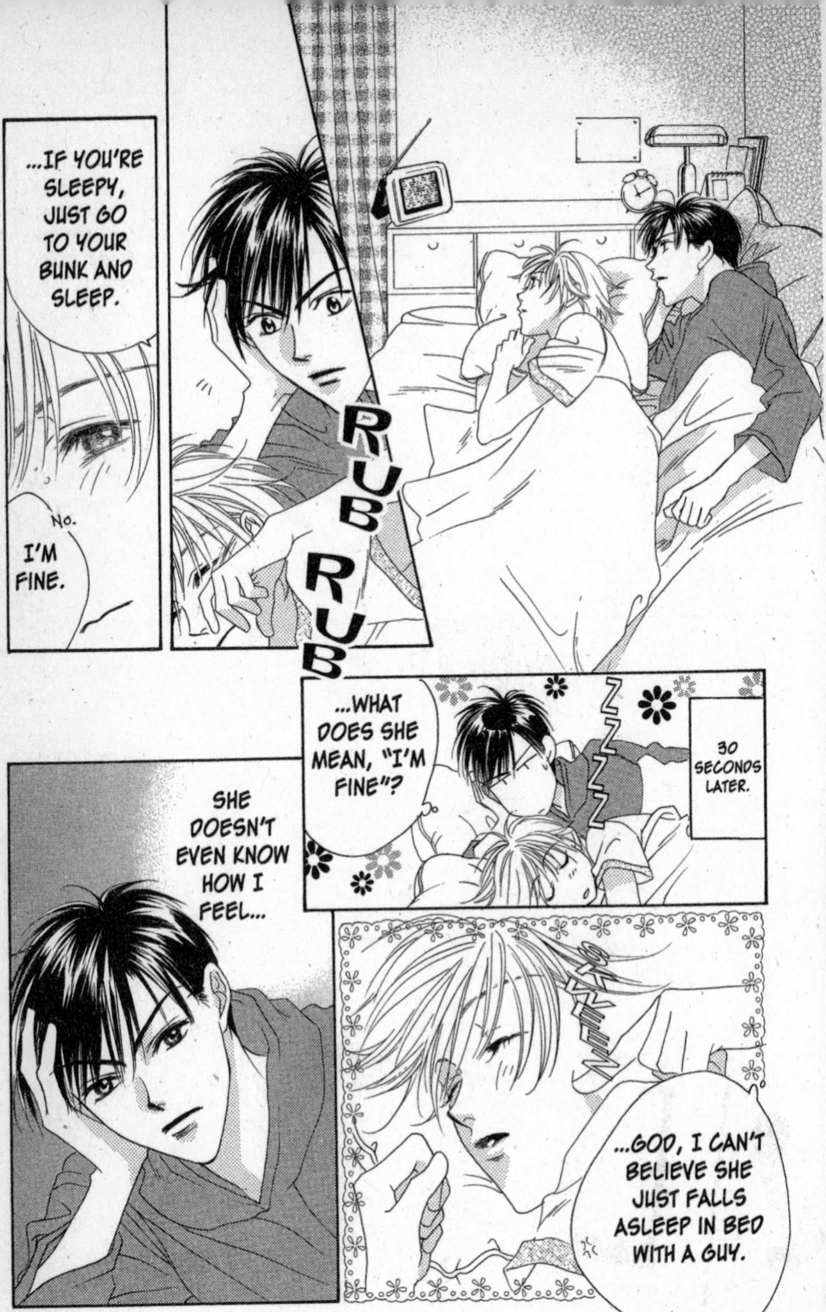
RUB RUB
...IF YOU'RE SLEEPY, JUST GO TO YOUR BUNK AND SLEEP.
No.
I'M FINE.
30 SECONDS LATER.
ZZZZ
...WHAT DOES SHE MEAN, "I'M FINE"?
...GOD, I CAN'T BELIEVE SHE JUST FALLS ASLEEP IN BED WITH A GUY.
SHE DOESN'T EVEN KNOW HOW I FEEL...

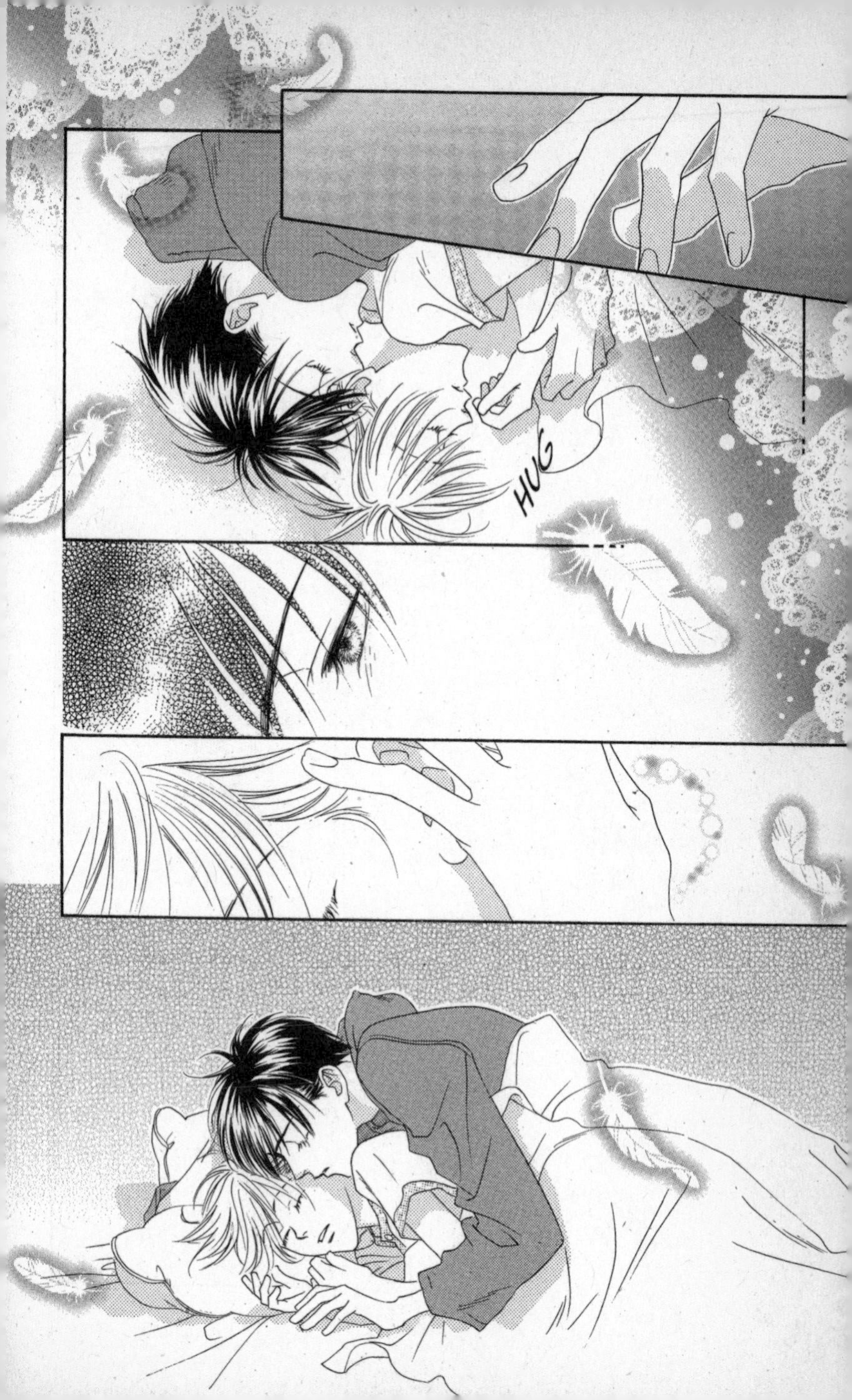
HUG

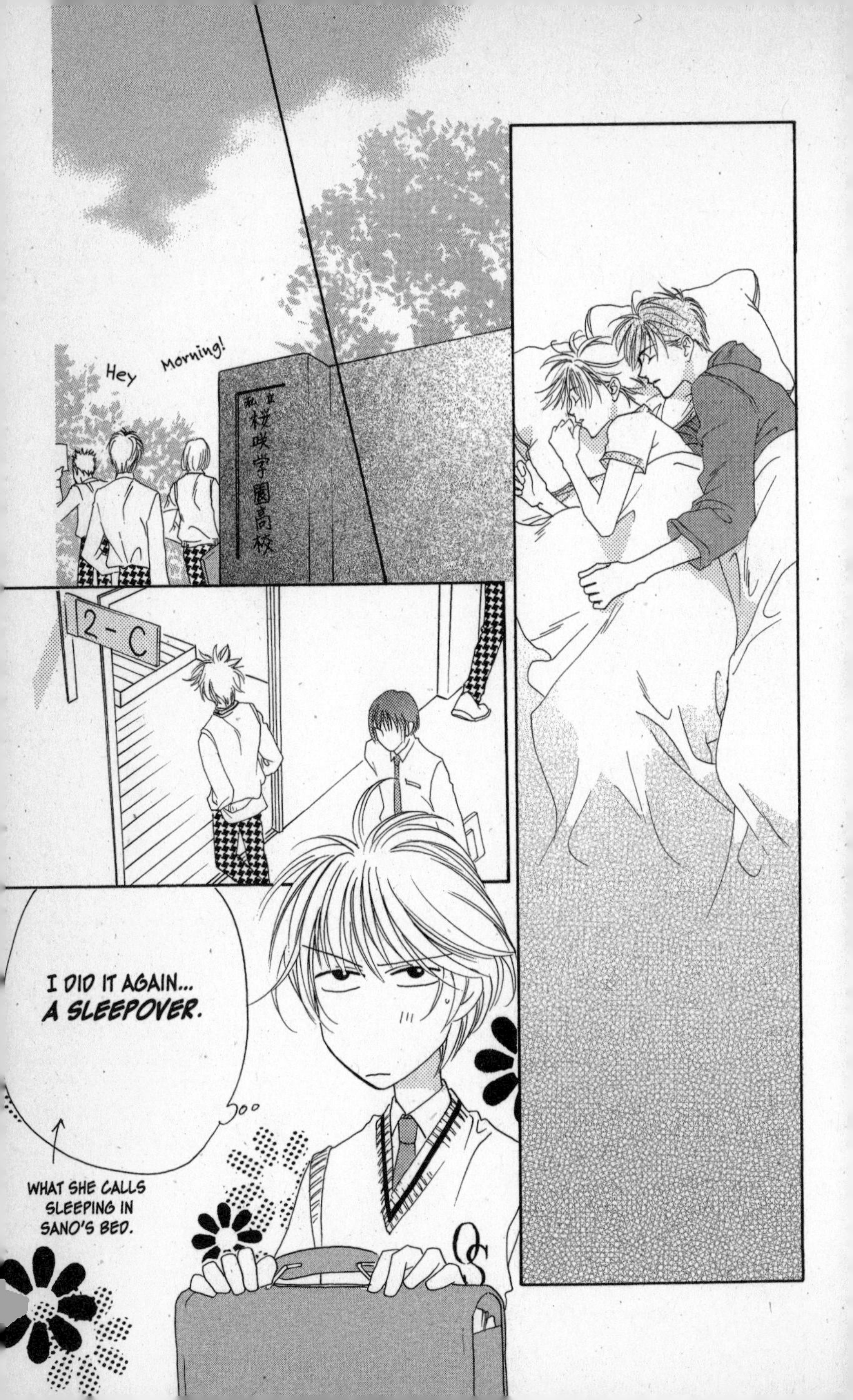

私立
桜咲学園高校
Hey
Morning!
2-C
I DID IT AGAIN... A SLEEPOVER.
SOO
WHAT SHE CALLS SLEEPING IN SANO'S BED.

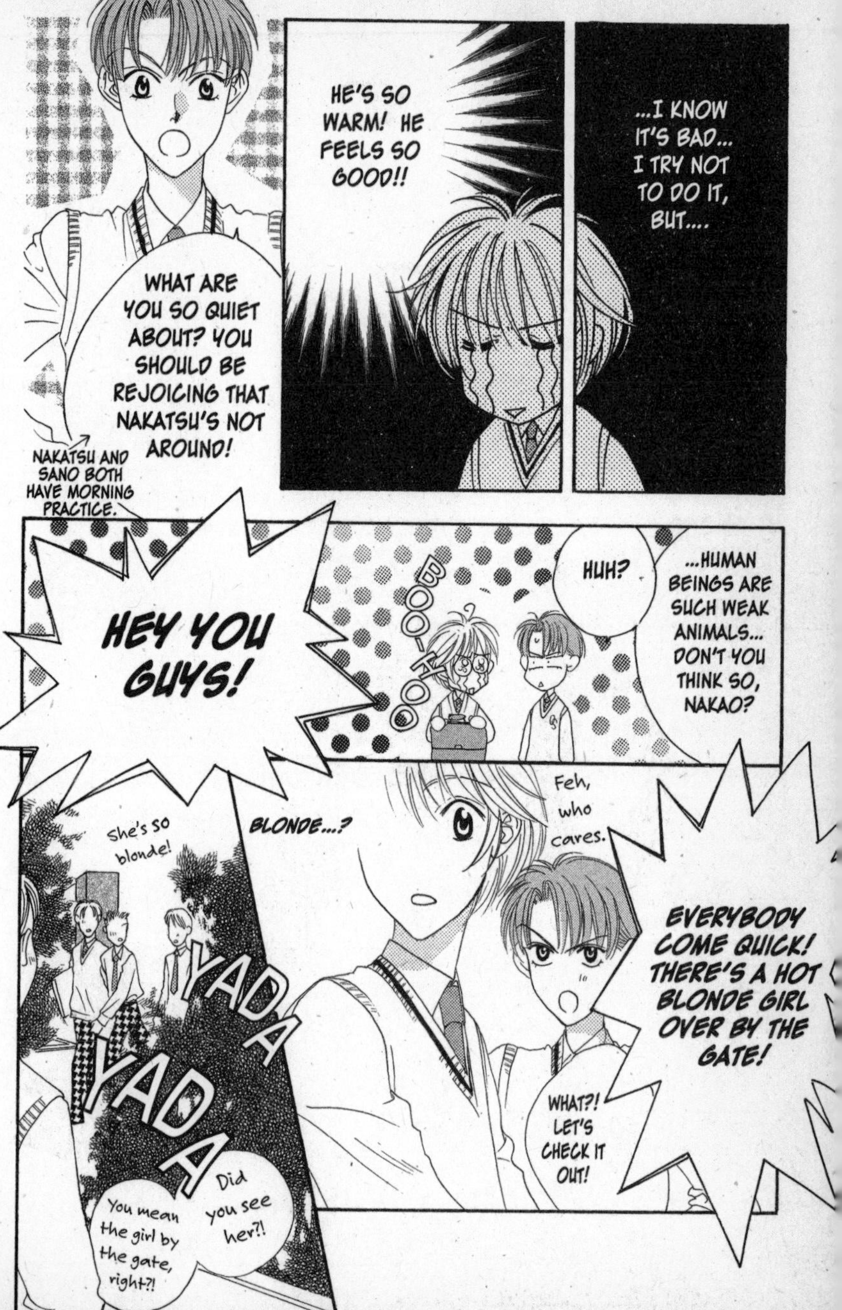
...I KNOW IT'S BAD... I TRY NOT TO DO IT, BUT....
HE'S SO WARM! HE FEELS SO GOOD!!
WHAT ARE YOU SO QUIET ABOUT? YOU SHOULD BE REJOICING THAT NAKATSU'S NOT AROUND!
NAKATSU AND SANO BOTH HAVE MORNING PRACTICE.
...HUMAN BEINGS ARE SUCH WEAK ANIMALS... DON'T YOU THINK SO, NAKAO?
HUH?
BOO-HOO
HEY YOU GUYS!
EVERYBODY COME QUICK! THERE'S A HOT BLONDE GIRL OVER BY THE GATE!
Feh, who cares.
WHAT?! LET'S CHECK IT OUT!
BLONDE...?
She's so blonde!
YADA YADA
Did you see her?!
You mean the girl by the gate, right?!

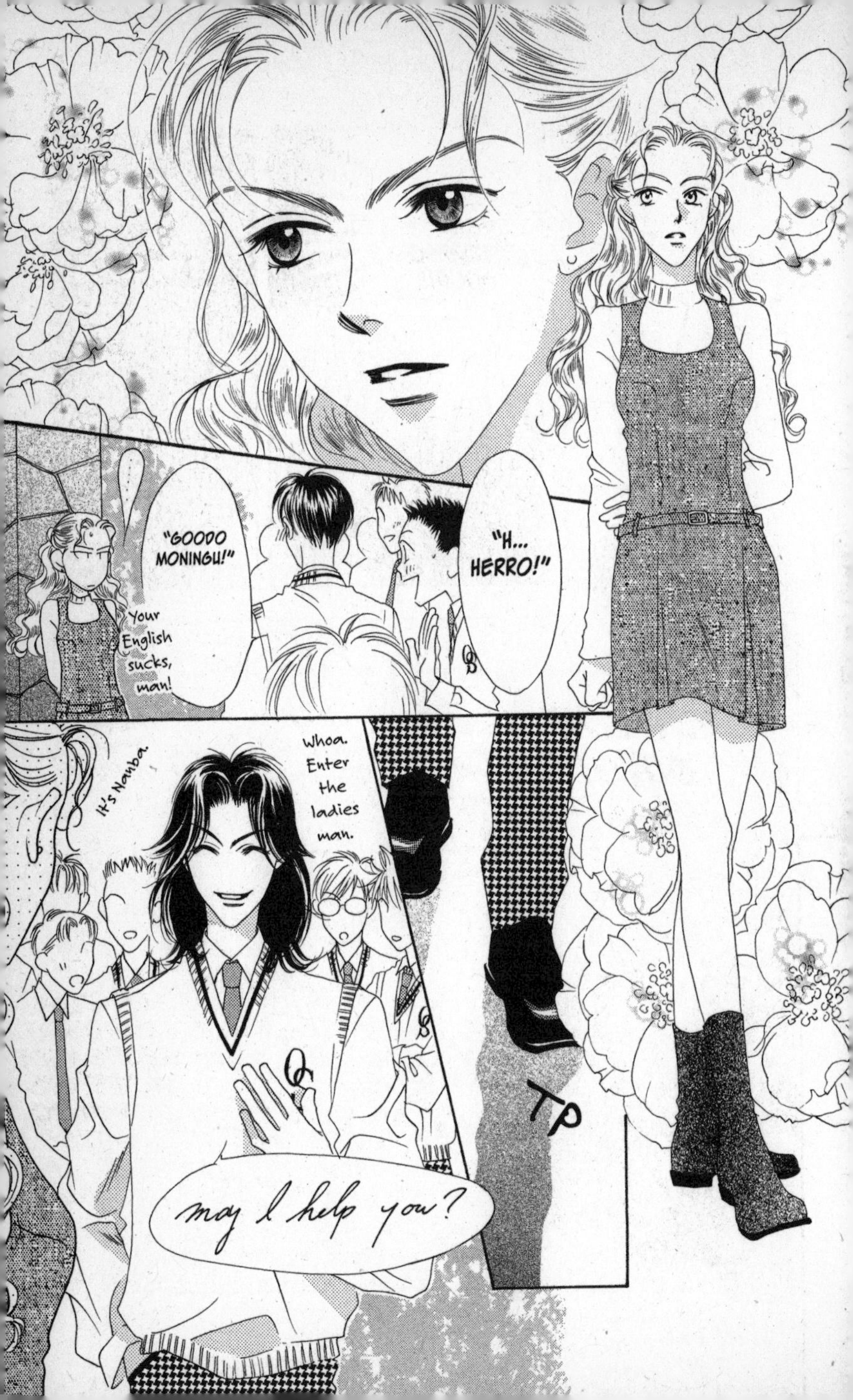
"H... HERRO!"
"GOODO MONINGU!"
Your English sucks, man!
TP
Whoa. Enter the ladies man.
It's Nanba.
may I help you?

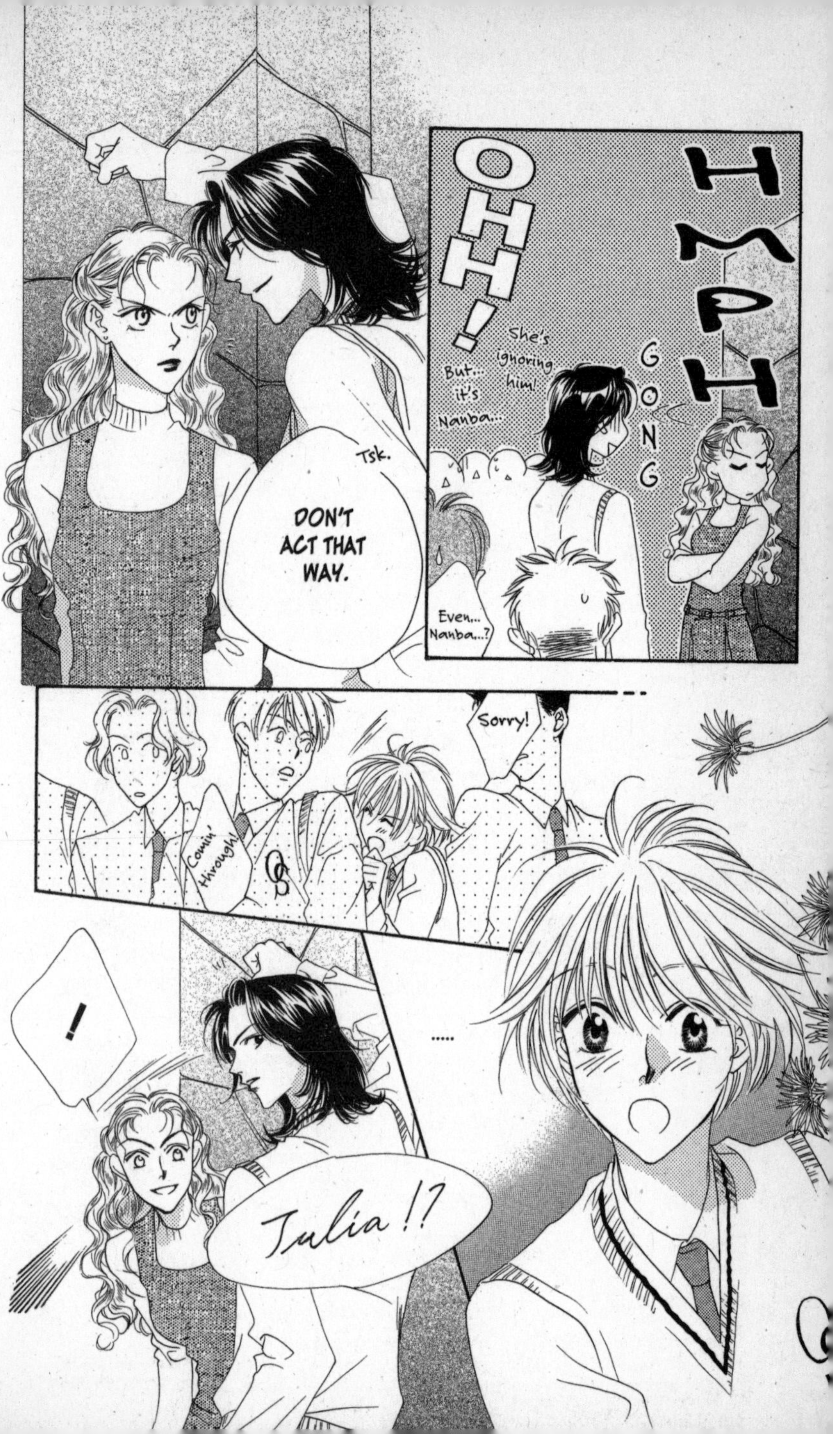
HMPH
GONG
OHH!
She's ignoring him!
But... it's Nanba...
Even... Nanba...?
Tsk.
DON'T ACT THAT WAY.
Sorry!
Comin' through!
.....
!
Julia !?

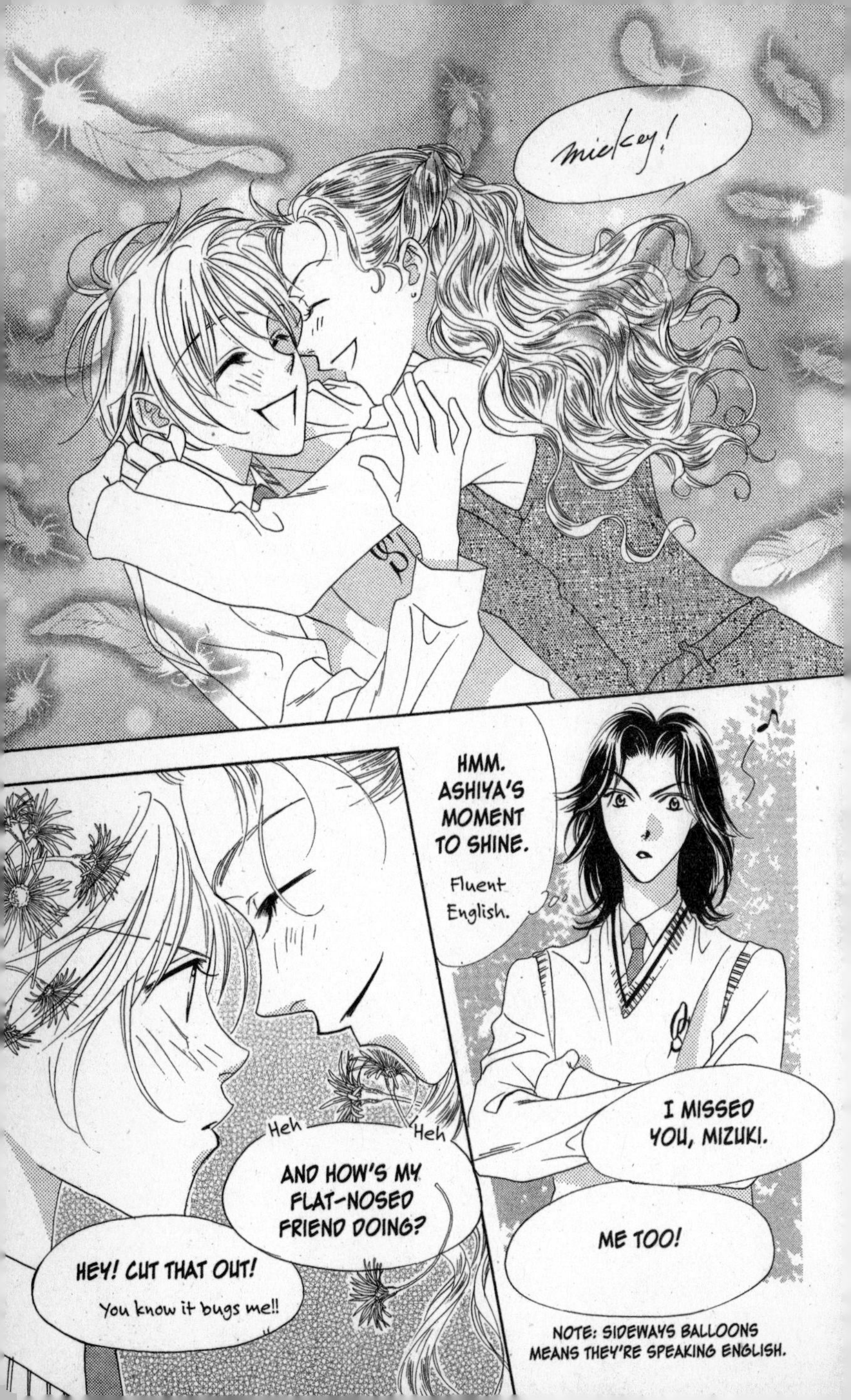
mickey!
HMM. ASHIYA'S MOMENT TO SHINE.
Fluent English.
I MISSED YOU, MIZUKI.
ME TOO!
Heh Heh
AND HOW'S MY FLAT-NOSED FRIEND DOING?
HEY! CUT THAT OUT!
You know it bugs me!!
NOTE: SIDEWAYS BALLOONS MEANS THEY'RE SPEAKING ENGLISH.

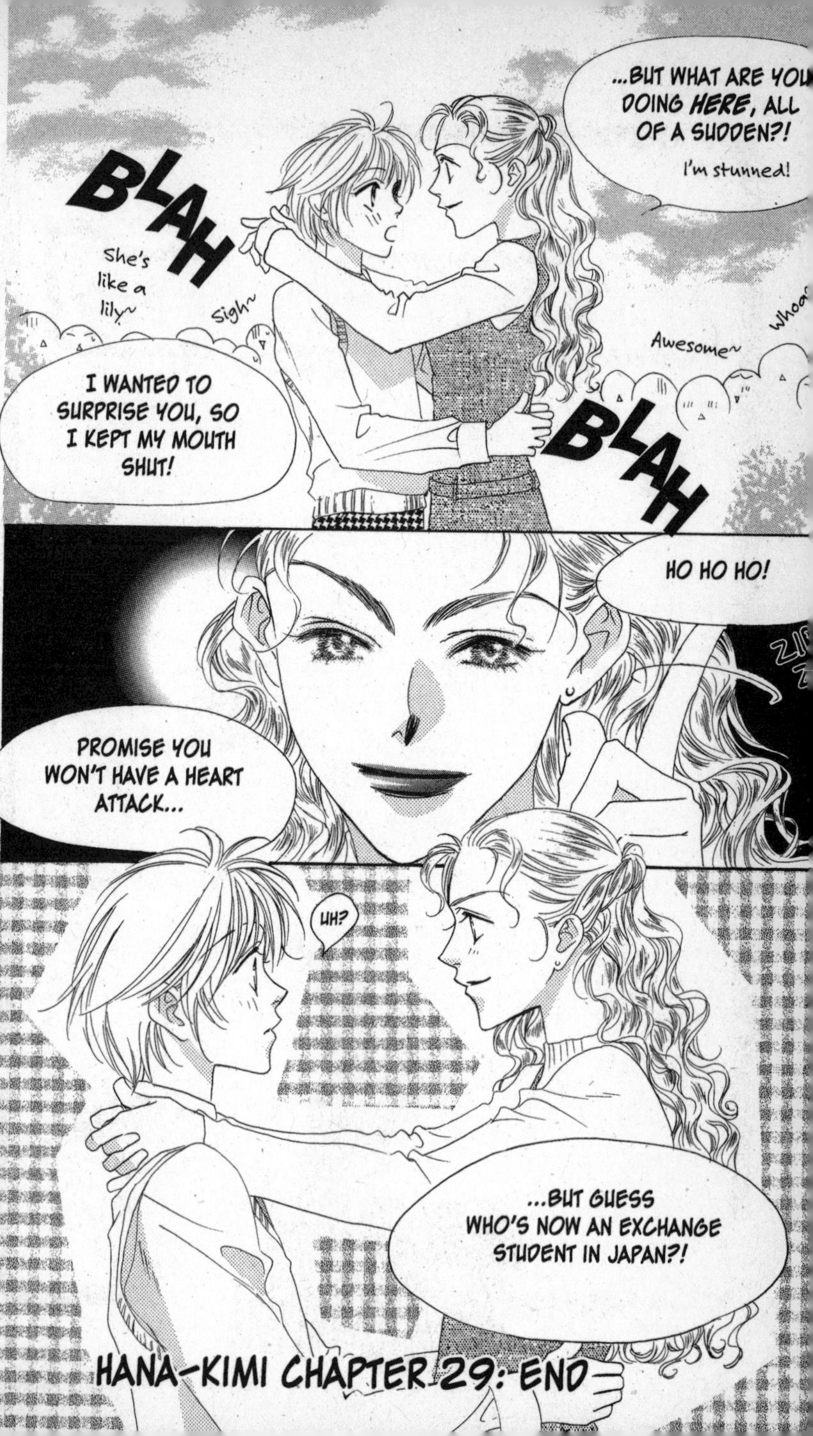
...BUT WHAT ARE YOU DOING *HERE*, ALL OF A SUDDEN?!
I'm stunned!
BLAH
Whoa
Awesome~
She's like a lily~
Sigh~
BLAH
I WANTED TO SURPRISE YOU, SO I KEPT MY MOUTH SHUT!
HO HO HO!
PROMISE YOU WON'T HAVE A HEART ATTACK...
UH?
...BUT GUESS WHO'S NOW AN EXCHANGE STUDENT IN JAPAN?!
HANA-KIMI CHAPTER 29: END

Hana-Kimi

For You in Full Blossom

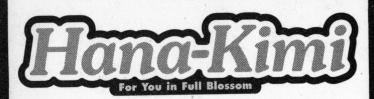

CHAPTER 30

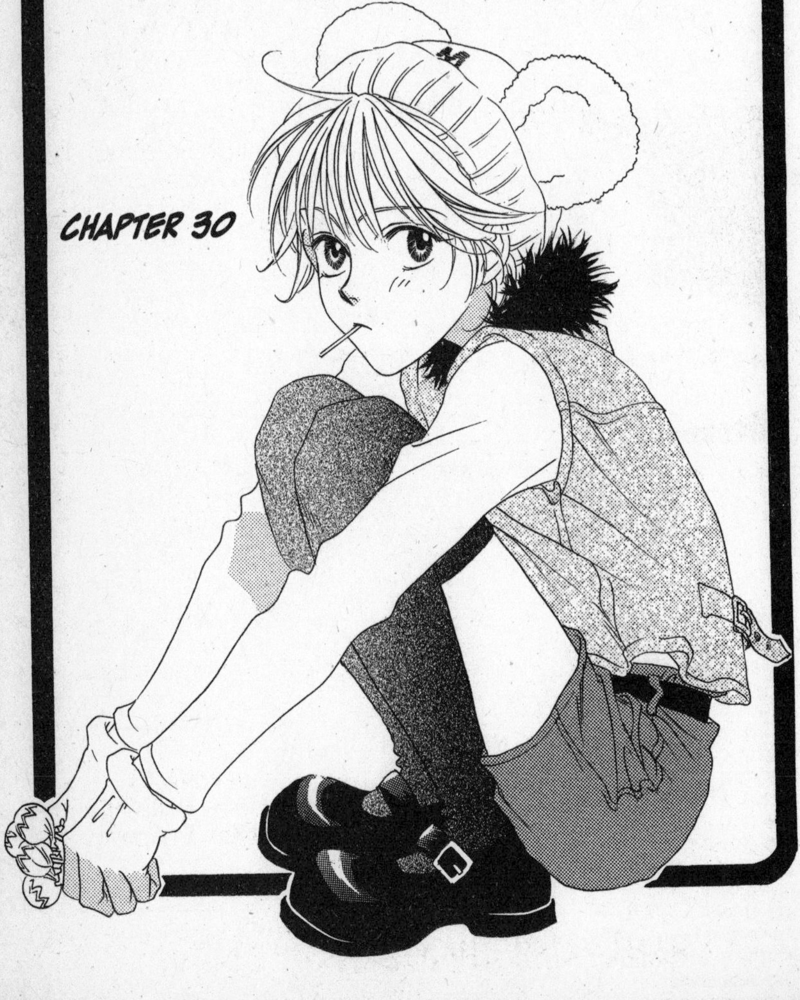

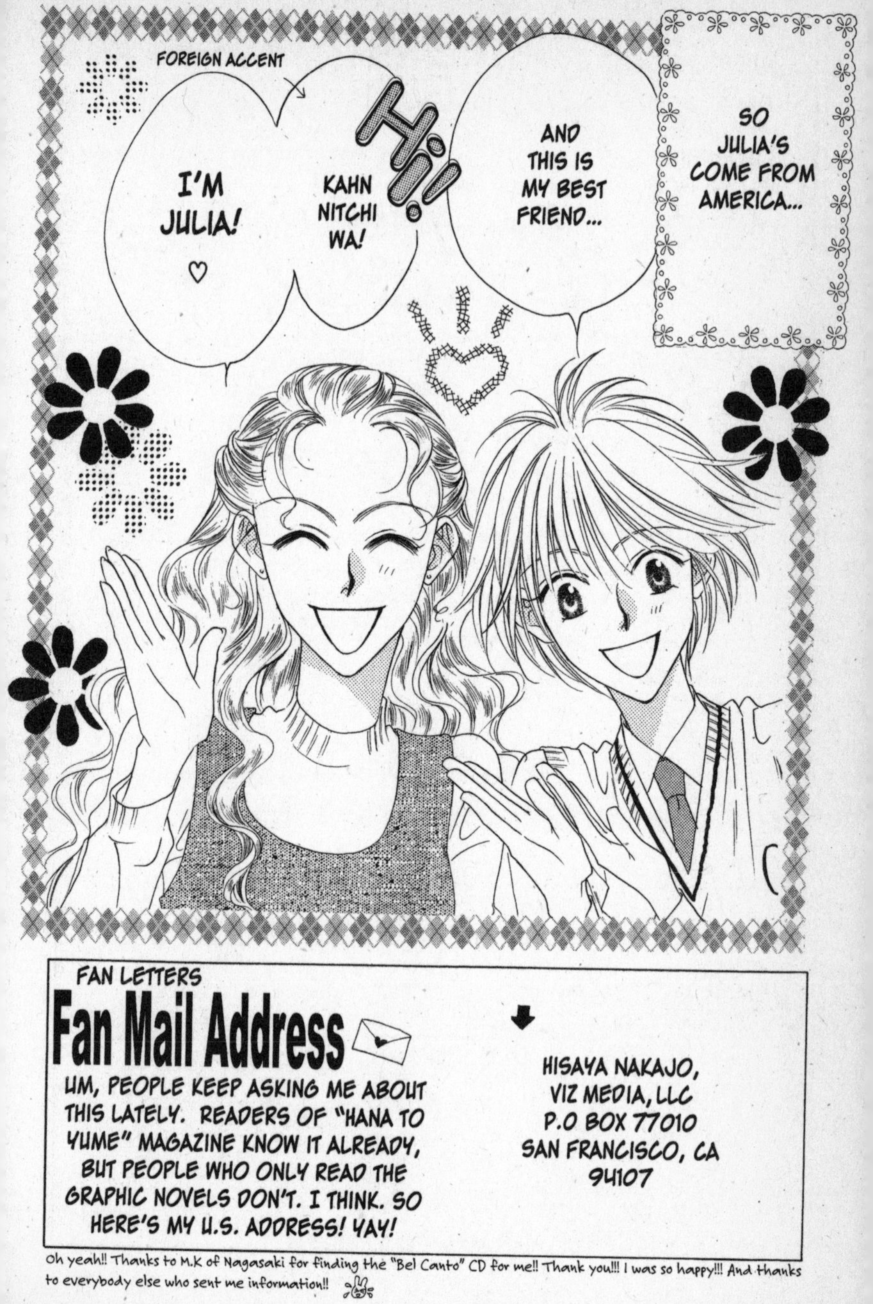
SO JULIA'S COME FROM AMERICA...
AND THIS IS MY BEST FRIEND...
Hi!!
KAHN NITCHI WA!
I'M JULIA! ♡
FOREIGN ACCENT

FAN LETTERS

Fan Mail Address

UM, PEOPLE KEEP ASKING ME ABOUT THIS LATELY. READERS OF "HANA TO YUME" MAGAZINE KNOW IT ALREADY, BUT PEOPLE WHO ONLY READ THE GRAPHIC NOVELS DON'T. I THINK. SO HERE'S MY U.S. ADDRESS! YAY!

HISAYA NAKAJO,
VIZ MEDIA, LLC
P.O BOX 77010
SAN FRANCISCO, CA
94107

Oh yeah!! Thanks to M.K of Nagasaki for finding the "Bel Canto" CD for me!! Thank you!!! I was so happy!!! And thanks to everybody else who sent me information!!

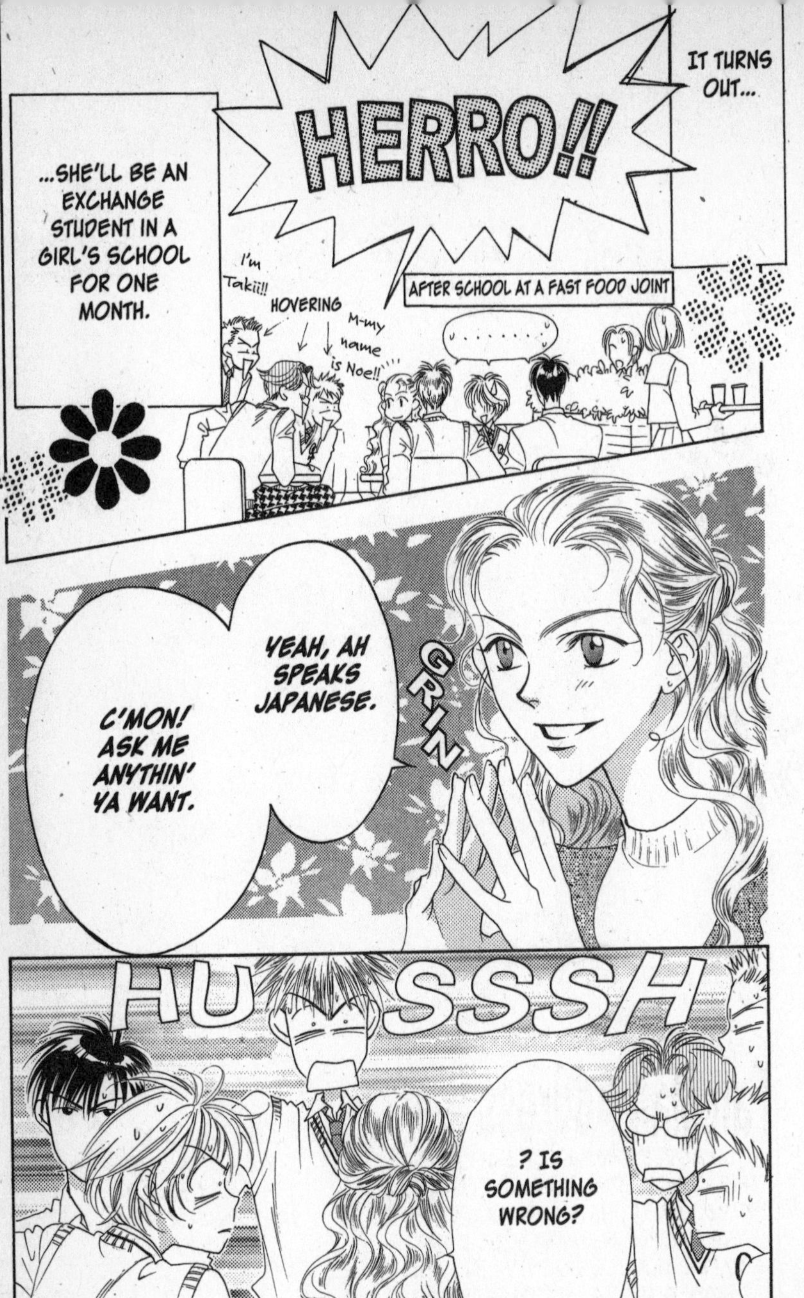
IT TURNS OUT...
HERRO!!
...SHE'LL BE AN EXCHANGE STUDENT IN A GIRL'S SCHOOL FOR ONE MONTH.
AFTER SCHOOL AT A FAST FOOD JOINT
u.......
M-my name is Noe!!
HOVERING
I'm Takii!!
GRIN
YEAH, AH SPEAKS JAPANESE.
C'MON! ASK ME ANYTHIN' YA WANT.
HUSSSH
? IS SOMETHING WRONG?

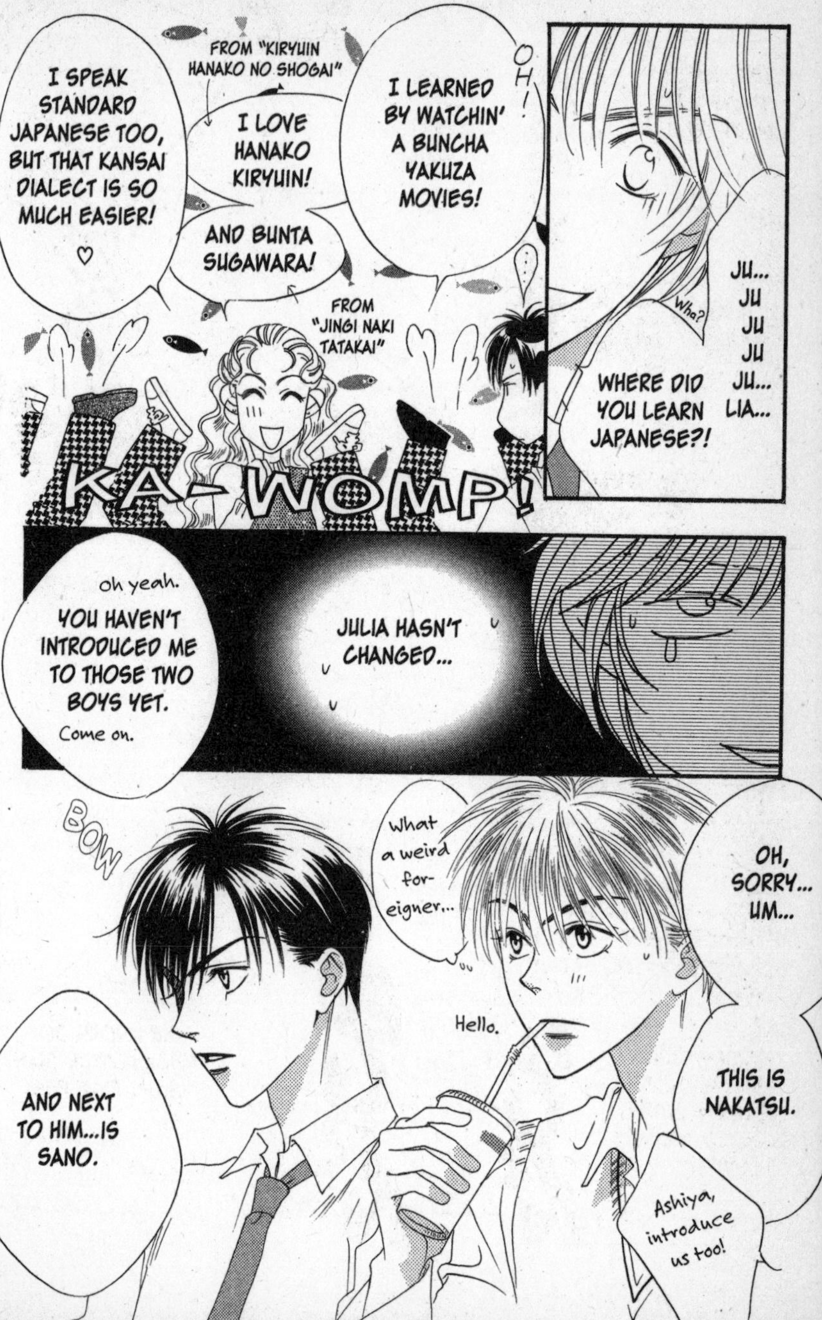
JU... JU JU JU JU... LIA...
Wha?
WHERE DID YOU LEARN JAPANESE?!
OH!
I LEARNED BY WATCHIN' A BUNCHA YAKUZA MOVIES!
I LOVE HANAKO KIRYUIN!
FROM "KIRYUIN HANAKO NO SHOGAI"
AND BUNTA SUGAWARA!
FROM "JINGI NAKI TATAKAI"
I SPEAK STANDARD JAPANESE TOO, BUT THAT KANSAI DIALECT IS SO MUCH EASIER! ♡
KA-WOMP!
JULIA HASN'T CHANGED...
oh yeah.
YOU HAVEN'T INTRODUCED ME TO THOSE TWO BOYS YET.
Come on.
OH, SORRY... UM...
THIS IS NAKATSU.
Ashiya, introduce us too!
What a weird foreigner...
Hello.
AND NEXT TO HIM...IS SANO.
BOW

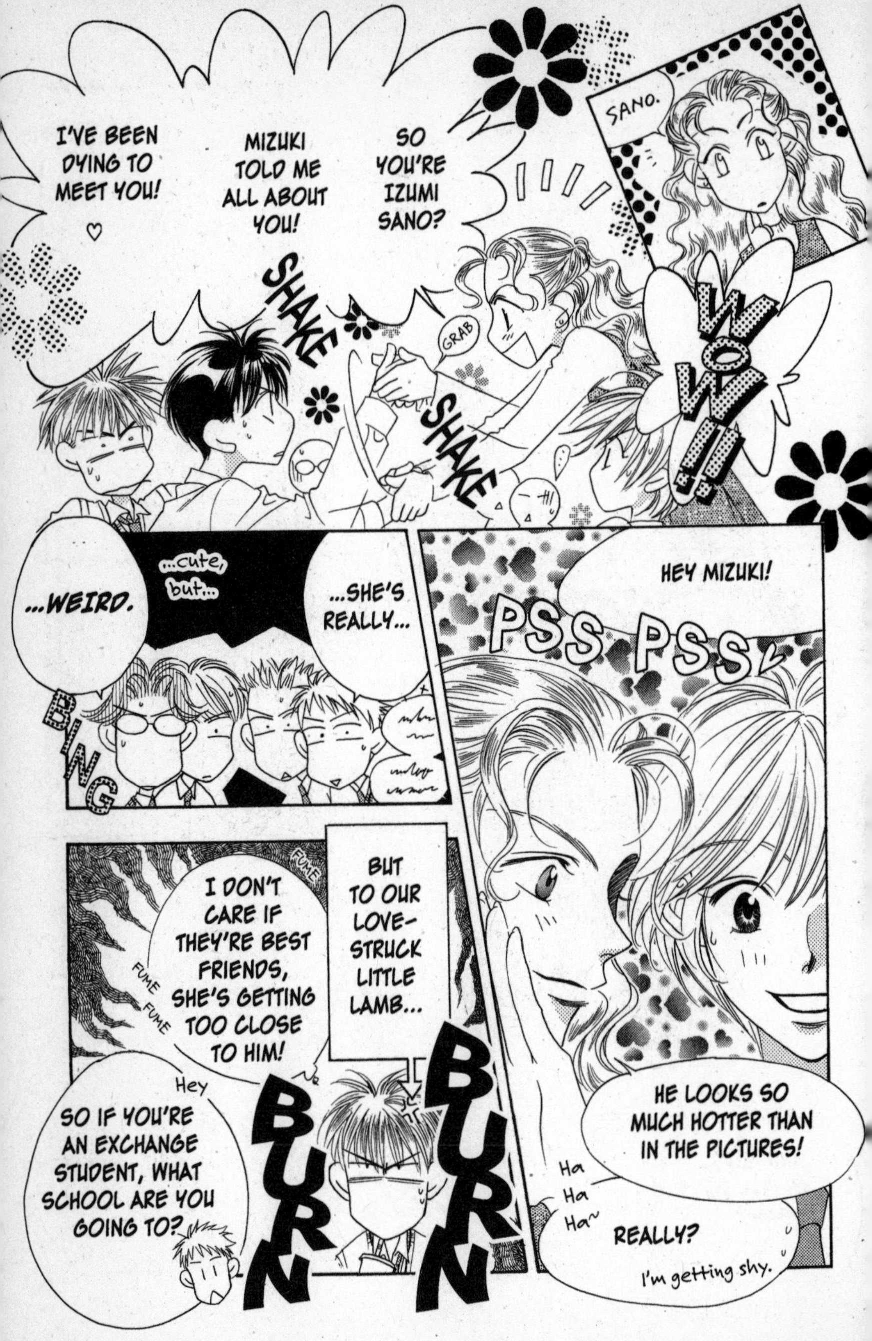
SANO.
WOW!!
SO YOU'RE IZUMI SANO?
MIZUKI TOLD ME ALL ABOUT YOU!
I'VE BEEN DYING TO MEET YOU! ♡
GRAB
SHAKE
SHAKE
HEY MIZUKI!
PSS PSS
HE LOOKS SO MUCH HOTTER THAN IN THE PICTURES!
Ha Ha Ha~
REALLY?
I'm getting shy.
...SHE'S REALLY...
...cute, but...
...WEIRD.
BWNG
BUT TO OUR LOVE-STRUCK LITTLE LAMB...
FUME
I DON'T CARE IF THEY'RE BEST FRIENDS, SHE'S GETTING TOO CLOSE TO HIM!
FUME FUME
BURN
BURN
Hey
SO IF YOU'RE AN EXCHANGE STUDENT, WHAT SCHOOL ARE YOU GOING TO?

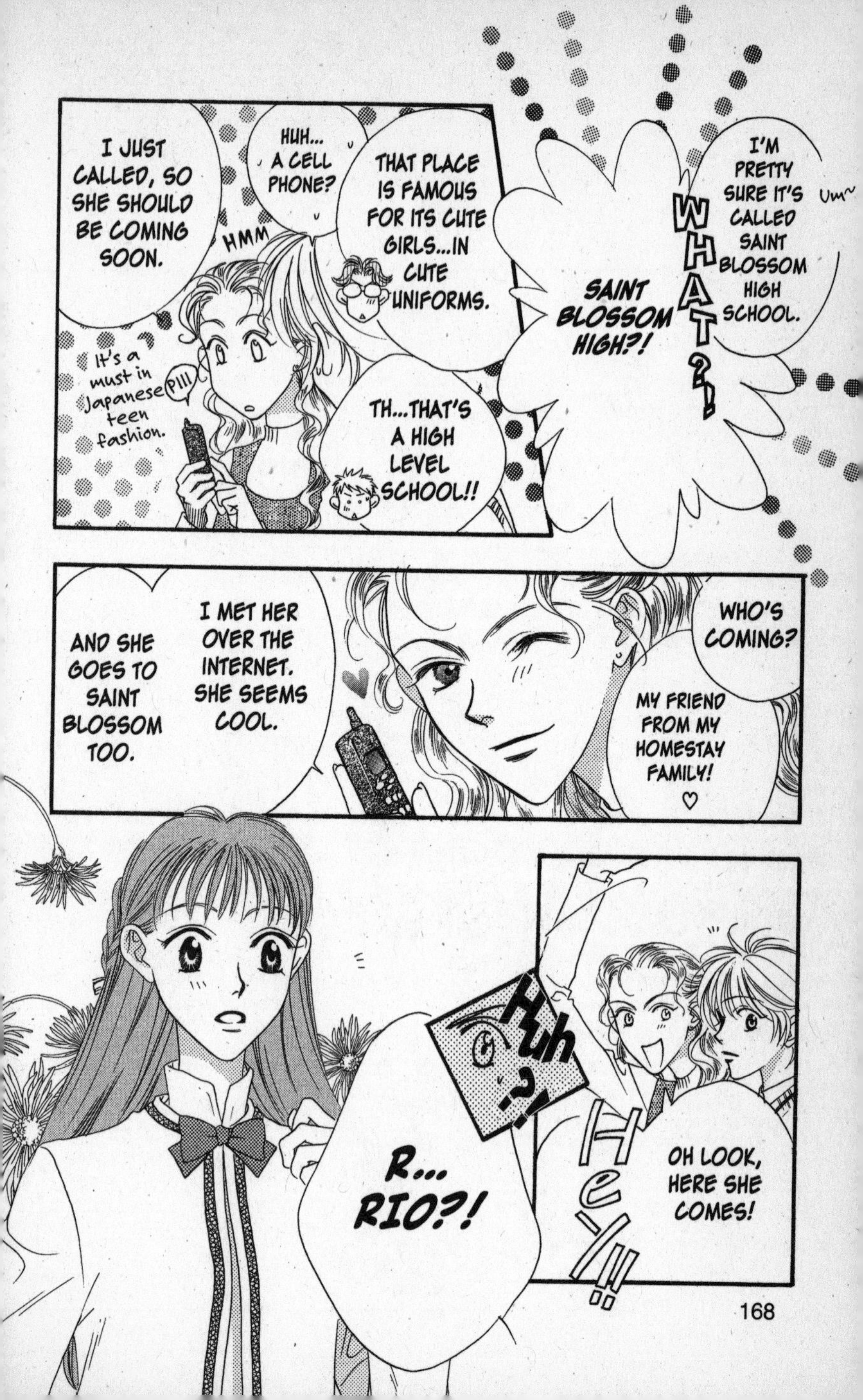

I'M PRETTY SURE IT'S CALLED SAINT BLOSSOM HIGH SCHOOL.
Um~
WHAT?!
SAINT BLOSSOM HIGH?!
THAT PLACE IS FAMOUS FOR ITS CUTE GIRLS...IN CUTE UNIFORMS.
HUH... A CELL PHONE?
I JUST CALLED, SO SHE SHOULD BE COMING SOON.
HMM
TH...THAT'S A HIGH LEVEL SCHOOL!!
PIII
It's a must in Japanese teen fashion.
WHO'S COMING?
MY FRIEND FROM MY HOMESTAY FAMILY! ♡
I MET HER OVER THE INTERNET. SHE SEEMS COOL.
AND SHE GOES TO SAINT BLOSSOM TOO.
HEY!!
OH LOOK, HERE SHE COMES!
HUH?!
R... RIO?!

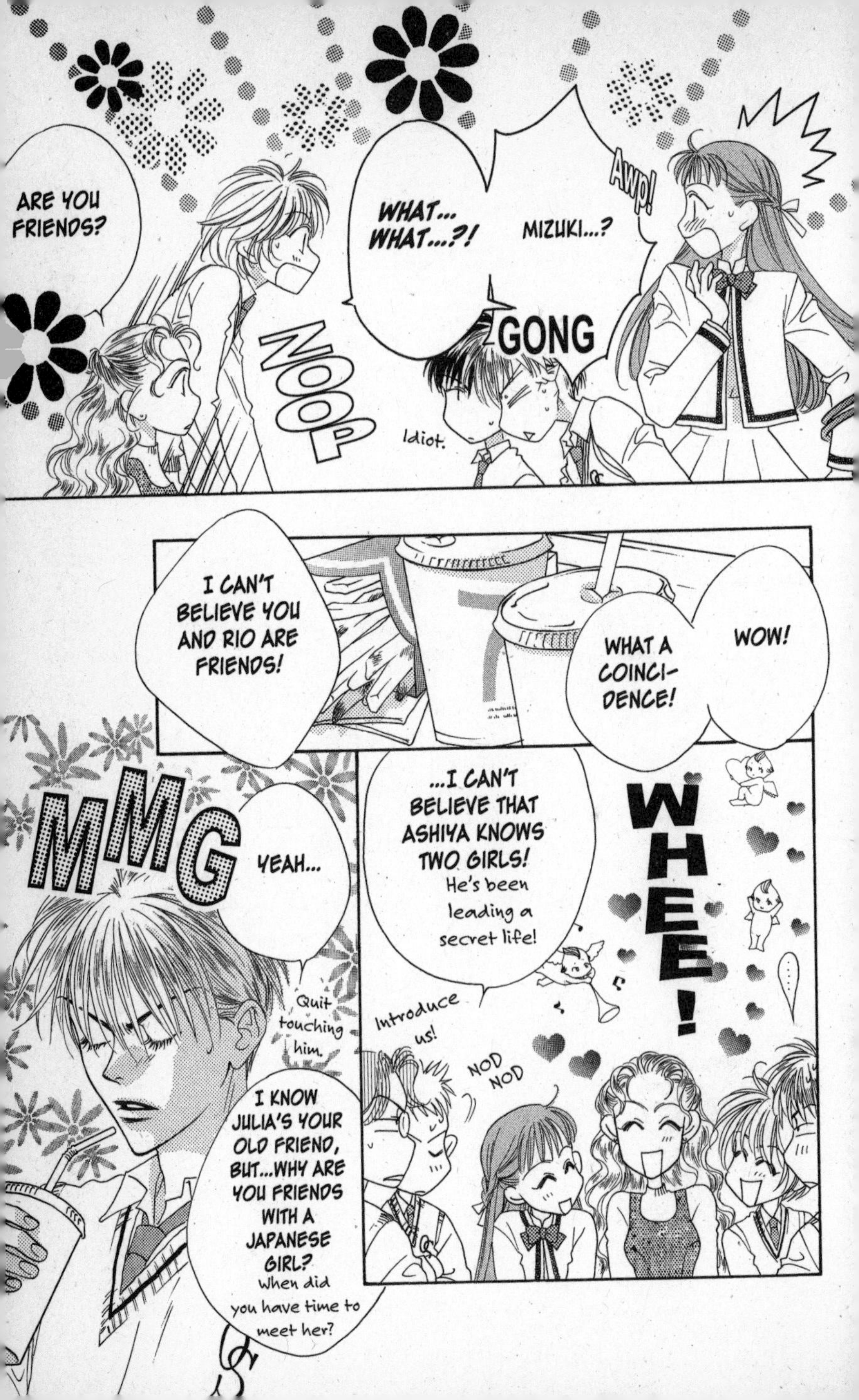
Awp!
MIZUKI...?
WHAT... WHAT...?!
ARE YOU FRIENDS?
GONG
NOOP
Idiot.
WOW!
WHAT A COINCI-DENCE!
I CAN'T BELIEVE YOU AND RIO ARE FRIENDS!
WHEE!
...I CAN'T BELIEVE THAT ASHIYA KNOWS TWO GIRLS!
He's been leading a secret life!
...
Introduce us!
NOD NOD
YEAH...
MMG
Quit touching him.
I KNOW JULIA'S YOUR OLD FRIEND, BUT...WHY ARE YOU FRIENDS WITH A JAPANESE GIRL?
When did you have time to meet her?

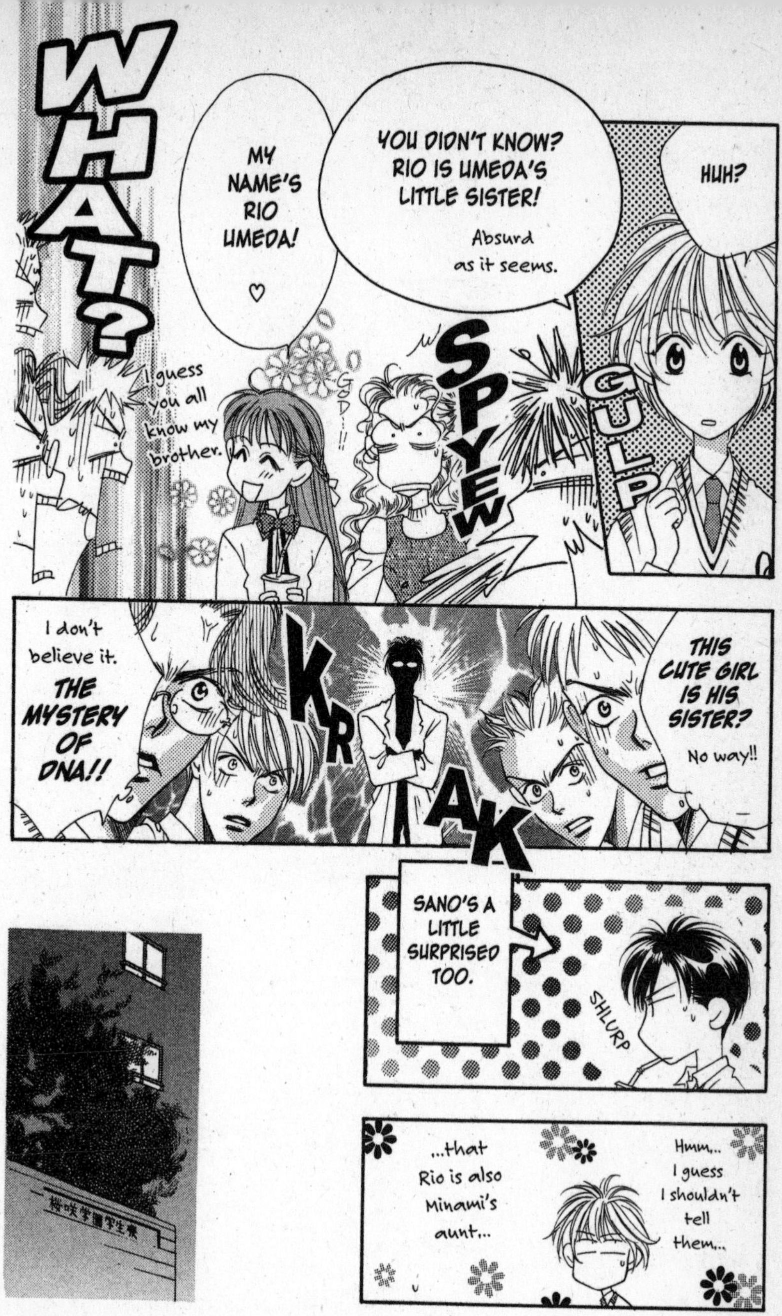
HUH?
GULP
YOU DIDN'T KNOW? RIO IS UMEDA'S LITTLE SISTER!
Absurd as it seems.
SPYEW
MY NAME'S RIO UMEDA! ♡
GOD...!!
WHAT?
I guess you all know my brother.
THIS CUTE GIRL IS HIS SISTER?
No way!!
KRAK
I don't believe it. THE MYSTERY OF DNA!!
SANO'S A LITTLE SURPRISED TOO.
SHLURP
Hmm... I guess I shouldn't tell them...
...that Rio is also Minami's aunt...

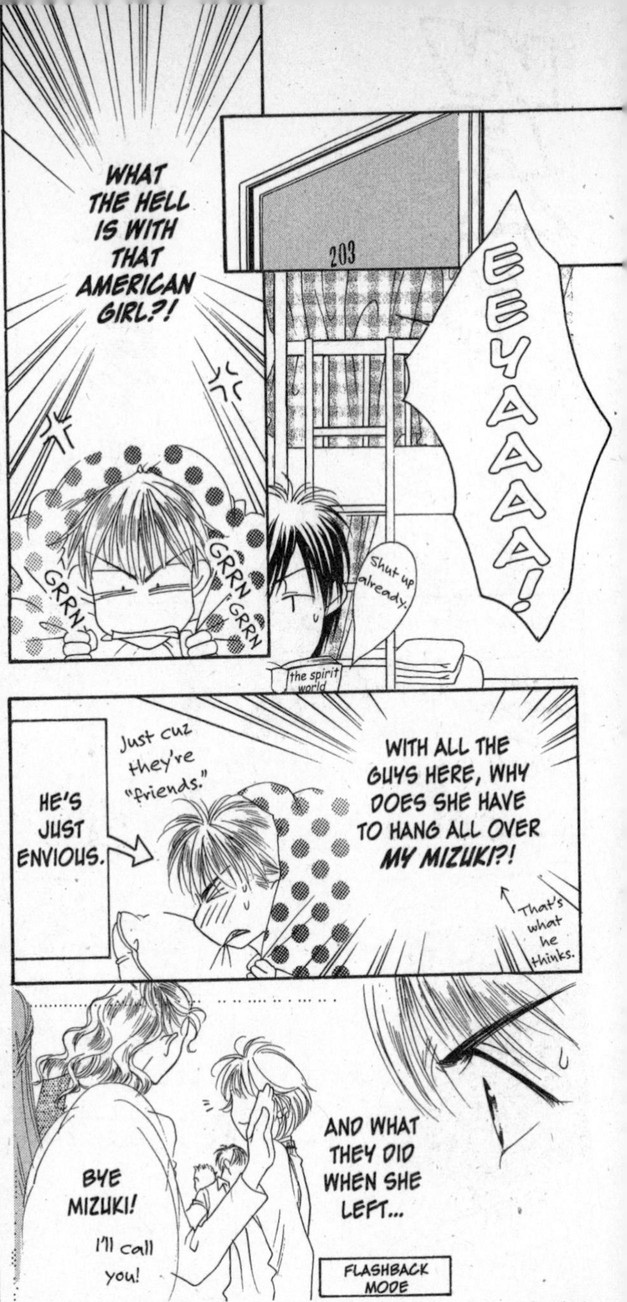
203
EEYAAAAA!
Shut up already.
the spirit world
WHAT THE HELL IS WITH THAT AMERICAN GIRL?!
GRRN GRRN
GRRN GRRN
WITH ALL THE GUYS HERE, WHY DOES SHE HAVE TO HANG ALL OVER MY MIZUKI?!
That's what he thinks.
Just cuz they're "friends."
HE'S JUST ENVIOUS.
AND WHAT THEY DID WHEN SHE LEFT...
FLASHBACK MODE
BYE MIZUKI!
I'll call you!

Whispered Secrets

BAD BACK

IT HAPPENED TO ME!! HA HA HA HA!! I HAD THIS PAIN THAT FELT LIKE SOMEBODY WAS GRABBING MY SPINE, BUT I IGNORED IT, THINKING IT WAS NO BIG DEAL. THEN IT REALLY STARTED TO HURT. I COULDN'T EVEN STAND UP BY MYSELF! THE DOCTOR SAID I HAD A SLIPPED DISC. I WAS SHOCKED! I CAN'T BELIEVE I HAVE BACK PAIN EVEN THOUGH I'M SO YOUNG!! ON TOP OF THAT, EVERYBODY TELLS ME THAT AFTER IT HAPPENS ONCE, IT'S MORE LIKELY TO HAPPEN AGAIN. SO I WORE A BACK BRACE WHEN I WENT TO MY BOOK SIGNING IN TOKYO (WHICH I TALKED ABOUT IN VOLUME 5).

It happened two days before the signing.

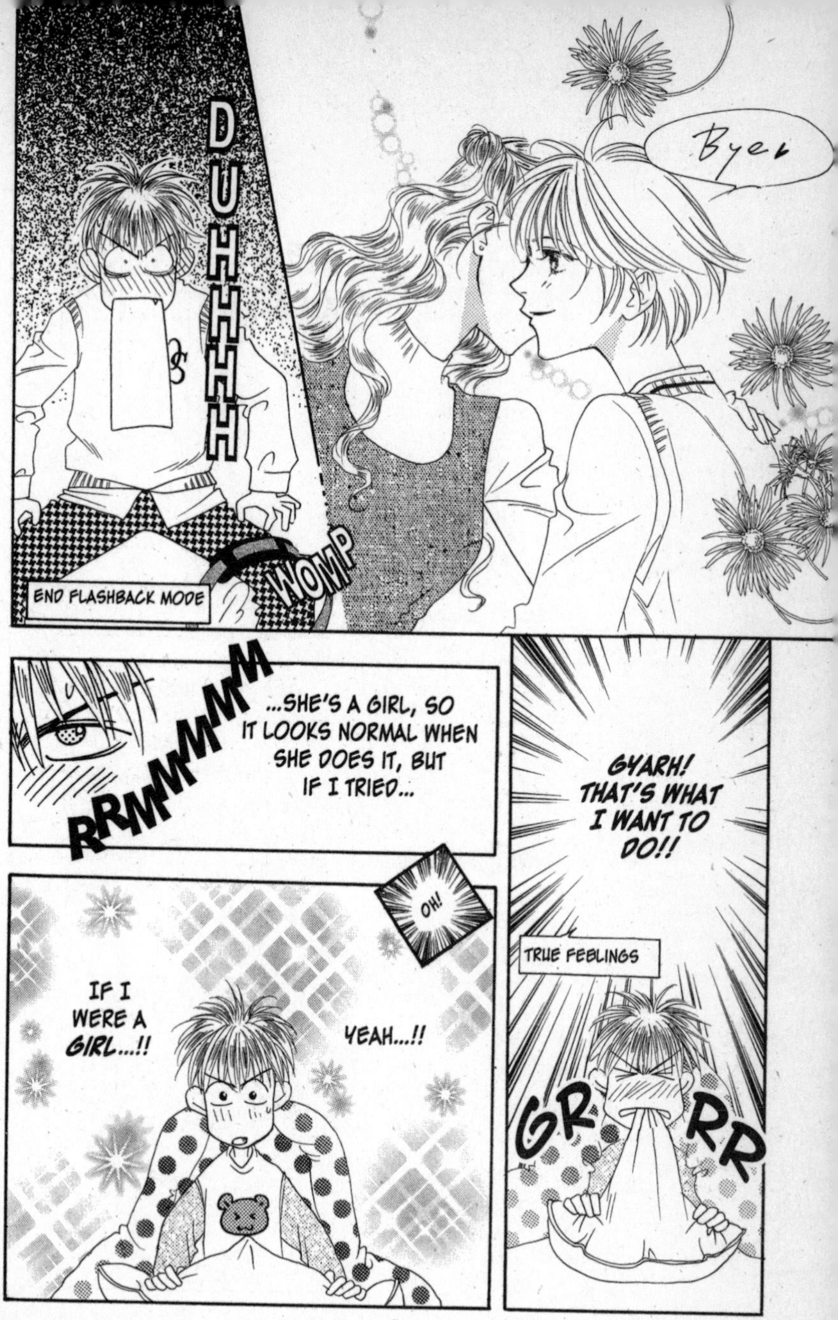
Bye
DUHHHHHH
WOMP
END FLASHBACK MODE
GYARH! THAT'S WHAT I WANT TO DO!!
TRUE FEELINGS
GRRR
...SHE'S A GIRL, SO IT LOOKS NORMAL WHEN SHE DOES IT, BUT IF I TRIED...
RRMMMMMM
OH!
YEAH...!!
IF I WERE A GIRL...!!

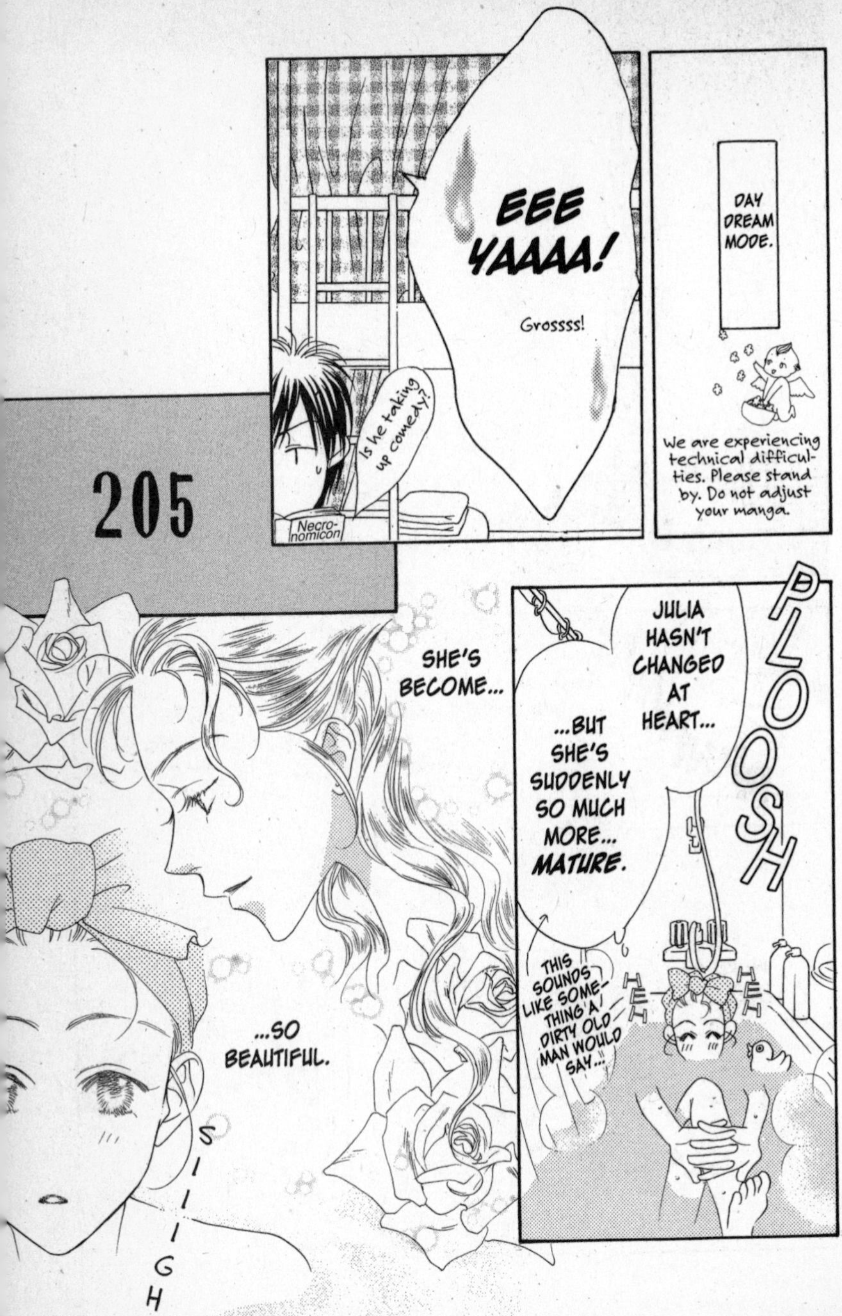
DAY DREAM MODE.
We are experiencing technical difficulties. Please stand by. Do not adjust your manga.
EEE YAAAA!
Grossss!
Is he taking up comedy?
Necronomicon
PLOOSH
JULIA HASN'T CHANGED AT HEART...
...BUT SHE'S SUDDENLY SO MUCH MORE... **MATURE**.
THIS SOUNDS LIKE SOMETHING A DIRTY OLD MAN WOULD SAY...
SHE'S BECOME...
...SO BEAUTIFUL.
SIIIGH

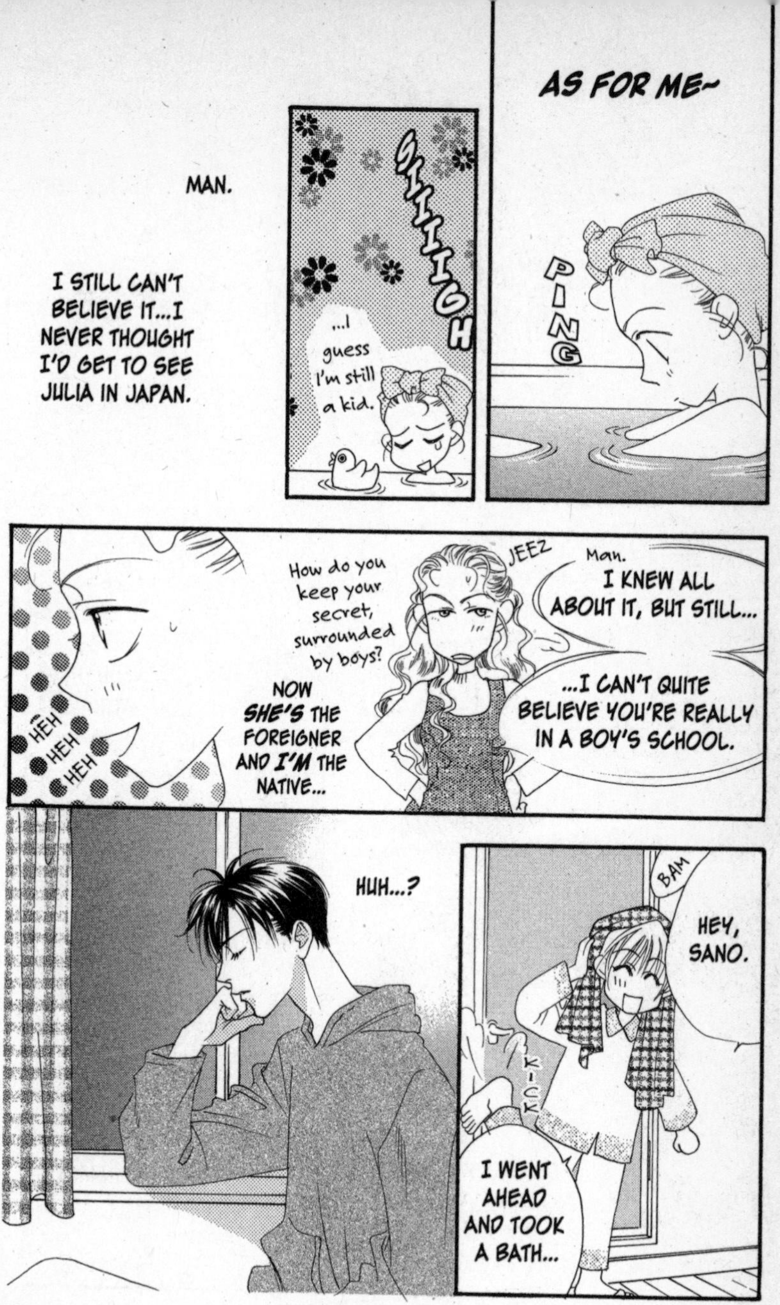
AS FOR ME~
PING
SIIIGH
...I guess I'm still a kid.
MAN.
I STILL CAN'T BELIEVE IT...I NEVER THOUGHT I'D GET TO SEE JULIA IN JAPAN.
Man.
I KNEW ALL ABOUT IT, BUT STILL...
...I CAN'T QUITE BELIEVE YOU'RE REALLY IN A BOY'S SCHOOL.
JEEZ
How do you keep your secret, surrounded by boys?
NOW SHE'S THE FOREIGNER AND I'M THE NATIVE...
HEH HEH HEH
BAM
HEY, SANO.
K-ICK
I WENT AHEAD AND TOOK A BATH...
HUH...?

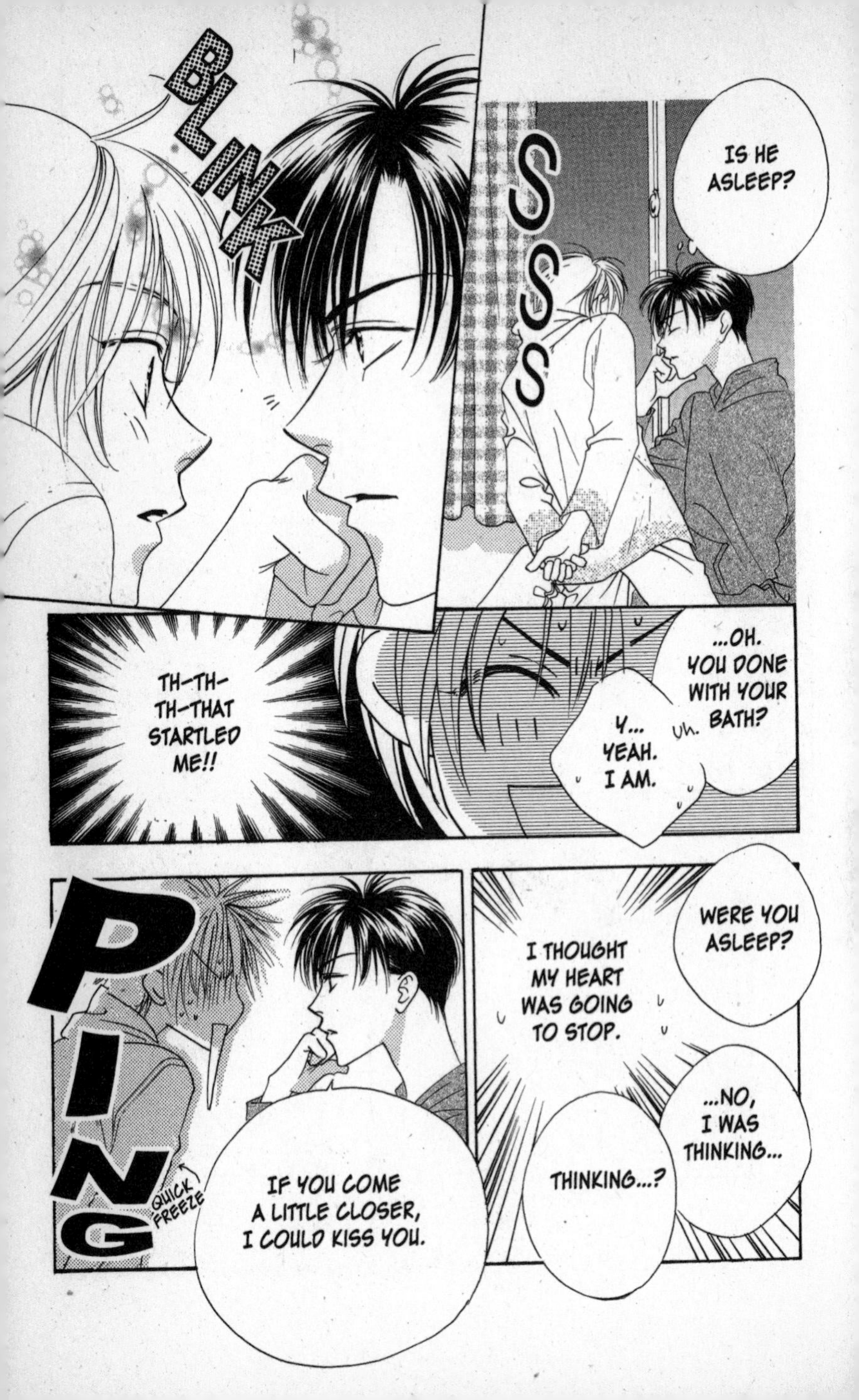
IS HE ASLEEP?
SSS
BLINK
...OH. YOU DONE WITH YOUR BATH?
UH.
Y... YEAH. I AM.
TH-TH-TH-THAT STARTLED ME!!
WERE YOU ASLEEP?
I THOUGHT MY HEART WAS GOING TO STOP.
...NO, I WAS THINKING...
THINKING...?
PING
QUICK FREEZE
IF YOU COME A LITTLE CLOSER, I COULD KISS YOU.

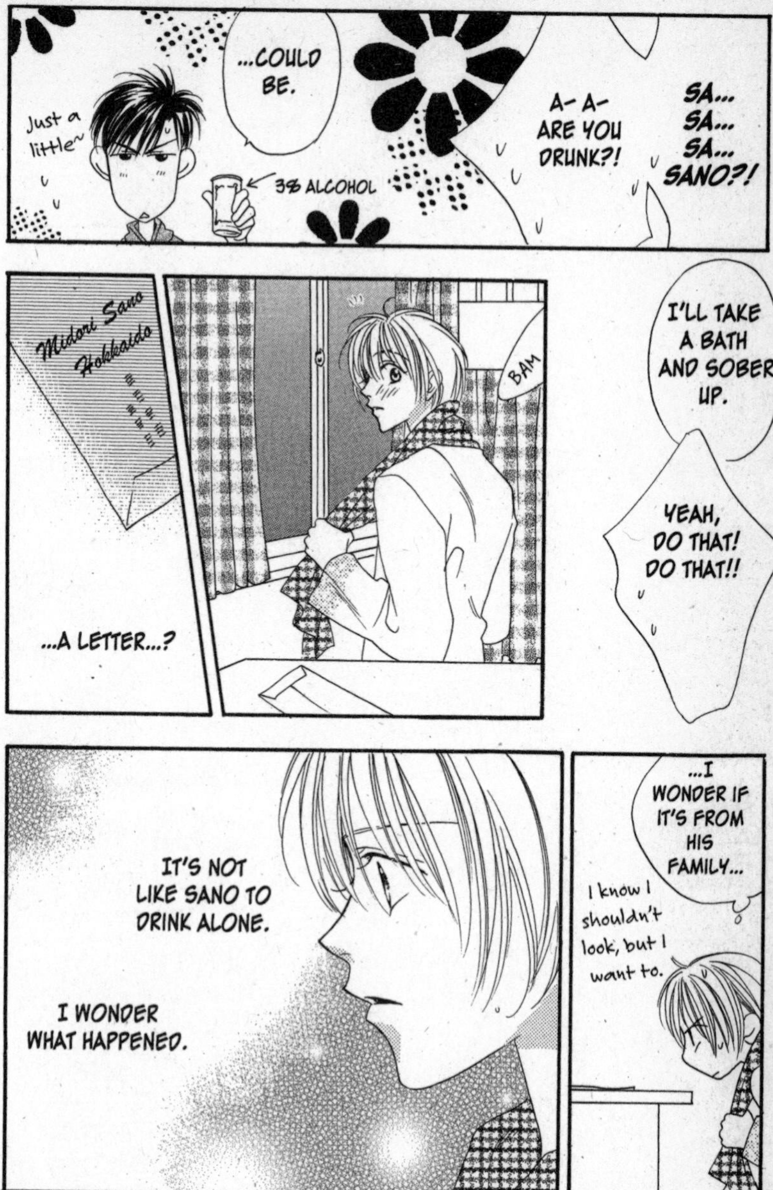
SA... SA... SA... SANO?!
A- A- ARE YOU DRUNK?!
...COULD BE.
3% ALCOHOL
Just a little~
I'LL TAKE A BATH AND SOBER UP.
YEAH, DO THAT! DO THAT!!
BAM
Midori Sano
Hokkaido
...A LETTER...?
...I WONDER IF IT'S FROM HIS FAMILY...
I know I shouldn't look, but I want to.
IT'S NOT LIKE SANO TO DRINK ALONE.
I WONDER WHAT HAPPENED.

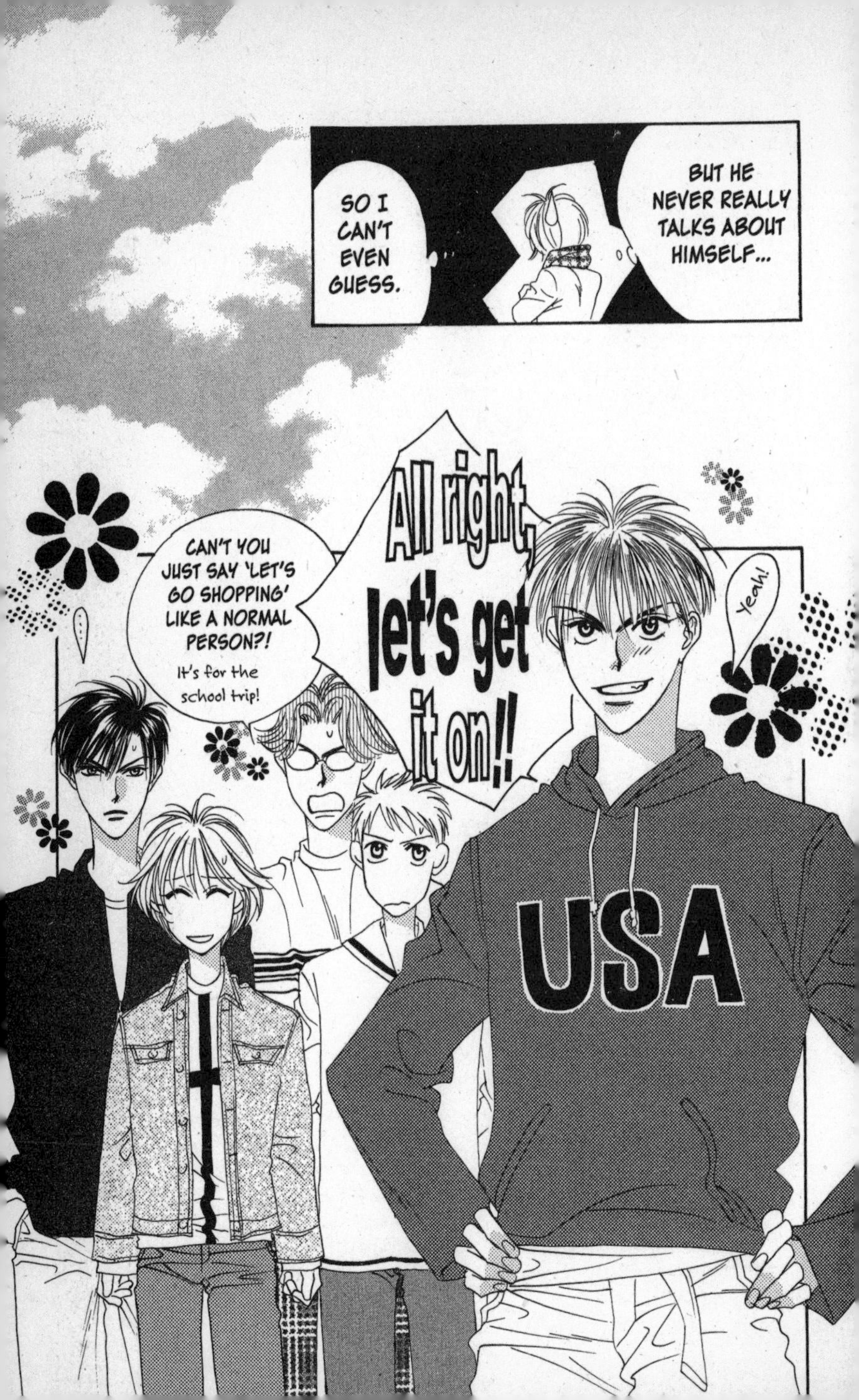
BUT HE NEVER REALLY TALKS ABOUT HIMSELF...
SO I CAN'T EVEN GUESS.
All right, let's get it on!!
Yeah!
CAN'T YOU JUST SAY 'LET'S GO SHOPPING' LIKE A NORMAL PERSON?!
It's for the school trip!
USA

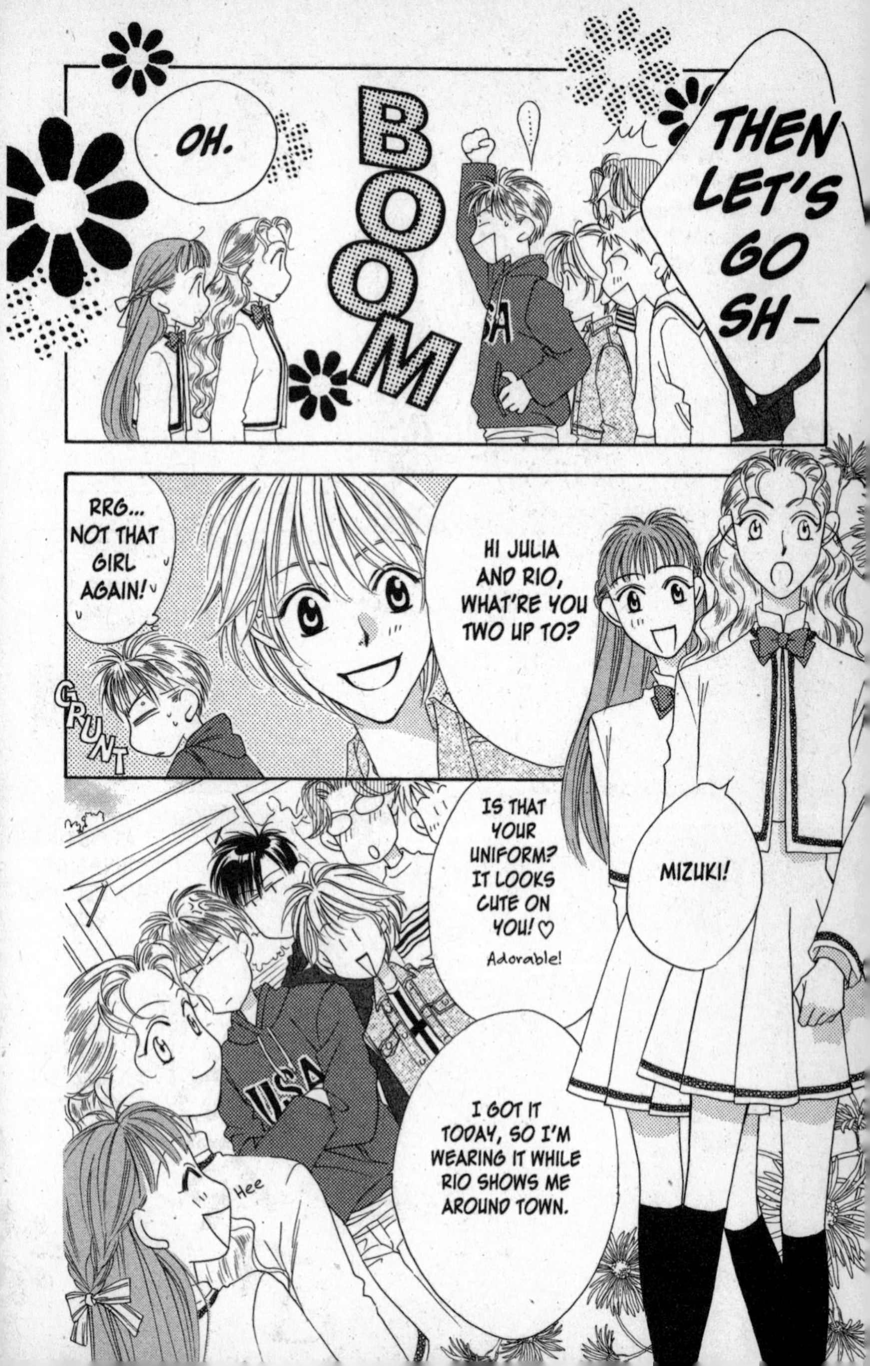
THEN LET'S GO SH-
BOOM
OH.
MIZUKI!
HI JULIA AND RIO, WHAT'RE YOU TWO UP TO?
RRG... NOT THAT GIRL AGAIN!
GRUNT
IS THAT YOUR UNIFORM? IT LOOKS CUTE ON YOU! ♡
Adorable!
I GOT IT TODAY, SO I'M WEARING IT WHILE RIO SHOWS ME AROUND TOWN.
Hee

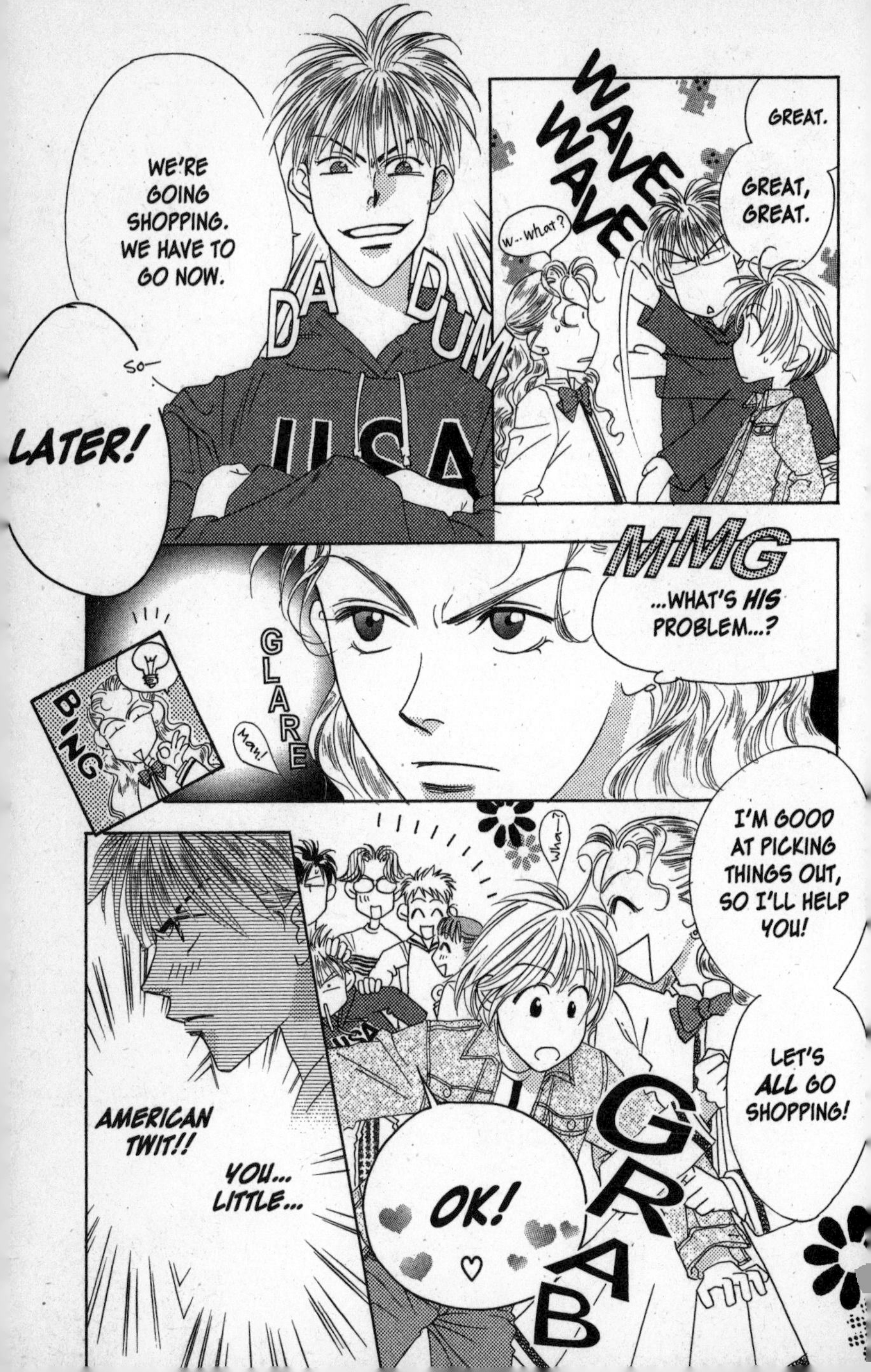
GREAT.
GREAT, GREAT.
WAVE WAVE
W... what?
WE'RE GOING SHOPPING. WE HAVE TO GO NOW.
DA DUM
So—
LATER!
MMG
...WHAT'S HIS PROBLEM...?
GLARE
Man!
BING
I'M GOOD AT PICKING THINGS OUT, SO I'LL HELP YOU!
What—?
LET'S ALL GO SHOPPING!
GRAB
OK!
YOU... LITTLE...
AMERICAN TWIT!!

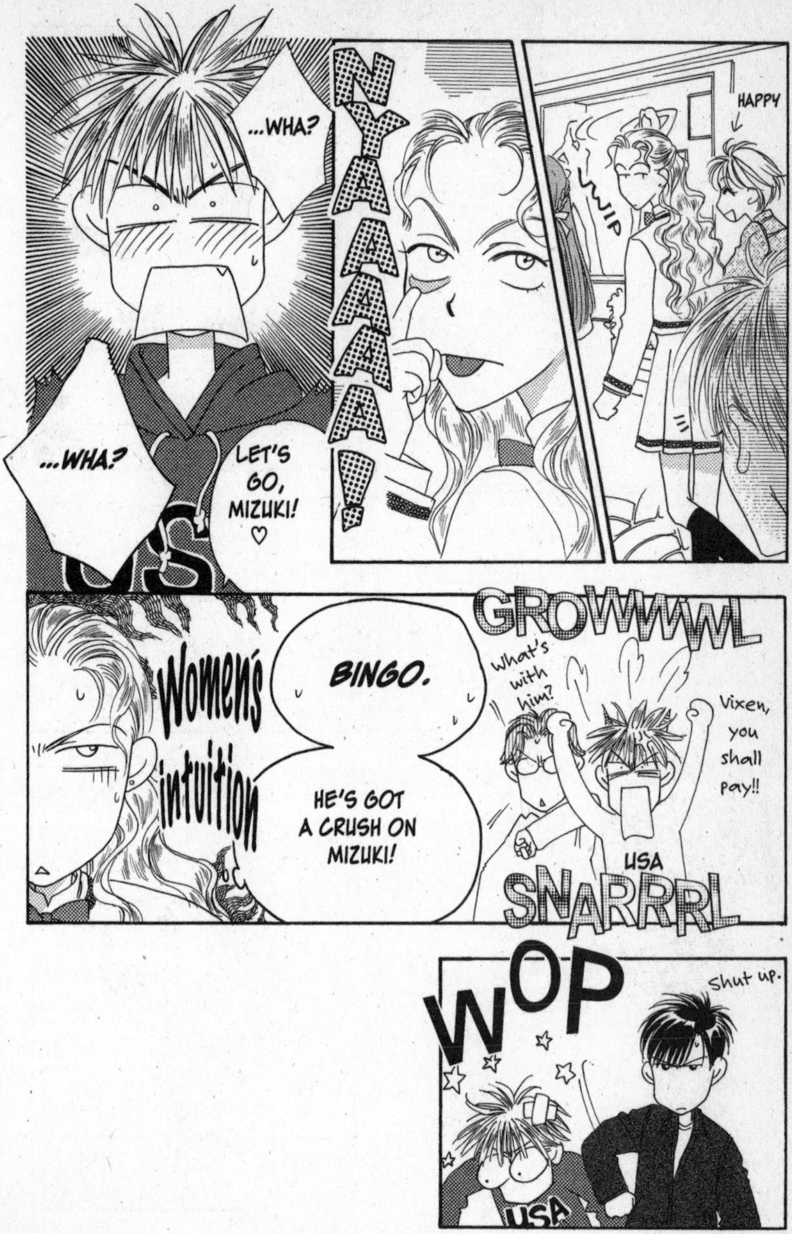
HAPPY
WIP
NYAAAAA!!
...WHA?
LET'S GO, MIZUKI! ♡
...WHA?
GROWWWWL
Vixen, you shall pay!!
What's with him?
BINGO.
HE'S GOT A CRUSH ON MIZUKI!
Women's intuition
USA
SNARRRL
Shut up.
WOP
USA

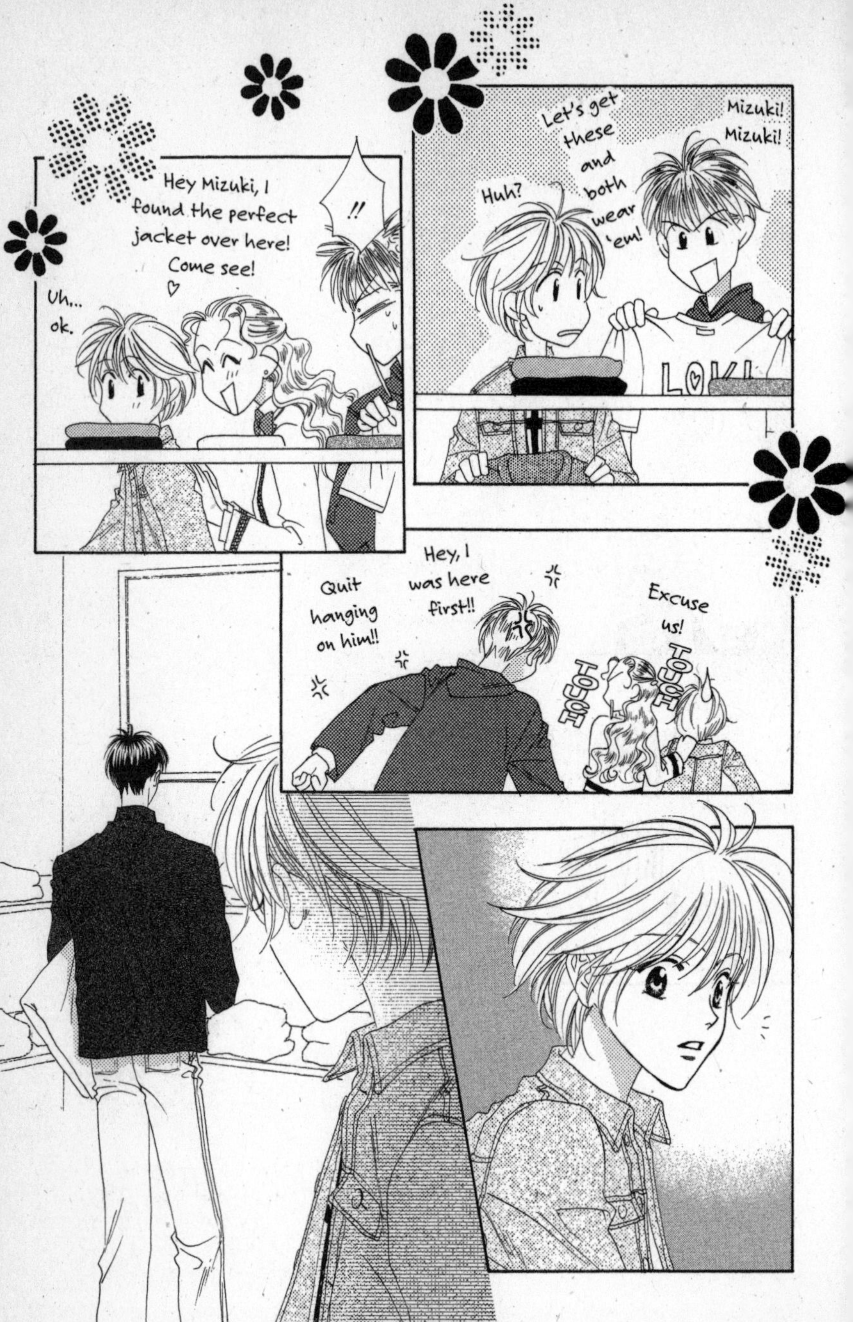

Mizuki! Mizuki!
Let's get these and both wear 'em!
Huh?
!!
Hey Mizuki, I found the perfect jacket over here! Come see! ♡
Uh... ok.
Excuse us!
TOUCH
TOUCH
Hey, I was here first!!
Quit hanging on him!!

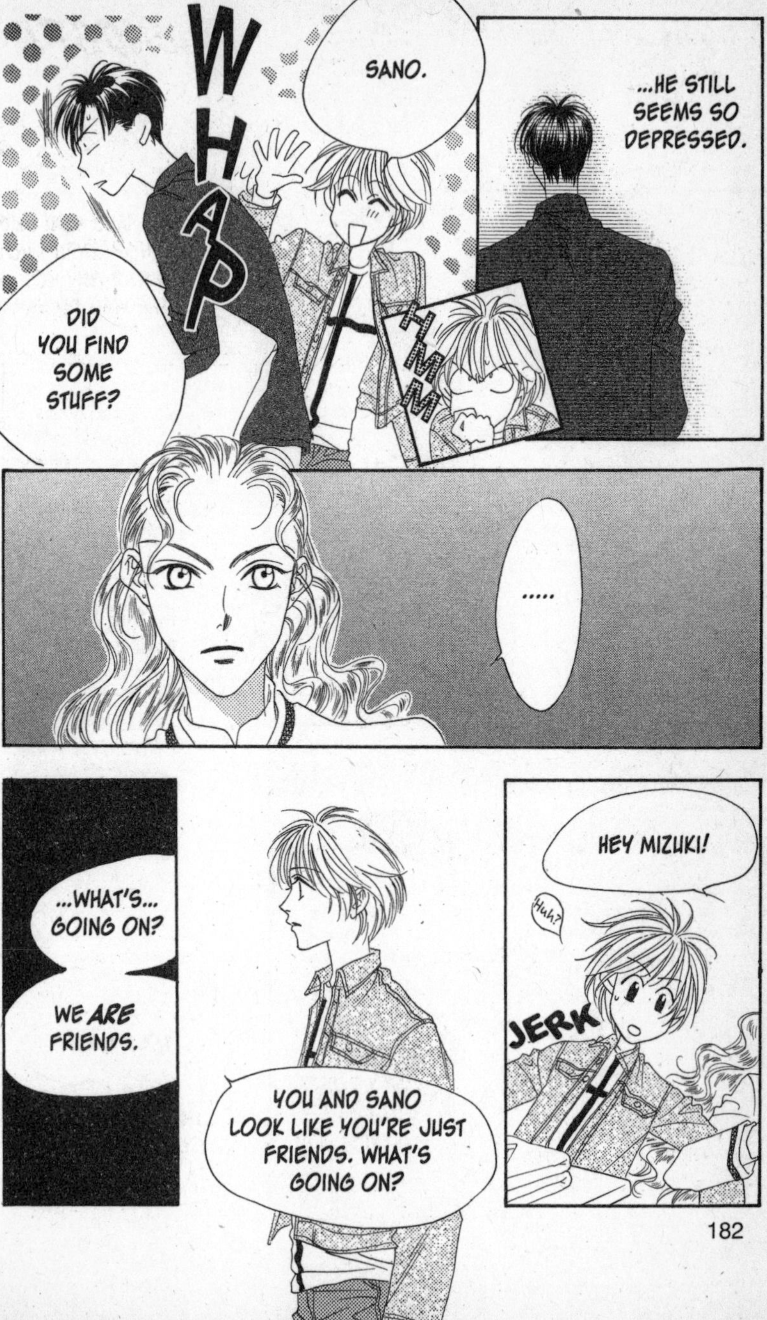
...HE STILL SEEMS SO DEPRESSED.
SANO.
WHAP
HMMM
DID YOU FIND SOME STUFF?
.....
HEY MIZUKI!
Huh?
JERK
YOU AND SANO LOOK LIKE YOU'RE JUST FRIENDS. WHAT'S GOING ON?
...WHAT'S... GOING ON?
WE *ARE* FRIENDS.

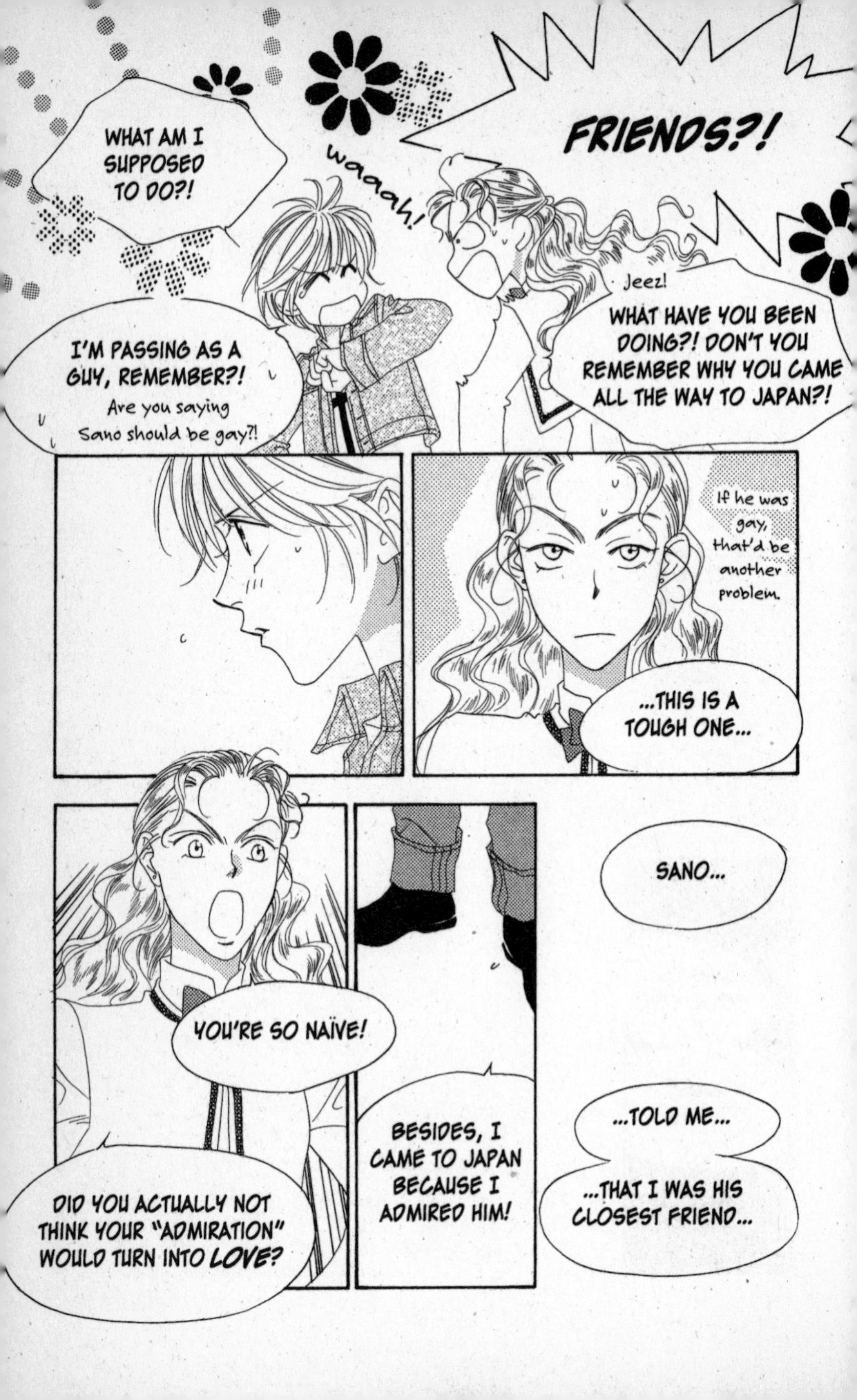

FRIENDS?!
Jeez!
WHAT HAVE YOU BEEN DOING?! DON'T YOU REMEMBER WHY YOU CAME ALL THE WAY TO JAPAN?!
WHAT AM I SUPPOSED TO DO?!
waaah!
I'M PASSING AS A GUY, REMEMBER?!
Are you saying Sano should be gay?!
If he was gay, that'd be another problem.
...THIS IS A TOUGH ONE...
SANO...
...TOLD ME...
...THAT I WAS HIS CLOSEST FRIEND...
BESIDES, I CAME TO JAPAN BECAUSE I ADMIRED HIM!
YOU'RE SO NAÏVE!
DID YOU ACTUALLY NOT THINK YOUR "ADMIRATION" WOULD TURN INTO *LOVE*?

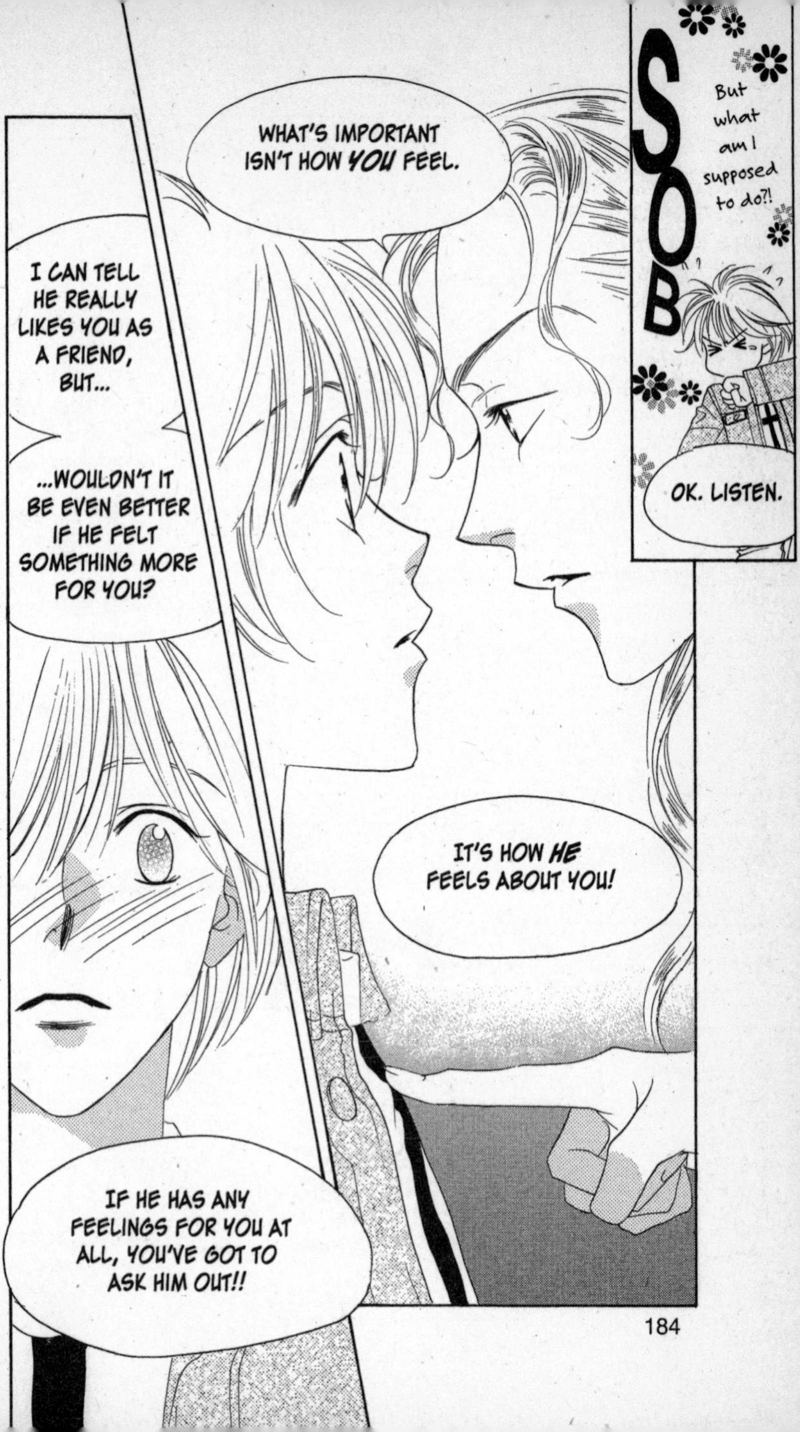
SOB
But what am I supposed to do?!
OK. LISTEN.
WHAT'S IMPORTANT ISN'T HOW *YOU* FEEL.
IT'S HOW *HE* FEELS ABOUT YOU!
I CAN TELL HE REALLY LIKES YOU AS A FRIEND, BUT...
...WOULDN'T IT BE EVEN BETTER IF HE FELT SOMETHING MORE FOR YOU?
IF HE HAS ANY FEELINGS FOR YOU AT ALL, YOU'VE GOT TO ASK HIM OUT!!

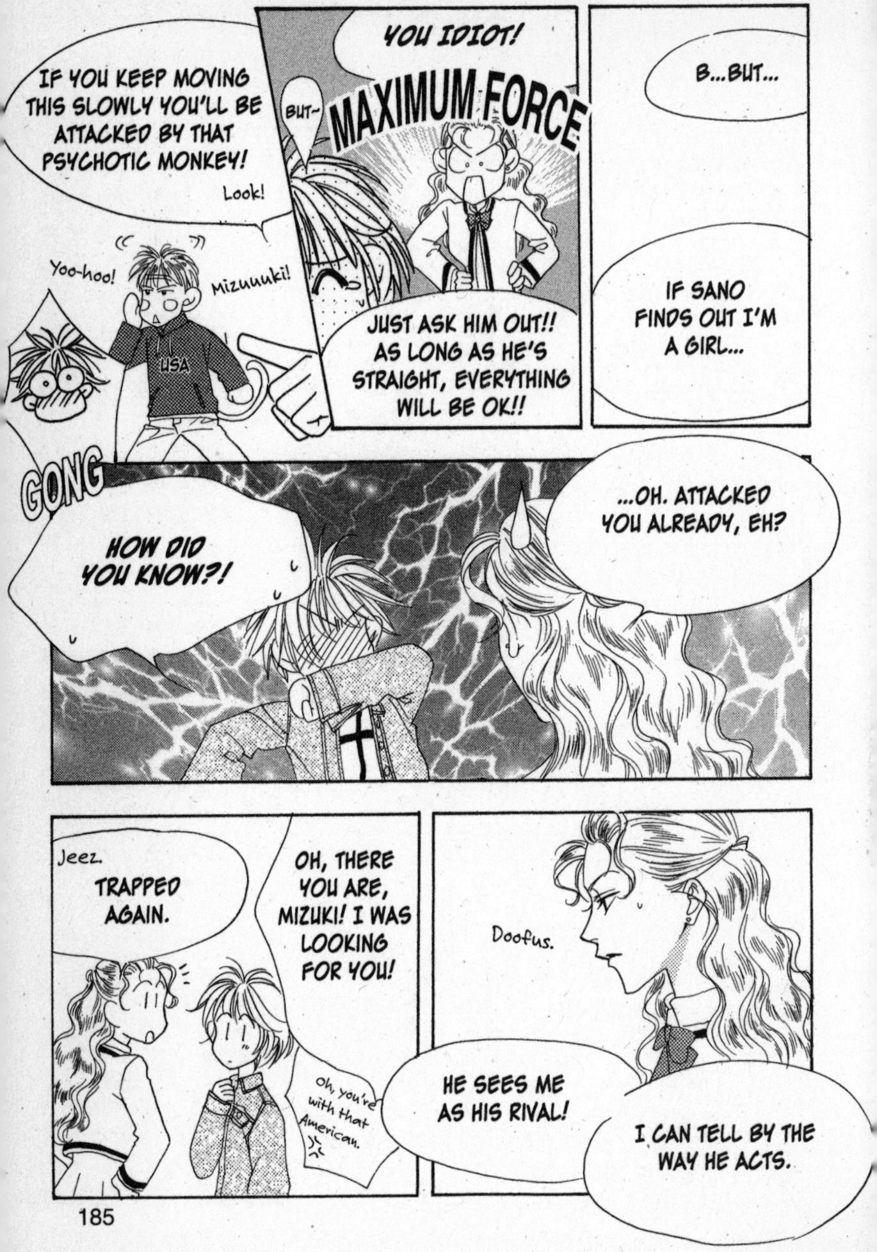
B...BUT...
IF SANO FINDS OUT I'M A GIRL...
YOU IDIOT!
MAXIMUM FORCE
BUT~
JUST ASK HIM OUT!! AS LONG AS HE'S STRAIGHT, EVERYTHING WILL BE OK!!
IF YOU KEEP MOVING THIS SLOWLY YOU'LL BE ATTACKED BY THAT PSYCHOTIC MONKEY!
Look!
Mizuuuki!
Yoo-hoo!
USA
...OH. ATTACKED YOU ALREADY, EH?
GONG
HOW DID YOU KNOW?!
Doofus.
HE SEES ME AS HIS RIVAL!
I CAN TELL BY THE WAY HE ACTS.
OH, THERE YOU ARE, MIZUKI! I WAS LOOKING FOR YOU!
Jeez.
TRAPPED AGAIN.
Oh, you're with that American.

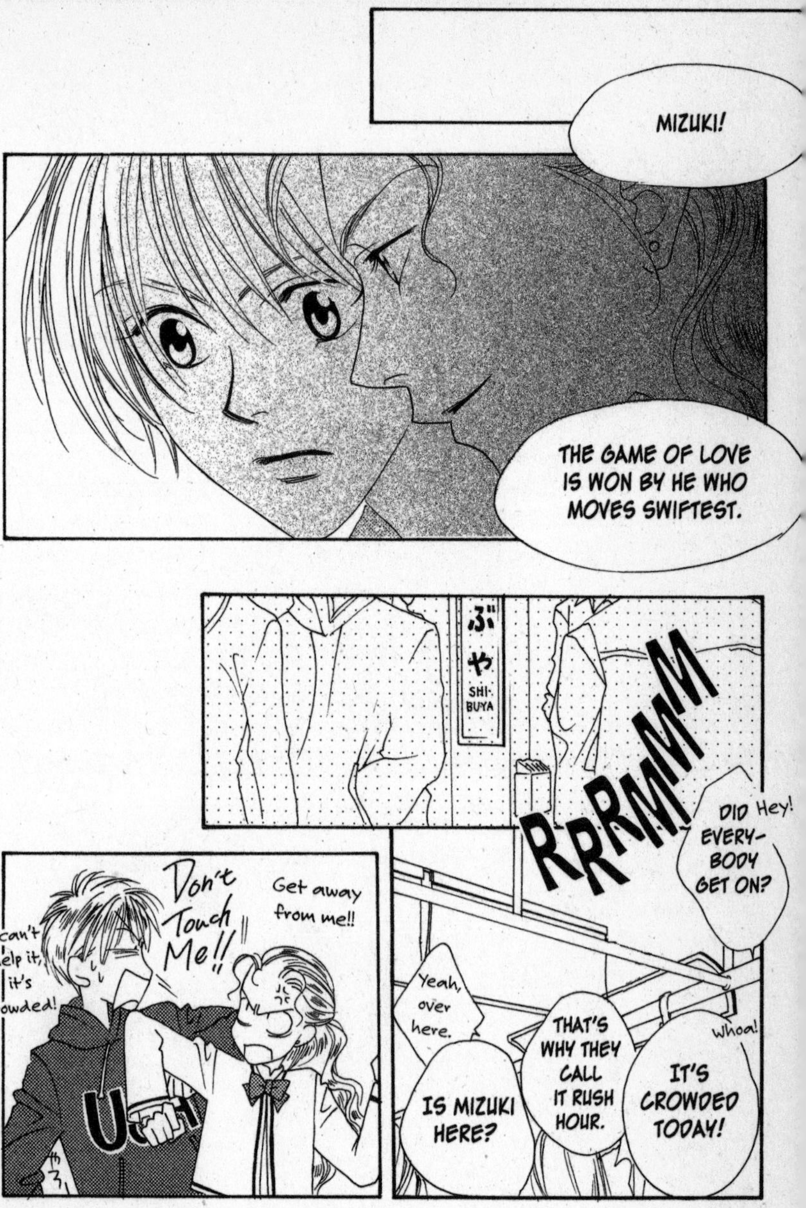
MIZUKI!
THE GAME OF LOVE IS WON BY HE WHO MOVES SWIFTEST.
ぶや
SHI-BUYA
RRRMMM
DID EVERY-BODY GET ON?
Hey!
Whoa!
IT'S CROWDED TODAY!
THAT'S WHY THEY CALL IT RUSH HOUR.
Yeah, over here.
IS MIZUKI HERE?
Get away from me!!
Don't Touch Me!!
I can't help it, it's crowded!

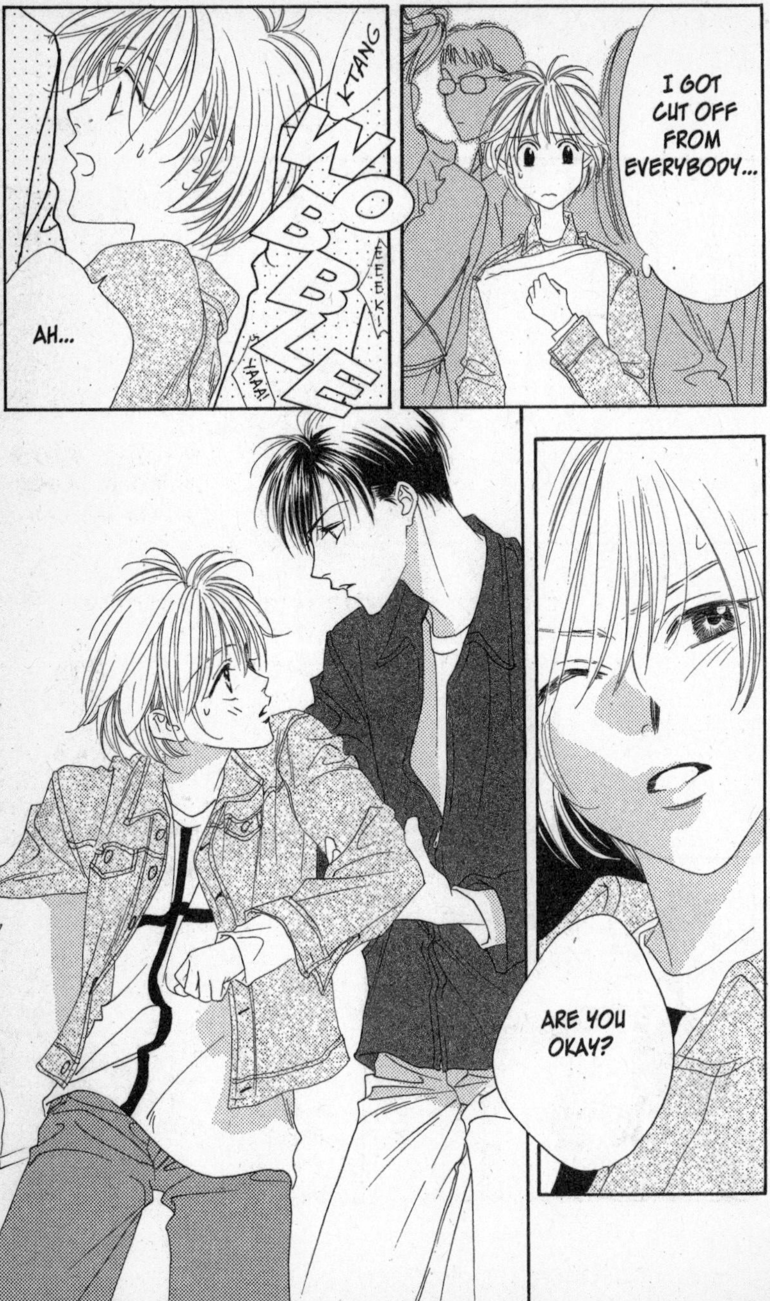
I GOT CUT OFF FROM EVERYBODY...
KTANG
WOBBLE
EEEK!
YAAA!
AH...
ARE YOU OKAY?

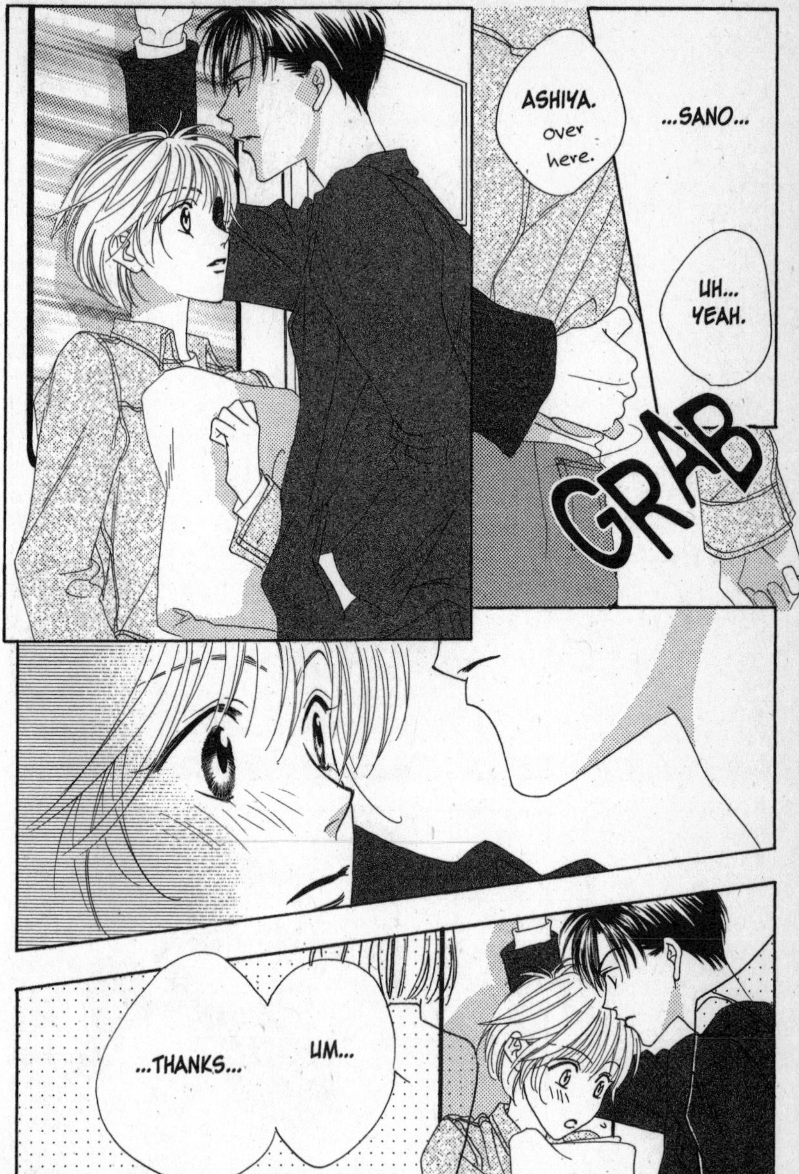
ASHIYA. over here.
...SANO...
UH... YEAH.
GRAB
UM...
...THANKS...

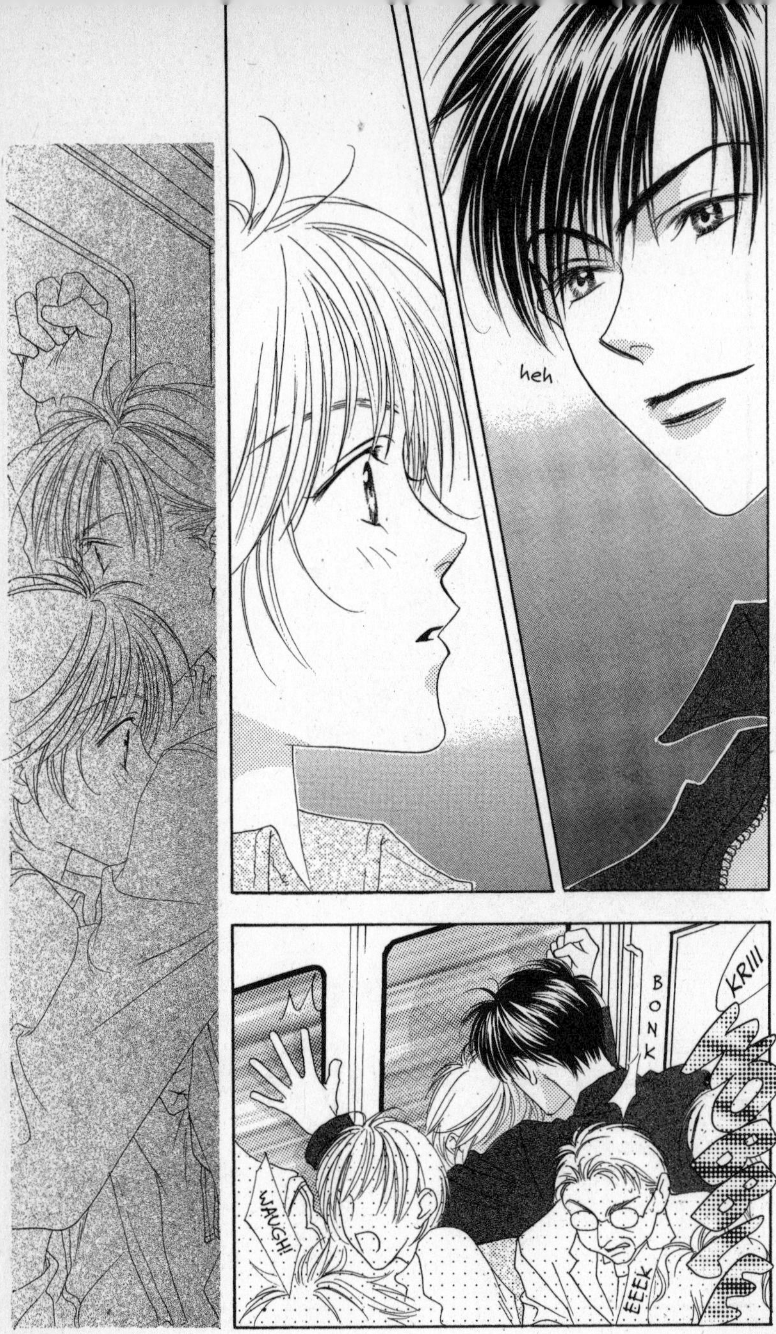
heh
KRIII
BONK
EEEK
WAUGH!

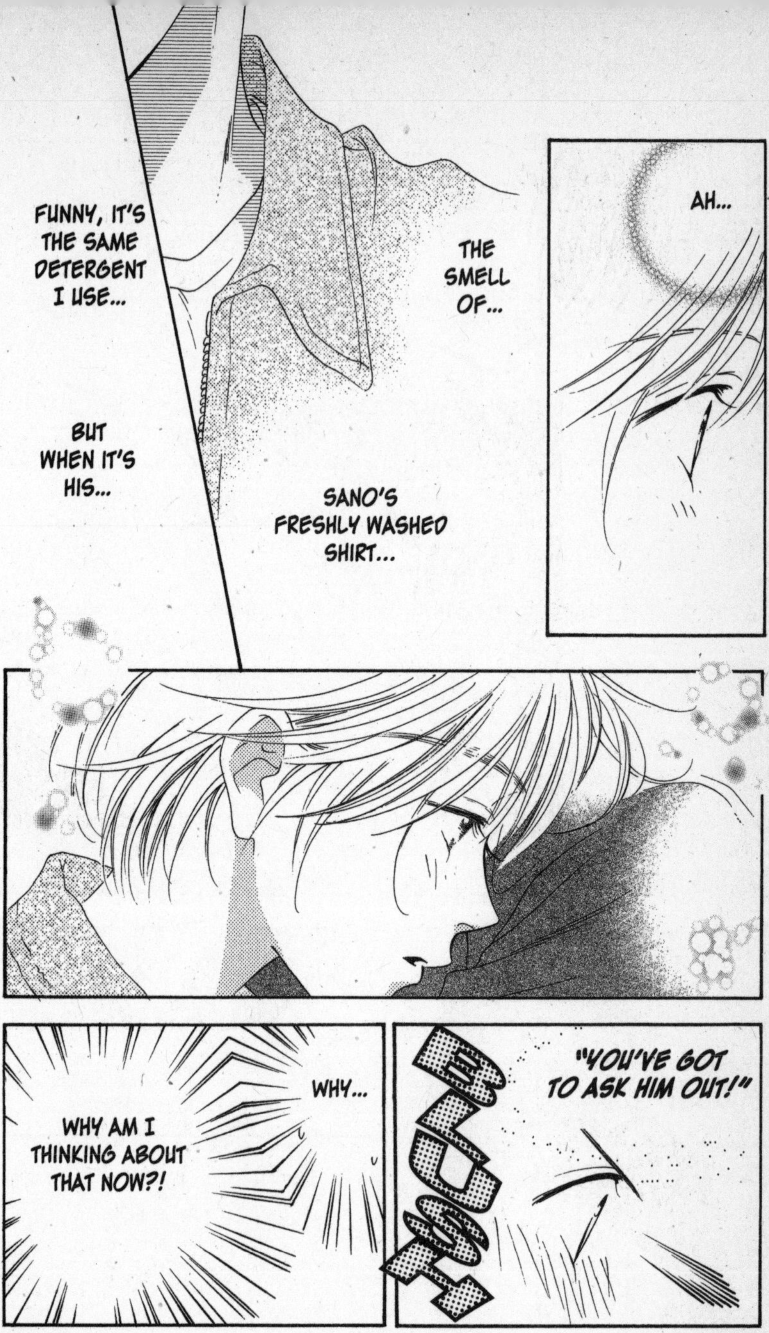
AH...
THE SMELL OF...
SANO'S FRESHLY WASHED SHIRT...
FUNNY, IT'S THE SAME DETERGENT I USE...
BUT WHEN IT'S HIS...
"YOU'VE GOT TO ASK HIM OUT!"
BLUSH
WHY...
WHY AM I THINKING ABOUT THAT NOW?!

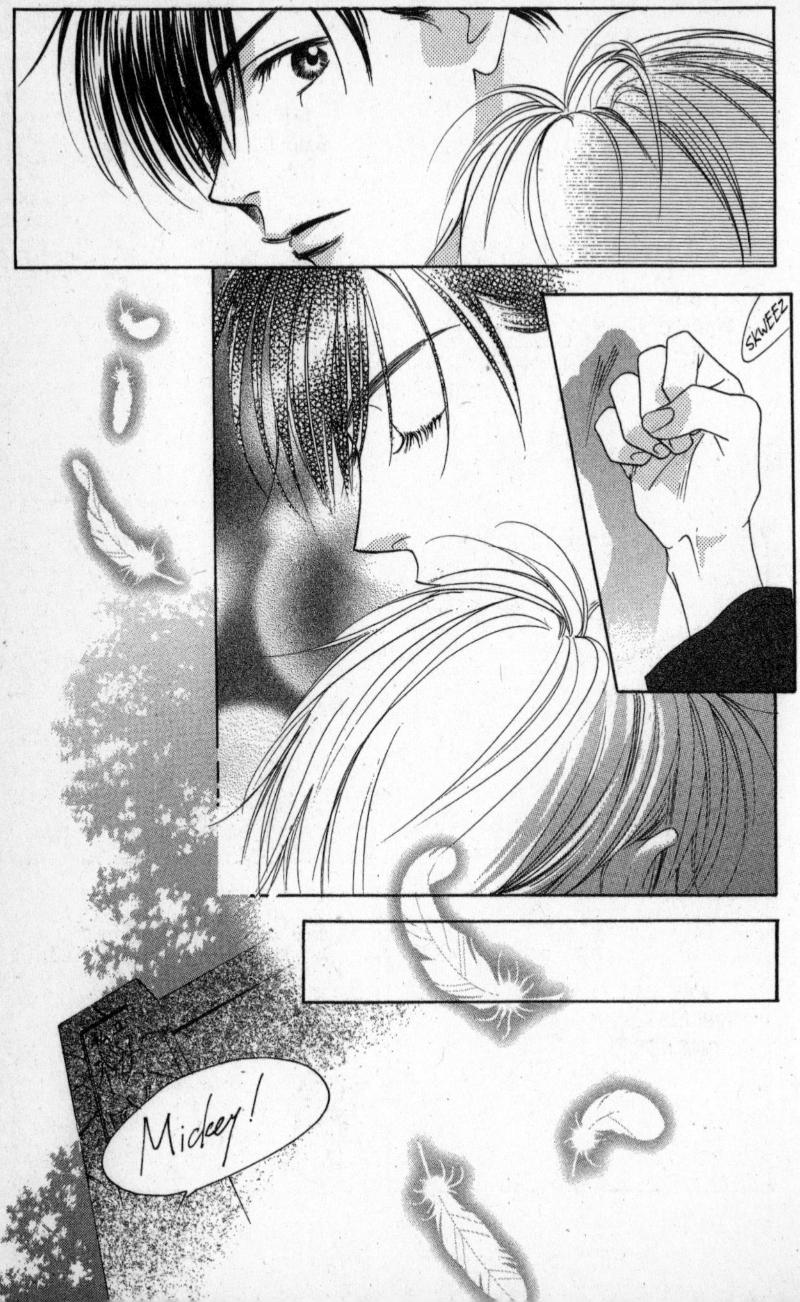
SKWEEZ
Mickey!

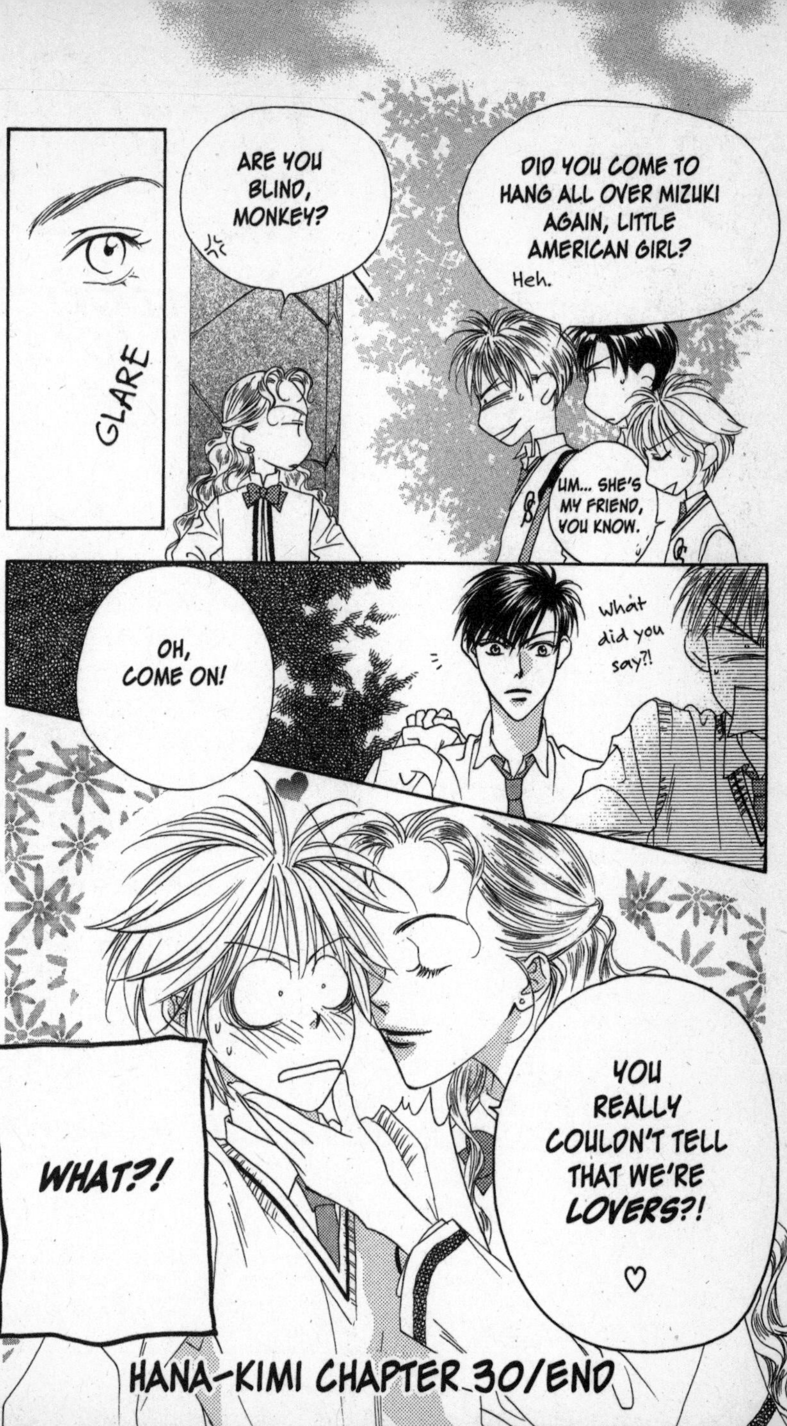
DID YOU COME TO HANG ALL OVER MIZUKI AGAIN, LITTLE AMERICAN GIRL?
Heh.
ARE YOU BLIND, MONKEY?
UM... SHE'S MY FRIEND, YOU KNOW.
GLARE
What did you say?!
OH, COME ON!
YOU REALLY COULDN'T TELL THAT WE'RE LOVERS?! ♡
WHAT?!
HANA-KIMI CHAPTER 30/END

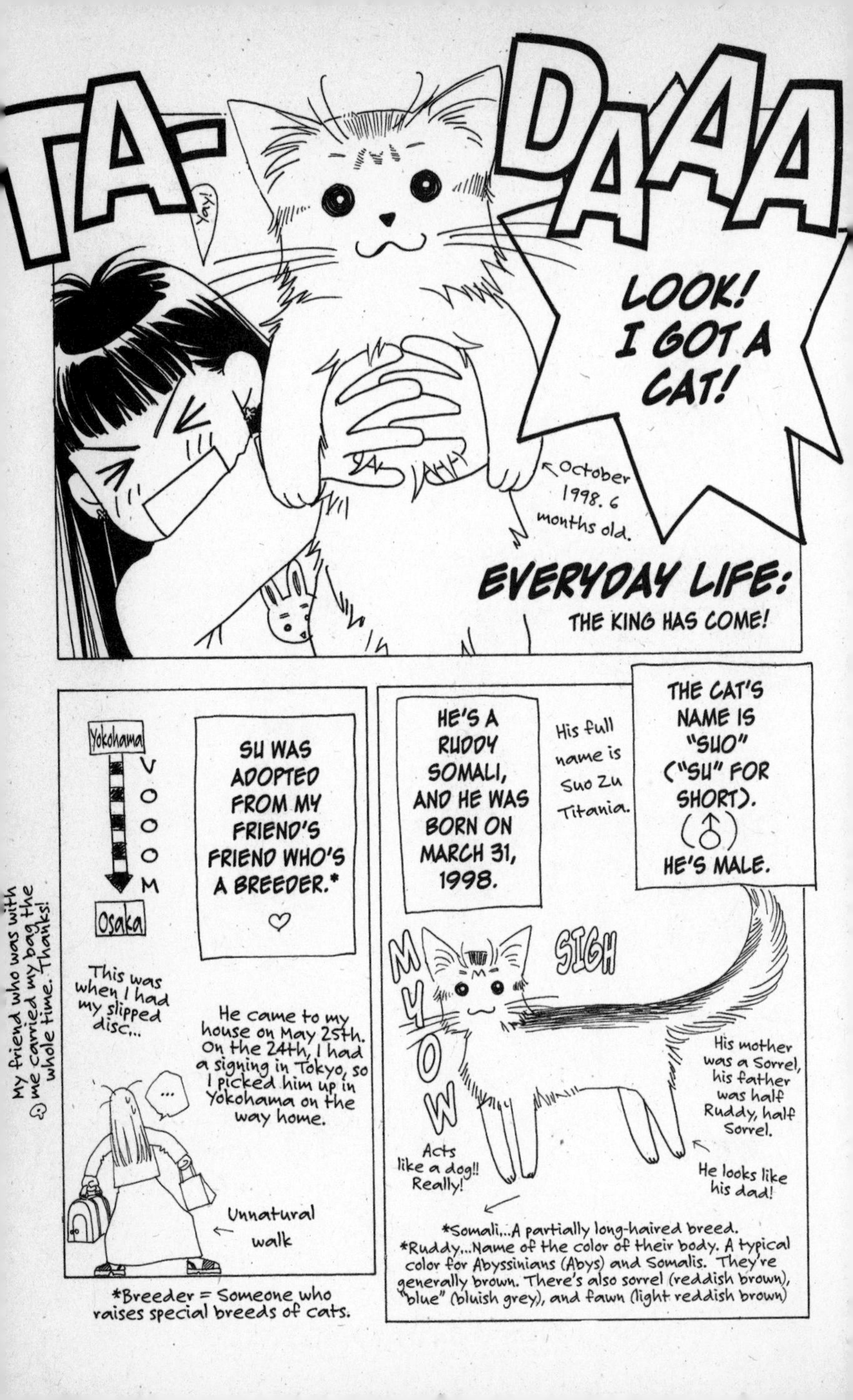
TA-DAAA
Yay!
LOOK! I GOT A CAT!
October 1998. 6 months old.
EVERYDAY LIFE:
THE KING HAS COME!
THE CAT'S NAME IS "SUO" ("SU" FOR SHORT). (♂) HE'S MALE.
His full name is Suo Zu Titania.
HE'S A RUDDY SOMALI, AND HE WAS BORN ON MARCH 31, 1998.
SIGH
MYOW
His mother was a Sorrel, his father was half Ruddy, half Sorrel.
He looks like his dad!
Acts like a dog!! Really!
*Somali...A partially long-haired breed.
*Ruddy...Name of the color of their body. A typical color for Abyssinians (Abys) and Somalis. They're generally brown. There's also sorrel (reddish brown), "blue" (bluish grey), and fawn (light reddish brown)
SU WAS ADOPTED FROM MY FRIEND'S FRIEND WHO'S A BREEDER.* ♡
Yokohama
VOOOOM
Osaka
He came to my house on May 25th. On the 24th, I had a signing in Tokyo, so I picked him up in Yokohama on the way home.
This was when I had my slipped disc...
...
Unnatural walk
*Breeder = Someone who raises special breeds of cats.
My friend who was with me carried my bag the whole time. Thanks!

ON THE FIRST DAY, HE WAS ALREADY USED TO MY HOUSE! (HA HA!)

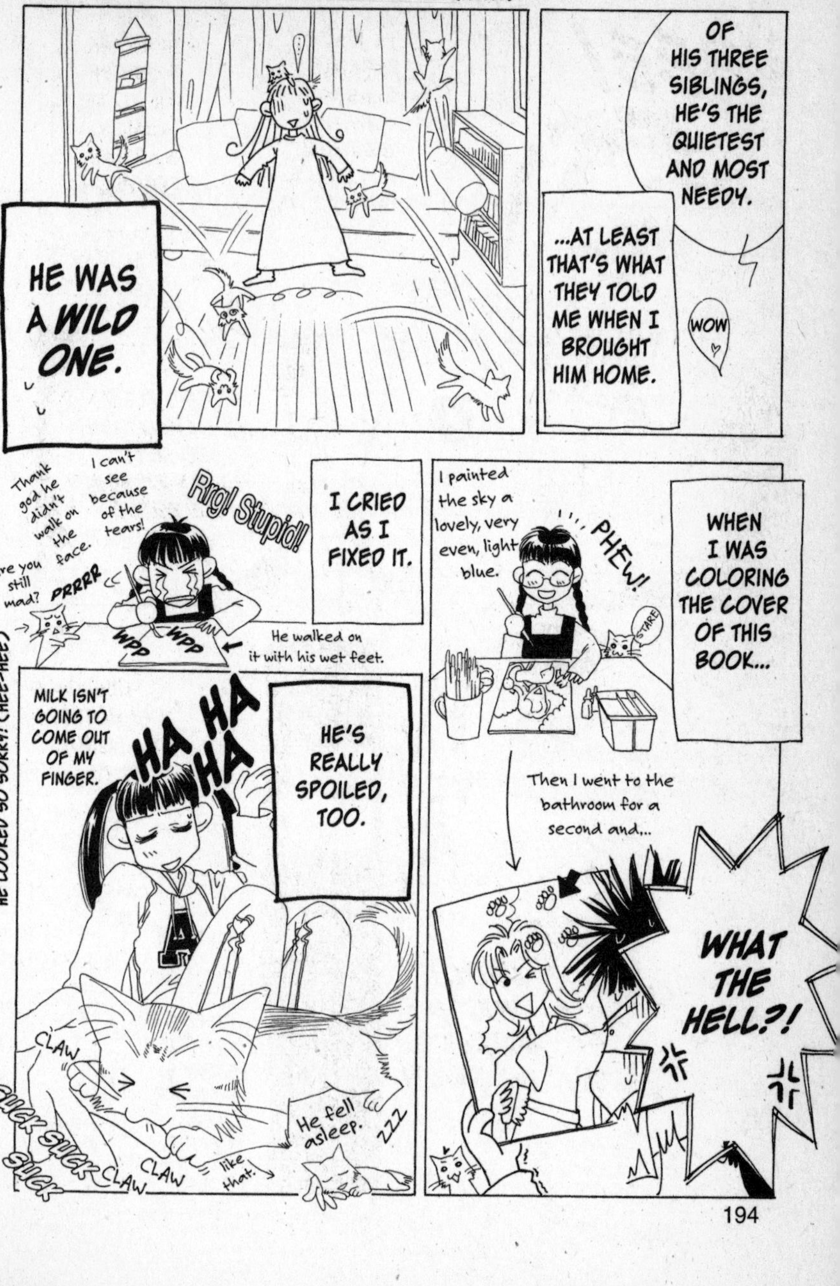
OF HIS THREE SIBLINGS, HE'S THE QUIETEST AND MOST NEEDY.
...AT LEAST THAT'S WHAT THEY TOLD ME WHEN I BROUGHT HIM HOME.
WOW
HE WAS A WILD ONE.
WHEN I WAS COLORING THE COVER OF THIS BOOK...
I painted the sky a lovely, very even, light blue.
PHEW!
STARE
Then I went to the bathroom for a second and...
WHAT THE HELL?!
I CRIED AS I FIXED IT.
Rrg! Stupid!
I can't see because of the tears!
Thank god he didn't walk on the face.
Are you still mad?
PRRRR
WPP
WPP
He walked on it with his wet feet.
HE'S REALLY SPOILED, TOO.
HA HA HA
MILK ISN'T GOING TO COME OUT OF MY FINGER.
CLAW
CLAW
CLAW
SUCK SUCK SUCK
He fell asleep.
zzz
like that.
HE LOOKED SO SORRY! (HEE-HEE)

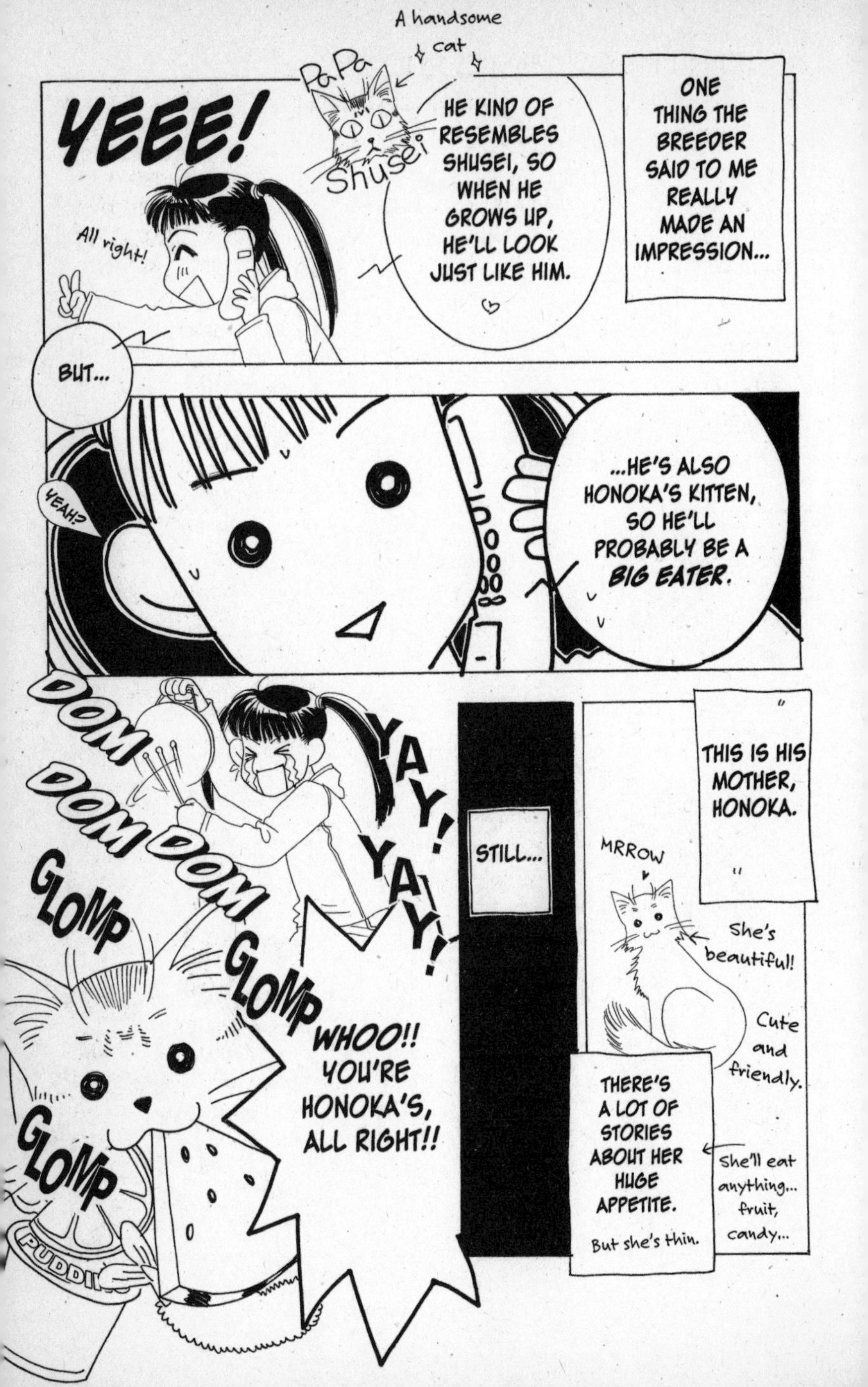
ONE THING THE BREEDER SAID TO ME REALLY MADE AN IMPRESSION...
A handsome cat
PaPa
Shusei
HE KIND OF RESEMBLES SHUSEI, SO WHEN HE GROWS UP, HE'LL LOOK JUST LIKE HIM.
YEEEE!
All right!
BUT...
...HE'S ALSO HONOKA'S KITTEN, SO HE'LL PROBABLY BE A *BIG EATER.*
YEAH?
THIS IS HIS MOTHER, HONOKA.
MRROW
She's beautiful!
Cute and friendly.
THERE'S A LOT OF STORIES ABOUT HER HUGE APPETITE.
She'll eat anything... fruit, candy...
But she's thin.
STILL...
YAY! YAY!
DOM DOM DOM DOM
GLOMP GLOMP GLOMP
WHOO!! YOU'RE HONOKA'S, ALL RIGHT!!

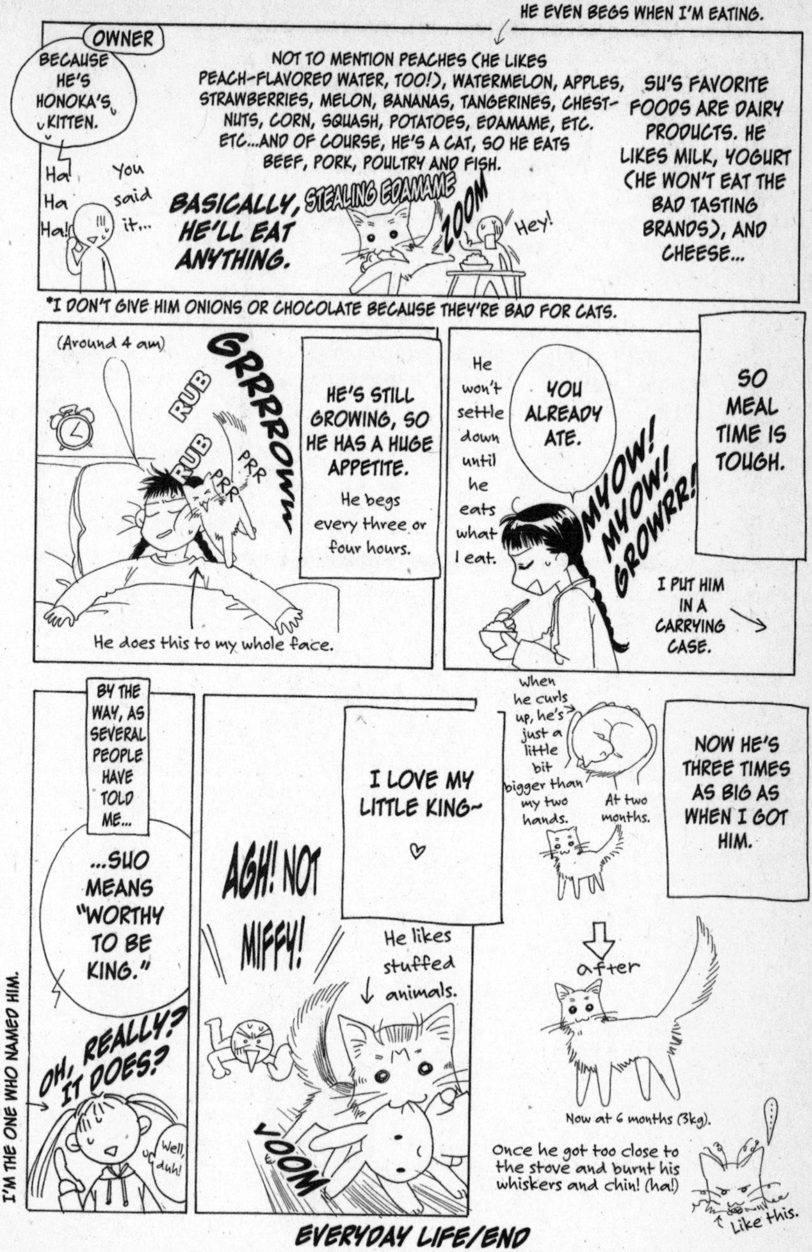
HE EVEN BEGS WHEN I'M EATING.
SU'S FAVORITE FOODS ARE DAIRY PRODUCTS. HE LIKES MILK, YOGURT (HE WON'T EAT THE BAD TASTING BRANDS), AND CHEESE...
NOT TO MENTION PEACHES (HE LIKES PEACH-FLAVORED WATER, TOO!), WATERMELON, APPLES, STRAWBERRIES, MELON, BANANAS, TANGERINES, CHEST-NUTS, CORN, SQUASH, POTATOES, EDAMAME, ETC. ETC...AND OF COURSE, HE'S A CAT, SO HE EATS BEEF, PORK, POULTRY AND FISH.
Hey!
ZOOM
STEALING EDAMAME
BASICALLY, HE'LL EAT ANYTHING.
OWNER
BECAUSE HE'S HONOKA'S KITTEN.
You said it...
Ha Ha Ha!
*I DON'T GIVE HIM ONIONS OR CHOCOLATE BECAUSE THEY'RE BAD FOR CATS.
SO MEAL TIME IS TOUGH.
YOU ALREADY ATE.
He won't settle down until he eats what I eat.
MYOW! MYOW! GROWRR!
I PUT HIM IN A CARRYING CASE.
HE'S STILL GROWING, SO HE HAS A HUGE APPETITE.
He begs every three or four hours.
GRRROWW
RUB RUB
PRR PRR
(Around 4 am)
He does this to my whole face.
NOW HE'S THREE TIMES AS BIG AS WHEN I GOT HIM.
When he curls up, he's just a little bit bigger than my two hands.
At two months.
after
Now at 6 months (3kg).
Once he got too close to the stove and burnt his whiskers and chin! (ha!)
Like this.
I LOVE MY LITTLE KING~ ♥
AGH! NOT MIFFY!
He likes stuffed animals.
ZOOM
BY THE WAY, AS SEVERAL PEOPLE HAVE TOLD ME...
...SUO MEANS "WORTHY TO BE KING."
OH, REALLY? IT DOES?
Well, duh!
I'M THE ONE WHO NAMED HIM.
EVERYDAY LIFE/END

ABOUT THE AUTHOR

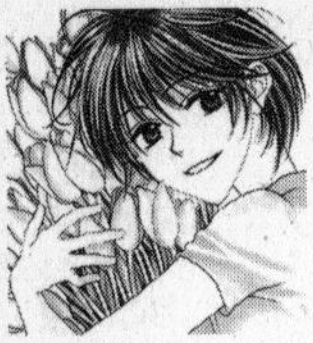

Hisaya Nakajo's manga series **Hanazakari no Kimitachi he** ("For You in Full Blossom," casually known as **Hana-Kimi**) has been a hit since it first appeared in 1997 in the shôjo manga magazine **Hana to Yume** ("Flowers and Dreams"). In Japan, a **Hana-Kimi** art book and several "drama CDs" have been released. Her other manga series include **Missing Piece** (2 volumes) and **Yumemiru Happa** ("The Dreaming Leaf," 1 volume).

Hisaya Nakajo's website:
www.wild-vanilla.com

IN THE NEXT VOLUME ...

Julia is Mizuki's girlfriend?! As the shocking lie tears Osaka High School apart, Mizuki's amorous classmates make their moves on the blonde, blue-eyed invader! Then, just before the Americans can finish taking over, the whole class leaves on a school trip to Hokkaido, complete with an overnight stay at the dream location of every romantic comedy manga...*the hot springs!* With their "chaperone" Dr. Umeda busy getting to know the locals, it isn't long before people start taking off their clothes (to *bathe,* all right?). But how long can Mizuki's gender stay secret inside the boy's bath?

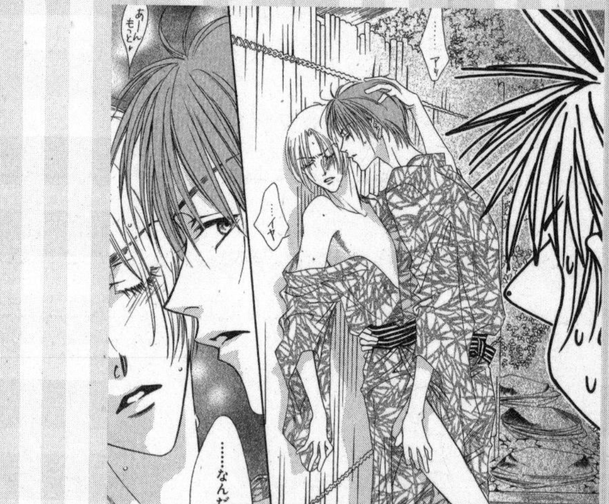
……アッ
……イヤ
あーん もっと
……なんだ芦屋か
入るならノックぐらいしろ
あ…っ
わ
ガゼーン
AVAILABLE NOW!